Psychology AS

The Complete Companion

WJEC CBAC

OXFORD UNIVERSITY PRESS

Cara Flanagan • Lucy Hartnoll • Rhiannon Murray

OXFORD
UNIVERSITY PRESS

Dedications

A Welsh book for my Welshman – Robert George Jones. Cara
Flanagan.

For my family: Dad, Mum, Lee. In particular to Mum: 'If I could
be "just half" the person you have been to me'. Lucy Hartnoll.

Thanks to my family, real and fake. You sustain and challenge
me every day. Rhiannon Murray.

Acknowledgements

An enormous thank you goes to Rick Jackman, our publisher, who
has managed the whole project from beginning to end – always
with enormous enthusiasm and good humour. We also wish to
thank Dave Mackin and Carrie Makin and the team at GreenGate
for the design of the text and their willingness to accommodate
all of our requests. Our thanks also to all those at Folens who
support our work in so many ways, most importantly Pat Catt, the
Sales Manager, and Peter Burton, Director of Publishing at Folens.
Finally, we would like to thank Alison George, the exam officer at
WJEC, who has encouraged and guided this project.

Cara Flanagan, Lucy Hartnoll and Rhiannon Murray

About our cover cat

Weighing in at little more than a couple of bags of sugar, Coco is a
pedigree Birman. She lives in a tiny Somerset village with her sister
Misty after they were rescued by their owner Sharon when they
were just two years old. Fourteen years later they divide their time
between proofreading their owner's business reports, sleeping
for England and drinking tea. Like her sister, Coco is a constant
reminder that you never own a cat, a cat always owns you.

Picture acknowledgements

Contents

How to use this book

The contents of this book are mapped exactly on to the WJEC AS specification. The book is divided into two units, matching the exam structure.

- **Unit 1 Approaches in Psychology** covers the four approaches you need to study. Each spread in this unit deals with one of the exam questions – the assumptions, theories, therapies, evaluation and methodology for each of the approaches.
- **Unit 2 Core Studies and Applied Research Methods** covers the 10 core studies in the specification, plus all the research method concepts.

Each **unit** begins with a detailed list of the **contents**. This is followed, on the next page, by the full details of the **specification** to be covered by the unit, along with information about the organisation of the unit.

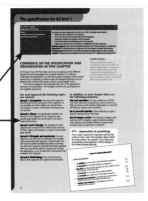

Throughout the book we have included:

Diagrammatic summaries

For example, for approaches…

…and for core studies

Review activities

Example exam questions with student answers (with examiner's comments at the end of the book)

On most spreads there is an **introduction** to the topic, at the top left. This explains what the topic is about and might identify some key issues or links to previous topics.

The **main text** for the spread is in the middle of the page.

On most spreads, there is a **Do It Yourself** box with ideas for activities that will increase your understanding of the topic.

The text is mapped closely on to the demands of the specification – for example, in Chapter 5 we have covered the **context and aims** of one core study that matches one of the exam questions.

Sometimes we've added a **comment** to enhance understanding.

In Chapter 6 we have often included **tables** to summarise advantages and disadvantages.

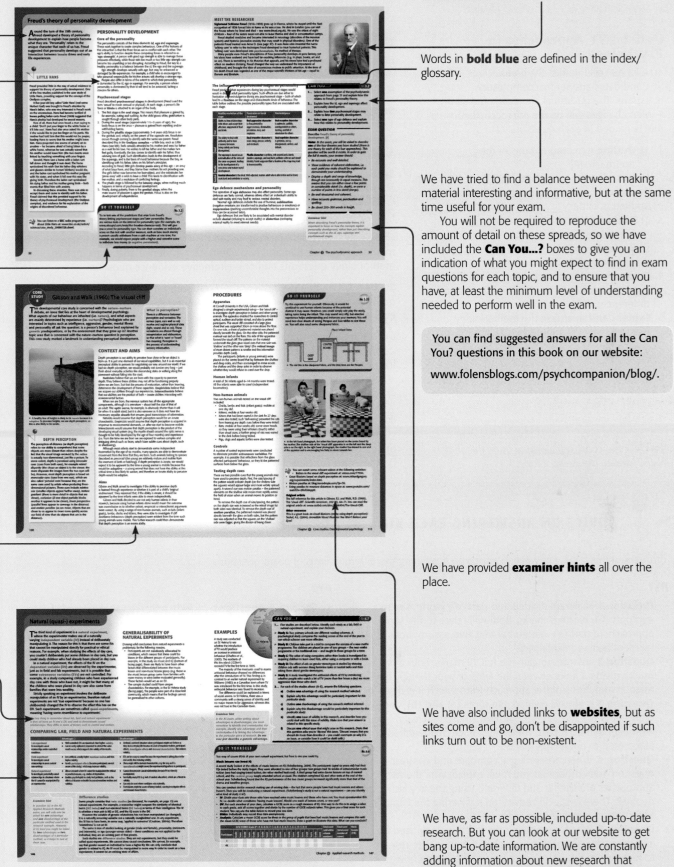

We have included brief biographical notes for some important psychologists in the **meet the researcher** boxes.

Words in **bold blue** are defined in the index/glossary.

We have tried to find a balance between making material interesting and informative, but at the same time useful for your exam.

You will not be required to reproduce the amount of detail on these spreads, so we have included the **Can You...?** boxes to give you an indication of what you might expect to find in exam questions for each topic, and to ensure that you have, at least the minimum level of understanding needed to perform well in the exam.

You can find suggested answers for all the Can You? questions in this book on our website:

www.folensblogs.com/psychcompanion/blog/.

We have provided **examiner hints** all over the place.

We have also included links to **websites**, but as sites come and go, don't be disappointed if such links turn out to be non-existent.

We have, as far as possible, included up-to-date research. But you can look at our website to get bang up-to-date information. We are constantly adding information about new research that we think might interest students. See: **www. folensblogs.com/psychcompanion/blog/**.

The WJEC AS examination

The AS examination consists of two papers:

Unit 1 PY1 Approaches in Psychology

40% of AS Level marks 1¼ hours

Candidates answer five compulsory questions. The questions are always the same – what changes will be the approach/theory that is named in each question.

1. a) **Outline** two assumptions of the ____ approach. [4]
   b) **Describe** the ____ theory. [8]
2. **Describe** how the ____ approach has been applied in either ____ or ____ therapy. [12]
3. a) **Evaluate** two strengths of the ____ approach. [6]
   b) **Evaluate** two weaknesses of the ____ approach. [6]
4. **Compare and contrast** the ____ and the ____ approaches in terms of similarities and differences. [12]
5. **Explain and evaluate** the methodology used by the ____ approach. [12]

Health warning

The exam information given on this spread is correct at the time of writing. However, exams evolve and there are often changes. You can find any updates on our website (folensblogs.com/psychcompanion/blog/), as well as on the official WJEC website (www.wjec.co.uk).

Unit 2 PY2 Core Studies and Applied Research Methods

60% of AS Level marks 1¾ hours

This paper is divided into **three** sections. In Sections A and B, the questions relate to identified core studies. Section C is on applied research methods.

Section A All three questions are compulsory and focus on **AO1**.
1. Summarise the aims **and** context of ____. [12]
2. Outline the procedures of ____. [12]
3. Describe the findings **and** conclusions of ____. [12]

Section B All three questions are compulsory and focus on **AO2**.
These three questions can be one of two types.
- Evaluate the methodology of ____. [12]
- With reference to alternative evidence, critically assess ____. [12]

There will always be a mixture of the two types of question: perhaps one methodology question and two alternative evidence questions; or two methodology questions and one alternative evidence question.

Section C Candidates answer one question from a choice of two. Each question will consist of a brief description of a study (experiment, observation, etc.) and be divided into parts (a)–(f).

a) Outline **one** advantage and **one** disadvantage of using [*the named method*] in this research. [3]
b) Identify **one** issue of reliability in this research and describe how you could ensure reliability. [3]
c) Identify **one** issue of validity in this research and describe how you could ensure validity. [3]
d) Outline **one** advantage and **one** disadvantage of [*the named sampling method*] in this research. [3]
e) Discuss **one** ethical issue that might arise in this research. [3]
f) State **one** conclusion that can be drawn from the [*the named data*] in this research. [3]

ADVICE ON ANSWERING EACH KIND OF QUESTION

Throughout this book you will find advice on answering the different kinds of exam questions.

PY1

- **Question 1** is always divided into part (a), worth 4 marks, and part (b), worth 8 marks. Both will relate to the same approach. In part (a), remember that **two** assumptions should be identified and explained.
- **Question 2** In order to gain the full 12 marks, your answer must provide a link between the aims of your therapy and the main assumptions of the approach from which it is derived.
- **Question 3** is always divided into parts (a) and (b), each worth 6 marks. Remember that **two** strengths/weaknesses are needed in each part. These must each be identified and elaborated to obtain full marks.
- **Question 4** When answering a 'compare and contrast' question, remember that you must explain *why* the two approaches are similar and different, using the key issues and debates. There is specific advice on answering the compare and contrast questions on pages 60–61.
- **Question 5** When considering the methodology used by an approach, use specific examples of appropriate research to highlight to the examiner that you understand how this method has been used within the specific approach. Generic descriptions of a method such as 'lab experiments' will gain very limited credit.

PY2

- **Section A questions** Include only relevant material. If the question is asking about findings and conclusions, any description of aims, context or procedures is irrelevant to the question being asked and will not be credited by the examiner. Including irrelevant material only wastes your time in the exam.
  Try to be as precise as you can when describing details of the core studies. Remember, top band answers need to be well detailed *and* accurate.
- **Section B questions** When evaluating the methodology of the core studies, use the themes in Section C questions to give your answer a coherent structure, i.e. include commentary on the method, reliability, validity, sampling and ethics.
  When assessing 'with reference to alternative evidence', make sure that you have made clear, overt links to the core study. Explain why the alternative evidence supports, contradicts or develops the core study.
- **Section C questions** In order to gain high marks, it is essential to make links between your methodological knowledge and the novel situation, i.e. *contextualise* your answers.

AO1 MARK SCHEME GRID

Some of the exam questions assess **AO1** (assessment objective 1), demonstrating your knowledge and understanding.

The **AO1** marking criteria below are used for **PY1 question 2**, and **PY2 questions 1, 2 and 3**.

Marks	Content	Material is used in…	Elaboration	Depth and range	Use of language (including grammar, punctuation and spelling)	For question 2: link between assumptions of the approach and therapy
10–12	Accurate and well detailed	…a highly effective manner	Coherent elaboration	Both depth **and** range	Relevant, well structured, coherent and accurate	Clearly demonstrated
7–9	Reasonably accurate, but less detailed	…an effective manner	Evidence of elaboration	Depth **or** range	Accurate, structured and clear	Evident
4–6	Basic detail	…a relevant manner but limited	Some elaboration		Some inaccuracies	Limited or none
1–3	Superficial	…muddled and/or incoherent at times	Little or none		Errors	Limited or none
0	No relevant knowledge or understanding					

PY1 question 1(a) carries a maximum of 4 marks (**AO1**). The mark scheme is:
- 3–4 marks for two relevant, detailed assumptions.
- 1–2 marks for one detailed, relevant assumption, **or** two assumptions identified briefly.

PY1 question 1(b) uses a mark scheme similar to the one above except that the five bands are:
7–8 marks, 5–6 marks, 3–4 marks, 1–2 marks and 0 marks.

*When both depth **and** range are required they do not both have to be given in equal measures in order to gain full marks. The same applies to similarities **and** differences.*

AO2 MARK SCHEME GRID

Some of the exam questions assess **AO2** (assessment objective 2), demonstrating your skill at analysis and evaluation.

The **AO2** marking criteria below are used for **PY1 question 4** and **PY2 questions 4, 5 and 6**.

Marks	Analysis and evaluation	Elaboration	Depth and range	For PY1 question 4	For PY2 questions: reference to alternative evidence
10–12	Clearly structured and thorough	Coherent elaboration	Depth **and** range	Similarities **and** differences	Overt, more than one
7–9	Reasonably thorough	Some coherence	Depth **or** range	Similarities **and** differences	Clear, more than one
4–6	Appropriate but limited			Similarities **and/or** differences	Some
1–3	Superficial and/or muddled	Muddled and/or incoherent			Muddled
0	No relevant evaluation or analysis				

For **PY1 question 3**, a total of 6 marks (**AO2**) is awarded for the strengths and for the weaknesses. The mark scheme is:
- 4–6 marks for **two** strengths/weaknesses, clearly and thoroughly explained.
- 1–3 marks for **one** strength/weakness (clearly and thoroughly explained), **or** two (lacking clarity/detail).

AO3 MARK SCHEME GRID

PY1 question 5 assesses **AO3** (assessment objective 3), demonstrating your understanding of research methodology.

The **AO3** marking criteria below are used for **PY1 question 5**.

Marks	Method(s)	Relevance to approach	Evaluation	Strengths and weaknesses
10–12	Appropriate and clearly explained	Relevance	Thorough, clearly structured	Clear evidence of strengths **and** weaknesses
7–9	Appropriate and reasonably explained	Has relevance	Reasonably thorough	Evidence of strengths **and** weaknesses
4–6	Appropriate and explained in a limited manner		Limited	Evidence of strengths **and/or** weaknesses
1–3	May be muddled and/or incoherent	May be inappropriate	Superficial	Superficial or absent
0	No relevant evaluation or analysis			

PY2 Section C

The marking criteria that are used for **PY2 Section C** are discussed in Chapter 6. See page 171 for a summary.

Effective revision

Get yourself motivated

People tend to do better when they are highly motivated. We have taught many mature students who all wished they had worked harder at school the first time around. You don't owe success to your teachers or your parents (although they would be delighted), you owe it to the person you will be 10 years from now. Think what you would like to be doing in 10 years' time, and what you need to get there, and let that thought prompt you into action now. It is always better to succeed at something you might not need later, than to fail at something you will.

Work *with* your memory

In an exam, it is harder to access information learned by rote. When people feel anxious, it is easier for them to recall knowledge they *understand* well. Just reading or writing out notes is likely to do little to help you create enduring memories or to understand the content. However, if you do something with your knowledge it will increase your understanding and make it more likely that material will be accessible when you need it. Psychologists call this 'deep processing', as opposed to the 'shallow processing' that takes place when you read something without really thinking about it. Constructing 'spidergrams' or mind-maps of the material, or even explaining it to someone else, involves deep processing and makes material more memorable.

Become multisensory

Why stick to using just one of your senses when revising? Visual learners learn best by seeing what they are learning, so make the most of text, diagrams, graphs, etc. In contrast, auditory learners learn best by listening (and talking), taking in material using their sense of hearing. You might associate more with one of these styles than the other, but actually we can make use of *both* these types of learning styles. As well as *reading* your notes and *looking* at pictures and diagrams, try *listening* to your notes and *talking* about topics with other people – and even *performing* some of the material such as role-playing a study.

Short bursts are best

One of the problems with revision is that you can do too much of it (at one go that is!). As you probably know all too well, your attention is prone to wander after a relatively short period of time. Research findings vary as to the optimum time to spend revising, but 30–45 minutes at a time appears to be the norm. What should you do when your attention begins to wander? As a rule, the greater the physiological change (i.e. go for a walk rather than surfing the internet), the more refreshed you will be when returning for your next 30–45 minute stint. There is another benefit to having frequent planned breaks – it increases the probability of subsequent recall.

Revisit regularly

Have you ever noticed that if you don't use an icon on your computer for a long time, the cunning little blighter hides it. Your computer seems to take the decision that as you are not using it regularly, it can't be that important, so neatly files it away somewhere. Your brain works in a similar way, knowledge that is not used regularly becomes less immediately accessible. The trick, therefore, is to review what you have learned at regular intervals. Each time you review material, it will take less time and will surely pay dividends later on!

Work with a friend

Although friends *can* be a distraction while you are trying to study, they can also be a very useful revision aid. Working together (what psychologists call 'collaborative learning') can aid understanding and make revision more interesting and more fun. Explaining something to someone else is a useful form of deep processing (see above), and by checking and discussing each other's answers to sample questions, you can practise your 'examiner skills' and therefore your understanding of what to put into an exam answer to earn the most marks.

Psychology is the science of human behaviour and experience. You have probably already studied science and therefore know some things about the **scientific method**. You know, for example, that scientists:
- Conduct experiments and other kinds of studies.
- Try to find out about the causes of things.

In order to explain the causes of behaviour, psychologists use different approaches. An 'approach' is a belief about the world and about what causes people to behave in certain ways. These beliefs will affect what they choose to study and how they choose to study it. Such beliefs are based on a set of assumptions – beliefs that are held without any need for proof.

The first unit of this book looks at four of the main approaches in psychology – the **biological**, **behaviourist**, **psychodynamic** and **cognitive** approaches. Each of these approaches has a set of assumptions that are the signature tune of the approach, and it is this tune that you need to understand in the first part of the course.

Cognitive Behaviourist Biological Psychodynamic

Psychology

APPROACHES IN PSYCHOLOGY

This is a very brief outline of the four main approaches.
- The **biological approach** believes that behaviour can be explained in terms of inheriting characteristics, such as the tendency to be aggressive.
- The **behaviourist approach** believes that the way a person is and behaves is due to life experiences. A person may be rewarded or punished for certain behaviour, and this determines how they behave in future. People might also imitate what they see others doing.
- The **psychodynamic approach** believes that our behaviour is influenced by emotions that are beyond our conscious awareness. Such emotions are buried in the **unconscious** mind as a result of events in early childhood.
- The **cognitive approach** believes that behaviour is best explained in terms of how a person thinks about their actions. For example, the expectation that a concert will be brilliant will increase the likelihood that it will be a great experience for you.

DO IT YOURSELF

Construct your own psychology timeline from the brief history below. Conduct some further research, finding out about the history of psychology.

A BRIEF HISTORY OF PSYCHOLOGY

Early thinking about human behaviour The Greeks considered questions about human behaviour. For example, Hippocrates (400BC) proposed that individual differences in personality were related to body 'humours' (fluids), for example too much black bile (in Greek *melan* [black] *kholé* [bile]) led to depression (melancholia). Until the late 19th century, human behaviour was the province of philosophers and physiologists. In the 17th century, the British philosopher John Locke argued that the human mind was a blank slate (*tabula rasa* in Latin), and that children were innately neither good nor bad.

The birth of psychology The origins of psychology are often traced to 1879, when Wilhelm Wundt, who had trained as a physiologist, set up the first psychology laboratory at Leipzig University in Germany. His aim was to make the study of mental processes more systematic using introspection. He trained psychology students to make objective observations of their thought processes, and used the results to develop a theory of conscious thought. Students from all over the world journeyed to Leipzig to learn about scientific psychology.

The behaviourist approach Many scientists were not impressed by the methods of introspection. Psychology probably owes its true claim to scientific status to John B.

Watson (1913), an American who recognised that the work of Ivan Pavlov could be used to create a really objective and therefore scientific psychology, which he called behaviourism (it is said that he suffered from 'physics envy'). Pavlov (1902), experimenting with salivation in dogs, developed the principles of classical conditioning that provided Watson with a simple observable behaviour – conditioned reflexes. Later, B.F. Skinner (1938) became the main advocate of behaviourism, introducing the concept of **operant conditioning**.

The psychodynamic approach At about the same time as behaviourism first took hold in the USA, Sigmund Freud (1856–1939) delivered his introductory lectures on **psychoanalysis** to audiences there, and soon became the second force in psychology.

The cognitive approach In the 1950s, the computer revolution changed the way people thought, including how they thought about human behaviour. Information processing offered an analogy for human thinking. In turn, this new cognitive approach influenced behaviourism, leading Albert Bandura to develop **social learning theory (SLT)** in the 1960s. SLT emphasised the importance of indirect reinforcement in the learning process. In order for social learning to take place, an individual must form mental representations of events. Therefore SLT, unlike behaviourism, includes the consideration of cognitive factors.

On this spread, we have introduced the four main issues and debates in psychology. They are issues, because they are so important that we can't really ignore them. They are debates, because there is no simple answer about which is right or wrong, better or worse. On the facing page is a scenario about a young boy called John. On the far right we have suggested how all four approaches might explain John's behaviour. The blank boxes are for you to fill in using the issues and debates introduced on this page – see the Do It Yourself box on the facing page.

ISSUES AND DEBATES

The issues and debates will be very important in helping you to evaluate each of the approaches studied in Unit 1 (and examined in PY1). They are also crucial for comparing and contrasting the approaches, another requirement of PY1. On this page, we explain the four main issues and debates in psychology, and on the facing page there is an activity to help you understand how the issues and debates relate to the approaches.

DETERMINISM OR FREE WILL

Determinism is the view that an individual's behaviour is shaped or controlled by internal or external forces rather than the individual's will to do something. This means that behaviour is predictable and lawful.

Free will is used to refer to the alternative end position in which an individual is seen as being capable of self-determination. According to this view, individuals have an active role in controlling their behaviour, i.e. they are free to choose and are not acting in response to any external or internal (biological) pressures.

Any approach such as behaviourism or the biological approach that takes the view that our behaviour is determined by factors other than our free will implies that people are not personally responsible for their behaviour. For example, according to the biological approach, low levels of **serotonin** may lead some individuals to behave aggressively. This poses a moral question about whether a person can be held personally responsible for his or her behaviour. We might argue that this is not acceptable, that people are responsible for their behaviour, and this kind of argument is therefore a limitation of such determinist explanations.

NATURE OR NURTURE

The **nature–nurture debate** suggests that people are either (mainly) the product of their **genes** and biology (**nature**) or of their environment (**nurture**). The term nature does not simply refer to abilities present at birth, but to any ability determined by the genes, including those that appear through maturation. 'Nurture' is everything learned through interactions with the environment, both the physical and social environment, and may be more widely referred to as 'experience'. At one time, nature and nurture were seen as largely independent and additive factors. However, a more contemporary view is that the two processes do not just interact, but are inextricably entwined. It is no longer really a debate at all but a new understanding of how genetics works.

REDUCTIONISM OR HOLISM

Reductionism involves breaking down a complex phenomenon into more simple components. It also implies that this process is desirable because complex phenomena are best understood in terms of a simpler level of explanation. Psychologists (and all scientists) are drawn to reductionist explanations and methods of research because reductionism is a powerful tool that underlies experimental research (reducing complex behaviour to a set of variables).

The 'opposite' of reductionism is **holism**, or the holistic approach. Holism is the view that systems should be studied as a whole rather than focusing on their constituent parts, and suggests that we cannot predict how the whole system will behave from a knowledge of the individual components. Cognitive systems such as memory and intelligence are examples of the value of a holistic approach. They are complex systems, the behaviour of which is related to the activity of neurons, genes and so on, yet the whole system cannot be simply predicted from these lower level units.

IDIOGRAPHIC OR NOMOTHETIC

The **idiographic** approach involves the study of individuals and the unique insights each individual gives us about human behaviour. The **nomothetic** approach involves the study of a large number of people and then seeks to make generalisations or develop laws/theories about their behaviour. This is the goal of the scientific approach – to produce general laws of behaviour.

John

John started stealing when he was just 10 years old. In the beginning, John just stole sweets from his local shop. However, by the time John was 17, he had joined a local gang. Along with the other members of the gang, he started stealing cars and breaking into houses to steal. An important part of being a gang member was acting tough and aggressive, regularly getting into fights with other gang members.

The biological approach might explain John's behaviour in terms of a physical cause. For example, he might have inherited aggressive genes from his father, or maybe John has particularly high levels of **testosterone**, which makes people behave more aggressively. Such high levels of testosterone might be inherited, or perhaps some environmental pollutants have raised his testosterone levels.

The behaviourist approach might say that John's behaviour is learned from the environment. He may have learned this directly because he got rewards such as gaining attention when he behaved aggressively. Or he may have learned to behave aggressively indirectly, by seeing others behaving like this and **modelling** his behaviour on them.

The psychodynamic approach would suggest that John's aggressive drives were **innate**, and that his early experiences had failed to channel them in a more positive direction. The psychodynamic approach might also suggest that his behaviour was driven by **unconscious** conflicts stemming from traumatic experiences in early childhood.

The cognitive approach would explain John's behaviour by looking at his internal thought processes. John's perception of stealing is that it is acceptable, and he has developed an expectation that aggression is the way to resolve conflicts such that he is 'programmed' to behave in an aggressive manner.

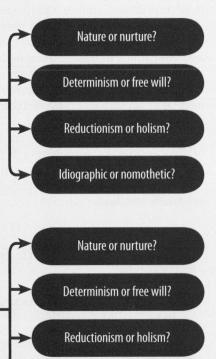

Nature or nurture?

Determinism or free will?

Reductionism or holism?

Idiographic or nomothetic?

Nature or nurture?

Determinism or free will?

Reductionism or holism?

Idiographic or nomothetic?

Nature or nurture?

Determinism or free will?

Reductionism or holism?

Idiographic or nomothetic?

Nature or nurture?

Determinism or free will?

Reductionism or holism?

Idiographic or nomothetic?

DO IT YOURSELF

1. In pairs or small groups, carry out some further research on the assumptions of the four approaches and then see if you can elaborate further the explanations on the right.
2. Fill in the empty boxes using the key issues and debates described on this page. Discuss how each approach fits in with these issues and debates.
3. Make up your own case histories like John's and use the four approaches – you may need to do some research on the internet.

There is one final issue/debate to consider – the question of whether an approach is scientific or not.

The reason science is desirable is because that is the only way to demonstrate whether a particular theory or explanation is 'true' – by testing the theory using a research study.

However, some theories (approaches) are not very easy to test, and we cannot therefore demonstrate their 'truthfulness'. Some people might argue that there are other ways to gather knowledge (such as through reasoned argument or simply because you believe in something). Scientists (and psychologists), however, aim to conduct well-controlled, objective and **empirical** studies. Such knowledge enables us to control our world, for example build bridges and treat schizophrenia. If the knowledge is not true, our bridges will collapse and our treatments won't work.

In order to uncover 'truths' about the world, scientists use the **scientific method**.

AN EMPIRICAL TEST

▲ The top picture is of a burger from a well known fast food outlet. This is what you are led to expect you will get. But what about the reality? You may think you know something, but unless you test this empirically you cannot know if it is true. The picture under it is the *empirical* evidence of what the burgers are really like. 'Empirical' refers to information gained through direct observation. Science uses empirical methods to separate unfounded beliefs from real truths.

(Thanks to Professor Sergio della Sala for this tasty and memorable example of empiricism.)

AN EXAMPLE OF THE SCIENTIFIC METHOD

1. **Observe behaviour in the natural world** The evolutionary psychologists John Lycett and Robin Dunbar (2000) observed two interesting facts about mobile phones. First, apparently a lot of people have fake mobiles. Second, they noticed (when sitting around in a pub) that men seem to play around with their phones more than women do. Men would take their phones out and place them on the bar counter or table for all to see. Women generally kept their phones in their handbags and only got them out if the phone rang or they wanted to make a call. Why would men be more interested in displaying their phones than women?

2. **Propose a theory** Lycett and Dunbar proposed that men were using mobile phones as a form of courtship display, in the same way that a male peacock displays his magnificent tail as an indicator to females that he is worth mating with (a phone advertises financial status and the owner's importance in a social network).

3. **Test a hypothesis** In order to test their theory, Lycett and Dunbar set up a study. Their hypothesis was: 'Men and women differ in their mobile phone behaviour – men are more likely to display their phones and also to "play" with them in public places.'
   The researchers observed the behaviour of men and women in pubs, recording who used their phones or displayed them, and how they handled the phone. Over their study period, 32% of the men were observed to display a mobile phone, whereas only 13% of the women did.
   The researchers also noted that the amount of time the men spent toying with and displaying their phones increased significantly as the number of men relative to women increased, rather as male peacocks fan open their feathers more vigorously the greater the number of competing suitors in view.

4. **Draw conclusions** These findings support the hypothesis proposed by Lycett and Dunbar that men use mobile phones in a different way than women, and support their explanation that this might be a form of mating display.

Science and pseudoscience

The two main features of science are:
- *It aims to be objective and systematic.*
- *It is verifiable, i.e. you can check the results of a study by repeating it, or cross-referencing it with another study in order to see whether the findings are true.*

Without science, people are susceptible to superstition and charlatans, beliefs in miracle cures and 'knowledge' of the future. Some people use science to sell their products or their services – they say this drug or that programme is 'scientifically proven' – but is it? One of the reasons for studying science is so that you, too, can learn to control your world and separate science from pseudoscience.

DO IT YOURSELF

1. From what you have learned about each psychological approach, discuss in small groups whether you would consider each one to be scientific or non-scientific. Explain your reasons.

2. Once you have decided, present your answers to the class. If you disagree, have a class debate.

3. Try some investigations yourself. Select some behaviour you have noticed about people. Perhaps it might also be related to the ways they use mobile phones, or behaviour on Facebook! Propose an explanation. Work out a way that you might test the behaviour and see what you discover.

4. Do some research on the internet to find out about psychological research. On Google, use search terms such as 'psychology experiments', 'classic psychology studies' or 'brilliant psychology studies'. Work in pairs. Find one study you think is really interesting, and then present it to your class.

Approaches in Psychology

UNIT 1

▲ Approaches in psychology were once called 'schools of thought', they embody a shared set of assumptions about human behaviour and the methods appropriate to its study. Adherents of any approach hold assumptions about the causes of behaviour and use a common set of concepts when giving an explanation. They also tend to use a common set of research methods.

The specification for AS Unit 1

PY1 20% 1¼ hours Approaches in Psychology	
Exam: Candidates answer five compulsory questions on psychology.	Four major psychological approaches form the basis of Unit 1. Candidates must be able to: ▶ Outline the main assumptions of each approach. ▶ Describe one theory and one therapy linked with each approach. ▶ Evaluate the strengths and weaknesses of each approach. ▶ Explain and evaluate the methodology used by each approach. ▶ Compare and contrast in terms of similarities and differences with other approaches. **Biological approach:** Selye's general adaptation syndrome (GAS) and psychosurgery or chemotherapy. **Behaviourist:** Social learning theory of aggression, aversion therapy or systematic desensitisation. **Psychodynamic:** Freud's theory of personality development and dream analysis or free association. **Cognitive:** Attribution theory and cognitive behavioural therapy (CBT) or rational emotive therapy (RET).

COMMENTS ON THE SPECIFICATION AND ORGANISATION OF THIS CHAPTER

In this part of your AS Psychology course you are going to study different approaches that psychologists use to explain behaviour. To help you understand the approaches, you will look at specific examples of the named approaches. For example, in order to study the biological approach you are going to look at Selye's GAS model, which is used to explain stress.

The first four chapters of this book deal with each of the approaches named in the specification – the biological, behaviourist, psychodynamic and cognitive approaches.

Health warning

The exam information given on this spread is correct at the time of writing. However exams evolve and there are often changes. We have a website (www.folensblogs.com/psychcompanion/blog/) where you can find any updates, as well as the official WJEC site (www.wjec.co.uk).

For each approach the following topics are covered

Spread 1: Assumptions We start each chapter by describing three key assumptions of the approach. As you read the rest of the chapter, you will see these assumptions 'in action' in the theory and therapy that are covered.

Spread 2: Theory The specification identifies one theory for each approach. This is covered on one double-page spread. You do not need to be able to evaluate this theory.

Spread 3 and 4: Therapy Two therapies for each approach are covered but you need to study only one of these. Again, each therapy is covered on one double-page spread.

Spread 5: Strengths and weaknesses For each approach, you also need to understand the strengths and weaknesses of the approach. In the AS exam you will never be asked to evaluate the theory or therapy, you will only be asked to evaluate the general approach. However, you will be asked to compare and contrast the approaches, so we consider this on the spread that evaluates each approach.

Spread 6: Methodology Two methods that are typical of the approach are explained and evaluated.

In addition, in each chapter there are the following elements.

Can you? questions On each spread you will find 'Can you?' questions, prepared by a senior examiner to help you focus on the content of the page in a way that will help you answer exam questions.

Do It yourself activities These will help you gain a deeper understanding of the topic.

End of chapter review This includes a diagrammatic summary of the chapter, a page of revision activities and exercises, and student answers to typical exam questions plus an examiner's comments.

PY1 – Approaches in psychology

This is what a typical set of questions will look like in the AS Unit 1 exam. The questions always follow the same pattern, e.g. question 1(a) is about two assumptions of one approach. All that changes is the theory/therapy/approach.

---

1 hour 15 minutes (60 marks)

Answer all questions.

1. (a) **Outline** two assumptions of the behaviourist approach. [4]
   (b) **Describe** the social learning theory of aggression. [8]
2. **Describe** how the biological approach has been applied to either Psychosurgery or Chemotherapy. [12]
3. (a) **Evaluate** two strengths of the cognitive approach. [6]
   (b) **Evaluate** two weaknesses of the cognitive approach. [6]
4. **Compare and contrast** the biological and psychodynamic approaches in terms of similarities and differences. [12]
5. **Explain and evaluate** the methodology used by the psychodynamic approach. [12]

Chapter 1 The biological approach

The **biological approach** aims to explain all behaviour and experience in terms of physical bodily processes. For example, when you feel stressed this usually involves a sensation of your heart pounding, your palms being sweaty and so on. These are physical symptoms created by activation of the nervous system. Your experience of stress is caused by biological processes. The nervous system is divided into the **central nervous system (CNS)** and the **autonomic nervous system (ANS)**, which is further subdivided into the **sympathetic** and **parasympathetic branches**. The CNS comprises the brain and spinal cord, containing about 12 billion nerve cells (neurons).

Assumption 1 Behaviour can be explained in terms of different areas of the brain

Many different areas of the human brain have been identified that are specialised for certain functions. The **cerebral cortex** covers the surface of the brain like a tea-cosy, and is much folded and grey in colour. This is the region of the brain responsible for higher cognitive functions. The cerebral cortex is divided into four lobes. The most important is the **frontal cortex** or **lobe** is responsible for fine motor movement and thinking. Other lobes include the occipital lobe, which is associated with vision.

   Underneath the cortex there are various **subcortical** structures, such as the **hypothalamus**, which integrates the ANS (important in stress and emotion).

Assumption 2 Behaviour can be explained in terms of neurotransmitters

Neurons are electrically excitable cells that form the basis of the nervous system. The flexibility of the nervous system is enhanced by having many branches at the end of each neuron (called *dendrites*) so that each neuron connects with many others. One neuron communicates with another neuron at a **synapse**, where the message is relayed by chemical messengers (**neurotransmitters**). These neurotransmitters are released from **presynaptic vesicles** in one neuron, and will either stimulate or inhibit receptors in the other neuron. The **synaptic cleft** or **gap** is about 20nm (nanometres) wide. Some common neurotransmitters are: **dopamine** (associated with rewards and also schizophrenia), **serotonin** (sleep and arousal), **adrenaline** (arousal) and **GABA** (decreases anxiety).

Assumption 3 Behaviour can be explained in terms of hormones

Hormones are biochemical substances that are produced in one part of the body (endocrine glands such as the pituitary and adrenal glands) and circulate in the blood, having an effect on target organ(s). They are produced in large quantities but disappear very quickly. Their effects are slow in comparison with the nervous system, but very powerful. Examples of hormones include **testosterone** (a male hormone) and **oestrogen** (female hormone). Some hormones such as **adrenaline** are also neurotransmitters.

Genetic explanations

*The biological approach also includes genetic explanations, i.e. that certain behaviours are inherited from your parents (**nature**). Some characteristics are determined by one **gene** (e.g. eye colour), whereas for most characteristics (e.g. intelligence or mental illness), many genes are involved. Genes generally create a predisposition to behave in a certain way rather than determining behaviour, and interact with life experiences.*

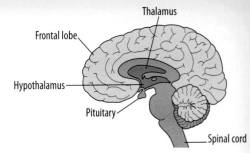

▲ Some important regions in the brain.

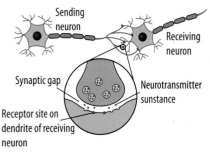

▲ A diagram of a neuron.

DO IT YOURSELF
No. 1.1

The brain is divided into two halves (or hemispheres), each of which has some special functions. If you perform two tasks that involve the same brain hemisphere, you should be slower at both tasks than if performing two tasks where one involves the right hemisphere and one the left. You can demonstrate this quite easily by doing the following experiment.

Tap your right finger while reading a page from a book (both involve the left hemisphere). And then repeat the finger-tapping with your right finger without doing any reading. On each occasion, count how many finger taps you manage in 30 seconds and compare these scores.

CAN YOU...?
No. 1.1

1... Name **two** areas of the brain and provide some extra information about each.

2... Explain the function of neurotransmitters and give **two** examples of neurotransmitters.

3... Give **two** examples of hormones and their functions.

EXAM QUESTION

Outline two assumptions of the biological approach. [4]

***Notes** In the exam, you will be asked to outline **two** assumptions of **one** of the four approaches. The question will be worth 4 marks. You should structure your answer in the following way.*

▶ *Identify one assumption.*

▶ *Explain/detail this assumption.*

▶ *Identify a second assumption.*

▶ *Explain/detail this assumption.*

Selye's GAS model

Stress is a good example of a behaviour that is explained using the **biological approach**. 'Stress' describes the way you feel when under pressure – when the perceived demands of a situation are greater than your perceived ability to cope, particularly when these demands are seen as endangering your well-being in some way. For example, a person who has built up an exam into something that is incredibly demanding and yet knows that he or she has done very little revision, will experience stress, *but only if* failing the exam will result in pretty unpleasant consequences for him or her.

The stress response is important to the survival of an animal because the bodily changes associated with stress are essential in conditions of fight or flight (i.e. attacking or running away). Without your stress response, you are in danger of being run over by a car or being attacked by an angry dog.

Much of our understanding of the nature of stress can be traced back to the pioneering work of Hans Selye, described on this page. He coined the use of the word 'stress' in this context, a practice extended to other languages where the same word is in use – *le stress* in French, *der Stress* in German, and so on.

▲ Modern humans face very different stressors to those faced by early humans, yet are equipped with the same stress response, which may not always be **adaptive**.

DO IT YOURSELF

No. 1.2

What happens when you feel stressed?
You have probably had the experience yourself many times – a racing heart, sweaty palms and a dry mouth. These are all characteristic changes of the stress response. Did you know, for example, that one of the selective advantages of sweating when faced with danger is that it makes the body slippery and more difficult to catch hold of!

The biological explanation for this is that the perception of a threat (stressor) arouses a part of your nervous system – the **sympathetic nervous system** – that produces adrenaline so you are ready for fight or flight.

Test out your own stress responses. Arrange for volunteers to engage in mildly stressful tasks, such as giving a presentation to the class or doing the particularly frustrating *Stroop task* (see faculty.washington.edu/chudler/words.html).

Take physiological measurements before, during and after (called **repeated measures**), e.g. pulse rate, size of pupils (when aroused they are dilated), dryness of mouth, sweat (check underarms!) and perhaps even blood pressure if you have a blood pressure monitor. For example, calculate mean heart rate for your volunteers and represent it on a graph.
- Analyse your findings by producing some graphs.
- You could also ask participants to produce a subjective report of their sensations. Were there any changes over the three phases?
- Did people's subjective reports match their physiological data?
- Did you find individual differences in your volunteers? For example, were males more or less stressed than females?
- What did you learn about the stress response from this activity?

THE GAS MODEL

Selye's (1936, 1950) research, such as the study on the facing page, led him to conclude that when animals are exposed to unpleasant stimuli, they display a universal response to all stressors. He called this the **general adaptation syndrome** (**GAS**).
- It is 'general' because it is the same response to all agents.
- The term 'adaptation' is used because it is adaptive – the healthiest way for the body to cope with extreme stress.
- It is a 'syndrome' because there were several symptoms in the stress response.

Selye proposed three stages that lead up to illness, thus linking stress and illness – stress results in a depletion of physiological resources, which lowers the organism's resistance to infection.

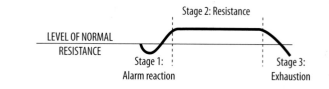

Stage 2: Resistance

LEVEL OF NORMAL RESISTANCE

Stage 1: Alarm reaction

Stage 3: Exhaustion

Stage 1: Alarm reaction

The threat or stressor is recognised and a response is made to the alarm. The **hypothalamus** in the brain triggers the production of **adrenaline** from the **adrenal glands** (which lie on top of the kidneys). Adrenaline causes sensations that are often labelled an 'adrenaline rush' – increased heart rate, sweaty palms, fast breathing and so on. This leads to readiness for 'fight or flight'.

Stage 2: Resistance

If the stress continues, then it is necessary to find some means of coping. The body is adapting to the demands of the environment, but at the same time resources are gradually being depleted. The body appears to be coping whereas, in reality, physiologically speaking, things are deteriorating.

Stage 3: Exhaustion

Eventually the body's systems can no longer maintain normal functioning. At this point, the initial symptoms may reappear (sweating, raised heart rate, etc.). The adrenal glands may be damaged from previous over-activity, and the **immune system** may not be able to cope because production of necessary proteins (e.g. **cortisol**) has been slowed in favour of other needs. The result may be seen in stress-related illnesses such as ulcers, depression, cardiovascular problems and other mental and physical illnesses.

MEET THE RESEARCHER

Hans Selye (pronounced sell-yeh) was born in Hungary but spent most of his working life in Canada. He came from a family of physicians, and trained as a medical doctor in Prague. His work as a doctor led him to observe that people who were sick all shared certain signs and symptoms, the first step to his recognition of the concept of 'stress'.

In Canada he was in charge of a large research lab, with 40 assistants and 15000 lab animals. One of his colleagues recalled the energy and dedication he displayed – typically he would rise at 5.00am, take a dip in his pool at home, and then cycle some 10km to his lab, where he would then work for up to 14 hours. He rarely had days off, and went in to work at weekends and on holidays.

The end result was a formidable list of publications – more than 1700 research papers and 40 books. He was nominated several times for a Nobel prize for the enormous contribution he made to our understanding of stress.

▼ Hans Selye 1907–1982.

HANS SELYE'S RESEARCH WITH RATS

Aims and context

Selye worked in a hospital and noted that all hospital patients shared a common set of symptoms (aches and pains, loss of appetite) no matter what was actually wrong with them. Later, when conducting research on the effects of hormones using rats, Selye (1936) again noticed this 'generalised' response. No matter what substance the rats were injected with, they always produced a similar response. He suggested that there was one internal mechanism for dealing with 'noxious agents' – which he called 'stressors'. The aim of this study was to test this hypothesis.

Procedures

Rats were exposed to various noxious agents: cold, surgical injury, production of spinal shock (cutting the spinal cord), excessive muscular exercise, or intoxications with sublethal doses of diverse drugs (adrenaline, morphine, formaldehyde, etc.).

Findings and conclusions

A typical syndrome was observed, the symptoms of which were independent of the nature of the damaging agent or the type of drug employed. This syndrome develops in three stages.

1. During the first stage (first 6–48 hours), all stimuli produced the same physiological triad:
   a) enlargement of the adrenal glands
   b) ulcers (open wounds) in the digestive system (stomach, intestines)
   c) shrinkage of the immune system.
2. If the treatment was continued, the appearance and function of the internal organs returned practically to normal.
3. With continued treatment, after one to three months (depending on the severity of the damaging agent) the animals lost their resistance and displayed the symptoms of the *physiological triad* seen in the first stage.

The results support the 'doctrine of non-specificity', that there is a non-specific response of the body to any demand made upon it. Selye suggested that the responses observed in rats to noxious agents might be similar to general defence reactions to illness.

Therapy 1   Psychosurgery

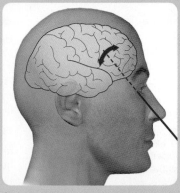

O n this spread and the next we look at two further examples of the **biological approach** in psychology. Both are examples of biological therapies that are used to treat mental disorders. On this spread, we look at **psychosurgery,** and on the next we will look at **chemotherapy**. You are required to study only one of these.

Views on psychosurgery tend to be extreme. There are those who are strongly in favour of this approach, and those who are vehemently against it, regarding it as nothing more than 'brain butchery'. However, it is important to remember that severe mental illness is also extremely disabling. Our society uses words like 'malignant' to describe cancer, but severe mental illness is possibly the most malignant disease you can have. Is it better to use methods that bring relief only sometimes and risk disastrous side effects, or to learn to tolerate mental problems?

▲ In the 1940s and 1950s, it was common to perform a lobotomy on patients with mental illness to control aggressive symptoms. One form of lobotomy – a transorbital lobotomy – was performed by inserting a sharp instrument into the brain through the eye socket. The prefrontal cortex, lying at the front, is thus damaged and this was thought to reduce aggressive behaviour.

HISTORY OF PSYCHOSURGERY

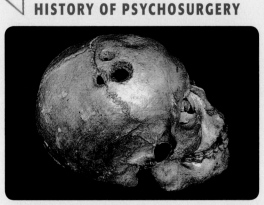

▲ Skull showing evidence of trepanning.

Psychosurgery goes back to the ancient practice of *trepanning* or *trephining*. Holes of about 4cm in diameter were cut in the skull of a living person using a sharp knife or special circular drill. The aim was to release evil spirits. The practice was common in Ancient Greece and Rome and into the Middle Ages in Europe, but it is much older than that – skulls dating back 40 000 years have been found showing signs of trepanning (Sabbatini, 1997).

In the 1940s and 1950s, a new form of psychosurgery was pioneered by Egas Moniz (see right). He heard about research where monkeys with aggressive tendencies were subdued after their **frontal lobes** were removed. He developed a similar operation for humans and was awarded the Nobel prize in 1949 for his work.

This method was popularised in the USA by Walter Freeman, who used the 'ice-pick technique', hammering an ice-pick into a patient's tear duct and wiggling it around to sever connections between the **prefrontal cortex** and the brain.

It is estimated that up to 50 000 lobotomies were performed, but ultimately the extreme side effects were recognised and the advent of **psychoactive drugs** for the treatment of mental disorders meant that the operation became unfashionable. Psychosurgery today is quite a different procedure.

PSYCHOSURGERY

Psychosurgery is a surgical procedure that is performed on the brain with the aim of treating mentally disordered behaviour. The term is not used in cases where there is a known organic cause of disturbed behaviour, such as when surgically removing a tumour or performing an operation to alleviate epilepsy. Psychosurgery may involve destroying sections of the brain, or, more commonly, severing fibres so that target areas of the brain are separated and 'functionally' removed.

Prefrontal lobotomy

The **prefrontal lobotomy** is a surgical procedure involving selective destruction of nerve fibres. It is performed on the frontal lobe of the brain, an area that is involved in impulse control and mood regulation. Its purpose is to alleviate some of the severe symptoms of mental illness. Initially, operations were performed on patients with *affective disorders* (i.e. various types of **depression**), other groups of patients included those with severe **obsessive-compulsive disorder** (**OCD**), and, less successfully, with **schizophrenia**. As a rule, the *severity* of the illness was a more important factor than the *type* of illness, along with consideration of how dangerous the patient was.

Moniz developed a surgical procedure called a **prefrontal leucotomy** in the 1930s. This involved drilling a hole on each side of the skull and inserting an instrument that resembled an ice-pick to destroy the nerve fibres underneath. Moniz later refined his technique by designing a 'leucotome', an instrument with a retractable wire loop that could cut into the white matter of the brain and sever nerve fibres. It was hoped that cutting into nerve pathways that carried thoughts from one part of the brain to the other, would relieve patients of their distressing thoughts and behaviours.

There is no doubt that the early practice of psychosurgery was both inappropriate and ineffective. Lobotomies had a fatality rate of up to 6%, and a range of severe physical side effects such as brain seizures and lack of emotional responsiveness (Comer, 2002). Modern psychosurgery is a different matter, although fundamentally the same objections could apply.

*Two of the mental disorders that psychosurgery is used on are **obsessive-compulsive disorder** (**OCD**) and **bipolar disorder**. OCD is anxiety disorder where an individual experiences recurrent obsessions – persistent ideas, thoughts, impulses and/or images that are seen as inappropriate or forbidden, and which cause intense anxiety. Compulsions develop as a means of controlling the obsessional thoughts. These compulsions are repetitive behaviours or thoughts such as repeated hand-washing. OCD can be severely debilitating.*

Bipolar disorder was previously referred to as manic-depression because sufferers oscillate between mania (being hyperactive, elated, making grandiose plans) and depression.

▶ The film *Frances* is about the Hollywood actress Frances Farmer. In the film, she is subject to a transorbital lobotomy. In real life, she did spend a number of years in a mental hospital but in fact never had a lobotomy. The film shows graphic detail of some of the horror of early lobotomies.

Recently Howard Dully (2007) produced a book called *My Lobotomy*, vividly describing his experiences as a lobotomy patient which gives disturbing insights into the whole process.

However, it is important to recognise that modern-day lobotomies are much less primitive, although the end result may be the same. For example, Mary Lou Zimmerman received psychosurgery (a cingulotomy and a capsulotomy) for untreatable OCD. Unfortunately, the operation resulted in crippling brain damage rather than a cure. Her family sued the US clinic that treated her, claiming they had not been informed of the dangerous and experimental nature of the surgery. A jury, after hearing expert witnesses, awarded her $7.5 million in damages.

Stereotactic psychosurgery

More recently, neurosurgeons have developed far more precise ways of surgically treating mental disorders such as OCD, bipolar disorder, depression and eating disorders that fail to respond to psychotherapy or other forms of treatment.

Instead of removing large sections of frontal lobe tissue, neurosurgeons nowadays use brain scanning, such as **MRI scans** to locate exact points within the brain and sever connections very precisely. The procedure is done using an anaesthetic.

In OCD, for example, a circuit linking the orbital **frontal lobe** to deeper structures in the brain, such as the **thalamus**, appears to be more active than normal. The bilateral **cingulotomy** is designed surgically to interrupt this circuit. Surgeons can either burn away tissue by heating the tip of the electrode, or use a non-invasive tool known as a *gamma knife* to focus beams of radiation at the target site.

In a **capsulotomy**, surgeons insert probes through the top of the skull and down into the capsule, a region of the brain near the **hypothalamus** that is part of the circuit connecting this area to the cortex. They then heat the tips of the probes, burning away tiny portions of tissue.

In a general review of research, Cosgrove and Rauch (2001) reported that cingulotomy was effective in 56% of OCD patients, and capsulotomy in 67%. In patients with major affective disorder, cingulotomy was effective in 65%, and capsulotomy in 55%. However, given that the authors claimed that only about 25 patients per year are currently treated in this way in the USA, the number of patients studied is very small. Also, Bridges *et al.* (1994) have pointed out that, as a treatment of last resort, no controlled trial against a comparable treatment is possible.

Deep brain stimulation

A possible alternative to psychosurgery is **deep brain stimulation** (**DBS**), where surgeons thread wires through the skull. No tissue is destroyed. The wires, which remain embedded in the brain, are connected to a battery pack implanted in the chest. The batteries produce an adjustable high-frequency current that interrupts the brain circuitry involved in, for example, OCD. If it doesn't work, it can always be turned off. Mayberg *et al.* (2005) found that four out of six patients with severe depression experienced a striking remission after treatment involving stimulation of a small area in the frontal cortex.

There are other similar techniques, including transcranial magnetic stimulation and vagus nerve stimulation.

DO IT YOURSELF

No. 1.3

Divide your class into groups. Each group should take one form of psychosurgery and prepare:
• an engaging and informative talk about that technique
• a poster display
• a handout of notes
• a quick quiz about the topic, including the answers.

Examiner hint

In order to gain the full 12 marks, your answer must provide a link between the aims of psychosurgery and the main assumptions of the biological approach.

CAN YOU...? No.1.3

1... Explain what psychosurgery is.

2... Outline the historical development of psychosurgery.

3... Briefly describe **three** different psychosurgery techniques.

4... Outline **two** findings from research studies and state what conclusion can be drawn from each of these studies.

EXAM QUESTION

Describe how the biological approach has been applied to either psychosurgery or chemotherapy. [12]

*Notes In the exam, you will be asked to describe **one** therapy. In total you will have studied four therapies (one for each of the four approaches). This question will be worth 12 marks. In order to gain the full 12 marks, your answer should satisfy the same criteria as those listed on page vii. You might include the following in an answer about psychosurgery.*

▶ *A brief outline of the aims of psychosurgery and how these link with the assumptions of the biological approach.*

▶ *The historical development of psychosurgery.*

▶ *Examples of how psychosurgery has been used.*

▶ *Research findings into psychosurgery.*

▶ *Your answer should be about 400–450 words in length.*

Therapy 2 Chemotherapy

Chemotherapy is the term used to describe the use of **psychoactive drugs** to treat mental disorders. 'Psychoactive' refers to drugs that affect psychological, as opposed to physical, conditions. In other words, drugs that treat, for example, **depression** rather than drugs that treat viral infections. A quarter of all the medication prescribed through the National Health Service (NHS) consists of psychoactive drugs – drugs that modify the working of the brain and affect mood and behaviour (SANE, 2009).

Such drugs were first developed in the 1950s, and revolutionised the treatment of mental disorder because they controlled many of the symptoms of serious disorders (such as hallucinations or crippling depression), enabling patients to conduct relatively normal lives. The use of these drugs is not restricted to adults. In 2003, it was estimated that more than 40 000 children and teenagers in the UK were taking drugs for the treatment of depression.

On the previous spread, we looked at **psychosurgery**, another technique used by the biological approach. The alternative is for you to study chemotherapy, discussed on this spread. You are required to study only one of these.

Schizophrenia

Schizophrenia is characterised by a profound disruption of thought and emotion, which affects a person's language, perception, affect, and even sense of self. The symptoms of schizophrenia are typically divided into positive and negative symptoms. Positive symptoms are those that appear to reflect an excess or distortion of normal functions, such as hearing voices or feeling controlled by aliens. Negative symptoms are those that appear to reflect a diminution or loss of normal functions, such as reduced emotional feelings and lack of goal-directed behaviour.

THE MECHANICS OF DRUG THERAPY

Before drugs can work, they have to enter the bloodstream and travel to the brain, which is protected from substances in the blood by the blood–brain barrier. When taken by mouth, drugs are absorbed by the gut and pass into the liver. This breaks down and destroys much of the active ingredients of the drug so that less is available to cross the blood–brain barrier. If the drug is injected, it enters directly into the bloodstream, bypassing the liver. This means that a given effect can be achieved with smaller doses when the drug is injected than when it is taken by mouth.

DO IT YOURSELF
No. 1.4

Divide your class into groups. Each group should take one form of chemotherapy and prepare:

- an engaging and informative talk about that technique
- a poster display
- a handout of notes
- a quick quiz about the topic, including the answers.

CHEMOTHERAPY (DRUGS)

The three main types of psychoactive drugs are antipsychotics, antidepressants and antianxiety drugs.

Antipsychotic drugs

Antipsychotic drugs treat **psychotic** mental disorders such as **schizophrenia**. A patient with a psychotic mental disorder has lost touch with reality and has little insight into his or her condition. **Conventional antipsychotics** (such as *chlorpromazine*, given a brand name such as *Largactil*) are used primarily to combat the positive symptoms of schizophrenia. These drugs block the action of the neurotransmitter **dopamine** in the brain by binding to, but not stimulating, dopamine receptors (see diagram above).

The **atypical antipsychotic drugs** (such as *clozapine*, given a brand name such as *Clozaril*) act by only temporarily occupying dopamine receptors, and then rapidly dissociating to allow normal dopamine transmission. This may explain why such atypical antipsychotics have lower levels of side effects (such as *tardive dyskinesia* – involuntary movements of the mouth and tongue) compared with conventional antipsychotics.

Antidepressant drugs

Depression is thought to be due to insufficient amounts of neurotransmitters such as **serotonin** being produced in the nerve endings (**synapse**). In normal brains, neurotransmitters are constantly being released from the nerve endings, stimulating the neighbouring neurons. To terminate their action, neurotransmitters are reabsorbed into the nerve endings and are broken down by an enzyme. Antidepressants work either by reducing the rate of reabsorption, or by blocking the enzyme that breaks down the neurotransmitters. Both of these mechanisms increase the amount of neurotransmitter available to excite neighbouring cells.

The most commonly prescribed antidepressant drugs are **selective serotonin reuptake inhibitors** (**SSRIs**) such as *Prozac*. These work by blocking the transporter mechanism that reabsorbs serotonin into the presynaptic cell after it has fired. As a result, more of the serotonin is left in the synapse, prolonging its activity and making transmission of the next impulse easier.

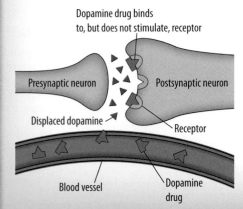

Dopamine drug binds to, but does not stimulate, receptor

Presynaptic neuron

Postsynaptic neuron

Displaced dopamine

Receptor

Blood vessel

Dopamine drug

◀ The diagram shows the synapse between two neurons. **Neurotransmitters** transmit information across the synapse. Drugs are delivered via blood vessels.

Conventional antipsychotics block the action of dopamine by binding to dopamine receptors. Other drugs, such as SSRIs (see below), also work by blocking the action of nervous transmission.

Antianxiety drugs

The group of drugs most commonly used to treat anxiety and **stress** are **benzodiazepines** (**BZs**). They are sold under various trade names such as *Librium*, *Valium*, *Halcion* and *Xanax*. BZs slow down the activity of the **central nervous system**. They do this by enhancing the activity of **GABA**, a biochemical substance (or neurotransmitter) that is the body's natural form of anxiety relief. About 40% of the **neurons** in the brain respond to GABA which, when released, has a general quietening effect on many of the neurons in the brain. It does this by reacting with special sites (called GABA receptors) on the outside of receiving neurons. When GABA locks into these receptors, it opens a channel that increases the flow of *chloride ions* into the neuron. Chloride ions make it harder for the neuron to be stimulated by other neurotransmitters, thus slowing down its activity and making the person feel more relaxed.

Beta-blockers (**BBs**) are also used to reduce anxiety. They reduce the activity of **adrenaline** and **noradrenaline**, which are part of the **sympathetic nervous system**'s response to stress. BBs bind to receptors on the cells of the heart and other parts of the body that are usually stimulated during sympathetic arousal. By blocking these receptors, it is harder to stimulate cells in this part of the body, so the heart beats slower and with less force, and blood vessels do not contract so easily. This results in a fall in blood pressure, and therefore less stress on the heart. The person feels calmer and less anxious. BBs are often used by sportsmen (e.g. snooker players) and musicians to reduce arousal because sympathetic arousal may have a negative effect on performance.

Effectiveness of chemotherapy

Drug therapies are popular with patients because they are easy to use, however they may have unpleasant or even dangerous side effects. For example, antipsychotic medications lead to *tardive dyskinesia* (uncontrollable movements) in 30% of those taking the drug (Hill, 1986) and research has found that patients taking SSRIs are twice as likely to commit suicide (Ferguson *et al.*, 2005).

Drugs are also popular because they reduce the symptoms of mental disorders. This is usually assessed by giving one group of patients the drug while another group is given a **placebo** – a substance that has no *pharmacological* effects (i.e. it has no effect on the body). Patients are given medication but do not know whether it is the real thing or the placebo. This enables us to determine whether the effectiveness of the drug is due its pharmacological properties or due to something psychological (e.g. simply believing that taking the drug will make you better).

There are thousands of studies looking at the effectiveness of drugs, and many of them indicate that drugs are superior to placebos. For example Kahn *et al.* (1986) followed nearly 250 patients over 8 weeks and found that BZs were significantly superior to a placebo. However, many other studies have found little or no benefits, suggesting that many of the benefits of drugs are due to the expectation that they will improve mental health rather than their pharmacological content.

Dopamine and *serotonin* are both neurotransmitters that have been associated with a number of behaviours. Dopamine is linked to schizophrenia. Low levels of serotonin are related to depression, and high levels have been linked to anxiety.

Examiner hint

In order to gain the full 12 marks, your answer must provide a link between the aims of chemotherapy and the main assumptions of the biological approach.

CAN YOU...?   No.**1.4**

1... Explain what chemotherapy is, including a definition of the term 'psychoactive'.

2... Describe **two** or **three** types of psychoactive drugs, explaining how they work and what disorders they are used to treat.

3... Describe at least **two** research findings related to the effectiveness of chemotherapy.

EXAM QUESTION

Describe how the biological approach has been applied to either psychosurgery or chemotherapy. [12]

*Notes In the exam, you will be asked to describe **one** therapy. In total you will have studied four therapies (one for each of the four approaches). This question will be*

worth 12 marks. In order to gain the full 12 marks, your answer should satisfy the same criteria as those listed on page vii. You might include the following in an answer about chemotherapy.

▸ *A brief outline of the aims of chemotherapy and how these link with the assumptions of the biological approach.*

▸ *Examples of different kinds of chemotherapy.*

▸ *Examples of how chemotherapy has been used.*

▸ *Research findings into chemotherapy.*

▸ *Your answer should be about 400–450 words in length.*

Evaluating the biological approach

You have studied two examples of the **biological approach** – one theory (the **GAS model**) and one therapy (either **psychosurgery** or **chemotherapy**). It is now time to use your understanding of the biological approach to consider its strengths and weaknesses. To help you, we have provided some additional examples of the biological approach.

➕ Strengths of the biological approach

1. Scientific approach

At the beginning of this chapter we looked at the assumptions of the biological approach, which were that behaviour can be explained in terms of the brain, **neurotransmitters** and **hormones** (i.e. biological systems). This means that biological explanations have clear variables that can be measured, tracked and examined. This enables psychologists to conduct scientific research studying these variables.

For example, psychosurgery involves functionally removing parts of the brain. Such procedures are based on earlier research that has linked areas of the brain to certain behaviours such as aggression.

In the case of chemotherapy, research has investigated the links between psychoactive drugs and the production of certain neurotransmitters (such as **dopamine**), and linked this to behaviour.

Selye exposed rats to certain noxious agents (such as drugs or extreme cold) and then observed the effects these 'agents' had on the behaviour and physiological responses of the animals.

All of these examples of research are scientific insofar as they fulfil the aims of scientific research – to conduct objective, well controlled studies and, ideally, to demonstrate causal relationships. Thus a strength of the biological approach is that it lends itself to scientific research that can then be used to support biological explanations.

2. Determinist approach

As well as being scientific, the biological approach is also **determinist**. One strength of being determinist is that if we know what 'predetermines' our behaviour, we are more likely to be able to treat people with abnormal behaviour. Psychologists seek, for example, to understand the functioning of neurotransmitters so they can predict the effects of neurotransmitters on normal and abnormal behaviour.

For instance, the neurotransmitter dopamine has been linked with the mental disorder of **schizophrenia**. The evidence comes from a number of sources. For example, the drug *amphetamine* is known to increase levels of dopamine and the large doses of the drug can cause some of the symptoms associated with schizophrenia (e.g. hallucinations). A second line of evidence comes from the drugs that are used to treat schizophrenia (**antipsychotics**), which reduce some of the symptoms and are known to reduce dopamine levels. This suggests that high levels of dopamine are causing the symptoms.

Similar research has been conducted in relation to psychosurgery. For example, **brains scans** have shown that certain areas of the brain are more active than others

▶ The biological approach sees behaviour as the consequence of biological systems, such as activity in the brain, neurotransmitters and hormones.

in patients with **OCD**. The **cingulotomy** (a form of psychosurgery) is therefore designed functionally to sever these areas in order to reduce the symptoms of OCD. The research suggests that OCD is caused by activity in these areas of the brain – a determinist explanation.

The strength of causal understandings is that they enable us to control our world. If we understand that prolonged stress causes physical illness, then we can reduce the negative effects by treating stress in the short-term. If mental illness is caused by biological factors, then we can treat mental illness using biological methods. Thus one strength of the biological approach is that it is determinist and provides explanations about the causes of behaviour so that we can use such understanding to improve people's lives.

3. Successful applications

The biological approach has led to many successful applications. For example, Selye's research had a major impact on our understanding of the link between stress and illness. It led to a large amount of other research that has demonstrated that people recover less quickly from wounds if they are stressed. Such understanding is applied in a hospital setting to reduce anxiety and stress in patients so that they recover more quickly.

The biological approach has also led to many forms of treatment for mental disorder, such as psychosurgery and chemotherapy. For example, the effectiveness of **capsulotomy** (a form of psychosurgery) in the treatment of OCD is discussed on page 7. Cosgrove and Rauch (2001) reported recovery rates of 67%, which is reasonable high.

Chemotherapy produces rather mixed results because drugs affect people differently. However, it is a particularly popular form of treatment because it is easy and enables many people with mental disorders to live relatively normal lives outside mental hospitals. For example, **bipolar disorder** (manic depression) has been successfully treated with drugs – Viguera *et al.* (2000), for instance, report that more than 60% of bipolar patients improve when taking lithium.

1. Reductionist approach

Biological explanations reduce complex behaviours to a set of simple explanations, for example reducing the experience of stress to the action of the hormone **adrenaline**.

Reductionism is a part of understanding how systems work, but the problem is that, in the process, we may lose a real understanding of the thing we are investigating. For example, the biological approach suggests that an illness such as schizophrenia is basically a complex physical–chemical system that has gone wrong. The psychiatrist R.D. Laing (1965) claimed that such an approach ignores the *experience* of distress that goes along with any mental illness, and is therefore at best an incomplete explanation.

Furthermore, a simplified explanation may prevent us reaching a true understanding of the target behaviour.

2. Nature rather than nurture

Mental illness has multiple causes, yet the biological approach focuses on just biology (**nature**), tending to ignore life experiences (**nurture**) and psychological factors such as how people think and feel.

For example, the biological approach to explaining schizophrenia is concerned with abnormal levels of certain neurotransmitters rather than with how patients feel about their illness. The biological approach to treatment is therefore concerned with adjusting the abnormal biological systems rather than with talking to patients about how they feel.

3. Individual differences

The biological approach is a **nomothetic** approach, looking to make generalisations about people and find similarities. It tends to ignore differences between individuals. For example, when stressed, some people produce higher levels of adrenaline than others, which, in turn, affects the long-term effects of stress.

Biological research studies a few individuals and assumes that everyone's biological systems behave in the same way. In fact, research on biological systems has tended to use male rather than female participants (animals and humans) because female hormone cycles may interfere with biological research. Such research bias could, however, produce an erroneous picture of behaviour: one with a male bias. For example, Taylor *et al.* (2000) suggest that men usually react to stress with a 'fight or flight' response, but women show a 'tend and befriend' response. This gender difference is seen in many species, with females responding to stressful conditions by protecting and nurturing their young (the 'tend' response), and by seeking social contact and support from other females (the 'befriend' response).

DO IT YOURSELF | No. 1.5

Compare and contrast

So far you have studied only one approach – the biological approach – and so you cannot compare and contrast it with the other approaches. However, you can lay the foundations for later chapters.

In the left-hand column below we have listed the issues and debates that were discussed in the introduction to this book. Some of these have been highlighted on this spread. Your task is to copy out this table and fill in the right-hand column in relation to the biological approach. We have filled in one entry for you as an example.

Issues and debates	The biological approach
Nomothetic/idiographic	
Nature–nurture	
Reductionism/holism	
Determinist/free will	Highly determinist. For example, suggests that neurotransmitters cause mental disorders such as depression and therefore chemotherapy can be used to alter or 'determine' neurotransmitter levels and reduce the symptoms of the mental disorder.
Scientific/non-scientific	
Methodology used	
Anything else	

The issues and debates listed in the table above are explained in the introduction to this book (see pages x–xi).

Compare and contrast

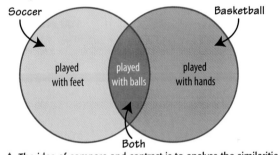

Soccer — played with feet · played with balls · Basketball — played with hands · Both

▲ The idea of compare and contrast is to analyse the similarities (compare) and differences (contrast) of two given ideas or things. Can you think of some other examples, such as comparing psychology and maths?

CAN YOU...? | No. 1.5

1... Identify **two** strengths of the biological approach.

2... Make **three** distinct points to explain each strength.

3... Identify **two** weaknesses of the biological approach.

4... Make **three** distinct points to explain each weakness.

EXAM QUESTIONS

Evaluate two strengths of the biological approach. [6]
Evaluate two weaknesses of the biological approach. [6]

*Notes In the exam, you are required to discuss **two** strengths and **two** weaknesses of **one** of the four approaches. For each strength and weakness, you should:*

▶ *Clearly identify the strength or weakness.*

▶ *Thoroughly explain why this is a strength or weakness in relation to the approach.*

▶ *Where appropriate, use examples drawn from theory/therapy to illustrate your answer.*

▶ *Think of each strength/weakness as being worth three marks (although, strictly speaking, this is not how they are marked).*

▶ *Write around 50–60 words on each strength/weakness.*

Methodology used by the biological approach

The final topic on the **biological approach** is a consideration of the methodology used by this approach. Obviously, researchers use all sorts of methods and techniques, but we have selected two that are particularly common in the biological approach – brain scanning and twin studies.

1. Brain scanning

The biological approach assumes that behaviour can be explained in terms of activity in the brain and nervous system. Therefore biological psychologists seek methods that allow them to view brain activity.

EEG – In the 1950s, the only method available for studying brain activity was the **electroencephalogram** (**EEG**). Electrodes are placed on the scalp, and electrical activity in different regions of the brain can be recorded. EEG was used in a classic study by Dement and Kleitman (1957) to detect different stages of sleep. As people go to sleep, their brain waves become slower. This can be detected by an EEG machine. During a night's sleep, this pattern occasionally changes to become very fast accompanied by the eyes darting about under closed lids. This is called **rapid eye movement** (**REM**) sleep. Dement and Kleitman woke participants up at various points during sleep and found that the participants were much more likely to report having a dream if they were awoken during REM sleep.

The development of brain scanning techiniques – In the past 30 years, much more precise methods of studying the brain have been developed.

▲ PET scans (see text) are usually shown as a coloured picture where the 'hot' colours, such as orange and red, are used to represent the areas where there is greatest activity, and the 'cold' colours, such as green and blue, represent the areas with least activity. PET scans tell us which bits of the brain are busy but not what they are doing. These PET scans show the difference between 'normal' brain activity (on the left) and that in a person with Alzheimer's disease (on the right). There is much less activity in the brain of the Alzheimer's patient.

CAT scans (computed axial tomography) – These involve taking a series of x-rays and combining them to form a comprehensive two- or three-dimensional picture of the area being scanned. Usually, a dye is injected into the patient as a contrast material and then he or she is placed in the cylindrical CAT scan machine that takes the pictures.

Strengths: CAT scans are useful for revealing abnormal structures in the brain such as tumours, or structural damage. The quality of the images provided by the CAT scan is much higher than that of traditional x-rays.

Weakness: CAT scans require more radiation than traditional x-rays, and the more detailed and complex the CAT scan is, the more radiation exposure the patient receives. Pregnant women are unable to be scanned this way, and repeated exposure should be avoided.

MRI scans (magnetic resonance imaging) – These involve the use of a magnetic field that causes the atoms of the brain to change their alignment when the magnet is on and emit various radio signals when the magnet is turned off. A detector reads the signals and uses them to map the structure of the brain.

A classic study by Maguire *et al.* (2000) used MRI scans to demonstrate that taxi drivers had larger **hippocampi** than non-taxi drivers, supporting the view that this area of the brain is important in spatial memories.

Functional MRI (**fMRI**) provides both anatomical and functional information by taking repeated images of the brain in action.

Strengths: MRI gives a more detailed image of the soft tissue in the brain than do CAT scans, and involves passing an extremely strong magnetic field through the patient rather than using x-rays. MRI is best suited for cases when a patient is to undergo the examination several times successively in the short term, because, unlike CAT, it does not expose the patient to the hazards of radiation.

Weakness: MRI scans take a long time and can be uncomfortable for patients.

PET scans (positron emission tomography) – This sort of scan involves administering slightly radioactive glucose (sugar) to the patient. The most active areas of the brain use glucose, and radiation detectors can 'see' the radioactive areas, so building up a picture of activity in the brain. The scans take between 10 and 40 minutes to complete and are painless.

Raine *et al.* (1997) used PET scans to compare brain activity in murderers and normal individuals. They found differences in areas of the brain such as the prefrontal cortex and the amygdala, regions previously associated with aggressive behaviour. However, they pointed out that such brain differences do not demonstrate that violence is caused by biology alone.

Strengths: PET scans reveal chemical information that is not available with other imaging techniques. This means that it can distinguish between benign and malignant tumours, for example. PET scans can also show the brain in action which is useful for psychological research.

Weaknesses: This is an extremely costly technique and therefore not easily available for research. Also, as the patient has to be injected with a radioactive substance, the technique can be used only a few times. Finally, PET scans are less precise than MRI scans.

DO IT YOURSELF

No. 1.6

Individually, or in groups, carry out research on a study that has made use of EEG, CAT, MRI, fMRI or PET scans.
- Note the aims of the research.
- Note the research findings.
- Evaluate the type of scanning device used.

You should prepare this information to present back to the group, and produce an overall handout on each type of scanning technique, along with its pros and cons.

2. Twin studies

One of the assumptions of the biological approach is the influence of **genes** on behaviour. Genes are the units of by which we inherit characteristics from our parents. Psychologists use **twin studies** to compare the effects of genetics (**nature**) versus experience (**nurture**).

Intelligence and twin studies – Bouchard and McGue (1981) studied the inheritance of IQ. They measured the intelligence of twins and compared their IQs (the score produced by an intelligence test). The degree to which two people are similar is expressed as a **concordance rate**. If two people have exactly the same IQ, the concordance rate is 100%, whereas 0% means absolutely no similarity.

Bouchard and McGue looked at **monozygotic (MZ)** twins. Such twins share 100% of their genes and are therefore called 'identical'. A review of more than 30 studies found a mean concordance rate of 86%. Even though this is not a perfect correlation, it suggests that a large part of intelligence appears to be inherited.

Research has also looked at **dizygotic (DZ)** twins, who are non-identical, sharing around 50% of their genes, the same as any two siblings. Research has found a mean concordance rate of 60% for DZ twins.

Twins reared apart – One of the problems with twin research is that twins not only share the same genes, but they also grew up in the same environment, and therefore any similarities may be due to environment as well as genetics. To try to separate these two influences, psychologists have looked at data from twins reared apart. Bouchard and McGue found 72% concordance for MZ twins reared apart. This continues to show a significant genetic contribution to intelligence.

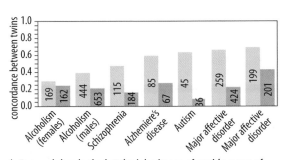

▲ Research has looked at the inheritance of a wide range of behaviours, including some of those shown in the graph. These studies have detected that some behaviours and disorders (e.g. schizophrenia) have a genetic link, but these concordance studies are based on correlational data, and this means that we can't really prove cause and effect as they neglect to consider the impact of the shared environment that twins have. They also overlook the fact that, although MZ twins do share 100% of their genes, they could be 'discordant' for a behaviour, not because they do not both have a gene that predisposes them to a behaviour or disorder, but because one of them may have been exposed to a 'trigger' that the other one has not.

Strengths

- As MZ twins share 100% of their genes, they make perfect participants for the study of genes on behaviour, and provide useful information for those that adopt the biological approach in psychology.
- Within the field of intelligence, for example, comparison between MZ twins reared together and apart has allowed psychologists to make sound assumptions about the relative importance of genes and environment on development (see research conducted by Bouchard and McGue, 1981).

Weaknesses

- Twins not only share between 50% (DZ) and 100% (MZ) of their genes, but are also often raised in exactly the same environment, and are treated in the same way in all areas of life (family, education, etc.). Concordance rates from psychological research should therefore be treated with caution, as it is difficult to untangle the relative effects of genetics versus environment.
- The study of twins reared apart is also problematic. Very often, twins separated at birth or at a young age will have been raised in very similar environments in terms of social class, education, family values, etc. Once again, in terms of looking at the **nature–nurture debate**, it is difficult to decipher the exact influence of genes/environment.

▲ Identical (MZ) twins are never totally identical despite having identical genes. Chance events throughout our lives have small effects – in fact, if you started all over again, you would turn out differently!

Genes contain instructions about the physical and behavioural characteristics of living things, such as your eye colour or the colour of a butterfly's wings. Offspring inherit these genes from their parents. The actual number of genes varies from one species to another. Humans have thousands of them.

Examiner hint

In order to ensure your answer to this question is thorough and relevant, you need to include examples of how the particular methodology is used within the approach. For example, when discussing the use of twin studies within the biological approach, you should bring in the work of Bouchard and McGue, or any other twin studies. This will help you explain the methodology thoroughly and coherently, and demonstrate to the examiner that you understand the methodology used within that particular approach. Answers where a candidate talks in a generic manner about certain research methods will not attract credit in the top two bands (see mark schemes on page vii).

CAN YOU...?

No.**1.6**

1... Identify **two** methods used by the biological approach, and for each describe an example of how this method was employed in a research study that used the biological approach.

2... For each method, outline and explain **two** strengths and **two** weaknesses of using this method in the study you described.

EXAM QUESTION

Explain and **evaluate** the methodology used by the biological approach. [12]

*Notes In the exam, you are required to explain and evaluate the methods used by **one** of the four approaches. It is vital that you clearly explain how the methods link*

with the assumptions of the approach, i.e. that they have clear relevance to the approach. A general guide in terms of structuring your answer is as follows.

▶ *Explain one method used by the approach (use examples that will highlight its relevance to the approach).*

▶ *Evaluate the strengths and weaknesses of this method.*

▶ *Explain a second method used by the approach (use examples that will again highlight its relevance).*

▶ *Evaluate the strengths and weaknesses of the second method.*

N.B. The top band of the mark scheme for this question requires: 'Methods are appropriate and clearly explained...and have clear relevance to the approach'.

Chapter 1 summary

Assumptions of the biological approach

Brain Different areas of the brain are linked to different functions, e.g. the frontal cortex is linked to thinking.

Neurotransmitters either stimulate or inhibit neurons in the brain, e.g. dopamine, adrenaline.

Hormones have an instant and short-lasting effect on target organs, e.g. testosterone, adrenaline.

Selye's GAS model

'General adaption syndrome' GAS
A general response to all stressors that is adaptive (helps the body cope); explains the link between stress and illness.

Three stages
1. Alarm: stressor perceived, adrenaline released for fight or flight.
2. Resistance: body adapts, apparently copes, but resources are depleted.
3. Exhaustion: initial symptoms reappear.

Research study
Selye (1936) Three stages of GAS occurred when he exposed rats to various noxious agents (e.g. cold, drugs); demonstrated the non-specific stress response.

Psychosurgery

Prefrontal lobotomy
Frontal lobe is functionally separated; involved in impulse control and mood. Early methods (e.g. Moniz) were primitive and ineffective.

Stereotactic psychosurgery
Precise location of target areas using MRI, e.g. capsulotomy where connections to region near thalamus are severed to relieve OCD; also cingulotomy.

Deep brain stimulation (DBS)
No tissue is destroyed; wires are placed through the brain tissue and high frequency current can be triggered to interrupt brain circuitry. Used successfully with depression.

Chemotherapy

Antipsychotic drugs
To treat psychotic disorders such as schizophrenia. Comprises conventional (e.g. chlorpromazine i.e. Largactil) and atypical (e.g. clozapine i.e. Clozaril) antipsychotics, which block the dopamine.

Antidepressant drugs
Raise levels of serotonin to reduce depression. SSRIs prevent the reuptake of serotonin at synapses. Other antidepressants block enzymes that break serotonin down.

Antianxiety drugs
Anxiety and stress are treated using benzodiazepines, which enhance GABA, or beta-blockers, which reduce adrenaline activity.

⊕ Strengths and weaknesses of the biological approach ⊖

Strengths
- A scientific approach – measurable variables enable well controlled, objective research.
- A determinist approach – causal relationships can be identified.
- Successful applications, e.g. Selye's research led to improved treatment for injured patients.

Weaknesses
- A reductionist approach – complex behaviour is reduced to actions of neurotransmitters and brain activity.
- Nature rather than nurture – ignores other factors such as life experiences and emotions.
- Tends to ignore individual differences, e.g. some people become more stressed than others.

Methodology of the biological approach

Brain scanning
Enables psychologists to measure brain activity.
- **CAT** scans take a series of x-rays showing brain structure.
- **MRI** scans detect brain structure using magnetic detectors, providing detailed information with no radiation.
- **fMRI** provides a picture of the brain in action.
- **PET** scans detect chemical and structural information and show the brain in action, but are very expensive and expose patients to radiation.

Twin studies
Enable psychologists to estimate the relative contribution of genetic (nature) and environmental (nurture) factors. High concordance rates for MZ twins demonstrate the importance of nature, especially when compared with DZ twins, and also with twins reared apart.
- **Strengths**: useful information, tells us about nature and nurture.
- **Weaknesses**: environments the same, twins reared apart share similar environments.

Review activities

Mind maps

A mind map is a visual representation of a topic, showing the links between the various elements. The links usually form a branching pattern, with the main topic in the centre and component elements/ideas radiating outwards. Small sketches/doodles can be added, as well as colours (highlighters, felt-tips). Each page of notes therefore has a unique, distinctive visual appearance (whereas pages of ordinary/linear notes all look very similar) (Buzan, 1993).

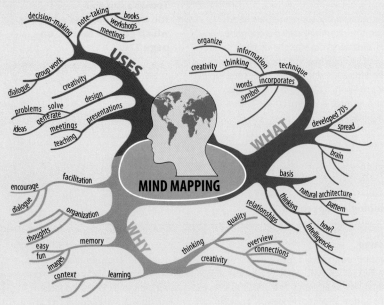

▲ A mind map about mind mapping.

The art of précis

Textbooks provide a large amount of text on the different topics you have to cover. Often there is more than you need for the exam. You need to select the 'golden nuggets' – the key pieces of information that must be remembered for the exam.

In this chapter, you have studied one theory (the GAS model) and one therapy. For each of these, list the golden nuggets of information that need to be remembered. You might select about 15–20 golden nuggets for each.

Now use these golden nuggets to construct:
- A 300-word account of the GAS model.
- A 400-word account of your therapy.

The assumptions of the biological approach

At the beginning of this chapter, we listed some assumptions of the biological approach. Draw a table like the one below and fill in examples from your studies.

	GAS model	Therapy (either psychosurgery or chemotherapy)
Assumption 1 Brain		
Assumption 2 Neurotransmitters		
Assumption 3 Hormones		

Key words

Go through the chapter and identify all the key terms in blue bold. Create a set of key cards for these words – write the key term on one card and write its definition on another card (you can find the definitions in the glossary/index).

One game you can play with these is called 'Concentration', which works best with two or three players. Place all the cards face down, with the key terms on the left and the definitions on the right. Turn over two cards – one from the left and one from the right. Do they match? If not, turn them face down again and let the next player have a go. If they do match, then you keep the cards.

Spot the mistakes

The text below contains a description of Selye's GAS model. Copy this text and identify all the mistakes! When you have finished compare your work with someone else and put the mistakes right.

Bill Selye conducted research in the 1920s on animals such as rats. It led him to conclude that, when animals are exposed to unpleasant stimuli, they display a universal response to all stressors. He called this the general adaptation system or GAS.

Selye proposed that this model can explain the link between stress and illness because stress results in a depletion of psychological resources and this lowers the organism's resistance to infection.

Stage 1 Alarm reaction

The threat or stressor is recognised and a response is made to the alarm. The hypothalamus in the brain triggers the production of dopamine from the adrenal glands. The effect is increased heart rate, sweaty palms, fast breathing and so on. This leads to readiness for 'fight or fidget'.

Stage 2 Acceptance

If the stress continues, then it is necessary to find some means of coping. The body is adapting to the demands of the environment, but at the same time resources are gradually being depleted. The body appears to be coping whereas, in reality, physiologically speaking, things are deteriorating.

Stage 3 Exhaustion

Eventually, the body's systems can no longer maintain normal functioning. At this point, new symptoms start (sweating, raised heart rate, etc.). The adrenal gland may be damaged from previous overactivity, and the immune system may not be able to cope because production of necessary proteins (e.g. adrenaline) has been slowed in favour of other needs. The result may be seen in stress-related illnesses such as ulcers, depression, cardiovascular problems and other mental and physical illnesses.

Example exam questions with student answers

Examiner's comments on these answers can be found on page 174.

EXAMPLE OF QUESTION 2

> **Describe** how the biological approach is applied to either psychosurgery or chemotherapy. [12]

Megan's answer

Chemotherapy can take many different forms. For example, antipsychotic drugs are used to treat things like schizophrenia. They do this by acting on the chemical called dopamine. Some antipsychotics have side effects though, such as involuntary movements of the mouth. Antidepressants are used to treat depression. One type of drug are the SSRIs which basically work by increasing the amount of serotonin in the bloodstream, these work for the patient as low levels of serotonin are thought to cause depression. Beta blockers are given to people with anxiety. These reduce levels of adrenaline and so help the person feel more calm and less stressed. Chemotherapy is therefore drug therapy.

Tomas's answer

You can read **Tomas's answer, which got full marks, on page 174.**

EXAMPLE OF QUESTION 5

> **Explain and evaluate the methodology used by the biological approach.** [12]

Megan's answer

The biological approach uses lab experiments so that they can manipulate the IV and observe the effects on the DV. This is done under very controlled conditions. There are lots of advantages to lab experiments. Firstly, there is a high control of variables, not only the IV but many EVs too. This allows cause–effect relationships to be established. Also because lab experiments follow standardised procedures, replication is possible, therefore increasing the experimental validity. However, there can be a problem of demand characteristics, where the participants may try and guess the purpose of the study, and behave in ways they might not normally. This also links to ecological validity – another problem with lab experiments. People who take part are unlikely to act in ways they normally would. Sometimes experimenter bias is a problem too, the experimenter may interpret the behaviour in ways that match the hypothesis, or even lead the participant into behaving in certain ways, for example, by reading a list of words really slowly so that participants will remember them.

Tomas's answer

The biological approach would make use of non-invasive methods such as brain scans; these include EEG, CAT, MRI and PET scans. EEG measures brain activity by placing electrodes onto the scalp, and are useful for investigating things like hemisphere function and stages of sleep. However, they do not provide us with images of the brain as do CAT, and MRI scans. CAT scans can show us an x-ray of the brain, and are used to look at brain structure, for example exact damage in brain damaged patients. MRI scans do not involve injecting a radioactive dye into the patient as do CAT scans, and are therefore good if a person has to be scanned several times in a short period. The most recent scanning device is known as PET – positron emission tomography. This type of scan differs from the others as it shows the chemical composition (metabolism) of the brain rather than just its structure. Therefore this is a more sophisticated scanning device, which can reveal information that the others cannot (such as whether a tumour is benign or not). Raine et al. studied criminal behaviour using PET scans; these were used to establish whether there were brain abnormalities in a sample of murderers. Advantages of these methods are that they are non-invasive in general, they do not cause permanent damage to the patient, yet they allow us to investigate the concept of localisation of function – the idea that certain areas of the brain are responsible for certain behaviours. PET scan s are effectively used to diagnose the early stages of neurological illnesses such as epilepsy, Alzheimer's disease, and other dementias. However, the radioactive exposure in PET imaging means that there is only a limited amount of times a patient can undergo this procedure. PET imaging is also extremely expensive, and for this reason is offered only in a limited number of medical centres in the world.

Twin studies are also of value to biopsychologists in investigating the assumption that behaviour is due to our genetic make-up. MZ twins share 100% of their genes, and so if behaviour is a product of our genes both twins should demonstrate the same behaviour. For example, Bouchard and McGue looked at both identical and non-identical twins when investigating whether intelligence could be due to nature. While twin studies provide useful information for the nature–nurture debate, and are able to help psychologists decipher whether certain disorders are genetic, they are not without criticism. Looking at concordance rates provides correlational data, and so cause–effect relationships cannot be established. For example, if twins have grown up in the same environment then they would have been exposed to the same social 'triggers', which could account for the similarities in their behaviour. This leads to another problem with comparing concordance rates in sets of twins, and that is that usually twins have grown up in exactly the same environment (or if not, very similar ones), and so the effects of biological versus environmental factors are difficult to untangle.

The essence of the **behaviourist approach** is that all behaviour is learned. The reason you tend to be aggressive or loving or interested in football or good at exams or suffer from a mental disorder can all be explained in terms of the experiences you have had, as opposed to any inherited dispositions. Behaviourists believe that we are born as a 'blank slate'. They also believe that behaviour is all that should concern psychologists – there is no need to search for the mind or analyse thoughts and feelings.

Assumption 1 Behaviour can be explained in terms of classical conditioning

New behaviours are acquired through *association*. Ivan Pavlov first described the process of classical conditioning in 1904 from his observations of salivation in dogs (see illustration on page 27). A 'behaviour' is a stimulus–response unit – food (a *stimulus*) produces salivation (a *reflex* response).

- Before conditioning, the food is an **unconditioned stimulus (UCS)** and salivation is an **unconditioned response (UCR)**.
- During conditioning, a **neutral stimulus (NS)**, such as the sound of a bell, occurs at the same time as the UCS and therefore acquires its properties.
- After conditioning, the sound of the bell is now a **conditioned stimulus (CS)**, which produces the salivation response, now a **conditioned response (CR)**.

Assumption 2 Behaviour can be explained in terms of operant conditioning

New behaviours are learned through *reinforcement*. At any time, an organism operates on the environment, resulting in positive consequences (rewards or **reinforcement**) or negative consequences (**punishments**).

Skinner (1938) demonstrated that an animal (e.g. pigeon or rat) in a Skinner box (shown below) randomly moves around the box. Occasionally an action will result in a food pellet being delivered. The food pellet acts as a **reinforcer**, so that the animal will increasingly repeat the behaviour that led to the reward (the food pellet). Reinforcers increase the probability that a behaviour will be repeated, punishers decrease the probability. Reinforcers can be **negative reinforcement** (escape from an unpleasant situation) or **positive reinforcement** (something pleasant).

Shaping explains how specific behaviours are learned – by reinforcing successively closer approximations to a desired performance.

Assumption 3 Behaviour can be explained in terms of social learning theory (SLT)

In SLT, learning is *primarily* through *observation*, i.e. indirect. Individuals observe role **models** (people with whom they identify) and learn about the consequences of behaviour through indirect or **vicarious reinforcement**. These consequences are represented as **expectancies of future outcomes** and stored as internal mental representations.

Observation may lead to learning (**observational learning**), but the *performance* of such behaviours is related to other factors. In the future, an individual will display the behaviour provided that the expectation of reward is greater than the expectation of punishment, and provided that the individual has the skills required to perform the behaviour.

The behaviour is maintained in the individual's repertoire if the individual is rewarded for his/her display of the behaviour; this is *direct* reinforcement. This will influence the value of the behaviour for that individual.

DO IT YOURSELF
No. 2.1

Try classical conditioning for yourself. If you blow air gently at someone's eye (using a straw), they will blink. This is a reflex response (UCR). The UCS is a puff of air.

Work in a group of three. Person 1 claps his or her hands (this is the NS), and immediately person 2 blows air at person 3's eye, causing them to blink. Before long you should find that clapping has become a CS.

CAN YOU...?
No. 2.1

1... Explain what is meant by classical and operant conditioning.

2... Explain the process of classical conditioning.

3... Describe the different kinds of reinforcement.

4... Explain the concepts of indirect learning and vicarious reinforcement.

EXAM QUESTION

Outline two assumptions of the behaviourist approach. [4]

Notes *In the exam, you will be asked to outline **two** assumptions of **one** of the four approaches. The question will be worth 4 marks. You should structure your answer in the following way.*

▶ *Identify one assumption.*

▶ *Explain/detail this assumption.*

▶ *Identify a second assumption.*

▶ *Explain/detail this assumption.*

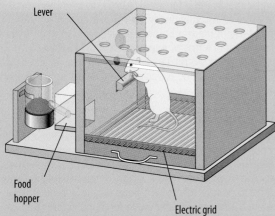

Lever

Food hopper

Electric grid

▲ A rat in a Skinner box. The rat might first be reinforced for pressing the lever, which over time should lead to a high frequency of lever-pressing. Then, we might begin to shock these rats after pressing the lever, which over time should lead to a reduced frequency of lever presses.

The social learning theory of aggression

Aggressive behaviour is viewed as one of the most disturbing forms of human social behaviour. Some psychologists believe that aggression is a legacy of our evolutionary ancestry, that people and animals behave aggressively because such behaviour is valuable for survival. In this view, aggression is **innate** and biological.

Behaviourists, however, see our aggressive behaviour arising out of our interactions with others in our social world. We learn when and how to behave aggressively by watching what other people do and then imitating this behaviour. This is the essence of the **social learning theory** of aggression.

Aggression is defined as behaviour between members of the same species that is intended to cause pain or harm.
- *Why do people behave aggressively?*
- *Why is one person more aggressive than another?*

MEET THE RESEARCHER

Albert Bandura was born in Canada in 1925. He lived in a small town where the school had only two teachers, so he found he had to do a lot of self-education. He observed: *'The content of most textbooks is perishable, but the tools of self-directedness serve one well over time'* (Pajares, 2004).

He first studied psychology by accident, but grew to like the subject, eventually working with some of the best known behaviourists of his day. However, he felt that direct reinforcement alone could not explain the complexity of human behaviour. In the 1960s, he developed his theory of social learning, and later developed this into social cognitive theory, which places emphasis on the self-regulating aspect of human behaviour – he believes that people are not just shaped by environmental forces but also have the capacity to direct themselves.

To students who are just beginning to study psychology, however, he is still best known for the Bobo studies he conducted nearly 50 years ago. *'The Bobo doll continues to follow me wherever I go … I recently checked into a Washington hotel only to have the clerk at the registration desk ask, "Did you do the Bobo doll experiment?" I explained: "I am afraid that will be my legacy." He replied: "Hell, that deserves an upgrade. I will put you in a suite in the quiet part of the hotel." So there are some benefits to the wide exposure'* (Bandura, 2004, page 626).

SOCIAL LEARNING THEORY (SLT)

Albert Bandura believed that aggression could not be explained using traditional learning theory where only *direct* experience was seen as responsible for the acquisition of new behaviours. Social learning theory suggests that we also learn by observing others. This enables us to learn the *specifics* of aggressive behaviour (e.g. the forms it takes, how often it is enacted, the situations that produce it and the targets towards which it is directed). This is not to suggest that the role of biological factors is ignored in this theory, but rather that a person's biological make-up creates a potential for aggression, and it is the actual *expression* of aggression that is learned. Bandura *et al.*'s classic study (1961, see facing page) illustrates many of the important principles of this theory.

Observation

Children primarily learn their aggressive responses through *observation* – watching the behaviour of role models and then *imitating* that behaviour. Whereas Skinner's **operant conditioning** theory claimed that learning takes place through direct reinforcement, Bandura suggested that children learn just by observing role models with whom they identify, i.e. **observational learning**.

Children also observe and learn about the consequences of aggressive behaviour by watching others being reinforced or punished. This is called indirect or **vicarious reinforcement**. Children witness many examples of aggressive behaviour at home and at school, as well as on television and in films. By observing the *consequences* of aggressive behaviour for those who use it, children gradually learn something about what is considered appropriate (and effective) conduct in the world around them. Thus they learn the behaviours (through observation), and they also learn whether and when such behaviours are worth repeating (through vicarious reinforcement).

Mental representation

Bandura (1986) claimed that in order for social learning to take place, children must form mental representations of events in their social environment. They must also represent possible rewards and punishments for their aggressive behaviour in terms of **expectancies of future outcomes**. When appropriate opportunities arise in the future, children will display the behaviour *provided* that the expectation of reward is greater than the expectation of punishment.

Maintenance through direct experience

If a child is rewarded (i.e. gets what he or she wants or is praised by others) for aggressive behaviour, they are likely to repeat the same action in similar situations in the future. This direct reinforcement then influences the value of aggression for that child. A child who has a history of successfully bullying other children will come to believe this to be a good way to get rewards. Aggression will, therefore, have considerable value for that child because of its association with the attainment of rewards.

Social learning theory is considered to be an example of the behaviourist approach – but it also has elements of the cognitive approach because of its emphasis on mental representations.

DIRECT AND INDIRECT REINFORCEMENT

Behaviourists believe that new behaviours are learned as a consequence of rewards (reinforcement). If a behaviour results in a 'pleasurable state of affairs' it is reinforced – more likely to be repeated. Such reinforcement can occur *directly* – for example, you might be rewarded for hitting your friend because he gives you a sweet. Or you may experience *indirect* reinforcement – you watch someone else hit a friend, which results in him getting a sweet. This is indirect or vicarious reinforcement and may lead you to repeat the behaviour yourself, in which case it is an example of observational learning. SLT involves both direct and indirect reinforcement – whereas Skinner's theory of operant conditioning was only concerned with direct reinforcement.

DO IT YOURSELF   No. 2.2

The TV programme *Supernanny* shows nanny Jo Frost taming troublesome children – her techniques involve both direct and indirect reinforcement (positive and negative), as well as punishment.

Look for some examples of the programme on YouTube, and produce a list of examples of the behaviourist approach in action. In particular, you should look for examples of indirect reinforcement (modelling) and direct reinforcement (both positive and negative).

THE BOBO DOLL STUDY

Albert Bandura and colleagues conducted a classic study to demonstrate that children learn aggressiveness through modelling – observing someone else behaving aggressively and later imitating this behaviour.

Bandura *et al.* (1961) arranged for some very young children (boys and girls aged 3–5 years) to watch an adult playing with some toys. Each child was taken individually to a room where there were toys. The child was joined by an adult who interacted with the child and played with the toys, one of which was a life-sized inflatable Bobo doll. Half of the children were exposed to adult models interacting aggressively with the Bobo doll, and half were exposed to models that were non-aggressive towards the doll.

The aggressive model displayed distinctive physically aggressive acts toward the doll, e.g. striking it on the head with the mallet and kicking it about the room, accompanied by verbal aggression such as saying 'POW'.

Following exposure to the model, the children were frustrated by being shown attractive toys that they were not allowed to play with. They were then taken to a room where, among other toys, there was a Bobo doll.

The children in the aggression condition reproduced a good deal of physically and verbally aggressive behaviour resembling that of the model. Children in the non-aggressive group exhibited virtually no aggression toward the doll.

The motivation for aggression

Although Bandura *et al.*'s study tells us that children do acquire aggressive responses as a result of watching others, it does not tell us much about *why* a child would be motivated to perform the same behaviours in the absence of the model. A classic experiment by Bandura and Walters (1963) fills this gap.

In this experiment, children were divided into three groups, each seeing a different ending to a film of an adult model behaving aggressively towards a Bobo doll.
- Group 1 saw the model rewarded for showing aggressive behaviour.
- Group 2 saw the model punished for showing aggressive behaviour.
- Group 3 observed the model with no subsequent consequences for the aggressive behaviour.

Bandura and Walters found that children's subsequent play with the doll was influenced by whichever film ending they had seen. Those who had seen the model being rewarded for aggressive acts, showed a high level of aggression in their own play. Those who had seen the model punished, showed a low level of aggression in their play, while those in the no-reward, no-punishment **control group** were somewhere in between these two levels of aggression. Bandura called this type of learning **vicarious learning** – the children were learning about the likely consequences of actions, and then adjusting their subsequent behaviour accordingly.

> **Examiner hint**
>
> *Note that Bandura's study of the imitation of aggression is a useful way to illustrate the theory of aggression but, in itself, it is not a description of social learning theory.*

▲ An adult 'model' displays aggression towards the life-sized Bobo doll, including punching the doll while saying 'POW'.

CAN YOU...?   No. 2.2

1... List the main features of the social learning theory of aggression.

2... Outline the procedures and findings of **one** of Bandura's studies of aggression.

3... Explain in what way Bandura's study supports the social learning theory of aggression.

4... Select **one** assumption of the behaviourist approach and explain how this relates to Bandura's explanation of aggression.

EXAM QUESTION

Describe the social learning theory of aggression. [8]

Notes *In the exam, you will be asked to describe **one** of the four theories you have studied (there is one theory for each of the four approaches). This question will be worth 8 marks. In order to gain the full 8 marks your answer should:*

▶ *Be accurate and well detailed.*

▶ *Show evidence of coherent elaboration, i.e. each point you make should be explained to demonstrate your understanding.*

▶ *Display a depth and range of knowledge, though not necessarily in equal measure. This means that you can either cover a few points in considerable detail (i.e. depth), or cover a number of points in less detail (range).*

▶ *Be well-structured and coherent.*

▶ *Have accurate grammar, punctuation and spelling.*

▶ *Be about 250–300 words in length.*

Therapy 1 Aversion therapy

On this and the next spread we look at two further examples of the **behaviourist approach** in psychology. Both of these are examples of behaviourist therapies that are used to treat mental disorders. According to the behaviourist approach, all behaviours are learned, including undesirable behaviours such as addictions. If such behaviours are learned through conditioning, then they can be unlearned in the same way.

On this spread, we look at **aversion therapy**, and on the next spread we look at **systematic desensitisation**. You are required to study only one of these.

> *Examiner hint*
>
> *Remember to link the aims of the therapy to the assumptions of the approach.*

BEHAVIOURAL THERAPIES

Behavioural therapy is the name given to a group of therapeutic techniques based on the principles of classical and operant conditioning. Behavioural therapies have a number of characteristics that distinguish them from other types of therapeutic approach (Sternberg, 1995).

- They are deliberately short-term, typically requiring only a relatively small number of sessions.
- Behaviour therapists target the *symptoms* rather than the underlying problem, believing that the original causes of a maladaptive behaviour may have little to do with the factors that are currently maintaining it.
- Behaviour therapies are intentionally directive, it is the therapist who formulates a treatment plan.

CLASSICAL CONDITIONING AND COUNTERCONDITIONING

Aversion therapy is an example of **counterconditioning**. An individual, for example, has learned to associate alcohol with pleasure. In aversion therapy the individual acquires a new stimulus–response link through classical conditioning, for example alcohol becomes linked with nausea. This new response runs *counter* to the original response of pleasure, therefore eliminating the initial undesirable association.

AVERSION THERAPY

MILK

www.cartoonstock.com

AVERSION THERAPY

Aversion therapy is a form of **psychotherapy** designed to cause a patient to reduce or avoid an undesirable behaviour pattern. The patient currently has an undesirable behaviour, such as alcoholism, which is associated with pleasure. The aim of the aversion therapy is to *condition* the patient to associate the undesirable behaviour with an undesirable (or *aversive*) stimulus (such as feelings of sickness). This leads to suppression of the undesirable behaviour.

The undesirable behaviours in question are usually alcoholism, smoking, drug abuse and overeating, although the technique has also been more controversially used for the 'treatment' of homosexuality, sexual perversions and aggressive behaviour. The NHS, following the decriminalisation of homosexuality in the UK in 1967, largely abandoned aversion therapy as a 'treatment' for homosexuality.

How it works

Aversion therapy is based on the principles of **classical conditioning**. Individuals are repeatedly presented with an aversive (i.e. unpleasant) stimulus, such as an electric shock or a drug that makes them feel nauseous, at the same time that they are engaging in the undesirable behaviour being treated. Note that the use of a shock is not the same as **electroconvulsive therapy** (**ECT**).

The aversive stimulus (the shock) is a **UCS**, which produces a **UCR**, such as avoidance. When the aversive stimulus is repeatedly paired with the unpleasant behaviour, the behaviour (e.g. violence, which was an **NS** and is now a **CS**), leads to the same consequences. As a result, patients lose their wish to engage in the undesirable behaviour.

Covert sensitisation

It is possible to deliver the aversive stimulus by verbal suggestion rather than any actual stimulus. For example, alcoholics are required to imagine upsetting, repulsive or frightening scenes while they are drinking. This form of therapy, called **covert sensitisation**, is used much less commonly than other forms of aversion therapy.

Nausea and alcohol

Those of you who have had the experience of drinking too much and becoming nauseous may wonder why such an aversive experience does not extinguish your desire to drink again: according to the principles of aversion therapy it should. One reason is that successful aversions after nausea are made only when a substance has a strong identity. People do often acquire a dislike for strongly flavoured alcoholic drinks after one bad experience.

This link between strong flavours and aversion has been called the 'sauce béarnaise syndrome' by the psychologist Martin Seligman, who first wrote about it after he had eaten a sumptuous dinner that included a rich sauce béarnaise. After the meal, he attended a concert with music by the composer Wagner. Later that night he developed stomach flu resulting in severe nausea and vomiting. For the next 10 years, he felt very queasy any time he smelled béarnaise sauce. This led him to reflect on the acquired association between sauce béarnaise and nausea. He had spent the evening listening to Wagner, but did not feel queasy when he heard that music again, but queasiness was strongly linked to the food. He therefore proposed that we have an innate predisposition to learn links between tastes and nausea, but only when the tastes are very strong.

◄ Stanley Kubrick's film *A Clockwork Orange*, an adaptation of the novel by Anthony Burgess, is set in a violent near-future UK, and portrays the extreme use of aversion therapy as social control. Alex, a teenage hooligan, is captured by the police and jailed. There he undergoes aversion therapy to make him unable to commit further violence. Alex is strapped into a chair in front of a large theatre screen. His head is tied down and his eyes are forced open with metal clips. He is then injected with a drug that makes him feel violently ill, and is forced to watch images of horrific violence. After a few weeks of treatment, Alex is ready to return to society, now conditioned so that violence makes him feel ill.

New developments

Recent developments in the treatment of alcoholism have refined the use of traditional aversion therapy. Researchers have discovered drugs that make users sick if they mix them with alcohol, but also reward abstinence by inducing feelings of tranquillity and well-being (Badawy, 1999). These compounds (known as *tryptophan metabolites*) prevent alcohol from being properly converted within the body, turning it into a chemical that causes unpleasant effects such as nausea, vomiting and hot flushes. Unlike conventional aversion compounds, however, these also offer an incentive for staying with the treatment.

Aversion therapy in action

In a study of alcoholics, Miller (1978) compared the effectiveness of three types of treatment:
- Aversion therapy (using shocks).
- **Counselling** therapy plus aversion.
- Counselling alone.

One year later, recovery was the same for all groups, indicating that aversion therapy offered no benefit.

In contrast, Smith *et al.* (1997) found that alcoholics treated with aversion therapy (using shocks or a drug to induce nausea) had higher abstinence rates after one year than those treated with counselling alone. Smith (1988) also reported success with a group of 300 smokers: 52% of those treated with shocks maintained abstinence after one year.

Aversion therapies often suffer from problems of patient drop-out. Bancroft (1992) reported that up to 50% of patients either refuse treatment or drop out of aversion therapy programmes, which makes it difficult to evaluate such therapies if only willing patients engage in the therapy in the first place.

A CASE STUDY

Mr Y had problem gambling behaviour. He was treated as an outpatient at a hospital clinic. His therapist began by asking Mr Y to keep a behavioural diary. The therapist used this information both to understand the seriousness of the problem, and as a baseline to measure whether change was occurring during the course of treatment.

Because electric shock is easy to use and is acceptable to the patient, the therapist chose it as the aversive stimulus. Mr. Y consented to this treatment. The shocks were administered on a daily basis for the first week, gradually tapering to once a week over a month. Sessions lasted about an hour. The shock was delivered by placing electrodes on the patient's wrist. The patient selected a level of shock that was uncomfortable but not too painful. This shock was then briefly and repeatedly paired with stimuli that the patient has chosen for their association with his problem gambling (such as slides of the race track, betting sheets, written descriptions of gambling). The timing, duration, and intensity of the shocks were carefully planned by the therapist to ensure that the patient experienced a discomfort level that was aversive so that the conditioning effect occurred.

After two weeks of treatment, Mr Y was provided with a portable shocking device to use on a daily basis for practice at home to supplement the outpatient treatment. The therapist visited Mr Y at home to monitor compliance as well as progress between outpatient sessions. Booster sessions in the therapist's office were scheduled once a month for six months.

Adapted from www.minddisorders.com/A-Br/Aversion-therapy.html.

Examiner hint

In order to gain the full 12 marks, your answer must provide a link between the aims of aversion therapy and the main assumptions of the behaviourist approach.

Therapy 2 Systematic desensitisation

Systematic desensitisation (SD) is a **behaviourist** therapy used mainly to treat **phobic disorders**. The therapy was developed by Joseph Wolpe in the 1950s. Wolpe's inspiration for SD came from experiments with cats. Masserman (1943) developed a phobia in cats by giving them an electric shock when they were put in a box. Thereafter, the cats displayed extreme anxiety when placed in the box but this disappeared if they were fed in the box. Wolpe (1958) explained this in terms of conditioning, and conducted further experiments, introducing the food more gradually (i.e. first at a distance from the box, and gradually closer until it was inside the box). The success of these experiments led Wolpe to suggest that a similar process could be used to treat phobic disorders.

On the previous spread, we looked at **aversion therapy**, another technique used by the behaviourist approach. The alternative is for you to study systematic desensitisation, discussed on this spread. You are required to study only one of these.

*The key features of phobic disorders are that a phobic is aware that his or her reaction is excessive, and the phobia interferes with normal everyday life. Phobic disorders include **specific phobias** (fear of specific objects, such as spiders, dogs, heights), agoraphobia (a fear of being trapped in a public place where escape is difficult or embarrassing), and **social phobia** (a phobia of situations involving other people, such as speaking in public or being part of a social group).*

How does it work

▲ **Problem –** patient is terrifed whenever she sees a spider.

▲ **Result –** After SD, patient has overcome her fear of spiders and feels relaxed in their presence.

Step 1: Patient is taught how to relax their muscles completely. (A relaxed state is incompatible with anxiety.)

Step 2: Therapist and patient together construct a desensitation heirachy – a series of imagined scenes, each one causing a little more anxiety than the previous one.

Step 3: Patient gradually works his/her way through desensitation heirachy, visualising each anxiety-evoking event while engaging in the competing relaxation response.

Step 4: Once the patient has mastered one step in the heirachy (i.e. they can remain relaxed while imagining it), they are ready to move onto the next.

Step 5: Patient eventually masters the feared situation that caused them to seek help in the first place.

CLASSICAL CONDITIONING AND COUNTERCONDITIONING

Pavlov's theory of **classical conditioning** explains how previously neutral stimuli (such as snakes, supermarkets, or even clocks) can provoke anxiety in some people because they have become associated with a different event that we naturally find distressing. A distressing event, e.g. being bitten (**UCS**), produces a natural fear response (**UCR**). An **NS**, e.g. the presence of a dog, becomes associated with the UCS, and thus the NS comes also to produce the UCR. They are now called the **CS** and the **CR**, respectively.

There is a reverse side to classical conditioning, called *counterconditioning*. This involves *reducing* a conditioned response (such as anxiety) by establishing an incompatible response (relaxation) to the same conditioned stimulus (e.g. snake, supermarket, or whatever).

SYSTEMATIC DESENSITISATION (SD)

An individual may learn that their feared stimulus is not so fearful after all – if only they could re-experience the feared stimulus. However, this never happens because the anxiety the stimulus creates, blocks any attempt to re-experience it. Joseph Wolpe developed a technique in the 1950s where phobics were *gradually* introduced to a feared stimulus, based on Masserman's research with cats (see top of page).

Counterconditioning

The diagram on the left shows the steps of SD. The process begins with learning relaxation techniques. The eventual aim is to acquire a new stimulus–response link, moving from responding to a stimulus with fear, to responding to the feared stimulus with relaxation. This is called **counterconditioning**, because the patient is taught a new association that runs counter to the original association. Wolpe also called this '**reciprocal inhibition**' because the relaxation *inhibits* the anxiety.

Desensitisation hierarchy

The diagram on the left also shows how learning proceeds through a **desensitisation hierarchy**, a series of gradual steps that are determined at the beginning of therapy when the patient and therapist work out a hierarchy of feared stimuli.

Different forms of SD

In the early days of SD, patients would learn to confront their feared situations directly (***in vivo** desensitisation*), by learning to relax in the presence of objects or images that would normally arouse anxiety. In more recent years, however, rather than actually presenting the feared stimulus, the therapist asks the subject to *imagine* the presence of it (***in vitro** or **covert desensitisation***).

Research has found that actual contact with the feared stimulus is most successful, so *in vivo* techniques are more successful than covert ones (Menzies and Clarke, 1993). Often a number of different exposure techniques are involved – *in vivo*, covert and also modelling, where the patient watches someone else who is coping well with the feared stimulus (Comer, 2002).

An alternative is self-administered SD. Humphrey (1973) reports that this has proved effective with, for example, social phobia.

DO IT YOURSELF

No. 2.4

1. Think of your own example of a phobia (this could be an object or a situation).
2. Learn some relaxation techniques. For example, look at: www.umm.edu/sleep/relax_tech.htm (useful for exam stress!).
3. Develop a desensitisation hierarchy for your phobia.
4. Practice systematic desensitisation!

BEHAVIOURAL THERAPIES

Behavioural therapy is the name given to a group of therapeutic techniques based on the principles of classical and operant conditioning. Behavioural therapies have a number of characteristics that distinguish them from other types of therapeutic approach (Sternberg, 1995).

- They are deliberately short-term, typically requiring only a relatively small number of sessions.
- Behaviour therapists target the *symptoms* rather than the underlying problem, believing that the original causes of a maladaptive behaviour may have little to do with the factors that are currently maintaining it.
- Behaviour therapies are intentionally directive, it is the therapist who formulates a treatment plan.

▲ American singer, actress and director Barbra Streisand developed a social phobia while giving a concert during which she forgot the words to several songs. For 27 years she avoided any public engagements. During an interview in 2006 with Oprah Winfrey, Barbra revealed that she had overcome her social phobia through the use of **antianxiety drugs** and by gradually exposing herself to more public performances, starting with a small warm-up show, then a national tour, and finally performing in front of a large television audience.

Another option is to skip the hierarchy and the relaxation, and just experience being with the feared stimulus. This is called **flooding**. The technique has been adapted for patients suffering with **obsessive-compulsive disorder** (**OCD**, see below). Known as '**exposure and response prevention**' (**ERP**), it involves exposing patients to the objects or situations that trigger obsessions (desensitisation), and then prohibiting them from engaging in the usual compulsive response.

Effectiveness of SD with phobias

Research has found that SD is successful for a range of anxiety disorders. McGrath *et al.* (1990) claim that about 75% of patients with phobias respond to SD.

In one piece of research by Capafóns *et al.* (1998), aerophobia (fear of flying) was treated with SD. A group of 41 aerophobics was recruited through a media campaign in Spain offering free treatment. Twenty-one participants were assigned to a waiting-**control group**, while the others received SD immediately. Treatment consisted of two one-hour sessions per week over a 12–15 week period. Both imagination and *in vivo* techniques were involved. Various measures were used to assess recovery, such as self-report scales and physiological measures of anxiety. Aerophobics who received treatment reported lower levels of fear (compared to with the control group) *and* lower physiological signs of fear during a flight simulation. However, one person in the control group showed similar levels of improvement (evidence of spontaneous recovery), and two patients in the treatment group showed no recovery, demonstrating that SD is not 100% effective.

Is counterconditioning necessary?

The success of SD may be more to do with exposure than relaxation, and it could also be that the expectation of being able to cope with the feared stimulus is most important. For example, Klein *et al.* (1983) compared SD with supportive **psychotherapy** for patients with either **social phobias** or **specific phobias**. They found no difference in effectiveness (those receiving supportive psychotherapy had also done well), suggesting that the 'active ingredient' in SD or any psychotherapy may simply be the generation of hopeful expectancies that the phobia can be overcome.

Obsessive-compulsive disorder *(OCD) is an anxiety disorder where patients experience recurrent obsessions and/or compulsions. Obsessions are persistent ideas, thoughts, impulses or images that are classed as inappropriate or forbidden and cause intense anxiety. Compulsions develop as a means of controlling the obsessional thoughts. These compulsions are repetitive behaviours or thoughts, such as repeated hand-washing. Most OCD patients recognise that their compulsions are unreasonable but cannot control them, which creates further anxiety.*

CAN YOU...?　No.2.4

1... Explain what systematic desensitisation is.

2... Explain how the principles of classical conditioning work in systematic desensitisation.

3... Describe the **three** main steps in systematic desensitisation.

4... Outline **two** findings from research into systematic desensitisation.

EXAM QUESTION

Describe how the behaviourist approach has been applied to either aversion therapy or systematic desensitisation. [12]

Notes *In the exam, you will be asked to describe **one** therapy. In total you will have studied four therapies (one for each of the four approaches). This question will be worth 12 marks. In order to gain the full 12 marks, your answer should satisfy the same criteria as those listed on page vii. You might include the following in an answer about systematic desensitisation.*

▶ *A brief outline of the aims of systematic desensitisation and how these link with the assumptions of the behaviourist approach.*

▶ *Examples of how systematic desensitisation has been used.*

▶ *Research findings into systematic desensitisation.*

▶ *Your answer should be about 400–450 words in length.*

Examiner hint

In order to gain the full 12 marks, your answer must provide a link between the aims of systematic desensitisation and the main assumptions of the behaviourist approach.

Evaluating the behaviourist approach

You have studied two examples of the **behaviourist approach** – one theory (**social learning theory**) and one therapy (either **aversion therapy** or **systematic desensitisation**). It is now time to use your understanding of the behaviourist approach to consider its strengths and weaknesses. To help you, we have provided some additional examples of the behaviourist approach.

People who believe that behaviour can only be explained in terms of learning theory are called ***radical behaviourists****, a rare group of psychologists today. 'Methodological behaviourism' is the view that learning theory is a part of any account of behaviour.*

➕ Strengths of the behaviourist approach

1. Scientific approach

Behaviourism was first introduced by John B. Watson at the beginning of the 20th century. He recognised that Pavlov's work on conditioned reflexes could be used to create a really objective, and therefore scientific, psychology. Behaviourism continues to embody the truly scientific approach, seeking to study behaviour that is observable and directly measurable. Intangible concepts such as feelings and thoughts are **operationalised** in terms of stimulus and response behaviours. Behaviourists believe that, through the use of the **scientific method**, we can analyse, quantify and compare behaviour.

Such a scientific approach is advantageous because it enables us to distinguish mere beliefs from real facts. For example, people may believe that wearing a gold token around your neck will ward off evil spirits, but how would we know this to be true without conducting **experiments**? When it comes to treatments for mental disorders, people want evidence to show that such treatments have been successful rather than just being asked to believe that they work. Therefore the scientific approach is desirable.

2. Successful applications

Behaviourist principles have been successfully applied in the real world, most notably in the treatment of mental disorders and in education. For example, **classical conditioning** principles are applied in aversion therapy to help people with addictions, and they have also been applied in systematic desensitisation to help people suffering from **phobias**.

In education, **operant conditioning** underlies successful teaching strategies. **Positive reinforcement** and punishment have helped shape behaviour in the classroom, as well as in the school environment in general.

B.F. Skinner specifically applied the principles of operant conditioning to teaching, designing a mechanical programmed instruction device (Skinner, 1954). Skinner believed that classroom teaching was often ineffective because different students learn at different rates, and reinforcements are therefore too variable to be effective. Reinforcements are also delayed due to the lack of individual attention. Skinner's concept of a teaching machine meant that each student could work at his/her own pace and receive reinforcements that would encourage future learning. Every time an answer is correct, the student is reinforced; and every time the answer is wrong, further explanation is offered. Feedback is immediate and therefore more effective. Feedback is also positive, which is more encouraging than negative feedback. The machine breaks down the learning process into small steps so that the student receives frequent rewards.

3. Focus on the here and now

The behaviourist approach is not concerned with events in a person's past. Other approaches in psychology seek to explain a person's behaviour in terms of things that happened in childhood or in terms of **innate** factors. The behaviourist approach means that the treatment of mental disorders does not have to look for complicated causes but just focuses on the current symptoms and trying to remove them.

For example, aversion therapy is used to treat alcoholism by teaching the person a new stimulus–response link between alcohol and nausea, thus reducing the undesirable behaviour. The treatment does not seek to understand why the person may have turned to alcohol.

Systematic desensitisation also seeks to treatment undesirable behaviour, such as a fear of social situations, by teaching a new stimulus–response link between the feared situation and relaxation. No attempt is made to understand why the phobia might have developed in the first place; removal of the symptoms is the sole aim of the treatment.

Some people prefer such a direct approach, and the success of such therapies suggests that it is not always necessary to look for deep meanings. On the other hand, the approach does not work for all people or all disorders. This suggests that a focus on the here and now is not always sufficient.

▲ The principles of behaviourism (such as reinforcement and punishment) are successfully used to train animals, for example training lions to perform in circuses or training dogs in the TV programme *Dog Borstal*. But to what extent are the same principles applicable to humans?

Weaknesses of the behaviourist approach

1. Emphasis on nurture

The behaviourist approach focuses exclusively on the surrounding environment as a means of shaping behaviour. Therefore, in terms of the **nature–nurture debate**, the role of **nature** is ignored. For example, behaviourists would not consider how our genetic make-up could influence personality and behaviour.

In addition, the role of external factors (i.e. **nurture**) is exaggerated within this approach. If learning was all that mattered, then everyone could become a surgeon or a rocket scientist. Our behaviour is governed by many internal factors, such as motivation and emotion and innate abilities.

2. Determinist approach

Behaviourists believe that behaviour is influenced almost exclusively by the associations we make between certain environmental stimuli (classical conditioning), or the rewards/punishments provided by our environment (operant conditioning). Thus people are controlled by external (environmental) factors.

This **determinist** approach does not consider the thought processes that occur before we behave in a certain way, and suggests that we are not making a choice when we behave. This view that our environment determines how we act, undermines the choice or **free will** that we have as human beings when making such decisions. It means that people cannot make choices and have no personal or moral responsibility for their behaviour. The implications of this are that people cannot be held responsible for any wrongdoing – instead they should simply be punished in order to change their behaviour rather than being taught to think responsibly.

3. More relevant to animals than humans

It is worth remembering that behaviourism has its roots in experiments with non-human animals, such as the research by Pavlov and Skinner. SD was also initially developed in research with animals. Wolpe (1958) created a phobia in cats by placing them in cages and administering repeated electric shocks. He then found he could reduce this learned anxiety response by placing food near a cage that was similar to the original. The act of eating apparently diminished their anxiety response (**reciprocal inhibition**), and gradually the cats could be placed in cages that were more and more similar to the original cages without symptoms of anxiety.

Human anxiety may not always respond in the same way. Wolpe (1973) treated one woman for a fear of insects and found SD did not cure her phobia. It turned out that her husband, with whom she had not been getting along, was nicknamed after an insect. So her fear was not the result of conditioning, but a means of representing her marital problems; Wolpe recommended marital **counselling**, which succeeded where SD failed.

An interesting book to read is B.F. Skinner's Walden Two (1948), which describes an ideal world where the environment is designed so that it shapes human behaviour in a desirable way.

CAN YOU...? No.2.5

1... Identify **two** strengths of the behaviourist approach.
2... Make **three** distinct points to explain each strength.
3... Identify **two** weaknesses of the behaviourist approach.
4... Make **three** distinct points to explain each weakness.

EXAM QUESTIONS

Evaluate two strengths of the behaviourist approach. [6]
Evaluate two weaknesses of the behaviourist approach. [6]

*Notes In the exam, you are required to discuss **two** strengths and **two** weaknesses of **one** of the four approaches. For each strength and weakness, you should:*

▶ *Clearly identify the strength or weakness.*

▶ *Thoroughly explain why this is a strength or weakness in relation to the approach.*

▶ *Where appropriate, use examples drawn from theory/therapy to illustrate your answer.*

▶ *Think of each strength/weakness as being worth three marks (although, strictly speaking, this is not how they are marked).*

▶ *Write around 50–60 words on each strength/weakness.*

DO IT YOURSELF No. 2.5

Compare and contrast

You have now studied two approaches – the **biological approach** and the behaviourist approach. You can now compare and contrast these two approaches.

1. First, copy out the table below and fill in the right-hand column in the table for the behaviourist approach.
2. Second, look at the answers you gave for the biological approach, and compare and contrast them with the behaviourist approach. For example, you might look at the issue of determinism and point out that both approaches are highly determinist (a similarity), although the biological approach suggests that we are determined by internal, physical factors whereas the behaviourist approach proposes that we are determined by external factors (a difference). Identify as many similarities and differences as you can, and make sure you explain each of them carefully.
3. Use this information to write an answer to the following exam question:

   Compare and contrast the biological and behaviourist approaches in terms of similarities and differences. [12]

Issues and debates	The behaviourist approach
Nomothetic/idiographic	
Nature–nurture	
Reductionism/holism	
Determinism/free will	
Scientific/non-scientific	
Methodology used	
Anything else	

The issues and debates listed in the table on the right are explained in the introduction to this book (see pages x–xi).

Examiner hint

There is a knack to writing answers to 'compare and contrast' questions – look at pages 60–61 for special advice on how to deal with these questions.

Methodology used by the behaviourist approach

The final topic on the **behaviourist approach** is a consideration of the methodology used by this approach. Obviously, researchers use all sorts of methods and techniques, but we have selected two that are particularly common in the behaviourist approach – **lab experiments** and studies using animals.

1. Lab experiments

▲ Albert Bandura conducted a series of experiments to support his **social learning theory** (see page 19). In the experiments, children observed an adult (the 'model') playing with various toys including a Bobo doll (shown above). In some conditions, the child saw the model behaving aggressively towards the Bobo doll, for example hitting it with a hammer. Later the children were given the chance to play with the toys. Those children who had observed the model behaving aggressively were much more likely to imitate the same behaviour. We can conclude from this that the observation of aggression *caused* the children to learn this behaviour through **modelling** – such causal conclusions can only be drawn from experimental research. In an experiment, the independent variable is manipulated in order to demonstrate what effect this has on the dependent variable.

Examiner hint

It is a good idea to use an example of a lab experiment to highlight for the examiner the fact that you understand how experiments have been used within the behaviourist approach.

DO IT YOURSELF

No. 2.6

One of the methods used by behaviourists is the study of animals – such as the classic research conducted by Pavlov (described on the facing page) and by Skinner (see page 17). In pairs or small groups, research the work carried out by Pavlov and Skinner.

1. What animals were used?
2. What behaviourist principles arose from their work?
3. How have such principles been applied in human learning?

Divide your class into two groups. Using the examples of Pavlov and Skinner, debate the advantages and disadvantages of using animal learning as a means of finding out about human learning.

Behaviourists believe that only observable behaviour is worthy of study because we cannot confirm what is going on in the mind. Early behaviourists at the beginning of the 20th century believed that if psychology were to be accepted as a science, then scientific methods should be used to study behaviour. Behaviourists therefore advocated an experimental approach to the study of human behaviour – one that is objective and quantifiable.

As behaviourists believe that our behaviour is shaped by our interactions with the environment, it would follow that if we manipulate our environment, we can establish the cause of certain behaviours. One of the main aims of the lab experiment is to establish cause–effect (stimulus–response) relationships. For example, in Bandura *et al.*'s experiment (see left), they manipulated the environment of the children (the **independent variable** was whether they observed an aggressive/non-aggressive role model, or whether the model was reinforced for their behaviour), and observed the effect of this on the children's behaviour (the **dependent variable** was whether the children displayed aggressive behaviour).

Strengths

- A lab experiment is the best way to study causal relationships because **extraneous variables** can be carefully controlled.
- Lab experiments offer an objective means of studying human behaviour. As the experimenter will follow set, standard procedures, this means the experiment can be repeated again (**replicated**) by others to demonstrate the **validity** of the findings.
- As data resulting from experiments can be quantified (e.g. the number/percentage of children in Bandura *et al.*'s experiments who copied the role model), it is easier to analyse and make comparisons.

Weaknesses

- The artificiality of the situation. It is unlikely that people will behave the same way in a contrived lab environment as they would in real life. This is known as **ecological validity** – the extent to which an environment shares the same characteristics as everyday life. The ecological validity of a lab experiment is generally very low.
- In a lab experiment, participants are likely to behave unnaturally because they will try and guess the purpose of the study, and conform to researcher's expectations. Alternatively, they may want to spoil the study on purpose – the 'screw you' effect. These problems are known as **demand characteristics**.
- **Experimenter bias** can also be a problem. The experimenter could (intentionally or unintentionally) display behaviour that influences participants to act in the desired way, e.g. by using tone of voice to influence participant feedback. This is possible due to the physical contact that occurs between experimenter and participant in a lab situation.

Many of the concepts discussed above are discussed in greater depth in Chapter 6. For example, lab experiments are discussed on pages 137 and 144. You can read about independent and dependent variables on page 136.

2. Use of animals in research

As behaviourists believe that there are only quantitative differences between humans and animals (e.g. brain size), they advocate studying animal learning and applying it to humans. Examples of such research include the work of Pavlov (see the panel on the right) and Skinner (see page 17).

Strengths

- Animal learning has been successfully applied to human behaviour. For example, **classical conditioning** principles were developed through Pavlov's study of dogs, and these principles have been successfully used in therapy, such as **systematic desensitisation** for the treatment of **phobias**.
- In practical terms, there is less emotional involvement with animals. This may result in greater objectivity on behalf of experimenters, and therefore less bias. Similarly, animals are not subject to demand characteristics, even though, like humans, they are likely to display behaviour that is not necessarily representative of how they behave in natural environments.

Weaknesses

- The issue of **generalisability** is a major problem. To what extent can we say that animals learn in the same way as humans? This may be true for some of the basic elements of human learning (e.g. reward/punishment), but human behaviour is more complex and governed by higher mental activity (e.g. having a sophisticated language system).
- **Ethical issues** are certainly raised by animal research. Animals cannot consent to taking part, they have no right to withdraw, and cannot understand why they are being confined to an experimental environment. This raises an important moral debate.

PAVLOV'S RESEARCH APPARATUS

◀ Ivan Pavlov was awarded a Nobel prize in 1904 for his work on the digestive system using apparatus like that pictured on left, which was devised to measure the production of saliva in dogs. When he received the award, he described a new finding – he had noticed that whenever he or an assistant entered the lab carrying meat powder, saliva began dripping out of the tube. Pavlov realised that the psychological state of anticipation was affecting the reflex response of salivation. How could this happen? Reflexes were biological, yet the reflex was influenced by psychological factors. To test his observation he tried a new association – he sounded a tone and then fed the dog meat powder. After repeating this a few times, he found that when the dog heard the tone, it would salivate. The diagram below illustrates this process.

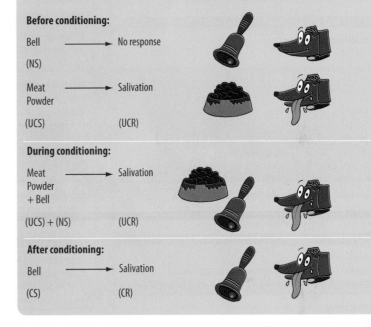

Before conditioning:

Bell ⟶ No response
(NS)

Meat Powder ⟶ Salivation
(UCS) (UCR)

During conditioning:

Meat Powder + Bell ⟶ Salivation
(UCS) + (NS) (UCR)

After conditioning:

Bell ⟶ Salivation
(CS) (CR)

Examiner hint

In order to ensure that your answer to this question is thorough and relevant, you need to remember to include examples of how the particular methodology is used within the approach. For example, when discussing the use of animal studies within the behaviourist approach, you should bring in the work of Pavlov or Skinner. This will help you explain the methodology thoroughly and coherently, and demonstrate to the examiner that you understand the methodology used within that particular approach. Answers where a candidate talks in a generic manner about certain research methods will not attract credit in the top two bands (see mark schemes on page vii).

CAN YOU...? No.2.6

1... Identify **two** methods used by the behaviourist approach, and for each describe an example of how this method was used in a research study that used the behaviourist approach.

2... For each method, outline and explain **two** strengths and **two** weaknesses of using this method in the study you described.

EXAM QUESTION

Explain and **evaluate** the methodology used by the behaviourist approach. [12]

*Notes In the exam, you are required to explain and evaluate the methods used by **one** of the four approaches. It is vital that you clearly explain how the methods link*

with the assumptions of the approach, i.e. that they have clear relevance to the approach. A general guide in terms of structuring your answer is as follows.

▶ *Explain one method used by the approach (use examples that will highlight its relevance to the approach).*

▶ *Evaluate the strengths and weaknesses of this method.*

▶ *Explain a second method used by the approach (use examples that will again highlight its relevance).*

▶ *Evaluate the strengths and weaknesses of this method.*

N.B. The top band of the mark scheme for this question requires: 'Methods are appropriate and clearly explained...and have clear relevance to the approach'.

Chapter 2 summary

Assumptions of the behaviourist approach

Classical conditioning
UCS → UCR, UCS paired with NS, NS becomes CS → CR.

Operant conditioning
Reinforcers can be positive (rewards) or negative (escape from aversive stimulus). Punishment decreases repetition of behaviour.

Social learning theory
See right.

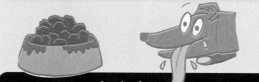

Social learning theory of aggression (Bandura)

Observation
Individual observes others being rewarded/punished.

Vicarious reinforcement
Indirect (vicarious) experience determines whether such behaviours are repeated.

Mental representation
Expectancies of future outcomes are stored.

Maintenance through direct experience
Future, direct rewards determine the value of the behaviour for the individual.

Aversion therapy

Classical conditioning and counterconditioning
Aversive stimulus (UCS) paired with undesirable behaviour (NS becomes CS) to produce avoidance (CR).

Covert sensitisation
Aversive stimulus delivered through verbal suggestion.

Applications
Smoking, drug abuse and overeating – paired with electric shock. Alcoholics are given a drug that induces nausea.

Systematic desensitisation

Counterconditioning
Relaxation is opposite to anxiety, therefore pairing feared stimulus with relaxation inhibits anxiety (reciprocal inhibition).

Desensitisation hierarchy
Patient and therapist construct hierarchy of fearful stimuli. Patient learns to relax at each stage of the hierarchy.

Different forms
In vivo (real life), *in vitro* or covert (imagined), self-administered.

➕ Strengths and weaknesses of the behaviourist approach ➖

Strengths
▶ Scientific approach – concepts easily operationalised.
▶ Successful applications to treatment of mental disorder and in education (e.g. programmed instruction device).
▶ Focus on here and now rather than seeking complex causes from past experience.

Weaknesses
▶ Emphasis on nurture, ignoring biological (nature) explanations; exaggerates environmental factors.
▶ Determinist approach – people controlled by environmental factors rather than free will.
▶ More relevant to animals than humans – but, for example, animal fear might be conditioned, human anxiety could have other causes.

Methodology of the behaviourist approach

Lab experiments
Manipulating the environment in highly controlled conditions can demonstrate causal relationships.
▶ **Strengths**: objective means of studying human behaviour, data can be quantified and easily analysed.
▶ **Weaknesses**: might lack ecological validity because artificial, and might have demand characteristics, also experimenter bias.

Use of animals in research
Animals and humans differ only quantitatively and therefore it is possible to generalise from animals to humans.
▶ **Strengths**: some principles (e.g. classical conditioning) clearly apply to both animals and humans; animals don't respond to, for example, demand characteristics.
▶ **Weaknesses**: generalisability in doubt because humans direct their own behaviour through, for example, thinking; there are ethical issues because animals can't provide informed consent.

Review activities

You can use some of the review activities described on page 15 with the content of this chapter. For example, you could construct mind maps or consider the assumptions of the behaviourist approach in relation to social learning theory and the therapy that you studied. You should certainly list again the key words in this chapter and make sure you understand them.

Revising social learning theory

Without looking back in your book, list as many key terms/concepts as you can remember, and for each one explain what the term/phrase means.

Afterwards, check what you have forgotten and add these to your list. You might repeat this task again until you can remember all the key concepts.

You could also repeat this task with the therapy you have learned.

Multiple choice questions

Working on your own or in groups, write multiple choice questions and answers related to the material in this chapter (and Chapter 1 if you wish). Then pool your questions with the rest of the class. You can answer the questions individually or in teams.

Writing exam advice

Several possible exam questions are listed below:

- **Describe** how the behaviourist approach has been applied to either aversion therapy or systematic desensitisation. [12]
- **Evaluate** two strengths of the behaviourist approach. [6]
- **Evaluate** two weaknesses of the behaviourist approach. [6]
- **Explain and evaluate** the methodology used by the behaviourist approach. [12]

1. Imagine that you are writing a book for AS level students. Write down **four** (or more) top tips for students about how to answer these questions in order to get maximum marks. Look at the section in this book on the exam and mark schemes (see page vii).

2. When you have finished writing the advice, select one of the questions and prepare two example answers for it:
   - An answer that *does not* follow your advice.
   - A model answer that does follow the advice.

3. After you have written both versions, give them to someone else to read and ask them to identify which is the better one, and explain to them why the essays are different.

4. Write notes for the model answer highlighting what makes it a model answer.

Fill in the blanks

Copy out the text below and try to fill in the blanks without looking back at the text. See how much you remember.

One method used by behaviourists is the _____ experiment. This method demonstrates _____ relationships because it shows the effect of the _____ variable on the _____ variable. In Bandura's study using the Bobo doll, the independent variable was _____, and the dependent variable was _____.

A particular strength of this kind of experiment is that _____ _____, but a weakness is that people don't behave the same way in a lab as they do in everyday life. This is referred to as a lack of _____ _____.

There are several reasons why people don't behave the same in a lab experiment as they would in everyday life, one is that they try to guess what the experimenter wants them to do. This is related to _____ _____. Another problem that can occur is that the experimenter may unintentionally communicate his/her expectations. This is called _____ _____.

Another method that is popular with behaviourists is the use of animals in research. The reason they feel justified in using animals is because they think there are only _____ differences between humans and animals. Pavlov's early experiments involved _____, and Skinner's experiments on operant conditioning involved _____.

One strength of research using animals is that _____ _____. One weakness is that we may not be justified in generalising from animal behaviour to human behaviour because human behaviour is _____ _____ _____.

Design your own crossword

There are many websites that will assist you in making your own crosswords, e.g. www.crosswordpuzzlegames.com/ (there are also sites to help make your own word search or other puzzles).

Are behaviourists SANE?

The acronym SANE may help you when you have to evaluate the behaviourist approach.
S = Scientific
A = Applications
N = Nurture
E = Environmental determinism

Write a short paragraph for each of these four topics. As always, try first to do this without looking at your notes.

Example exam questions with student answers

Examiner's comments on these answers can be found on page 174.

EXAMPLE OF QUESTION 1(a) AND (b)

> (a) **Outline** two assumptions of the behaviourist approach. [4]
> (b) **Describe** the social learning theory of aggression. [8]

Megan's answer to 1(a)

One assumption of the behaviourist approach (BA) is that we learn through classical conditioning. This is based on the principle of association. Pavlov showed (through his research with dogs) that if two stimuli are presented at the same time (e.g. food and sound of bell), and this happens repeatedly, then they become associated with each other. Through this process, we can learn new responses to environmental stimuli, as the behaviourist approach says all behaviour is learned.

The BA says that we also learn through the consequences of our actions. This is known as operant conditioning. We learn through reinforcement and punishment (one increases the likelihood the behaviour will happen again, the other decreases it). Reinforcement can be positive or negative. Positive reinforcement is where we receive a reward for our behaviour, negative reinforcement is where we manage to avoid something unpleasant happening.

Tomas's answer to 1(a)

The behaviourist approach thinks that we learn everything from our environment and that we are born as blank slates. It also thinks that we learn from other people, and this is known as observational learning.

Megan's answer to 1(b)

The SLT of aggression would consider how children could learn aggression both directly and indirectly. For example, a child may be given attention for throwing a temper tantrum, and this is positively reinforcing for them, as it acts as a reward (learn aggression directly).

SLT mainly would focus on how children would learn aggression from seeing others (indirect learning). For example, a child may observe their older sibling having a tantrum and receiving sweets from their mum to pacify them. Due to vicarious reinforcement, the younger child will think that if they behave like this too, they will also receive sweets. This is known as observational learning or modelling.

Such observational learning and vicarious reinforcement means that a child learns about the reinforcements they are likely to receive if they repeat the behaviour (expectancy of future outcomes). Such expectancies are mental concepts and will change if the child repeats the behaviour. The child will be directly rewarded which will increase or decrease future expectancies depending on whether such actions are reinforced or punished.

Studies carried out by Bandura illustrate how children will imitate the behaviour of others, and model their behaviour on them. In one study, it was found that children were more likely to behave aggressively if they had seen an adult being rewarded for their aggression. The study supports the SLT of aggression, as it shows that children will learn through vicarious reinforcement, i.e. seeing others being rewarded for their behaviour.

The SLT of aggression, like SLT in general focuses on how we think about our own and other people's behaviour, and consider the consequences of aggressive acts. It therefore adds a cognitive element to the traditional behaviourist view.

Tomas's answer to 1(b)

Bandura did a study on aggression where children who were 3–5 years old watched a video of an adult and a Bobo doll, which is a plastic inflatable doll. There were three conditions. In one, the adult punched and kicked the Bobo doll, and was rewarded by another adult for this. In another, the adult was aggressive toward the doll, but was punished by another adult who shouted at them. The third condition was a control, where the adult was not rewarded or punished for their aggressive behaviour.

Bandura found that children who had seen the adult rewarded were more likely to behave aggressively later on when placed in a room with a Bobo doll, compared with the children who had seen the adult be punished. This study shows that children will copy an adult, or role model, especially if they see the model being rewarded for their behaviour. This is known as observational learning.

The essence of the **psychodynamic approach** is to explain behaviour in terms of its *dynamics*, i.e. the forces that drive it. The best known example of this approach is Freud's psychoanalytic theory of personality, although there are many other psychodynamic theories based on Freud's ideas (such as Jung's theory).

Sigmund Freud was the first to challenge the view that mental disorders were caused by physical illness. Instead, he proposed that *psychological* factors were responsible.

WHAT'S ON A MAN'S MIND

SIGMUND FREUD

Assumption 1 Behaviour is influenced by the three parts of the mind (i.e. tripartite personality)

Freud believed that the adult personality is structured into three parts that develop at different stages in our lives.

- **Id** This is the impulsive (and unconscious) part of our personality, and is present at birth. It demands immediate satisfaction, which can be referred to as the **pleasure principle**. The main aim of the id is to gain pleasure and gratification at any cost.
- **Ego** This is the conscious, rational part of the mind that develops around the age of two years. Its function is to work out realistic ways of balancing the demands of the id in a socially acceptable way. It is governed by the **reality principle**.
- **Superego** This is the last part of our personality to develop. Forming at around the age of four years, it embodies the child's sense of right and wrong as well as his or her ideal self. The superego seeks to perfect and civilise our behaviour. It is learned through identification with one's parents and others.

DO IT YOURSELF No. 3.1

There is a wide array of terms (and associated concepts) on this page. Make a mobile or a mind map (or any visual representation) to illustrate these concepts and the connections between them.

Assumption 2 Behaviour is influenced by different levels of consciousness and ego defences

Freud proposed that the mind is like an iceberg – much of what goes on inside the mind lies under the surface. This is the **preconscious** and **unconscious** mind. The conscious mind is logical, whereas the unconscious mind is not and is ruled by pleasure-seeking. The unconscious mind cannot be directly accessed, but expresses itself indirectly through, for example, dreams.

The unconscious is also related to **ego defence mechanisms**. Conflicts between the id, ego and superego create anxiety. The ego protects itself with various ego defences. These defences can be the cause of disturbed behaviour if they are overused. For example, a boy who cannot deal with what he perceives as maternal rejection when a new baby brother is born may **regress** to an earlier developmental stage, soiling his clothes and becoming more helpless. Other examples of defence mechanisms include:

- **Displacement** (transfer of impulses from one person or object to another).
- **Projection** (undesirable thoughts are attributed to someone else).
- **Repression** (pushing painful memories deep down into our unconscious mind, so they are effectively forgotten).

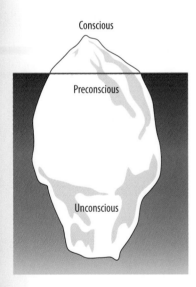

Conscious

Preconscious

Unconscious

Assumption 3 Behaviour is influenced by early childhood experiences

In childhood, the ego is not developed enough to deal with traumas, which are therefore repressed. For example, a child may experience the death of a parent early in life and repress associated feelings. Later in life, other losses may cause the individual to re-experience the earlier loss, and can lead to depression. Previously unexpressed anger about the loss is directed inwards, towards the self, causing depression.

There are key developmental stages in early childhood (described on the next spread). **Fixation** on any one of these stages (through frustration or overindulgence) may have a lasting affect on the individual's personality.

CAN YOU...? No.3.1

1... Name **three** structures of the mind and write a sentence about each.

2... Identify and explain **one** ego defence.

3... Explain the importance of early experience.

EXAM QUESTION

Outline two assumptions of the psychodynamic approach. [4]

Notes *In the exam, you will be asked to outline **two** assumptions of **one** of the four approaches. The question will be worth 4 marks. You should structure your answer in the following way.*

▶ *Identify one assumption.*

▶ *Explain/detail this assumption.*

▶ *Identify a second assumption.*

▶ *Explain/detail this assumption.*

Freud's theory of personality development

Around the turn of the 19th century, Freud developed a theory of personality development to explain how people become what they are. 'Personality' refers to the unique character that each of us has. Freud suggested that personality develops out of an interaction between **innate** drives and early life experiences.

LITTLE HANS

Freud provided little in the way of actual evidence to support his theory of personality development. One of the few studies published is the case study of Little Hans, providing support for the concept of the Oedipus complex.

A five-year-old boy called 'Little Hans' (real name Herbert Graf) was brought to Freud's attention by Hans's father, who was very interested in Freud's work on the unconscious. Hans had become terrified of horses pulling laden carts. Freud (1909) suggested that Hans's phobia had developed for several reasons.

First of all, Hans had once heard a man saying to a child: 'Don't put your finger to the white horse or it'll bite you'. Hans had also once asked his mother if she would like to put her finger on his penis. His mother had told him that this would not be proper, leading Hans to worry that his mother might leave him. Hans projected one source of anxiety on to another – he became afraid of being bitten by a white horse, whereas he was actually scared that his mother would leave him (the two events were linked by touching something with your finger).

Second, Hans saw a horse with a laden cart fall down and thought it was dead. The horse symbolised his wish that his father (big whiskers and glasses similar to horses' blinkers) would die, and the laden cart symbolised his mother pregnant with his sister, and when it fell over this was like giving birth. Therefore the laden cart symbolised his dying father and his mother giving birth – both events that filled him with anxiety.

In discussing these anxieties, Hans was able to accept them and came to identify with his father. Freud claimed that this provided support for his theory of psychosexual development (the Oedipus complex), and evidence for his explanation of the origins of disordered behaviour.

You can listen to a BBC radio programme about Little Hans at: www.bbc.co.uk/radio4/science/case_study_20080528.shtml.

PERSONALITY DEVELOPMENT

Core of the personality

The personality consists of the three elements **id**, **ego** and **superego**. These work together to create complex behaviours. One of the features of this interaction is that the three forces are in conflict with each other. The ego's ability to function despite these competing forces is referred to as **'ego strength'**. A person with good ego strength is able to manage these pressures effectively, while those with too much or too little ego strength can become too unyielding or too disrupting. According to Freud, the key to a healthy personality is a balance between the id, the ego and the superego.

Ego strength develops naturally with age, but may be enhanced or damaged by life experiences. For example, a child who is encouraged to take personal responsibility for his/her actions will develop a stronger ego.

People also differ in terms of the extent to which their personality is dominated by the id, ego or superego. For example, a person whose personality is dominated by their id will tend to be antisocial, lacking a concern for others.

Psychosexual stages

Freud described **psychosexual stages** in development (Freud used the term 'sexual' to mean sensual or physical). At each stage, a person's life force or **libido** is attached to an organ of the body.

1. The first stage is the **oral stage**. This means that pleasure is gained by, for example, eating and suckling. As the child grows older, gratification is sought through other body parts.
2. During the **anal stage** (approximately 1½–3 years of age), the body focus is on the anus – pleasure is gained from expelling and/or withholding faeces.
3. During the **phallic stage** (approximately 3–6 years old) focus is on the genitals and, initially, on the parent of the opposite sex. Resolution occurs through coming to identify with the same-sex parent. Freud described this in the **Oedipus complex** – a little boy, such as Little Hans (see left), feels sexually attracted to his mother and sees his father as a rival for his love. He wishes to kill his father and this makes him feel guilty. Eventually, the boy comes to identify with his father, thus relieving him of guilt. Such identification leads to the development of the superego, and is the basis of moral behaviour because the boy, in identifying with his father, takes on his father's principles.
   According to Freud, little girls develop **penis envy** at this age – an envy of what boys have, and they blame their mothers for not providing one. The girl's father now becomes her love-object, and she substitutes her 'penis envy' with a wish to have a child. This leads to identification with her mother, and a resolution of conflicting feelings.
4. The phallic stage is followed by the **latency stage**, when nothing much happens in terms of psychosexual development.
5. Finally, during puberty, there is the **genital stage**, when the main source of pleasure is again the genitals. Focus is also on the development of independence.

DO IT YOURSELF

No. 3.2

Try to test one of the predictions that arise from Freud's theory linking psychosexual stages and later personality. There are various tests on the internet for personality type (for example, try www.okcupid.com/tests/the-freudian-character-test). This will give you a score for personality type. You can then correlate an individual's score on this test with another measure, such as how much money a person usually withdraws from a cash machine at one time. For example, we would expect people with a higher anal retentive score to withdraw less money (a **negative correlation**).

Sigismund Schlomo Freud (1856–1939) grew up in Vienna, where he stayed until the Nazi occupation of 1938 forced him to leave as he was a Jew. He died in London (you can visit the house where he lived and died – see www.freud.org.uk). He was the eldest of eight children – four of his sisters were not able to leave Vienna and died in concentration camps.

Freud studied medicine and became interested in neurology (disorders of the nervous system) and hysteria (excessive anxiety that may result in physical disorders). One of the patients Freud treated was Anna O. (see page 37). It was Anna who invented the name 'talking cure' to refer to the technique Freud developed to treat hysterical patients. This 'talking cure' was developed into **psychoanalysis**, his method of therapy.

Many people view Freud's descriptions of how personality develops as pure fantasy, yet his ideas have endured and have had far-reaching influences (e.g. in plays, books, art and so on). There is something in his theories that appeals, and his views have had a profound effect on modern thinking. Freud changed the way we understand the importance of childhood, and brought the idea of unconscious motives to public attention. At the time of his death Freud was regarded as one of the major scientific thinkers of his age – equal to Darwin and Einstein.

The influence of psychosexual stages on personality

Freud predicted that experiences during key psychosexual stages would result in distinct adult personality types. Such effects are due either to frustration or overindulgence during any psychosexual stage – both of which lead to a **fixation** on the stage and characteristic kinds of behaviour. The table below outlines the possible personality types that are associated with each stage.

	Healthy resolution of the stage	Frustration or harsh treatment	Overindulgence
Oral	Ability to form relationships with others and accept their affection; enjoyment of food and drink.	**Oral aggressive character** is characterised by aggressiveness, domination, pessimism, envy, and suspicion.	**Oral receptive character** is optimistic, gullible, overdependent on others, trusting, and full of admiration for others.
Anal	The ability to deal with authority and to have a balance between being orderly and being disorganised.	**Anal retentive character** is neat, stingy, precise, orderly, and obstinate.	**Anal expulsive character** is generous, messy, disorganised, careless, and defiant.
Phallic	The superego is based on an internalisation of the views of the same-sex parent, leading to the development of a conscience and mature moral development.	**Phallic character** is reckless, self-assured and a harsh, punitive superego, and may have problems with sex and sexual identity. Freud suggested that a fixation at this stage may lead to homosexuality.	
Genital	**Genital character** is the ideal. Well-adjusted, mature adult who is able to love and be loved, work hard and contribute to society.		

Ego defence mechanisms and personality

The operation of **ego defences** may also affect personality. Some ego defences are fairly normal, whereas others affect an individual's ability to deal with reality and may lead to serious mental disorders.

'Normal' ego defences include the use of humour, **sublimation** (negative emotions are transformed to positive behaviours or emotions) or **suppression** (pushing uncomfortable thoughts into the preconscious so they can be accessed later).

Ego defences that are likely to be associated with mental disorder include **denial** (refusing to accept reality) or **distortion** (reshaping external reality to meet internal needs).

CAN YOU...? No.3.2

1... Select **one** assumption of the psychodynamic approach from page 31 and explain how this relates to Freud's personality theory.

2... Explain how the id, ego and superego affect personality development.

3... Explain how **two** psychosexual stages may relate to later personality development.

4... Select **one** type of ego defence and explain how this relates to personality development.

EXAM QUESTION

Describe Freud's theory of personality development. [8]

Notes In the exam, you will be asked to describe **one** of the four theories you have studied (there is one theory for each of the four approaches). This question will be worth 8 marks. In order to gain the full 8 marks, your answer should:

▶ Be accurate and well detailed.

▶ Show evidence of coherent elaboration, i.e. each point you make should be explained to demonstrate your understanding.

▶ Display a depth and range of knowledge, though not necessarily in equal measure. This means that you can either cover a few points in considerable detail (i.e. depth), or cover a number of points in less detail (range).

▶ Be well structured and coherent.

▶ Have accurate grammar, punctuation and spelling.

▶ Be about 250–300 words in length.

Examiner hint

When describing Freud's personality theory, it is important to focus on how the concepts explain personality development, rather than just describing concepts such as the id, ego, superego and psychosexual stages.

Therapy 1 Dream analysis

On this spread and the next, we look at two further examples of the **psychodynamic approach** in psychology. Both of these are techniques that are used in **psychoanalysis** – the method developed by Freud to treat mental disorder. Psychoanalytic therapy is based on the assumption that individuals are often unaware of the influence of **unconscious** conflicts on their current psychological state. The aim of psychoanalysis is to help bring these conflicts into the conscious mind, where they can be dealt with. On this spread we look at **dream analysis**, and on the next we consider **free association**. You are required to study only one of these.

Before Freud, the Greeks and Egyptians sought to discover the hidden meaning of dreams believing that they were sent from God. Freud was greatly influenced by these classical cultures in his thinking.

> **Examiner hint**
>
> *Remember to link the aims of the therapy to the assumptions of the approach.*

Freud famously described dreams as 'the royal road to a knowledge of the unconscious activities of the mind' (Freud, 1900, page 769).

▲ Surrealist artists tried to recreate the nonsensical but meaningful experience of dreams in their paintings.

NIGHTMARES

It is difficult to see how nightmares would be wish fulfilments or how they might protect the sleeper (because they wake you up rather than enable you to sleep unworried). Freud did suggest that there is a class of dreams that do not seem to be fulfilments of wishes. He gave the example of one of his own dreams of a time when he was working in a chemistry lab, work that he was not good at. He regarded this dream as a 'sensible warning' rather than wish fulfilment. Freud considered that the experience of anxiety dreams and nightmares was the result of failures in dreamwork. Such phenomena did not contradict the wish-fulfilment theory, but instead demonstrated how the ego reacted to the awareness of repressed wishes that were too powerful and insufficiently disguised.

DREAM ANALYSIS

Freud proposed that the unconscious mind expresses itself through dreams, and that the content of a person's dreams can therefore reveal what is in their unconscious. Dream analysis is the process of assigning meaning to dreams.

Dreams as primary-process thought (repression)

Freud believed that personality consists of three basic structures: the **id**, **ego** and **superego**. Most important in the explanation of dreaming is the id. This is the unconscious source of our impulses, and is also the source of the wishes and fantasies that derive from these. The id is associated with irrational, instinct-driven unconscious thought called **primary-process thought**. This form of thought is unacceptable to the adult conscious mind, and so is relegated to our dreams (Freud referred to this as **repression**), where we can act out our wishes and desires. Freud believed that if we did not dream, the energy invested in these desires would build up to intolerable levels and so threaten our sanity.

Dreams as wish fulfilment

Freud believed that all dreams were the unconscious fulfilment of wishes that could not be satisfied in the conscious mind. Dreams therefore protect the sleeper (primary-process thought), but also allow some expression to these buried urges (wish fulfilment).

The symbolic nature of dreams

According to Freud, although dreams represent unfulfilled wishes, their contents are expressed *symbolically*. The real meaning of a dream (**latent content**) is transformed into a more innocuous form (**manifest content**, the content you actually experience) that may be meaningless to anybody but a psychoanalyst trained to interpret these symbols. For example, a penis may be represented by a snake or a gun, a vagina by a tunnel or a cave. In order to understand the meaning of dream symbols fully, however, Freud believed it was necessary to consider them in the context of a person's life. For example, a fish could represent a person's friend who is a fisherman or another friend who has a Piscean star sign. Freud did not support the idea of dream dictionaries. Freud also recognised that not everything in a dream is symbolic, as Freud himself said, *'sometimes a cigar is just a cigar'*.

Dreamwork

The latent content of a dream is transformed into manifest content through the process of **dreamwork**. Dreamwork consists of the various processes listed below. These processes are applied to repressed wishes to produce the content of the dream that is experienced. The processes include the following.

- **Condensation** Dream thoughts are rich in detail and content but these are condensed to the brief images in a dream where one dream image stands for several associations and ideas.
- **Displacement** The emotional significance of a dream object is separated from its real object or content and attached to an entirely different one so that the dream content is not 'censored'. (Freud used the concept of a 'censor' who prevents disturbing thoughts reaching the conscious mind except in a disguised form.)
- **Representation** A thought is translated into visual images.
- **Symbolism** A symbol replaces an action, person or idea.
- **Secondary elaboration** The unconscious mind collects all the different images and ties them together to form a logical story, further disguising the latent content.

The actual dream material may be supplied from recent events in a person's waking life.

An example of dream analysis

Dream *I had a dream where I was on a cruise ship in a foreign country and we landed and embarked. There was a scavenger hunt that everyone had to participate in. We all went into town and I bought some pretty shoes. There was only one restaurant in town and everyone went there to drink and eat. Everyone ate dinner and got really drunk from beer and shots of tequila.*

Personal interpretation Perhaps being on a ship signifies that I feel scared and trapped in the middle of an ocean or a big decision, and that landing signifies making a decision. Shoes may signify being grounded with the decision. Eating and being merry may signify being content with the decision.

Freud might say Do the cruise ship/foreign location/scavenger hunt have personal associations, or are they associated with any current reality shows or other indirect context? Knowing this could deeply affect the meaning of these pieces of manifest content. The shoes and the merry-making may be interpreted straightforwardly as what the dreamer thinks, except that wish fulfilment requirements would make it a dream about wishing the dreamer is happy and grounded with his or her decision.

Adapted from www.alexfiles.com/otiod.shtml#samples.

DO IT YOURSELF No. 3.3

Try to analyse one of your own dreams.
1. Record your dream, including as much detail as possible.
2. Break the report down into specific items and events.
3. For each item/event, write down any associations, such as recent events, old memories and personal interests. These should point to the latent content of your dream. (Remember the processes of dreamwork and try to ignore the 'logic' of the manifest content.)
4. Find the wish fulfilment in your dream.

If your dreams aren't very interesting (!), try the internet for dream reports. For example: www.edgarcayce.org/dreams/categories/dreams-relantionships.asp.

Using dream analysis in therapy

The process of dream analysis consists largely of reversing the processes that created the manifest content. Freud suggested that a therapist should disregard any apparent connections between elements in the manifest content. The process of free association (see next spread) can be used to uncover the latent content, i.e. the patient should be allowed to discuss each element of the dream, expressing any thought that occurs to them.

A psychoanalyst does not offer any one particular interpretation of a dream – dream analysis involves suggesting various interpretations based on the patient's free associations and knowledge of their life experiences, and allowing the patient to select the interpretations that make sense.

Research evidence

Recent research has provided support for Freud's link between dreaming and primary-process thinking. Solms (2000) used **PET scans** to highlight the regions of the brain that are active during dreaming. The results showed that the rational part of the brain is indeed *inactive* during **rapid eye movement** (**REM**) **sleep**, whereas the **forebrain** centres concerned with memory and motivation are very active. In Freud's language, the ego (rational and conscious thought) becomes suspended while the id (the more primitive, unconscious-'driven' parts of the mind) is given free reign.

Another source of support comes from earlier research by Hopfield *et al.* (1983) on **neural networks** – computer simulations that aim to mimic the action of the brain. Such computer simulations show that neural networks deal with an overloaded memory by conflating or condensing 'memories'. This supports Freud's notion of condensation – when unacceptable desires are censored and dealt with by recombining fragments until they emerge in a new form (the manifest content of the dream).

> **Examiner hint**
>
> *Remember that in order to be able to gain the full 12 marks, your answer must provide a link between the aims of dream analysis and the main assumptions of the psychodynamic approach.*

> **Examiner hint**
>
> *Even though free association is part of dream analysis, it is important, when answering an exam question, to ensure that your response is clearly focused on dream analysis rather than the alternative therapy, free association.*

CAN YOU...? No.3.3

1... Explain the purpose of dream analysis.

2... Explain how dreams are wish fulfilments.

3... Explain the difference between the latent and manifest content of dreams.

4... Identify and describe **three** processes involved in dream analysis (i.e. the process of transforming the manifest content back to the latent content).

5... Outline **two** findings from research studies and state what conclusion can be drawn from each of these studies.

EXAM QUESTION

Describe how the psychodynamic approach has been applied to either dream analysis or free association. [12]

Notes *In the exam, you will be asked to describe **one** therapy. In total you will have studied four therapies (one for each of the four approaches). This question will be worth 12 marks. In order to gain the full 12 marks, your answer should satisfy the same criteria as those listed on page vii. You might include the following in an answer about dream analysis.*

▶ *A brief outline of the aims of dream analysis and how these link with the assumptions of the psychodynamic approach.*

▶ *Explanations of how manifest content can be turned back into latent content.*

▶ *A description of the process of dream analysis.*

▶ *Research findings into dream analysis.*

▶ *Your answer should be about 400–450 words in length.*

Therapy 2 Free association

Free association is one of the techniques used in **psychoanalysis**, the method developed by Freud to treat mental disorder. Psychoanalytic therapy is based on the assumption that individuals are often unaware of the influence of **unconscious** conflicts on their current psychological state. The aim of psychoanalysis is to help bring these conflicts into the conscious mind, where they can be dealt with.

On the previous spread we looked at **dream analysis**, another technique used in psychoanalysis. The alternative is for you to study **free association**, discussed on this spread. You are required to study only one of these.

▲ Freud's couch and analyst's chair (Freud Museum, London). The patient lay on the couch, facing away from Freud, to help them focus inwards. Freud believed this arrangement helped patients to relax and explore their unconscious thoughts through free association.

Examiner hint

Remember to link the aims of the therapy to the assumptions of the approach.

DO IT YOURSELF   No. 3.4

Many students are somewhat dismissive of Freudian psychology. Perhaps the following activity may help you be convinced, '**The Story of Your Life'**.

Freud thought that making sense of our past – especially, the events of our childhood – would help us to resolve present conflicts and open up more possibilities for ourselves in the future. Write a short story about yourself. The story should show you in the past, the present, and the future. You can include the following details.
- A scene from your early childhood.
- A scene about a conflict in your current life.
- A scene from your imagined future where the conflict is resolved and elements of the first two scenes are also present.

You may present the scenes in the story in any order you choose. You might then share your story with other students and consider what you learned from the exercise.

Did you make unconscious thoughts and feelings conscious? Do you think this may be helpful? If so, in what way? Has the task changed what you think about psychoanalysis?

FREE ASSOCIATION

Free association is one of the most important and central techniques used in psychoanalysis, the therapy developed by Sigmund Freud to make the unconscious conscious.

Repression and the unconscious mind

As a therapy, psychoanalysis is based on the idea that individuals are unaware of the many factors that cause their behaviour, emotions and general mental health. Such factors operate at an unconscious level, and are the result of **repressed** memories or unresolved conflicts from childhood. During psychoanalysis, the therapist attempts to trace these unconscious factors to their origins, and then helps the individual to deal with them. The therapist uses a variety of different techniques to uncover repressed material and help the client deal with it. Free association is one of these techniques (as is dream analysis, which was discussed on the previous spread).

Using free association

In free association, patients express their thoughts exactly as they occur, even though the thoughts may seem unimportant or irrelevant. Patients should not censor their thoughts in any way. Freud believed that the value of free association lies in the fact that the patients are making links (or associations) as they express their thoughts, and these associations are determined by the unconscious factors that the analysis is aiming to uncover. This procedure is designed to reveal areas of conflict, and to bring into consciousness those memories that have been repressed. The therapist helps interpret these for patients, who correct, reject, and add further thoughts and feelings.

Therapist interpretation

Therapists listen carefully as their patients talk, looking for clues and drawing tentative conclusions about the possible cause(s) of the problem. Patients may initially offer resistance to the therapist's interpretations (e.g. changing the subject to avoid a painful discussion), or may even display **transference**, where they recreate feelings and conflicts and transfer these on to the therapist (e.g. acting towards the therapist as if, for example, *he* or *she* was the despised parent).

Working through

Psychoanalysis (and free association) is not a brief form of therapy. Together, patients and therapist examine the same issues over and over again, sometimes over a period of years, in an attempt to gain greater clarity concerning the causes of their neurotic behaviour.

An example of free association

I am thinking of the fluffy clouds I seem to see with my very eyes. They are white and pearly. The sky is full of clouds but a few azure patches can still be seen here and there…

Clouds keep changing their shapes. They are fluid because they are condensed water particles…

I am thinking I may have an obsession about this water. The doctor has told me I am dehydrated; there's not enough water in my body. He suggested I should drink two to three litres of water every day. Mineral water or tea!

I thought there is a connection between my need to add salt to my food and thirst. My body has found itself a pretext – salty food – to make me drink more water. I have a lot

ANNA O.

One of Freud's early patients was Anna O. She suffered severe paralysis on her right side as well as nausea and difficulty drinking. Freud demonstrated, by using the technique of free association, that these physical symptoms actually had a psychological cause.

During his therapeutic sessions with her, it became apparent that she had developed a fear of drinking when a dog she hated drank from her glass. Her other symptoms of paralysis originated from when she was caring for her sick father, because she could not express her anxiety about his illness and, instead, her anxiety was expressed as a physical paralysis.

During psychoanalysis, she was able to understand her fear of water, and was also able to express her feelings of anxiety about her father. As soon as she had the opportunity to make these unconscious thoughts conscious, her fears and paralysis disappeared.

▲ Anna O. (real name Bertha Pappenheim).

The writing cure

Anna O. (see box above) is one of Freud's most famous patients. She described free association as the 'talking cure'. Freud also used writing as a means of expressing free association, suggesting that patients perform a kind of self-analysis by writing down whatever came into their mind. The method was further developed by Pickworth Farrow (1942), who found it an effective way to analyse himself.

Research evidence

Pole and Jones (1998) recorded more than 200 sessions of psychoanalysis with a single patient. They compared the complexity of the free associations with the symptoms the patient was experiencing, and found that the symptoms were reduced during periods of particularly rich free associations, suggesting that free association does have a beneficial effect.

Other evidence for the effectiveness of free association comes from reviews of psychoanalysis in general. Bergin (1971) analysed the data from 10 000 patient histories, and estimated that 80% benefited from psychoanalysis compared with 65% from eclectic therapies (therapies based on a number of different approaches). Bergin concluded that this is modest support for psychoanalysis.

Tschuschke *et al.* (2007) carried out one of the largest studies investigating long-term **psychodynamic** treatment. More than 450 patients were included in the study, which showed that the longer **psychotherapeutic** treatments take, the better the outcomes are. This supports the need for a prolonged therapy.

Beyond Freud

Free association is not a technique that is exclusive to psychoanalysis. In fact, it has been used beyond the therapeutic context, for example Hollway and Jefferson (2000) suggested its use as a method of collecting information from research participants. They developed the '*free-association narrative interview method*'. This method is particularly useful with interviewees who are 'defended', i.e. are reluctant to reveal their true thoughts and feelings. This **qualitative** method also has the advantage of acknowledging the unconscious dynamics between interviewer and interviewee.

of thoughts about the manifestations of my body, which seem logical and aim at inner balance. Everybody has in fact got an inner physician in oneself. What need is there of an outside doctor then? If you allow yourself to be at the will of your free inclinations, with no assumptions whatsoever, you will have the intuition of making things that may surprise you, nevertheless useful to your body and securing your health and high spirits.

I read somewhere that one can be one's own doctor... Everybody can be one's own doctor.

From www.freudfile.org/psychoanalysis/free_associations.html.

Lion Kimbro spent three months writing down every one of his thoughts (and published it for all to read). He reported that the outcome was an incredible clarity about his own views and feelings, and said he emerged from this process as a changed man. You can read more at www.speakeasy.org/~lion/.

CAN YOU...?   No.3.4

1... Describe the aim of free association.

2... Describe how free association allows the unconscious mind to reveal itself.

3... Describe the therapist's role in free association.

4... Identify and describe **three** key features of free association.

5... Outline **two** findings from research studies and state what conclusion can be drawn from each of these studies.

EXAM QUESTION

Describe how the psychodynamic approach has been applied to either dream analysis or free association. [12]

Notes *In the exam, you will be asked to describe* **one** *therapy. In total you will have studied four therapies (one for each of the four approaches). This question will be worth 12 marks. In order to gain the full 12 marks, your answer should satisfy the same criteria as those listed on page vii. You might include the following in an answer about free association.*

▶ *A brief outline of the aims of free association and how these link with the assumptions of the psychodynamic approach.*

▶ *Examples of how free association is conducted.*

▶ *Research findings into free association.*

▶ *Your answer should be about 400–450 words in length.*

Examiner hint

Remember that to gain the full 12 marks, your answer must provide a link between the aims of free association and the main assumptions of the psychodynamic approach.

Evaluating the psychodynamic approach

You have studied two examples of the **psychodynamic approach** – one theory (Freud's theory of personality development) and one therapy (either **dream analysis** or **free association**). It is now time to use your understanding of the psychodynamic approach to consider its strengths and weaknesses. To help you, we have provided some additional examples of the psychodynamic approach.

➕ Strengths of the psychodynamic approach

1. Nature and nurture

One strength of the psychodynamic approach is that it takes into account both sides of the **nature–nurture debate**. Freud claimed that adult personality is the product of **innate** drives (**nature**) and childhood experiences (**nurture**). These innate drives include the structures of the personality (id, ego and superego), as well as the psychosexual stages that every child passes through. In each of these stages, frustration or overindulgence may lead to a fixation on that stage and predictable adult personality characteristics. Freud's theory therefore considers the influence of nature (things we are born with) and nurture (things that develop through experience). The *interactionist* nature of this approach is a key strength.

2. Usefulness

The psychodynamic approach has proved to be useful in several ways.
- It highlights the fact that childhood is a critical period in development; who we are and become is greatly influenced by our childhood experiences.
- Ideas put forward by Freud have greatly influenced the therapies used to treat mental disorders. Freud was the first person to recognise that psychological factors could be used to explain physical symptoms such as paralysis. **Psychoanalysis** (the general term for therapy developed from this approach) has been widely used to help people overcome psychological problems. There is research evidence to support this (see pages 34–35 and 36–37).
- Generally, this is a useful approach for helping to understand mental health problems, i.e. that mental health can be caused by childhood trauma and/or unconscious conflicts.

3. Reflects the complexity of human behaviour

One of the common criticisms of the other approaches in this unit is that the explanations of behaviour are **reductionist**. In contrast, Freud's explanations reflect the complexity of human behaviour and experience.
  This can be seen in the ways the different approaches treat mental disorder. For example, the **behaviourist approach** proposes that recovery from mental disorder can be achieved through re-learning, and does not require any consideration of what may have caused the disorder in the first place. The problem with this approach is that the original symptoms may simply reappear again because the actual cause has been ignored (called '**symptom substitution**'). Freud's method of psychoanalysis seeks to uncover deep meanings and acknowledges that understanding behaviour is a lengthy process.

The issues and debates listed in the table on the facing page are explained in the introduction to this book (see pages x–xi).

"AND THEN INSTEAD OF FEEDING ME HE WOULD RING A LITTLE BELL."

www.cartoonstock.com

DO IT YOURSELF

Compare and contrast

You have now studied three approaches – the biological, behaviourist and psychodynamic approaches. You can compare and contrast these three approaches.

1. Copy out the table on facing page and fill in the right hand column (the psychodynamic approach).
2. Look at the answers you gave for the **biological approach** on page 11 (in Chapter 1), and compare and contrast them with those for the psychodynamic approach. For example, you might look at the issue of reductionism and point out that the biological approach is reductionist, whereas the psychodynamic approach is, in some ways, not reductionist. Explain this difference, and then do the same for as many similarities and differences as you can.

1. Reductionist approach

On the facing page, we identified one of the strengths of the psychodynamic approach being that it reflects the complexity of human behaviour and experience. However, in some ways the psychodynamic approach can also be seen as being reductionist. It can be accused of 'mechanistic reductionism' because it simplifies complex human behaviour to the mechanics of the mind (i.e. the battle between the **id**, **ego** and **superego**) and early childhood experience (**psychosexual stages**). This approach thus ignores other important influences on behaviour, such as biochemistry and genetics. For example, during the 1950s and 60s, one of the main explanations for **autism** was that some mothers were very distant from their children ('refrigerator mother') and autism was a withdrawal from the lack of involvement. Such a psychodynamic explanation was an oversimplification of the underlying processes of autism. Therefore, in some ways, this approach does have the weakness of being reductionist.

2. Determinist approach

Freud saw infant behaviour as determined by innate forces (**libido**), and adult behaviour as determined by childhood experiences. It therefore follows that we have no **free will** (choice) in who we become or how we behave. We call this a **determinist** viewpoint, as it sees our personality as shaped (pre-determined) by forces that we cannot change or do not have a choice about – as humans we have no free will when it comes to our personality and behaviour. This is a weakness, as we *are* able to change the way we behave if we want to. This determinist viewpoint may give some people a plausible excuse for behaving unreasonably (*'I can't help the way I am'*) or an excuse for criminal behaviour (*'It's not my fault'*). It also implies that people cannot be held responsible for their behaviour.

3. Cannot be proven wrong

The major objection to Freud's theory is that it is difficult to **falsify**. A good theory is one that can be tested to see if it is wrong. Popper (1935) argued that falsification is the only way to be certain, *'no amount of observations of white swans can allow the inference that all swans are white, but the observation of a single black swan is sufficient to refute that conclusion'.* In other words, you can't prove that a theory is right – you can only falsify a theory.

Many of Freud's predictions are notoriously 'slippery'. For example, his view that all men have repressed homosexual tendencies cannot be disproved. If you do find men who have no repressed homosexual tendencies then it could be argued that they have them, it's just they are so repressed they are not apparent. In other words, the prediction cannot be falsified.

However, while it is difficult to generate testable hypotheses from Freud's theory of personality, it is not impossible. For example, research has looked at the relationship between guilt and wrongdoing – Freud predicted an inverse relationship, and MacKinnon (1938) did find that individuals who cheated at a task tended to express less guilt when questioned about life in general than those who did not cheat.

▶ A person might believe all swans are white, and this picture appears to support this hypothesis – but it does not prove it to be right. In fact, you cannot prove that this hypothesis is right, you can only prove it wrong (falsify it) by seeing a black swan.

CAN YOU...? No.**3.5**

1... Identify **two** strengths of the psychodynamic approach.

2... Make **three** distinct points to explain each strength.

3... Identify **two** weaknesses of the psychodynamic approach.

4... Make **three** distinct points to explain each weakness.

EXAM QUESTIONS

Evaluate two strengths of the psychodynamic approach. [6]
Evaluate two weaknesses of the psychodynamic approach. [6]

Notes *In the exam, you are required to discuss **two** strengths and **two** weaknesses of **one** of the four approaches. For each strength and weakness, you should:*

▶ *Clearly identify the strength or weakness.*

▶ *Thoroughly explain why this is a strength or weakness in relation to the approach.*

▶ *Where appropriate, use examples drawn from theory/therapy to illustrate your answer.*

▶ *Think of each strength/weakness as being worth three marks (although, strictly speaking, this is not how they are marked).*

▶ *Write around 50–60 words on each strength/ weakness.*

Examiner hint

There is a knack to writing answers to 'compare and contrast' questions – look at pages 60–61 for special advice on how to deal with these questions.

No. 3.5

3. Repeat step 2, this time comparing the **behaviourist** (page 25 in Chapter 2) and psychodynamic approaches.
4. Use this information to write an answer to the following exam question:

   Compare and contrast the behaviourist and psychodynamic approaches in terms of similarities and differences. [12]

Issues and debates	The psychodynamic approach
Nomothetic/idiographic	
Nature–nurture	
Reductionism/holism	
Determinism/free will	
Scientific/non-scientific	
Methodology used	
Anything else!	

Methodology used by the psychodynamic approach

The final topic on the **psychodynamic approach** is a consideration of the methodology used by this approach. Obviously researchers use all sorts of methods and techniques, but we have selected two that are particularly common in the psychodynamic approach – **case studies** and the **clinical interview**.

Case studies in general are discussed on page 163.

1. Case studies

The psychodynamic approach to studying behaviour is generally focused on the individual, observing particular 'cases' in great detail. This is known generally as an **idiographic** approach. The idiographic approach emphasises the uniqueness of each individual, and so the case study method would be the main way that a psychodynamic psychologist would study human behaviour. Case studies involve studying one person in great detail, which often involves spending a lot of time with the person, interviewing and observing him or her. Freud based his theory of personality development on several clinical cases. For example, the case of Little Hans was used to develop his ideas about the Oedipus conflict (see page 32 and the box on the right).

Strengths

- A true insight into behaviour can be obtained, as case studies involve spending time with the person, rather than gaining a 'snap shot' of his or her behaviour, which is what would be produced by a **lab experiment**.
- Descriptive, **qualitative** data is obtained, which is important in trying to understand the reasons behind a person's behaviour. We may be more able to draw valid conclusions about behaviour if we take the time to study it in detail.
- Idiographic research addresses the wholeness and uniqueness of the individual, and aims to give a complete in-depth picture. This is invaluable if it is these unique qualities that are important in understanding why a person behaves in the way they do.

Weaknesses

- Because case studies relate to single instances, it is not possible to generalise to other people. The results of a study are only valid when applied to that case.
- As case studies rely on qualitative rather than **quantitative** analysis, there is a danger that behaviour is interpreted in the way the researcher wants (**subjective**). Researchers alone decide how they are to interpret what they observe/hear, what they include in their descriptions, and what they leave out. It is therefore easy to select information in support of the theory that is put forward.
- The individuals studied by Freud hardly formed a representative sample of the population. They were largely middle-class Viennese women suffering from neurotic disorders living in a sexually suppressed culture in the 19th century. This raises the issues of gender, **culture** and historical bias.

> **Examiner hint**
>
> *Remember to use an example of a case study to highlight to the examiner that you understand how case studies have been used within the psychodynamic approach.*

THE CASE STUDY OF LITTLE HANS

The complete case study of Little Hans covers almost 150 pages. In many places Hans's father produced a detailed record of conversations he had with Hans. For example:

I:	*Did you often get into bed with Mummy at Gmunden?*
Hans:	*Yes.*
I:	*And you used to think to yourself you were the Daddy?*
Hans:	*Yes.*
I:	*And then you felt afraid of Daddy.*
Hans:	*You know everything; I didn't know anything.*
I:	*What carts are you still afraid of?*
Hans:	*All of them.*
I:	*You know that's not true.*
Hans:	*I'm not afraid of carriages and pair or cabs with one horse. I'm afraid of buses and luggage-carts, but only when they are loaded up, not when they're empty.*

(Freud, 1909, pages 90–91)

Such conversations demonstrated the inner workings of Hans's mind to Hans's father and Freud. However, what Hans said may not truly represent his feelings – it certainly seems from the extract above that Hans's father often used '**leading questions**' (questions that may 'suggest' a certain answer from the respondent – see study by Loftus and Palmer on page 92 for more on leading questions). This meant that Hans's answers may well have been influenced by his father's expectations.

The case study also included other details, such as this drawing by Hans.

▲ A reproduction of a drawing made by Hans. He asked his father to add the widdler but his father said '*Draw it yourself*'.

Interviews in general are discussed on page 159.

2. Clinical interviews

Psychoanalysis, the general name for psychodynamic therapies, makes much use of the clinical interview technique, where the client is encouraged to talk about his or her past and emotions. Clinical interviews will usually follow an unstructured format. The therapist may begin with some predetermined questions, but further questions arise in response to what the patient says. The patient is free to talk about anything they wish; the therapist can guide the interview as they see fit, following up any relevant issues that arise. Freud used this clinical interview technique as a means of making a diagnosis of his patients during **dream analysis** and **free association**.

Strengths

- Clinical interviews allow the facilitation of good relationships between clients and therapists. Clients are therefore more likely to open up and be honest about their emotions.
- Clinical interviews allow the therapist to tap in to both verbal and **non-verbal behaviour**, such as tone of voice and body language.
- As with case studies, clinical interviews allow rich, qualitative data to be gathered, which is more likely to facilitate the understanding of the reasons behind a person's behaviour.

Weaknesses

- Once again, there is a problem with **generalisability**, but this time in a different way. Clinical interviews tend to produce qualitative data, which is difficult to summarise and difficult to detect any trends in the data. This makes it hard to produce generalisations.
- There is also a danger of subjectivity and **interviewer bias**. A therapist may be extremely keen to guide the interview as they 'see fit', and interpret the client's answers in a way that supports a particular hypothesis they may have.

▲ You are probably very familiar with the clinical interview – when you visit your doctor he or she will start by asking some fairly routine questions, such as 'What's wrong with you?' or 'Have you been running a high temperature?'. Your answers to these initial questions will determine the subsequent questions that are asked by the doctor.

The same technique is used by interviewers in some psychological research. In such cases, the interviewer has the freedom to vary questions so that he/she can elicit the most from interviewees. Such interviews are called '**unstructured interviews**' and are discussed again on pages 159–161.

DO IT YOURSELF

No. 3.6

Obtain a copy of Freud's case study of Little Hans (Freud, 1909, pages 5–147). Or you might look at some other of his case studies. The Rat Man is reported in the same volume as Little Hans.
- Go through the case study finding your own examples.
- Make notes about the techniques used in case studies, including where possible examples of the strengths and weaknesses.
- Do the same for clinical interviews.

You can do this individually, or in groups. You should prepare this information to present back to the group, and produce an overall handout on the examples you have identified.

Examiner hint

In order to ensure your answer to this question is thorough and relevant, you need to include examples of how the particular methodology is used within the approach. For example, when discussing the use of case studies within the psychodynamic approach, you could bring in Freud's case study of Little Hans or Anna O. This will help you to explain the methodology thoroughly and coherently, and demonstrate to the examiner that you understand the methodology used within that particular approach. Answers where a candidate talks in a generic manner about certain research methods will not attract credit in the top two bands (see mark schemes on page vii).

CAN YOU...? No.3.6

1... Identify **two** methods used by the psychodynamic approach, and for each describe an example of how this method was used in a research study that used the psychodynamic approach.

2... For each method outline and explain **two** strengths and **two** weaknesses of using this method in the study you described.

EXAM QUESTION

Explain and **evaluate** the methodology used by the psychodynamic approach. [12]

*Notes In the exam, you are required to explain and evaluate the methods used by **one** of the four approaches. **It is vital that you clearly explain how the methods link with the assumptions of the approach, i.e. that they have clear relevance to the approach.** A general guide in terms of structuring your answer is as follows.*

- *Explain one method used by the approach (use examples that will highlight its relevance to the approach).*
- *Evaluate the strengths and weaknesses of this method.*
- *Explain a second method used by the approach (use examples that will again highlight its relevance).*
- *Evaluate the strengths and weaknesses of this method.*

N.B. The top band of the mark scheme for this question states: 'Methods are appropriate and clearly explained…and have clear relevance to the approach'.

Chapter 3 summary

Assumptions of the psychodynamic approach

Tripartite personality
Id (pleasure principle), ego (reality principle), superego (conscience and ideal self).

Levels of consciousness
Conscious, preconscious and unconscious mind. Unconscious is related to ego defences, e.g. regression, displacement, repression.

Early childhood
Young children greatly affected by anxiety, therefore ego defences act. Psychosexual stages have great influence.

Freud's theory of personality development

Core of the personality
Id, ego, superego managed by strength of ego.

Psychosexual stages
Oral, anal, phallic (Oedipus conflict or penis envy), latent, genital stages.

Personality types
Oral aggressive or receptive, anal retentive or expulsive, phallic and genital characters.

Ego defences
May lead to mental disorders.

Dream analysis

Primary-process thought
Dreams are expression of id thoughts (irrational, instinct-driven) that are unacceptable to the conscious mind.

Wish fulfilment
Dreams are unconscious fulfilment of wishes denied by the conscious mind.

Dreamwork
Latent content transformed to manifest through condensation, displacement, representation, symbolism and secondary elaboration.

Free association

Repression
Unresolved conflicts are repressed to the unconscious mind, but exert negative influence, resulting in disordered behaviour.

Free association
Patient relates thoughts as they occur; uncensored thoughts reveal unconscious feelings.

Therapist interpretation
Therapist draws tentative conclusions.

Working through
Psychoanalysis takes many years.

Strengths and weaknesses of the psychodynamic approach

Strengths
► Nature and nurture – an interactionist approach.
► Usefulness – importance placed on childhood, value as a therapy and explanation of behaviour.
► Reflects complexity of human behaviour – reductionism prevents true understanding.

Weaknesses
► Reductionist approach – behaviour simplified to mechanics of id, ego, superego and importance of childhood.
► Determinist approach – behaviour determined by innate forces and childhood.
► Cannot be proved wrong – a 'good' theory should be falsifiable.

Methodology of the psychodynamic approach

An idiographic approach observing one case in detail.
► **Strengths**: true insight because greater time spent with participant, rich qualitative data, emphasises uniqueness of individuals.
► **Weaknesses**: lacks generalisability, subjective interpretations, unrepresentative sample.

Clinical interview
Interviewer starts with fixed questions and then adapts to responses from patient.
► **Strengths**: facilitates patient/interviewer relationship, therapist can acknowledge non-verbal behaviour, qualitative data.
► **Weaknesses**: lacks generalisability because qualitative data is hard to summarise, interviewer bias leads to subjective findings.

Review activities

Y‌ou can use some of the review activities described at the end of Chapters 1 and 2 (see pages 15 and 29) with the content of this chapter. For example, you could construct mind maps or write multiple choice questions. You should certainly list again the key words in this chapter and make sure you understand them.

The id, ego and superego

1. In pairs, decide what your id, ego and superego would be telling you to do in the following scenarios (or this can be done as a role play).
   a) You haven't got any money but you go into your favourite clothes shop anyway, and try on a lovely item. You discover the item is not tagged, and no one saw you take it into the changing room.
   b) Your best friend has just split up from their boyfriend/girlfriend and is devastated. The problem is the ex-boyfriend/girlfriend has asked you out on a date, and you have secretly liked them for ages.
   c) In your psychology test, you realise that you have left some revision notes in your pencil case, which is on the desk in front of you. Your teacher is busy marking some work at the front of the classroom.

2. Create a chart with the headings, 'id', 'ego' and 'superego' and, working in pairs, place the following phrases under the appropriate headings. Try to think of some more of your own as well.
   - Demands immediate pleasure.
   - Function is to control the impulses of the id, especially those that society forbids.
   - Concerned with devising a realistic strategy to obtain pleasure.
   - Not concerned with the consequences of an action.
   - Can punish the ego through causing feelings of guilt.
   - Works out realistic ways of satisfying the id's demands.
   - Develops in order to mediate between the unrealistic demands of the id and the superego.

Ego defences

1. Decide which defence mechanisms are being used in the examples below (repression, displacement, denial, projection):
   a) Sarah really wants to punch her cheeky little brother in the face. Instead she punches her pillow.
   b) Mandy refuses to accept her boyfriend doesn't want to be with her anymore so carries on texting him.
   c) Tommy constantly accuses his girlfriend of cheating on him.
   d) Julie suddenly remembered as an adult, while talking about her feelings in therapy, that her father had committed suicide when she was a girl.

2. List all of the ego defences mentioned in this chapter and think of examples for each of them.

Fill in the blank

Copy out the text below and try to fill in the blanks without looking back in the book to see how much you remember.

One assumption of the psychodynamic approach is that each child moves through five _____ _____ of development. He or she moves through these in the same _____. The stages are known as _____, _____, _____, _____ and _____. At each stage, a child's energy or _____ is attached to a body region. If conflicts occur at any stage and are not overcome or dealt with, _____ can occur, which may be due to _____ or _____ at a stage of development. This will affect our _____ later on in life. One example is the _____ _____ character. Such people typically have some of the following characteristics _____, _____ and _____. Another personality type is the _____ _____ character. Such people typically have some of the following characteristics: _____, _____ and _____.

Is Freud a NURD?

The acronym NURD may help you to evaluate the psychodynamic approach.
N = Nature and nurture
U = Usefulness
R = Reductionist
D = Determinist

Write a short paragraph for each of these four topics. As always, try first to do this without looking at your notes.

Writing and marking essays

Task 1 Write your essay

It is very important to practise writing essay answers to time. You have about 15 minutes to answer a 12-mark question, and should write about 400–450 words.

Students often have a false idea of what they can do because, before the exam, they have plenty of time to write quite reasonable essays, and they also use their notes. Write an answer to the following question without any notes and allow yourself only 15 minutes.

Compare and contrast the behaviourist and psychodynamic approaches in terms of similarities and differences. [12]

NB Before you begin, write a very short plan of the key points to be covered – you might use a **writing frame** to identify each of your key points. A writing frame is a table where each box is one element of your answer. For example, divide your table into 3 columns and 5 rows. In the first row, in box 1 identify your point, in box 2 explain this and in box 3, give an example. Repeat this on each line. You are following the **PEE rule** (point, explain, example).

Task 2 Mark your essay

When you have finished, you should swap your essay with someone else so that you can each mark the other's essay. You can find example mark schemes on page vii.

Remember that no credit is given in this essay for descriptive (AO1) material – so be careful not to give credit if the approaches are only described. AO2 marks can be given only for looking at similarities and differences and explaining why the approaches are similar/different.

Task 3 Improve your essay

With your marking partner, you should discuss the marks each of you gave to the other's essay and then spend time improving both essays. You can use your textbook or class notes to improve the essays. You will probably find that you will take out as much material out as you put in – students often include irrelevant material just to pad out an essay.

Example exam questions with student answers

Examiner's comments on these answers can be found on page 175.

Examiner hint

Remember that in the exam, question 1(a) will always be paired with 1(b), which will ask about the theory associated with this approach and be worth 8 marks.

EXAMPLE OF QUESTION 1(a)

Outline two assumptions of the psychodynamic approach. [4]

Megan's answer

The psychodynamic approach says that we are influenced by things that happen to us during our childhood, and that these will affect us later on in life. Also this approach says that our mind is made up of 3 things – an id, ego and superego. These constantly battle and cause us conflict within the mind.

Tomas's answer

One assumption of this approach is that personality is made up of three parts: the id (which demands pleasure at any cost), the superego (which is our sense of right and wrong, our morals), and the ego (which is in touch with reality and largely part of the conscious mind). The ego essentially acts as a referee between the id and superego, as they are in constant conflict, where one may be saying 'I want to do/have it now', and the other, 'You cannot have it now'.

The psychodynamic approach also assumes that in order to cope with the demands of the id, the ego uses defences – known as defence mechanisms, to prevent us from anxieties caused by the id–superego battle. One example of a defence mechanism is known as displacement, which is the act of taking out our feelings for someone or something on some substitute object (e.g. punching our pillow instead of our boyfriend who we are angry at).

EXAMPLE OF QUESTION 2

Describe how the psychodynamic approach has been applied in either dream analysis or free association. [12]

Megan's answer

Free association was a technique used by Freud in order to help treat his clients. Free association involves the patient sitting on a reclining couch and talking freely about whatever comes into their mind. The therapist encourages the client to be as open and honest as possible, however trivial or insignificant their thoughts may seem. Freud believed that by doing this, the ego, which normally censors threatening thoughts from the unconscious mind, would be by-passed.

During the therapy, the analyst usually sits behind the patient, and does not in general communicate verbally or non-verbally with them, but does sometimes need to repeat what the client is saying, just for clarification. The patient may avoid talking about certain things, or may change or skim over a topic if it comes up. Freud called this resistance, and saw this as being important to the therapy, as it reveals to the client and therapist possibly what the underlying problems might be.

When the therapist eventually discusses his (or her) thoughts with the client, transference could occur. This is where the patient will displace their feelings onto the therapist. For example, they may become very angry with the therapist if it has come to light that they are extremely angry about the way their parents behaved toward them in their childhood.

Tomas's answer

One of the main assumptions of the psychodynamic approach is that our behaviour is largely driven by the thoughts and feelings that lie in our unconscious mind. Therefore the aim of any therapy based on this approach would be to access the unconscious mind, and bring these feelings into the conscious mind, so they can be addressed.

Dream analysis is one form of psychoanalysis. Freud believed dreams to be a significant source of information in relation to our personality, essentially they are the 'royal road to the unconscious'. For Freud, dreams represented our underlying wishes and desires (wish fulfilment), which would come to light during dreaming as this was when our ego defences were at their lowest, and therefore would not censor important information. However, Freud said that this information is presented in a dream in a disguised form, called the manifest content, which is the storyline that you recall. The true meaning of the dream, which is likely to be hidden, is known as the latent content. It is the process of 'dreamwork' that disguises the latent content, and allows the dream to continue, forming a more acceptable storyline. For example, during dreamwork, displacement may occur where our true feelings for someone will be transferred onto someone or something else. Also symbolisation will disguise the meaning of the dream, this is where an object in a dream may symbolise something else. For example, a snake may really represent a penis, or a train going through a tunnel may represent sexual intercourse.

The role of the dream analyst is to decode the manifest to the latent content. They must merely suggest ideas about the interpretation to the patient who can accept or deny this as accurate. Freud himself did accept that not everything in a dream was symbolic, and famously stated that 'sometimes a cigar is just a cigar'. While some symbols do have a universal meaning, it is important to interpret the dream in the context of the patient's current life.

The emphasis of the **cognitive approach** is on how thinking shapes our behaviour – quite the opposite of the **behaviourist approach** where the concept of the mind was banished from any explanations. The cognitive approach is more recent than the others examined so far, emerging in the 1950s along with the information processing/computer revolution. Cognitive psychologists explain all behaviour in terms of thoughts, beliefs and attitudes, and study how these direct our behaviour, i.e. they look at the *internal* processes of the mind.

▲ *Always Look on the Bright Side of Life*, the song sung at the end of Monty Python's film *The Life of Brian*, is an example of the cognitive approach: dealing with a problem by thinking about it differently.

Assumption 1 Behaviour can be explained by mental processes

This approach sees human beings basically as information processors, where essential cognitive processes all work together to enable us to make sense of, and respond to, the world around us. Some of the most well studied cognitive processes include **perception**, attention, memory and language. These processes all relate to each other, and constantly work together to help individuals understand their environment. It is possible to see how these processes work if you consider the experience of recognising a dog. When we see a dog, what enables us to know it is a dog? We have to pay attention to it, perceive its features (e.g. four legs, tail, fur), search through our memory store to see if the object matches an existing **schema** (a mental structure that represents an aspect of the world). In order to be able to name it, we use our knowledge of language. Our mental processes work together within a split second to allow us to respond to the world around us. This is also known as information processing.

Assumption 2 Human mind is compared to a computer

The notion of the 'computer analogy' has become well accepted within the cognitive approach. Cognitive psychologists have often compared the human mind with a computer. In very basic terms, they compare how we take in information (*input*), change it/store it (*process*), and then recall it when necessary (*output*). During the process stage, we actively use the cognitive processes of perception, attention, memory and so on. Thus the mind is compared with the hardware of a computer, and the cognitive processes with a computer's software.

One example of this approach is the **multistore model** of memory (Atkinson and Shiffrin, 1968). In this theory, it was proposed that information enters the brain through the senses (eyes, ears, etc.) and moves to the short-term memory (STM) store and then to the long-term memory (LTM) store. It is output when required.

DO IT YOURSELF

No. 4.1

Try the following activity. Each student should think of a word related to 'bank robbery' and write it on a Post-it note. Then stick the Post-it on your forehead and see if you can find others in the class with the same Post-it word on their foreheads.

Consider all the words that people selected – these represent our schema of a bank robbery.

In future, you may find that when you think of a bank robbery, you also think of the word 'schema' because that has now become part of your bank robbery schema!

CAN YOU...?

No. 4.1

1... Explain the term 'schemas', using examples.

2... Explain in what way the human mind is like a computer (you might use the example of the multistore model of memory to help your explanation).

3... How could the multistore model be investigated in an objective, scientific way.

EXAM QUESTION

Outline two assumptions of the cognitive approach. [4]

*Notes In the exam, you will be asked to outline **two** assumptions of **one** of the four approaches. The question will be worth 4 marks. You should structure your answer in the following way.*

▶ *Identify one assumption.*

▶ *Explain/detail this assumption.*

▶ *Identify a second assumption.*

▶ *Explain/detail this assumption.*

Assumption 3 Psychology is a science, and behaviour should be studied in an objective, measurable way

Although cognitive psychologists focus on our internal, mental processes, they would still advocate a scientific approach to the study of human behaviour, one that should be conducted under controlled experimental lab conditions. Although we cannot see cognitive processes occurring within the mind, and we certainly cannot measure internal processing, we can measure the results of these processes in a scientific, objective way. In other words, what people say and how they respond can be taken as valid measures of their thought processes. For example, if we want to find out about the capacity of STM under controlled lab conditions, we ask participants to recall as many words as possible from a word list. Then we can make inferences about the capacity of STM from their responses. We have therefore made an assumption about the memory system from measuring people's responses to a task.

Attribution theory

There are many theories that illustrate the **cognitive approach**, such as the **multistore model** of memory mentioned on the previous page. **Attribution theory** is another excellent example of the cognitive approach. **Attribution** is the process of explaining causes of behaviour. When we observe someone else's behaviour, we unconsciously think of explanations for their behaviour, i.e. we *attribute* causes. For example, a friend buys you a gift: you think, 'What a kind person'. You have explained your friend's behaviour in terms of their personality. In the 1950s, cognitive psychologists drew our attention to the fact that we do not observe personality traits (such as kindness or stinginess), what we do is observe *behaviours* and from these draw inferences about personal attributes. This process is so ingrained that we even do it when shown a film of triangles and circles (see below)!

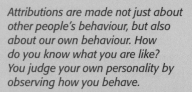

Attributions are made not just about other people's behaviour, but also about our own behaviour. How do you know what you are like? You judge your own personality by observing how you behave.

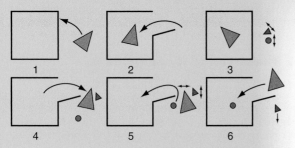

▲ In 1944, Fritz Heider and Marianne Simmel conducted a classic study in psychology. They showed a group of more than 100 women a silent film of two triangles (one large and one small) and a circle (see diagram above). The film lasted two and a half minutes and showed the triangles and circles moving against and around each other (you can see the film on YouTube: www.youtube.com/watch?v=sZBKer6PMtM).

One group of participants was asked simply to write a description of what had happened, whereas a second group was asked to interpret the movements of the figures as if they were the actions of people. For example, participants variously described the triangle as aggressive, warlike, irritable, dumb, stupid, ugly, shy, sly and quick to take offence (watch the film and you'll see why).

This shows how ready people are to attribute personality traits even to inanimate objects.

REAL-WORLD APPLICATIONS

One of the attractions of attribution theory is that it has produced some intriguing applications. One of these is a method for treating insomnia. Insomniacs often have difficulty sleeping because they have come to expect that they won't be able to go to sleep, and so when they go to bed they are therefore tense, which in itself prevents sleep. In terms of attribution theory, insomniacs have learned to *attribute* their sleep difficulties to 'insomnia'. If they can be convinced that the source of the difficulty lies elsewhere, this should end their maladaptive attribution.

In one study, insomniacs were given a pill and told that the pill would either stimulate them or act as a sedative. Those who expected arousal actually went to sleep faster because they attributed their arousal to the pill and therefore actually relaxed (Storms and Nisbett, 1970)!

ATTRIBUTION THEORY

Attribution theory was first developed by Fritz Heider in the 1950s. Further theories have been proposed by a number of psychologists, including Edward E. Jones and Harold Kelley.

Internal and external attributions

The origins of attribution theory lie with an amusing study by Heider and Simmel (1944, see left). This led Heider (1958) to propose that people have a strong tendency to attribute causes to behaviour. Heider suggested that people are like amateur (or 'naïve') scientists, trying to understand other people's behaviour by piecing together information until they arrive at a reasonable explanation. These explanations come from two sources.

- The *person*: internal or dispositional factors, such as a person's traits. For example, we might explain a person's loud behaviour in terms of their extrovert personality.
- The *situation*: external or situational factors, such as social norms or luck. For example, we might explain a person's loud behaviour in terms of the noisy environment. Or we might explain getting a good exam result in terms of having a good teacher (a **situational attribution**) rather than in terms of a student's ability (which would be a **dispositional attribution**).

Heider suggested that people prefer to make dispositional attributions. This is called the **fundamental attribution error** (**FAE**), i.e. it is a basic (fundamental) mistake that people make. For example, when served in a shop by an assistant who is very rude, people tend to assume that it is in the assistant's nature (dispositional explanation) rather than wondering if the assistant has been having a bad day (situational explanation).

Ross *et al.* (1977) demonstrated the FAE. Observers watched contestants giving answers to a quiz and were asked to rate their ability. They knew that some of the contestants had actually made up the questions (which would explain why they did well on the quiz), but nevertheless rated these contestants more highly.

However the FAE does not occur in all **cultures**. In **collectivist** cultures, people tend to make situational attributions, whereas in an **individualist** society people are more concerned with individual character because individualist cultures (such as that in the USA) emphasise the rights and interests of the individual. In a collectivist culture, individuals share tasks, belongings and income.

DO IT YOURSELF

No. 4.2

Imagine that one of your fellow students walks into class 10 minutes late in the morning. Think of what your initial reaction might be about why he or she was late. Compare your responses with those of other members of your class and list them on the board. In pairs, decide whether each of these reasons represents an internal or an external attribution.

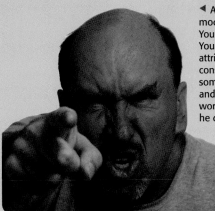

◀ An example of the covariation model. Imagine you are at work. Your manager gets angry with you. You would make a dispositional attribution if he often yells at you (high consistency), he yells at other workers sometimes (low distinctiveness), and no one else yells at you for bad work (low consensus). However, if he doesn't yell at other workers (high distinctiveness), this might lead you towards a situational attribution – it's something about your behaviour. This would be especially likely if he rarely yelled at you (low consistency).

Covariation model

Kelley (1967) suggested that attributions can be explained in terms of covariation. Things that covary are things that tend to happen at the same time, such as grey clouds and rain, or drinking and hangovers. Their covariance leads us to expect that the one causes the other. Kelley proposed that attributions are determined by the covariance of three factors or axes.

- **Consistency** Behaving the same way all the time, the extent that behaviour between one person and one stimulus is the same across time. For example, John always laughs at a particular comedian (high consistency), or John sometimes finds this comedian funny (low consistency).
- **Distinctiveness** Considering the extent to which any behaviour is unique, the extent that one person behaves the same to different stimuli. For example, John laughs only at this comedian (high distinctiveness), or John laughs at most comedians (low distinctiveness).
- **Consensus** The extent to which there is agreement among other people. For example, everyone laughs at this comedian (high consensus), or only some people find this comedian funny (low consensus).

Internal (dispositional) attributions occur when consistency is high and distinctiveness and consensus are low (HLL). External (situational) attributions are made when consistency is low, distinctiveness is high and consensus is low (LHL) or all three are high (HHH).

One study that supported this was by McArthur (1972), who gave participants 12 event-depicting sentences that contained information (high or low) about all three axes. Participants attributed external or internal causes as the model predicted.

One of the criticisms of this model is that it is a very mechanistic approach. Kelley believed that human behaviour is, for the most part, accurate and logical, but this may not be true. People often behave irrationally.

Errors and biases in the attribution process

The fundamental attribution error is an example of the predictable tendencies that people display when making attributions, which lead them to make mistaken attributions. There are several other errors or biases in the attribution process, two of which are described below.

Actor/observer bias We prefer to explain our own (the actor's) behaviour in terms of situation, and the behaviour of others (those we are observing) in terms of disposition. Nisbett *et al.* (1973) asked students to provide an explanation for selecting a particular course of study, relating to both themselves and to a friend. They made situational attributions about themselves (e.g. what the course had to offer), but dispositional ones about the friend.

Self-serving bias We take credit for our successes and disassociate from our failures, blaming external factors. This protects self-esteem, and gives us a sense of control. Jones *et al.* (1968) arranged for participants to teach two pupils. The 'teachers' attributed improved performance to themselves, but blamed the pupils for failure.

DO IT YOURSELF
No. 4.3

Think of your own examples for the covariation model. For each row in the table below, think of an example. An example for row 5 could be: Bill sometimes buys his wife a present for her birthday (low consistency). He never buys other friends a present (high distinctiveness), and other men usually don't buy presents for their wives (high consensus).

Then see whether people would make an internal or external attribution. For example, is Bill's behaviour due to his disposition (he is mean) or to the situation (he doesn't love his wife)?

	Consistency	Distinctiveness	Consensus
1	H	H	H
2	H	H	L
3	H	L	H
4	H	L	L
5	L	H	H
6	L	H	L
7	L	L	H
8	L	L	L

CAN YOU...?
No. 4.2

1... Describe what is meant by the term 'attribution'.

2... Describe the difference between 'internal' and 'external' attributions.

3... Write **three** sentences relating to the FAE.

4... Write **one** paragraph on Kelley's covariation model.

5... Select **one** assumption of the cognitive approach from page 45 and explain how this relates to attribution theory.

EXAM QUESTION

Describe attribution theory. [8]

*Notes In the exam, you will be asked to describe **one** of the four theories you have studied (there is one theory for each of the four approaches). This question will be worth 8 marks. In order to gain the full 8 marks, your answer should:*

▶ *Be accurate and well detailed.*

▶ *Show evidence of coherent elaboration, i.e. each point you make should be explained to demonstrate your understanding.*

▶ *Display a depth and range of knowledge, though not necessarily in equal measure. This means that you can either cover a few points in considerable detail (i.e. depth), or cover a number of points in less detail (range).*

▶ *Be well-structured and coherent.*

▶ *Have accurate grammar, punctuation and spelling.*

▶ *Be about 250–300 words in length.*

Therapy 1 Cognitive behavioural therapy

We have considered one theory illustrating the **cognitive approach** and will now look at therapies based on this approach. On this spread and the next, we look at examples of **cognitive behavioural therapy** (**CBT**). Such therapies combine cognitive therapy with behavioural techniques (related to the **behaviourist approach**). CBT involves identifying maladaptive *thinking* and then developing coping strategies (i.e. *behavioural* change).

On this spread we look at CBT, including the specific examples of Beck's cognitive therapy and Meichenbaum's **stress inoculation training** (**SIT**). On the next spread, we look at another specific example of CBT – Ellis's **rational emotive therapy** (**RET**). You are required to study only this spread (CBT and examples) or the next (RET).

Examiner hint

Can you recall the general assumptions of the cognitive approach? You will need to link the aims of the therapy to the assumptions of the whole approach.

It may seem strange that two such contrasting approaches (the cognitive and behavioural approaches) appear to work together. Behaviourists reject the use of any mental concepts, whereas cognitive psychologists base their whole approach on explaining behaviour in terms of such concepts. In the 1950s, these two traditions found some common ground when considering the treatment of mental disorders. Both cognitive and behaviourist therapies focus on the 'here and now' (compared, for example, with the psychodynamic approach, which is concerned with uncovering past influences).

Both cognitive and behaviourist therapies also focus more on the removal of symptoms than on seeking to discover what caused the behaviour in the first place. Some CBT methods are more predominantly cognitive, while others are more behaviourally oriented.

REAL-WORLD APPLICATIONS

Liverpool footballer Ryan Babel admitted that he has always been susceptible to pressure from the crowd, and struggled to handle fans turning against him. That is now a thing of the past thanks to manager Rafa Benitez. 'He [Benitez] told me that the abuse ought to make me stronger, saying the more the opposing fans swore at me, the more afraid of me they were'.

Many sportsmen and women unwittingly respond to stress with maladaptive thoughts that greatly hinder their performance. Once they understand how this way of thinking is keeping them from reaching their full potential, they begin to develop new coping strategies that can have a profoundly positive impact on their performance. Studies on the effects of stress inoculation training (SIT, see facing page) on sports performance have generally been very positive. SIT has been linked with improved performance during cross-country running, squash and basketball, and has been particularly effective at boosting the performances of gymnasts (Kerr and Leith, 1993). If Ryan Babel's performances for Liverpool are anything to go by, it has worked pretty well in football as well!

COGNITIVE BEHAVIOURAL THERAPY (CBT)

CBT is used in the treatment of a wide range of different mental disorders as well as for 'normal' problems such as in marriage guidance and improving exam performance. It is a cost-effective therapy because it is relatively short-term (usually between 16 and 20 sessions), and it is popular because it doesn't involve searching for deep meanings. CBT involves both cognitive and behaviourist approaches.

The cognitive approach

The cognitive approach believes that the key influence on behaviour is how an individual *thinks* about a situation. Therefore cognitive *therapy* aims to change unwanted or maladaptive thoughts and beliefs. Various psychologists have used different terms for such faulty thinking. Beck (1976) called them '*dysfunctional automatic thoughts*', and Ellis (1962) called them '*irrational assumptions*' (see next spread). Meichenbaum (1977) called the products of this faulty thinking '*counterproductive self-statements*'.

The aim of CBT is to identify and challenge these negative thoughts and replace them with constructive, positive thinking that will lead to healthy behaviour. For example, a patient may believe that everyone hates him or her. It is this *belief* (cognition) that is causing his or her problems. If the belief can be changed by challenging it (e.g. 'Where is your evidence for this?', 'Why does it matter to you?'), then the problem will disappear.

The cognitive approach does consider the *causes* of behaviour to some extent – faulty thinking is seen as the initial cause of maladaptive (unhealthy) behaviour. However, cognitive therapists are not focused on the original source of the irrational assumptions, whereas a psychoanalyst would be.

The behaviourist approach

The behaviourist approach believes that undesirable behaviours have been learned, therefore behaviourist *therapy* aims to reverse the learning process, and produce a new set of more desirable behaviours. Behaviourist therapeutic techniques include rewarding desirable behaviours and the use of models for modelling desirable behaviours.

One of the problems with behaviourist therapies is that they simply replace undesirable behaviours and don't consider the causes of such behaviours, which may mean that further unhealthy behaviours will appear (called **symptom substitution**). Combining behaviourist therapies with cognitive therapies can be an effective way of dealing with the problem of symptom substitution because cognitive therapies tackle some aspects of causation.

Research evidence for CBT

There is a large body of evidence that suggests that CBT is the most effective of all therapies. For example, David and Avellino (2003) report that CBT has the highest overall success rate of all therapies. However, Wampold *et al*. (2002) suggest that this may be because non-bona fide treatments (i.e. those with no theoretical framework) are included in the comparison therapies; when they are excluded from analysis, CBT does not appear superior to these other therapies. On the other hand, such apparent lack of success may be due to the fact that effectiveness varies considerably in relation to therapist competence. Kuyken and Tsivrikos (2009) concluded that as much as 15% of the variance in outcome may be attributable to therapist competence.

▲ Aaron Beck (1921–).

▲ Donald Meichenbaum (1940–).

MEET THE RESEARCHERS

Aaron Beck trained as a psychoanalyst but found, through his research with depressed patients, that psychodynamic explanations were inadequate and that he could better explain his patients' experiences in terms of negative thoughts. This led to his being one of the first to develop cognitive therapy. He now runs the *Beck Institute for Cognitive Therapy and Research* in Philadelphia, USA, with his daughter, Dr Judith Beck.

Donald Meichenbaum was voted 'one of the 10 most influential psychotherapists of the century' by US clinicians. He worked with victims of the Oklahoma bombing in 1993 and Hurricane Katrina in 2005, as well as with Canadian soldiers serving in Afghanistan and the native Inuit population in northern Canada.

Beck's cognitive therapy

Beck (1967) believed that depressed individuals feel as they do because their thinking is biased towards negative interpretations of the world. For example, he suggested that depressed people have acquired a negative **schema** (a tendency to adopt a negative view of the world) through their interactions with other people. Beck suggested that they have a *negative triad*, a pessimistic view of the self, the world (not being able to cope with the demands of the environment), and the future. In his therapy, Beck recommended the use of various techniques to challenge this negative triad, such as a *dysfunctional thought diary*.

Dysfunctional thought diary As 'homework', clients are asked to keep a record of the events leading up to any unpleasant emotions experienced. They should then record the automatic 'negative' thoughts associated with these events and rate how much they believe in these thoughts (on a scale of 1–100%). Next, clients are required to write a rational response to the automatic thoughts and rate their belief in this rational response, again as a percentage. Finally, clients should re-rate their beliefs in the automatic thoughts.

Therapy during therapy A client may feel distressed about something they have overheard, assuming that another person (person X) was talking about them. During CBT, that client is taught to challenge such dysfunctional automatic thoughts, for example by asking themselves: 'Where's the evidence that X *was* talking about me? What is the worst that can happen if X was?'. By challenging these dysfunctional thoughts, and replacing them with more constructive ones, clients are able to try out new ways of behaving.

Meichenbaum's SIT

Meichenbaum (1985) developed a form of CBT to deal with stress. He believed that we cannot (usually) change the *causes* of stress in our life (e.g. a stressful job is still a stressful job), but we can change the way that we *think* about those stressors. Negative thinking (e.g. 'I failed to hit a deadline, people must think I'm hopeless') may lead to negative outcomes such as anxiety, whereas positive thinking (e.g. 'OK, so I missed a deadline, my boss will still be delighted by what I've achieved') leads to more positive attitudes and feelings.

Meichenbaum suggested that people could *inoculate* themselves against stress in the same way that they could receive inoculations against infectious diseases such as measles. There are three main phases to this process.

1. **Conceptualisation phase** The therapist teaches the client to view perceived threats as problems-to-be-solved and to break down global stressors into specific components that can be coped with.
2. **Skills acquisition phase (and rehearsal)** This includes positive thinking, relaxation, social skills, and using social support as well as coping self-statements (see right). These skills are cognitive because they encourage the client to think in a different way, and behavioural because they involve learning more adaptive behaviours.
3. **Application phase (and follow through)** Clients are given opportunities to apply the newly learned coping skills in different situations, which become increasingly stressful. Various techniques may be used, such as modelling (watching someone else cope with stressors and then imitating this behaviour).

> **Examiner hint**
>
> In order to gain the full 12 marks, your answer must provide a link between the aims of CBT and the main assumptions of the cognitive approach.

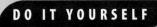

CAN YOU...?   No.4.3

1. Outline the aims of CBT.
2. Explain the cognitive approach to therapy.
3. Explain the behaviourist approach to therapy.
4. Select **two** or **more** techniques used in CBT and explain each of them, using examples.

EXAM QUESTION

Describe how the cognitive approach has been applied to either CBT or RET. [12]

Notes *In the exam, you will be asked to describe **one** therapy. In total you will have studied four therapies (one for each of the four approaches). This question will be worth 12 marks. In order to gain the full 12 marks, your answer should satisfy the same criteria as those listed on page vii. You might include the following in an answer about CBT.*

▶ *A brief outline of the aims of CBT and how these link with the assumptions of the cognitive approach.*

▶ *An explanation of the cognitive and behavioural components of CBT.*

▶ *Examples of how CBT has been used.*

▶ *Research findings into CBT.*

▶ *Your answer should be about 400–450 words in length.*

Examples of SIT coping self-statements

• *To help prepare for a stressful situation, you could say: 'You can develop a plan and deal with it'.*
• *When confronting and handling a stressful situation, you could say: 'Relax, you're in control, take a slow breath'.*
• *An example of a reinforcing self-statement would be: 'It wasn't as bad as you expected'.*

Therapy 2 Rational emotive therapy

Rational emotive therapy (**RET**) is a form of **cognitive behavioural therapy** (**CBT**). The primary focus of this treatment approach is to suggest changes in thinking that will lead to changes in behaviour, thereby alleviating or improving symptoms. The therapy aims to change irrational thinking patterns that cause emotional distress into thoughts that are more reasonable and rational. CBT is not solely focused on thinking (the **cognitive** component). It also encompasses the **behaviourist approach**, which believes that undesirable behaviours have been learned. Behaviourist therapy aims to reverse the learning process and produce a new set of more desirable behaviours.

On the previous spread, we looked at CBT (including the therapies of Beck and Meichenbaum). The alternative is to study Ellis's RET therapy. You are required to study only one of these, and must not muddle CBT and RET together when answering an exam question.

On the previous spread, we presented a general account of CBT that may be worth reading to increase your understanding of the basics.

> **Examiner hint**
>
> *Can you recall the general assumptions of the cognitive approach? You will need to link the aims of the therapy to the assumptions of the whole approach.*

▲ 'Beauty is in the eye of the beholder'. This sums up the cognitive approach – there is no 'reality', what matters is the way you think about reality.

DO IT YOURSELF   No. 4.5

1. Think of a situation where you feel frustrated or unhappy.
2. Identify the *activating event*, *self-defeating thoughts*, and *consequences* of this irrational thinking.
3. How might RET (see below) be used to change this irrational thinking and bring about more productive consequences for you?

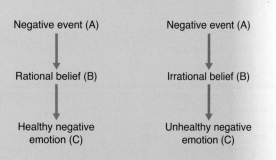

▲ We experience negative events all the time, such as being given a low grade on an essay or seeing a sad movie. Such negative events lead to negative emotions only if they are followed by an irrational belief instead of a rational one.

RATIONAL EMOTIVE THERAPY (RET)

In the 1950s, Albert Ellis was one of the first psychologists to develop a form of CBT. He first called it '*rational* therapy' to emphasise the fact that, as he saw it, psychological problems occur as a result of irrational thinking – individuals frequently develop self-defeating habits because of faulty beliefs about themselves and the world around them. The aim of therapy is to turn these *irrational* thoughts into rational ones, therefore it was first called '*rational* therapy'. Rational beliefs are flexible, realistic and undemanding, whereas irrational beliefs are rigid, unrealistic and demanding.

Ellis renamed his therapy 'rational *emotive* therapy' (RET) because the therapy focuses on resolving emotional problems, and, even later, he renamed it '**rational emotional behaviour therapy**' (**REBT**) because the therapy also resolves behavioural problems.

Mustabatory thinking

The source of irrational beliefs lies in mustabatory thinking – thinking that certain ideas or assumptions *must* be true in order for an individual to be happy. Ellis identified the three most important irrational beliefs.

- *I must* be approved of or accepted by people I find important.
- *I must* do well or very well, or I am worthless.
- The world *must* give me happiness, or I will die.

Other irrational assumptions include:

- Others *must* treat me fairly and give me what I need, or they are absolutely rotten.
- People *must* live up to my expectations or it is terrible!

An individual who holds such assumptions is bound to be, at the very least, disappointed; at worst, depressed. An individual who fails an exam becomes depressed not because they have failed the exam but because they hold an irrational belief regarding that failure (e.g. 'If I fail people will think I'm stupid'). Such 'musts' need to be challenged in order for mental healthiness to prevail.

The ABC model

Ellis (1957) proposed that the way to deal with irrational thoughts was to identify them using the ABC model. (A) stands for the activating event – a situation that results in feelings of frustration and anxiety. Such events are quite real and will have caused genuine distress or pain. These events may lead to irrational beliefs (B), and these beliefs lead to self-defeating consequences (C). For example:

- A (activating event) → friend ignores you in the street
- B (belief) → he must have decided he doesn't like you; no one likes you and you are worthless
- C (consequences) → avoid social situations in future.

Albert Ellis held open audiences demonstrating his ABC approach until his death at the age of 93 in 2007. Every Friday night, there were lively sessions with audience volunteers at the Albert Ellis Institute in New York for only $5.00 including cookies and coffee!

Like many psychologists, Ellis became interested in an area of behaviour that was personally challenging. His own experiences of unhappiness (for example his parents divorced when he was 12) led him to develop ways to help others. Initially, he trained as a psychoanalyst, but gradually became disillusioned with the Freudian approach and started to develop his own methods. Over the course of half a century, he wrote 54 books and published 600 articles on RET/REBT, as well as advice on good sexual relationships and good marriage.

▲ Albert Ellis (1913–2007).

A film was produced of Albert Ellis interviewing a client named Gloria, which you can see on YouTube in four segments (search YouTube for 'Albert Ellis Gloria'). It provides useful insights into the process of RET.

ABCDE – disputing and effects

The ABC model was extended to include D and E – disputing beliefs and the effects of disputing. The key issue to remember is that it is not the activating events that cause unproductive consequences, it is the *beliefs* that lead to the self-defeating consequences. RET therefore focuses on challenging or disputing the beliefs and replacing them with effective, rational beliefs. For example:

- **Logical disputing** Self-defeating beliefs do not follow logically from the information available (e.g. 'does thinking this way make sense?').
- **Empirical disputing** Self-defeating beliefs may not be consistent with reality (e.g. 'where is the proof that this belief is accurate?').
- **Pragmatic disputing** This emphasises the lack of usefulness of self-defeating beliefs (e.g. 'how is this belief likely to help me?').

The effect of disputing is to change self-defeating beliefs into more rational beliefs. The individual can move from *catastrophising* ('no one will ever like me') to more rational interpretations of events ('my friend was probably thinking about something else and didn't even see me'). This, in turn, helps the client to feel better and, eventually, to become more self-accepting.

Unconditional positive regard

Ellis (1994) came to recognise that an important ingredient in successful therapy was convincing the client of their value as a human being. If the client feels worthless, they will be less willing to consider changing their beliefs and behaviour. However, if the therapist provides respect and appreciation regardless of what the client does and says (i.e. **unconditional positive regard**), this will facilitate a change in beliefs and attitudes.

Research evidence

RET has generally done well in outcome studies (i.e. studies designed to measure the outcome of treatment). For example, in a **meta-analysis**, Engels *et al.* (1993) concluded that RET is an effective treatment for a number of different types of disorder.

Ellis (1957) claimed a 90% success rate, taking an average of 27 sessions to complete. However, he recognised that the therapy was not always effective, and suggested that this could be because some patients did not put their revised beliefs into action (Ellis, 2001). Ellis also explained a possible lack of success in terms of suitability – some people simply do not want the direct sort of advice that RET practitioners tend to dispense. They prefer to share their worries with a therapist without getting involved in the cognitive effort that is associated with recovery (Ellis, 2001).

Examples of disputing irrational beliefs
- 'Why must I do very well?'
- 'Where is it written that I am a bad person?'
- 'Where is the evidence that I must be approved or accepted?'

Examples of exchanging for effective rational beliefs
- 'I'd prefer to do very well but I don't have to'.
- 'I am a person who acted badly, not a bad person'.
- 'There is no evidence that I have to be approved of, although I would like to be'.

CAN YOU...? No.4.4

1... Outline the aims of RET.
2... Explain the cognitive and behavioural elements of RET.
3... Select **two** or **more** techniques used in RET and explain each of them, using examples.
4... Outline **two** findings from research studies and state what conclusion can be drawn from each of these studies.

EXAM QUESTION

Describe how the cognitive approach has been applied to either CBT or RET. [12]

Notes *In the exam, you will be asked to describe **one** therapy. In total you will have studied four therapies (one for each of the four approaches). This question will be worth 12 marks. In order to gain the full 12 marks, your answer should satisfy the same criteria as those listed on page vii. You might include the following in an answer about RET.*

▶ *A brief outline of the aims of RET and how these link with the assumptions of the cognitive approach.*

▶ *The historical development of RET.*

▶ *Examples of how RET has been used, emphasising the cognitive and behavioural components.*

▶ *Research findings into RET.*

▶ *Your answer should be about 400–450 words in length.*

Examiner hint

In order to gain the full 12 marks, your answer must provide a link between the aims of RET and the main assumptions of the cognitive approach.

Evaluating the cognitive approach

You have studied two examples of the **cognitive approach** – one theory (**attribution theory**) and one therapy (either **CBT** or **RET**). It is now time to use your understanding of the cognitive approach to consider its strengths and weaknesses. To help you, we have provided some additional examples of the cognitive approach.

➕ Strengths of the cognitive approach

1. Mediational processes

One major advantage of the cognitive approach, especially when compared with **behaviourism**, is the focus on the important 'processes' that occur between stimulus and response. Whereas behaviourists did not attempt to investigate what goes on inside the 'black box', cognitive psychologists have gone some way to explaining how important *mediational* processes such as **perception** and memory affect the way we respond to the world around us.

This has helped explain practical elements of human behaviour. For example, cognitive psychologists look at ways of improving memory using retrieval cues (see study below). Such research can show us why we need to make shopping lists before going to the local supermarket.

THE VALUE OF RETRIEVAL CUES

Can't remember something? If someone gives you a clue the memories might come flooding back.

- Research has shown that people can remember more than they think they know – if they are given the right cue. Tulving and Psotka (1971) conducted an experiment that demonstrated this.
- They gave participants six different word lists to learn, each containing 24 words.
- Each list was divided into six different categories (so over the six lists there were 36 categories, such as kinds of tree and names of precious stones).
- After all the lists had been presented, the participants were asked to write down all the words they could remember (called 'free recall').
- Then they were given cues – the names of the different categories (e.g. 'trees' or 'precious stones'), and asked to recall the words again (called 'cued recall').
- The key finding was that people remembered about 50% of the words when initially tested in the free recall condition, but this rose to 70% when given cued recall. It shows that there is often more in your head than you think there is, if someone would just give you the right cues!

2. Important contributions

The cognitive approach has influenced many areas of psychology. As well as being usefully applied in therapy, such as in CBT to successfully treat disorders such as depression, it has also been applied to the field of developmental psychology. For example, theories about how children's thinking develops have guided teaching practices in schools. Piaget (1970) developed one such theory, suggesting that children's thinking is not the same as that of adults. For example, children aged around eight or nine years old cannot think in the abstract. If they want to solve a mathematical problem, they need to see it in a concrete form, such as manipulating counting sticks. Piaget's ideas had a major effect on teaching in primary schools because teachers realised it was important to use concrete examples with younger children.

Additionally, within social psychology, much of the thinking is 'cognitive' in nature, as it involves looking at the mental processes involved in understanding the social world and people around us. For example, why we form certain **stereotypes**, and why **attributional biases** occur.

3. Scientific approach

Like many of the approaches, another strength of the cognitive approach is that it lends itself to scientific research. For example, the various attribution theories that were described on pages 46–47 provide clear predictions that can be tested in experimental research. This means that psychologists can test such theories and demonstrate whether they are true or not.

One of the other advantages of the scientific approach is that it seeks to control variables as far as possible, and we are therefore more likely to discover causal relationships.

DO IT YOURSELF

No. 4.6

Answering the questions below will help you to understand how we can measure memory in a 'scientific way'. With reference to the study by Tulving and Psotka above:

1. Identify the **independent variable (IV)** in this study.
2. Identify the **dependent variable (DV)** in this study.
3. What conclusions can be drawn from this study in relation to memory.

Discuss (in groups) whether you think we can measure memory scientifically.

DO IT YOURSELF

Compare and contrast

You have now studied all four approaches – the biological, behaviourist, psychodynamic and cognitive approaches. You can compare and contrast these four approaches.

1. Copy out the table on facing page and fill in the right hand column in the table for the cognitive approach.
2. Look at the answers you gave for the **biological approach** (page 11) and compare and contrast them with the cognitive approach, as you have done before.
3. Repeat step 2, this time comparing the **behaviourist** (page 25) and cognitive approaches.
4. Finally repeat step 2 for the **psychodynamic** (page 39) and cognitive approaches.
5. Use this information to write an answer to the following exam question.

1. Nature and nurture

While the cognitive approach does consider the influence of both internal and external factors on behaviour (e.g. processes within the mind are 'internal' and the role of experience in the formation of **schemas** is 'external'), it fails to consider important elements of **nature** and **nurture**. For example, the role of **genes** in human cognition is ignored, yet research into intelligence has consistently looked at the influence of genes, through the use of twin studies (see page 13).

Additionally, important social and cultural factors (nurture) are often ignored, which seems unrealistic. For example, within the field of cognitive development, key theorists such as Piaget failed to consider the role of culture and gender on the development of thinking in children.

2. Determinist approach

As we have seen, 'schemas' are an important assumption of the cognitive approach (see page 45). People acquire such schemas through direct experience. For example, Piaget suggested that cognitive development is essentially the development of schemas. At a young age a child might call everything with four legs and hair a 'dog'. Later the child learns various related schemas – one for a dog and one for a cat and so on.

Another important way in which we acquire schemas is through our social interactions. We acquire stereotypes about people and situations, such as the belief that women with blonde hair are stupid but fun, or that people with glasses are intelligent. These are cultural stereotypes and such stereotypes (or schemas) may *determine* the way that we interpret situations.

A father was taking his son to school when they were involved in a serious car accident. Sadly, the father was killed instantly, but the son was alive and rushed to hospital, where he was taken immediately to the operating theatre because of his serious injuries. The surgeon arrived to conduct the operation but said, 'I cannot operate on this person – he is my son!'.

What happened? Was the father alive after all? No, the surgeon was the boy's mother. People tend to find the story confusing because they have a schema of a surgeon that leads them to expect that the surgeon will be a man.

Examiner hint

When answering a 'compare and contrast' question, remember that in order to gain marks, you must explain the similarities and differences between the two approaches using the key issues and debates discussed in the introduction to this book (see page x–xi). There is also specific advice on answering the compare and contrast questions on pages 60–61.

No. 4.7

Compare and **contrast** the behaviourist and cognitive approaches in terms of similarities and differences. [12]

(You can, of course, do the other two essays as well, comparing the biological with the cognitive approach, and the psychodynamic with the cognitive approach.)

Issues and debates	The cognitive approach
Nomothetic/idiographic	
Nature–nurture	
Reductionism/holism	
Determinism/free will	
Scientific/non-scientific	
Methodology used	
Anything else!	

3. Mechanistic approach

Another criticism of the cognitive approach is that it is 'mechanistic' – it portrays human behaviour as being like that of a machine. Indeed, the cognitive approach is based on the 'behaviour' of computers, so it is inevitable that the outcome would be a rather mechanistic view of human behaviour. This criticism was made of Kelley's covariation model that explained the process of attribution (see page 47).

The main objection to such mechanistic explanations is that they ignore social and emotional factors. In fact, in general, they oversimplify behaviour and are therefore **reductionist**. For example, attribution theory suggests that there are certain rules that predict when people will make dispositional or situational attributions. However, research has found that there are many exceptions to these rules. This shows that human behaviour is not as simple or predictable as cognitive theories suggest.

CAN YOU...? No.4.5

1... Identify **two** strengths of the cognitive approach.

2... Make **three** distinct points to explain each strength.

3... Identify **two** weaknesses of the cognitive approach.

4... Make **three** distinct points to explain each weakness.

EXAM QUESTIONS

Evaluate two strengths of the cognitive approach. [6]

Evaluate two weaknesses of the cognitive approach. [6]

Notes In the exam, you are required to discuss **two** strengths and **two** weaknesses of **one** of the four approaches. For each strength and weakness, you should:

▶ *Clearly identify the strength or weakness.*

▶ *Thoroughly explain why this is a strength or weakness in relation to the approach.*

▶ *Where appropriate, use examples drawn from theory/therapy to illustrate your answer.*

▶ *Think of each strength/weakness as being worth three marks (although, strictly speaking, this is not how they are marked).*

▶ *Write around 50–60 words on each strength/ weakness.*

Methodology used by the cognitive approach

The final topic on the **cognitive approach** is a consideration of the methodology used by this approach. Obviously, cognitive researchers use all sorts of methods and techniques, but we have selected two that are particularly common in this approach – **lab experiments** and **case studies** of brain-damaged individuals.

Lab experiments in general are discussed in Chapter 6 (see pages 138 and 144–145). The other research method concepts identified on this page are also explained in Chapter 6.

1. Lab experiments

One of the main methods of investigation used by cognitive psychologists is lab experiments. This is due to the belief that psychology is a pure science, and therefore behaviour should be studied objectively and scientifically. How can we study thought processes in a lab? Cognitive psychologists believe that they can make inferences about the processes in a person's mind on the basis of observations of the person's behaviour, and also by asking people to answer questions (such as asking people to study word lists and report which words they can remember).

For example, on the previous spread we described a lab experiment by Tulving and Psotka about forgetting. Another example is the classic study by Loftus and Palmer, which you will read about in Chapter 5. In fact, Loftus conducted a variety of different experiments to examine whether people's memory for an event can be distorted by leading questions. She studied participants' responses as a means of testing whether their memory for an event had been distorted under certain conditions. This area of research is particularly relevant to our understanding of the reliability of eyewitness testimony.

Another area of research that Loftus has investigated is the **weapon effect** (see below), which is again related to eyewitness testimony and the accuracy of memory.

THE WEAPON EFFECT

In a study in 1987, Loftus *et al.* identified the weapon effect. They suggested that one explanation for the fact that eyewitnesses are often not especially good at identifying criminals is that, at the time of the crime, eyewitnesses are focusing on the weapon the criminal was holding rather than on the criminal's face. The eyewitnesses can't recall facial information because they weren't looking at the face!

In their initial experiment, Loftus *et al.* used two conditions, one involving a weapon and one not. In both conditions, participants heard a discussion in an adjoining room. In condition 1, a man emerged holding a pen and with grease on his hands. In condition 2, the discussion was rather more heated and a man emerged holding a paperknife covered in blood.

When asked to identify the man from 50 photos, participants in condition 1 were 49% accurate, compared with 33% accuracy in condition 2. This suggests that the weapon may have distracted attention from the person holding it and may therefore explain why eyewitnesses sometimes have poor recall for certain details of violent crimes.

Strengths

- The lab experiment is the best way to study causal relationships because **extraneous variables** can be carefully controlled.
- Lab experiments offer an objective means of studying human behaviour. As the experimenter will follow set, standard procedures, this means the experiment can be repeated again (**replicated**) by others to demonstrate the **validity** of the findings.
- As data resulting from experiments can be quantified (e.g. the percentage of participants in Loftus and Palmer's study who said there was a headlight), it is easier to analyse and make comparisons.

Weaknesses

- Lab experiments such as those carried out by Loftus may not represent everyday life because people don't take the experiment seriously and/ or they are not emotionally aroused in the way that they would be in a real accident, i.e. such experiments lack **ecological validity**. Foster *et al.* (1994) found that if participants thought they were watching a real life robbery, and also thought that their responses would influence the trial, their identification of a robber was more accurate.
- In a lab experiment, participants are likely to behave unnaturally because they will try to guess the purpose of the study and conform to researchers' expectations. Alternatively, they may want purposefully to spoil the study – the 'screw you' effect. These problems are known as **demand characteristics**.
- **Experimenter bias** can also be a problem. The experimenter could (intentionally or unintentionally) display behaviour that influences participants to act in the desired way. For example, by using tone of voice to influence participant feedback, or interpreting behaviour in a way that fits in with the hypothesis. This is possibly due to the physical contact that occurs between experimenter and participant in a lab situation.

Examiner hint

Remember to use an example of an experiment to highlight to the examiner that you understand how lab experiments have been used within the cognitive approach.

Case studies in general are discussed on page 163.

2. Case studies of brain-damaged individuals

Case studies are in-depth investigations of a particular person, group or event. Within cognitive psychology, case studies of individuals with damage to their brain can give researchers unique insights into the workings of the mind.

Take the classic case study of HM, who suffered from permanent memory loss as a result of brain surgery (see right). HM could remember events that occurred before the operation, but had trouble storing information for events occurring after the operation. This case study has been used to support the idea of the **multistore model** of memory, namely, that we possess both a short-term and a long-term memory.

Strengths

- A true insight into behaviour can be obtained, as case studies involve spending time with the person, rather than gaining a 'snap shot' of his or her behaviour, which is what would be produced by a lab experiment.
- Descriptive, **qualitative** data is obtained, which is important in trying to understand the reasons behind a person's behaviour. We may be more able to draw valid conclusions about behaviour if we take the time to study them in detail.

Weaknesses

- **Generalisability** because case studies relate to single instances, it is not possible to generalise to other people. The results of a study are only valid when applied to that case.
- Case studies rely on qualitative rather than **quantitative** analysis, there is a danger that behaviour is interpreted in the way the researcher wants (**subjective**). Researchers alone decide how they are to interpret what they observe/hear, what they include in their descriptions, and what they leave out. It is therefore easy to select information in support of the theory that has been put forward.

CAN YOU...? No.**4.6**

1... Identify **two** methods used by the cognitive approach, and for each describe an example of how this method was used in a research study that used the cognitive approach.

2... For each method outline and explain **two** strengths and **two** weaknesses of using this method in the study you described.

EXAM QUESTION

Explain and **evaluate** the methodology used by the cognitive approach. [12]

*Notes In the exam, you are required to explain and evaluate the methods used by **one** of the four approaches. **It is vital that you clearly explain how the methods link with the assumptions of the approach, i.e. that they have clear relevance to the approach.** A general guide in terms of structuring your answer is as follows.*

▶ *Explain one method used by the approach (use examples that will highlight its relevance to the approach).*

▶ *Evaluate the strengths and weaknesses of this method.*

▶ *Explain a second method used by the approach (use examples that will again highlight its relevance).*

▶ *Evaluate the strengths and weaknesses of this method.*

N.B. The top band of the mark scheme for this question states: 'Methods are appropriate and clearly explained ... and have clear relevance to the approach'.

THE FASCINATING CASE OF HM

In the 1940s, **psychosurgery** (see page 6) was at its peak. Dr William Scoville was one of the surgeons at the forefront of this work, and was called in to help a patient known simply as Henry M. or HM (Henry Gustav Molaison, 1926–2008). On his 16th birthday, HM experienced his first severe epileptic fit. For the next few years, these fits became progressively more debilitating and uncontrollable by medication. Scoville believed that HM's epilepsy may be cured by removing the parts of his brain thought to be causing the fits (the **hippocampus**).

The effect on HM's epilepsy is not clear. It seems to have got slightly better, but this was overshadowed by a much greater problem: HM was no longer able to form any new memories. His personality and intellect remained intact, but he had lost some of his memories from the 10 years prior to the operation (*anterograde amnesia*). More importantly, he lost the ability to form any new long-term memories (*retrograde amnesia*). For many years, he reported that his age was 27 and the year was 1953. After a while, he realised that this was absurd and tried guessing the answer. He watched the news every night, yet had no recall for major events. He happily reread magazines with no loss of interest. He couldn't memorise lists of words or recall the faces of people he met. He didn't remember that his mother had died, and every time they told him, he mourned all over again.

This outcome of the operation was clearly a disaster for HM, although he only vaguely understood it. He wrote: *'Right now, I'm wondering, have I done or said anything amiss? You see, at this moment everything looks clear to me, but what happened just before? That's what worries me. It's like waking from a dream. I just don't remember'* (Hilts, 1995).

DO IT YOURSELF No. 4.8

This task involves looking at YouTube. Type in *Life without memory: the case of Clive Wearing (parts a and b)*, and watch the films about Clive Wearing who, like HM, also experienced memory loss. Use this case study, and that of HM, to discuss the strengths and weaknesses of using case studies to tell us about how our memory works.

Examiner hint

In order to ensure your answer to this question is thorough and relevant, you need to include examples of how the particular methodology is used within the approach. For example, when discussing the use of case studies within the cognitive approach, you should bring in the study of HM, Clive Wearing, or any other cognitive case studies. This will help you to explain the methodology thoroughly and coherently, and demonstrate to the examiner that you understand the methodology used within that particular approach. Answers where a candidate talks in a generic manner about certain research methods will not attract credit in the top two bands (see mark schemes on page vii).

Chapter 4 summary

Assumptions of the cognitive approach

Mental processes
Cognitive (mental) processes include perception, attention, memory and language, which help us to create and use schemas.

Computer analogy
The human mind is like a computer. Thinking involves input, process and output.

Mental behaviour can be objectively measured
Measurements of external behaviours can be used to infer internal mental processes.

Attribution theory

Internal and external attributions
Heider (1958) identified these two sources, and suggested a tendency to make internal/dispositional attributions (the FAE).

Covariation model
Kelley (1967) proposed that high consistency, low distinctiveness and low consensus (HLL) lead to dispositional attributions.

Errors and biases
Such as the fundamental attribution error (FAE), actor/observer bias and self-serving bias.

CBT

Cognitive approach
Emphasises thinking. Aims to change maladaptive thoughts and beliefs into more positive, constructive ones.

Behaviourist approach
Emphasises behaviour. Unhealthy behaviours can be replaced in therapy through rewards and modelling.

Beck's cognitive therapy
Negative schemas lead to dysfunctional automatic thoughts that can be challenged, e.g. using a thought diary.

Meichenbaum's stress inoculation training (SIT)
Inoculation achieved through:
1. Conceptualisation.
2. Skills acquisition (e.g. coping self-statements and modelling).
3. Application.

RET

Mustabatory thinking
People hold beliefs about what must be true if they are to be happy; such assumptions are irrational.

The ABCDE model
Activating event à belief à consequences à disputed à effect. Disputing may be logical, empirical or pragmatic.

Unconditional positive regard
Therapist gives client a sense of value and respect that will assist in changing beliefs and behaviour.

Strengths and weaknesses of the psychodynamic approach

Strengths
- Mediational processes: explains what goes on in the 'black box'.
- Important contributions: to therapy, education and understanding social processes.
- Scientific approach: theories produce clear predictions that can be tested so theory can be 'proven'.

Weaknesses
- Nature and nurture: some aspects not acknowledged, e.g. genetics and social/cultural influences.
- Determinist approach: schemas are partly learned through social stereotypes and these determine our beliefs.
- Mechanistic approach: the approach is based on computers; leads to machine-like explanations lacking emotion.

Methodology of the psychodynamic approach

Lab experiments
Manipulating the environment in highly controlled conditions can demonstrate causal relationships.
Strengths: objective, controlled means of studying human behaviour, data can be quantified and easily analysed.
Weaknesses: may lack ecological validity because artificial; may have demand characteristics; could also have experimenter bias.

Case studies of brain-damaged individuals
An idiographic approach observing one case in detail.
Strengths: true insight because greater time spent with participant; rich qualitative data.
Weaknesses: lacks generalisability, unrepresentative sample, subjective interpretations.

Review activities

You can use some of the review activities described at the end of Chapters 1, 2 and 3 (see pages 15, 29 and 43) with the contents of this chapter. For example, you could consider the assumptions of the cognitive approach in relation to attribution theory and the therapy that you studied, or you could set and mark each other's essays. You should certainly list again the key words in this chapter and make sure you understand them.

▲ In the jigsaw technique each person is responsible for a piece of the jigsaw and then, as a group, you put the pieces of the jigsaw together.

The jigsaw technique

Divide your class into groups with four members in each group. It is best if the groups are not 'friendship groups'. Give each person in your group a letter – A, B, C and D. Each person has to perform the task specific to the letter they have been assigned – possible examples are listed below.

Person A: Assumptions of the cognitive approach.
Person B: Kelley's covariation model.
Person C: Beck's cognitive therapy or Ellis's RET.
Person D: Cognitive methodology.

For example, people with the letter A must prepare material on the assumptions of the cognitive approach. They can do this by meeting with all the other As in the class. They must:

a) Prepare a set of brief and memorable notes on their topic.
b) Brief the group on their topic.
c) Write three (or more) questions for a test on their topic.

Your teacher should collect all the questions that have been written and use them to produce a class test. Each person will take the test individually – your performance will depend on how well you were briefed by your group members!

Is the cognitive approach about the MIND?

The acronym MIND may help you evaluate the psychodynamic approach:

M = Mediational
I = Important contributions
N = Nature and nurture
D = Determinist.

Write a short paragraph for each of these four topics. As always, try first to do this without looking at your notes.

True or false?

Decide which of the statements below are true or false. If the statement is false, correct it.

		True or false?
1	The experiment with two triangles and a circle was conducted by Heider and Simmel.	
2	The letters FAE stand for fundamental attribution error.	
3	Kelley's covariation model suggested that consistency, distinctiveness and collaboration are used to determine internal and external attributions.	
4	The self-serving bias refers to making dispositional attributions about failures but not successes.	
5	One strength of the cognitive approach is that it is mechanistic.	
6	One of the methods commonly used by cognitive psychologists is case studies.	

Post-it fun

Each student should have a pile of Post-its. Think of all the specialist terms you have learned when studying the cognitive approach and write each one on a Post-it.

Each class member should then place their Post-its on one wall in the classroom so that the notes are organised in some way. For example, all Post-its related to assumptions should go together, and all Post-its on the therapy you studied should go together. Within each of these you can further organise the Post-its. In the end, you will have created a mind map of the chapter!

You could then do the same thing for the other chapters you have studied.

Rolling shows

A rolling show* is a series of images, each placed on one PowerPoint slide, that automatically changes after a period of time (such as five seconds). Working in groups, students can produce a rolling show about the cognitive approach (or just one of the topics in this chapter), and then show this to students in other groups, who have to guess what the images represented.
*Thanks to Mike Griffin and Cath Gellis for this idea from Psychology AS: The Teacher's Companion for AQA 'A', published by Folens.

▶ What does this picture represent? An image is a very powerful way to remember something – this rolling show task will help you build up some very useful memory cues. Once again, you could do this for all the other approaches in this chapter.

Example exam questions with student answers

Examiner's comments on these answers can be found on page 175.

EXAMPLE OF QUESTION 1(b)

Examiner hint

Remember that in the exam, question 1(b) will always be paired with 1(a), which will ask for two assumptions of the approach, and be worth 4 marks.

Describe attribution theory. [8]

Megan's answer

Attributions are the beliefs that we hold about the causes of a person's behaviour. Heider proposed a simplistic model of attribution. He said that our beliefs about the causes of a person's behaviour can be categorised in two main ways. Firstly, we use an internal attribution, whereby we believe that the person themselves is responsible for their behaviour, for example, it is their personality. Or we can make an external attribution, whereby we see external factors as responsible for a person's behaviour, for example, the environment or situation they are in.

Kelley proposed a more complex model known as the covariation model. Kelley said that attributions are determined by the covariance of three factors: Consistency – does the person always behave in this way when faced with similar situations? Distinctiveness – does the person always behave in this way when in the same situation? Consensus – do other people behave in the same way in similar situations?

According to Kelley, internal attributions are made when distinctiveness and consensus are low, but consistency is high. For example, John always laughs at comedians (high consistency), he doesn't just laugh at one particular comedian (low distinctiveness) and not everybody laughs at all comedians (low consensus). Therefore, we can conclude that John is a happy-go-lucky guy who is always happy (internal attribution).

We often make errors in our attributions, one of which is known as the Fundamental Attribution Error (FAE). This is where we tend to offer internal attributions for other peoples behaviour, even when external causes are equally more likely. This doesn't occur in all cultures though, but is more likely to occur in individualist ones.

Tomas's answer

Attribution is all about saying what the cause of someone's behaviour is. For example, do we think that the person is responsible for their behaviour – an internal cause, or do we think that something outside of the person has caused their behaviour – an external cause? Say if someone does badly in an exam. If we think 'they didn't do any revision', this would be an internal attribution, but if we thought 'the teacher is really bad', this would be an external attribution.

Kelley came up with the covariation model. He said that attributions are influenced by three things, and these are consistency, distinctiveness and consensus. If a person always behaves in a particular way then there is high consistency, and if a person behaves in a way that is unique then this is distinctive.

We make many errors in our attributions too, such as self-selecting bias where we tend to blame external factors for our behaviour, for example, if we do fail an exam, we blame the teacher.

EXAMPLE OF QUESTION 3

(a) **Evaluate two strengths of the cognitive approach. [6]**
(b) **Evaluate two weaknesses of the cognitive approach. [6]**

Megan's answer to 3(a)

One strength of the cognitive approach is that it does consider what goes on inside the mind to be important. Unlike the behaviourist approach, which did not see the mind as worthy of study, cognitive psychologists believe that important processes such as perception and thinking shape our behaviour, and so should be studied. in other words, they are interested in what goes on inside the 'black box'. This has led to important advances in our understanding and improvement of memory. Another important strength to this approach is the way that it has influenced different areas of psychology, and the impact that it has had in everyday life. For example, therapies like CT and CBT have greatly helped people overcome psychological problems; in fact CBT is extremely widely used now in the UK for treating depression. Cognitive psychology has greatly influenced the thinking within the field of developmental psychology too. For example, Piaget's theory of cognitive development has been most influential within education.

Tomas's answer to 3(a)

The cognitive approach looks at what goes on inside the mind, and says that the mind is like a computer, in that it takes in information, stores it and then can recall it.

The cognitive approach is scientific though, and this is good because it would say we should study behaviour in a lab, where we can control the situation and be objective. It is also better than some other approaches as it does try to explain behaviour using conscious thought processes, whereas other approaches ignore these.

Megan's answer to 3(b)

A problem with this approach is the comparison that it makes between the human mind and a computer (computer analogy). This is too 'mechanistic', as human beings have emotions and feelings that greatly affect how they respond to situations, and how they store information (for example when we witness a traumatic event). So it seems a bit naïve to reduce the mind to a machine as there are many differences.

The cognitive approach can also be considered a bit simplistic. It does say that both internal and external factors shape our behaviour, but also ignores some important other factors that are likely to affect how we behave. For example, it fails to consider the role that genetics have on behaviour, and it also ignores important social factors on behaviour, such as a person's upbringing. In summary, not all aspects of the nature–nurture debate are considered by this approach, in fact the approach ignores this debate completely.

Tomas's answer to 3(b)

This isn't good as there are many ways our mind is not like a computer. For example, we often forget, whereas computers do not and also we have feelings that will affect the way we remember things.

EXAMPLE OF QUESTION 5

Explain and evaluate the methodology used by the cognitive approach. [12]

Megan's answer

The cognitive approach would make use of case studies in order to understand cognitive processes such as memory. Case studies of individuals with damage to their brain can help psychologists further understand mental processes. For example, take the case of HM whose memory became impaired as a consequence of psychosurgery. HM had trouble laying down new memories after his operation, and this case has been used to support the multistore model of memory. Case studies have the advantage that they allow us to gain in-depth, unique insight into a person's behaviour. Also, qualitative data can be obtained which allows us to draw valid conclusions, as we have taken time to study behaviour in detail.

Case studies do have their disadvantages though. The main issue being that we cannot generalise from them. Take the case of HM, his brain damage was unique, and it is unlikely that we can draw general conclusions about memory from this case alone. There is also a danger of researcher bias and subjectivity. Researchers may only select the information they want in their descriptions, in order to support a theory or hypothesis. This means case studies are not as objective as, say, experiments.

Another method used by the cognitive approach would be lab experiments. Cognitive psychologists believe that psychology is a pure science and that we should study behaviour in an objective manner. Lab experiments have proved useful in studying memory processes. For example, Loftus conducted many experiments into the role of leading questions in distorting memory. Lab experiments have the advantage of allowing us to draw conclusions about causal relationships, as variables can be tightly controlled. Further, as they follow standardised, objective procedures, they are easy to replicate in order to validate findings. They produce quantitative data (for example in the Loftus experiments, the percentage of people who had been influenced by a leading question) that is easy to analyse and compare.

However, lab experiments can lack ecological validity, for example, it is questionable whether Loftus' research is valid as participants were unlikely to be as emotionally aroused during the study as they would have been if they had witnessed real life traumatic events. Also, demand characteristics can be a problem, where participants try and 'act up' to the experiment, therefore behaving unnaturally. Finally, the experimenter may intentionally or unintentionally bias the outcome, and encourage the participant to behave/respond in the desired way. This can occur due to the close proximity between experimenter and participant.

Tomas's answer

This approach would use lab experiments to study behaviour, as it believes we should study behaviour in a scientific way. This is because as many variables as possible can be controlled and behaviour can be studied scientifically. Experimenters can manipulate the IV, and measure its effect on the DV to establish cause–effect relationships. Advantages of this method include the fact that due to the procedures being standardised, they can be replicated to validate the findings. Also, objectivity is a key advantage due to the maximum control that the experimenter can have over extraneous variables. Experiments are high in validity that is also a good thing.

However, experiments are said to be low in ecological validity because they do not represent how a person is likely to behave in the real world. It is an artificial situation – behaviour is not natural. There may also be ethical issues involved if participants are unaware of the aims, such as lack of informed consent. Demand characteristics can also occur whereby those taking part may feel the need to change their behaviour – either to be 'good' participants or to spoil the results on purpose. This again will mean that the situation is not representative of real world behaviour.

One of the questions on the Unit 1 exam is the **'compare and contrast'** question. It is always question 4. It will ask you to compare and contrast two of the approaches covered in this unit. Throughout the chapter we have been preparing you for this question in the Do It Yourself activities on the evaluation spreads (see pages 11, 25, 39 and 53).

On this spread, we have given you some special advice on how to tackle the compare and contrast (C&C) questions, plus two example student answers.

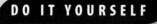

DO IT YOURSELF
No. 4.9

On pages x and xi we introduced the issues and debates. We have used these throughout this unit as a means of evaluating each approach. You have also used them as the basis for making comparisons between the different approaches. An understanding of the issues and debates is vital for being able to answer the C&C questions.

Revisit the Do It Yourself activity on page xi and see if you can provide some more sophisticated and informed responses – you should be able to because, by now, you know a lot more about the issues, debates and approaches.

KEY TIPS FOR ANSWERING THE C&C QUESTION

The C&C question is an **AO2** question, which means that it focuses on your *evaluation* skills.

> **Compare and contrast approach 1 and approach 2 in terms of similarities and differences. [12]**

The exam question emphasises similarities *and* differences, and so you must include both to gain credit in the top two bands. Throughout the chapters in this unit, you have practised comparing and contrasting the approaches and you should have recognised that the best way to do this is to consider how each approach 'fits in' with the key issues and debates.

The AO1 description trap

Students often make the mistake of *describing* each approach or each issue/debate. This is easy to do because 'description' (**AO1**) is a simpler skill than evaluating. However, such descriptions will not gain credit in the C&C question. You must focus on explaining *how* the two stated approaches are similar and different. For example:

> *The behaviourist approach suggests that all behaviour is learned from the environment. The psychodynamic approach suggests that we are born with innate drives, but also that the environment plays a role in that early experiences/relationships are important.*

This paragraph merely presents a *description* of the assumptions, i.e. demonstrates **AO1** and therefore would gain no credit as an answer to a C&C question. Consider the second example:

> *One key difference between the behaviourist and the psychodynamic approaches is where they stand in terms of the nature–nurture debate. The behaviourist approach supports the nurture side of the debate, as it believes that all behaviour is learned from the environment. However, the psychodynamic approach takes an interactionist perspective in that it believes we are born with the innate drives of the id (nature) but also that childhood experiences are important because fixations may develop (nurture).*

This paragraph clearly *contrasts* the two approaches in terms of a key psychological debate, i.e. demonstrates **AO2**.

How to write AO2 comments

One way to avoid the **AO1** description trap is to use certain key sentences at the beginning of each paragraph.
- One key similarity (or difference) between the X and Y approaches is…
- One key comparison between the X and Y approaches lies in the fact that…
- One means of contrasting (or comparing) the X and Y approaches is to consider the determinist debate…
- Another similarity (or difference) between the X and Y approaches is…
- Finally, the X and Y approaches are similar (or different) because…

Timing and length

Most importantly, you need to focus on answering this question in the time allocated (15 minutes). The bullet points above suggest that five paragraphs (i.e. five points of comparison/contrast) will be sufficient for marks in the top band. You don't have to follow the bullet points exactly but five points will be about right. You should write about 80–100 words for each paragraph, making a total of 400–500 words for your answer.

Note – you don't have to cover all five of the bullet points; you could, for example, repeat the first two. You must, however, cover similarities **and** differences.

AN EXAMPLE OF A C&C QUESTION

> **Question 4 Compare and contrast** the biological and psychodynamic approach in terms of similarities and differences. **[12]**

This question would be marked using the marking bands below.

Marks	AO2
10–12	Analysis is thorough, clearly structured and there is evidence of coherent elaboration of relevant similarities **and** differences. Depth and range of analysis is displayed, though not necessarily in equal measure.
7–9	Analysis is thorough and coherent, with evidence of both similarities **and** differences. Depth **or** range of analysis is displayed.
4–6	Analysis is basic/limited, with evidence of similarities **and/or** differences.
1–3	Analysis is superficial. Material is muddled. Very limited analysis.
0	No relevant analysis.

Two example student answers

These examples will help you to understand what you need to do to get good marks when answering a **compare and contrast** question.

Megan's answer

The biological approach thinks that we behave the way we do because of our biological make-up. Things like genes, chemicals and hormones all influence the way we behave rather than external things. It believes we need to look at the brain too as a way of understanding behaviour because different areas of the brain can influence our behaviour, for example some people who have had a stroke have problems with their speech.

The psychodynamic approach thinks that our childhood is very important and that our relationship with our parents will influence how we grow up. Freud talked about the stages of development, oral, anal, phallic and genital as being important, because we could get 'stuck' in these stages.

This is a difference between the two approaches, one focuses mainly on internal influences on behaviour and the other mainly on external influences. They are both also reductionist and determinist.

Examiner's comments

Megan has spent most of the time outlining the assumptions of the approach and there is little comparison. **AO1** is not credited in this question, and so it is a waste of a candidate's time *describing* the assumptions of the approach; the focus should be on explaining why the approaches are similar and different. Megan has attempted to 'compare and contrast' at the end of the essay, but this is in very limited detail. Overall this answer would attract credit in the lowest band – **3 out of 12 marks**.

Tomas's answer

One difference between the biological approach (BA) and the psychodynamic approach (PA) is where they stand in terms of the nature–nurture debate. The BA believes that behaviour can be explained in terms of our physiological and genetic make-up, and so lends itself to the 'nature' argument, while the PA looks at the interaction between innate drives (nature) and childhood experiences (nurture) as the cause of behaviour.

Another major difference is in terms of the methods they use to study behaviour. The BA is totally a scientific approach and therefore would aim to study human behaviour objectively through methods such as lab experiments. The PA is relatively unscientific in its approach and relies on using case studies to study behaviour, whereby an individual would be asked about their past experiences, feelings etc., and it would be left to the researcher to provide an interpretation of the causes of behaviour. This is a very subjective way to study behaviour, and so is different from the biological approach. The BA would also believe that we can study animals as a way of finding out about human behaviour (e.g. Selye), whereas the PA wouldn't as animals can express thoughts, feelings etc.

One similarity is that both approaches are determinist. The BA sees behaviour as determined by our genes and the physiology we are born with; while the PA sees adult behaviour as determined by the experiences we have as children. Both therefore deny us humans as having free will.

Another similarity is that they are both reductionist. As explained, the BA can be seen to display 'physiological reductionism' as it simplifies our behaviour to the level of functioning of biological systems. The PA can be seen to display 'mechanistic reductionism' as it simplifies our behaviour to the mechanics of the mind (interaction of id, ego, superego). Although you could argue that the PA is less reductionist as it does look at a number of factors that influence our behaviour, and recognises that understanding behaviour is a complex process.

Finally I feel both approaches have proved useful in their contributions to society in general. The biological assumptions have been important in influencing chemotherapy, whereby drugs such as antidepressants have been widely used to help those with depression. Psychoanalysis has also been used to help people overcome psychological problems, and has helped us to recognise that many psychological illnesses are rooted in childhood experience.

Examiner's comments

Tomas has effectively compared the approaches in terms of similarities and differences. The answer displays both range and depth, and shows coherent elaboration. A thorough, clearly structured answer that would attract maximum credit – **12 out of 12 marks**.

Y ou've reached the end of the first unit and you're ready to take the exam: congratulations! On this spread, we have provided lots of ideas that you can use in class and on your own to review and revise what you have learned.

Theories to remember

Create a spider diagram like the one on the right, with four branches and a further six legs. Label the four branches with the four theories you have studied – Selye's GAS model, the social learning theory of aggression, Freud's theory of personality and attribution theory.

Each theory is linked to six legs – at the end of each leg write down six things you know in relation to this theory.

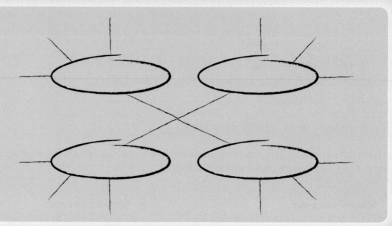

Whose therapy am I?

In pairs, choose a therapy that you have studied. One person in the pair is to play the therapist, and the other plays the client/patient. Write a script for a scene from a therapy session and then act this out in front of your class. The rest of the class has to guess which therapy is being acted out.

Assumptions

Draw a table with four columns like the one below. Under the table we have listed a number of sentences. Place the sentences in the appropriate columns of the table. (No looking at your notes!)

Biological approach	Behaviourist approach	Psychodynamic approach	Cognitive approach

1. The mind is like a computer.
2. Early experiences are very important.
3. Different areas of the brain influence behaviour.
4. The mind has both conscious and unconscious parts.
5. Behaviour is learned through conditioning.
6. Hormones can influence behaviour.
7. The mind can be studied scientifically.
8. We learn behaviour through observing others.

Now, in pairs, try to write two sentences in relation to each assumption.

Try to think of some other assumptions yourself.

Your chance to be a psychologist

On the right is a list of common human behaviours. Divide your class in groups and each group should select a behaviour, and also select one of the four approaches. Use the assumptions of your chosen approach to explain the behaviour. The rest of the class should guess which approach you used and rate the success of your explanation.

Evaluation – key issues and debates

Throughout the 'approaches' chapters in this unit, you have learned about some key psychological issues and debates. Take the first letter of each one, i.e.

Nomothetic/idiographic,
Nature–nurture,
Reductionism/holism,
Determinism/free will,
Scientific/non-scientific,
Methodology used.

- In pairs, try to think of a mnemonic that will help you remember these key issues/debates.
- Now, individually, write **two** sentences on each debate, explaining their nature.
- Divide the class in half. Each half is to prepare a speech arguing the benefits of each issue/debate. For example, one half prepares an argument in favour of 'reductionism', the other in favour of 'holism'; or the benefits of studying behaviour 'scientifically' versus 'non-scientifically; or the pros and cons of a particular methodology.

The best team could receive a prize.
(This will help your understanding of these issues/debates and improve your marks on questions 3 and 4 in the exam.)

Mix it up

Take any theory or therapy that you have studied and write six sentences about it on six slips of paper. Now mix them up and get someone else to try to put them in an order that makes sense. You may not realise it, but just reordering the sentences will help you remember them.

Test it out: try remembering the sentences after you have done this task.

Love	Aggression	Eating habits
Prejudice	Dreams	Addiction
Altruism	Depression	Football

Get your answers here

Divide your class into five groups. Each group should choose (or randomly select) one of the four approaches in the specification. The group should prepare a model essay plan for each of the exam-style questions below. You should use the PY1 mark schemes given on page vii to help you produce answers that would attract top band marks.

1 (a) **Outline** two assumptions of the _____ approach. [4]
  (b) **Describe** the _____ theory. [8]

2 **Describe** how the _____ approach has been applied in the _____ or the _____ therapy. [12]

3 (a) **Evaluate** two strengths of the _____ approach. [6]
  (b) **Evaluate** two weaknesses of the _____ approach. [6]

4 **Compare and contrast** the _____ and the _____ approaches in terms of similarities and differences. [12]

5 **Explain and evaluate** the methodology used by the _____ approach. [12]

By the end of the activity, each student will have a model answer for every possible question!

Linking the approaches and issues/debates

Create a table like the one on the right using A3 paper (a large space!).

Divide your class into four groups. Each group should be given one of the four approaches in this unit and prepare a presentation about how that approach fits in with each of the five issues/debates listed in the table.

After each presentation, all students should fill in the relevant column in their table. At the end of all four presentations, everyone in the class should have completed the table.

	Biological approach	Behaviourist approach	Psychodynamic approach	Cognitive approach
Nomothetic/idiographic				
Nature–nurture				
Reductionism/holism				
Determinism/free will				
Scientific/non-scientific				
Methodology used				

Dominoes

Students should work in pairs and produce 20 questions and answers, such as 'The innate, unconscious part of the mind is known as what?'

Prepare 20 'dominoes' (a piece of paper or preferably card with a line down the middle). On the left hand side write one question. On the right hand side write an answer to a different question, as shown below.

| psychosexual | The innate, unconscious part of the mind is known as the _____. | id | The opposite of free will is know as _____. |

Swap your dominoes with another pair of students and play the game.

Or you can use them to play a game of question and answer. Put all the dominoes together and deal them out around the class. One student starts by reading the question on one of their cards. The student who has the answer calls it out, and then reads the question on their card. This game can be timed, and the challenge is to get through all the cards within, say, two minutes.

▲ Psychologists have shown that people who are successful believe in themselves – they value themselves and have high self-esteem. If you want to do well in exams, love yourself!

End of Unit 1 review CROSSWORD

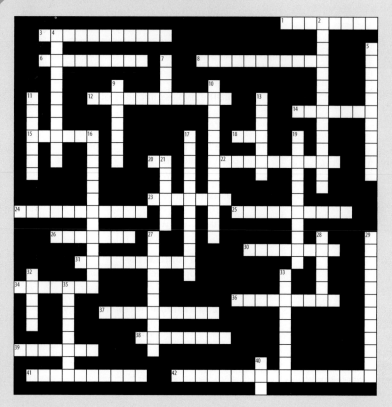

Answers on page 179.

The template for this crossword can be found on the Folens blog website (www.folensblog.com/psychcompanion/blog/).

Across

1. Cognitive psychologists suggest the way the human mind works can be compared to a _____. (8)
3. Luck is an example of a _____ attribution. (11)
6. Indirect reinforcement. (9)
8. The part of the nervous system involved in the fight or flight response. (11)
12. Approach that explains behaviour in terms of learning and experience. (12)
14. Psychologist who developed social learning theory. (7)
15. A mental structure that represents an aspect of the world. (6)
18. Type of brain scan that involves the use of a radioactive dye. (3)
20. The impulsive, unconscious part of our personality. (2)
22. The opposite of the free will position. (11)
23. Name given to the conditioned stimulus before conditioning takes place. (7)
24. Kelley suggested that internal attributions are made if _____ is high. (11)
25. Approach that explains behaviour in terms of physical bodily processes. (10)
26. Psychologist who introduced the concept of operant conditioning. (7)
30. Kind of interviewing method used by Freud. (8)
31. Case study used to support Freud's Oedipus complex. (6, 4)
34. The ego deals with anxiety using ego _____ mechanisms. (7)
36. Approach that explains behaviour in terms of how thinking shapes our behaviour. (9)
37. An approach to research that focuses on formulating general laws of behaviour. (10)
38. Hormone produced when a person is stressed. (8)
39. The ego is driven by the _____ principle. (7)
41. Hormone that is produced in the adrenal gland, associated with stress. (10)
42. Serotonin, dopamine and GABA are all _____. (17)

Down

2. Therapy developed by Freud. (14)
4. An approach to research that focuses more on the individual than on general laws. (11)
5. The area of the brain involved in higher cognitive functions. (7, 4)
7. Doll used in classic social learning experiment. (4)
9. Freud's third stage of psychosexual development. (7)
10. Approach that explains behaviour in terms of the unconscious mind. (13)
11. Popper proposed that you cannot prove a theory correct, you can only _____ it. (7)
13. The term used to describe environmental explanations of behaviour. (7)
16. Personality character that is stingy and orderly, _____ _____ character. (4, 9)
17. Explanations that break complex phenomenon into more simple components are _____. (12)
19. Identical twins. (11)
21. Social learning theory proposes that reinforcement is both indirect and _____. (6)
27. The third stage of the GAS model. (10)
28. Psychologist who developed the concept of classical conditioning. (6)
29. The level of consciousness between the conscious and unconscious. (12)
32. The psychologist who developed the GAS model. (5)
33. The film made by Heider and Simmel (1944) involved a circle and two _____. (9)
35. Kind of reinforcement that involves escaping from an unpleasant situation. (8)
40. Abbreviation for the common mistake of explaining a person's behaviour in terms of internal rather than external factors. (3)

The specification for AS Unit 2

PY2 60% 1¾ hour
Psychology: Core Studies and Applied Research Methods

Section A and Section B are based on the core studies, and candidates answer three compulsory questions in each section. Section C is based on research methods, and candidates answer one question from a choice of two.	**Core studies:** Ten core studies drawn from five main areas	
	▶ Asch ▶ Milgram ▶ Rahe, Mahan and Arthur ▶ Bennett-Levy and Marteau ▶ Loftus and Palmer ▶ Gardner and Gardner ▶ Langer and Rodin ▶ Gibson and Walk ▶ Buss ▶ Rosenhan	For each core study, candidates should know: ▶ Aims and context. ▶ Procedures. ▶ Findings and conclusions. ▶ Evaluation of the methodology. ▶ Critical assessment of research in comparison with alternative evidence.
	Applied research methods	

	Apply knowledge of research methods to novel situations:
	▶ Qualitative and quantitative research methods (define and give advantages and disadvantages): lab, field and natural (quasi-) experiments, correlations, observations, questionnaires, interviews and case studies.
	▶ Reliability and ways of dealing with this (split half, test-retest, inter-rater).
	▶ Validity (experimental and ecological) and ways of dealing with these (content, concurrent, construct).
	▶ Ethical issues relating to research, including lack of informed consent, use of deception, a lack of the right to withdraw from the investigation, a lack of confidentiality, a failure to protect participants from physical and psychological harm.
		▶ Different sampling methods (define and give advantages and disadvantages), including opportunity, quota, random, self-selected (volunteer), stratified and systematic.
		▶ Define and offer advantages and disadvantages, and draw conclusions from the following ways of describing data:
		  ▶ Development of a coding system.
		  ▶ Content analysis.
		  ▶ Categorisation.
		  ▶ Mean, median, mode.
		  ▶ Range.
		  ▶ Scattergraphs, bar charts, histogram.

COMMENTS ON THE SPECIFICATION AND ORGANISATION OF THIS UNIT

Unit 2 is divided into two chapters: Chapter 5 on the Core Studies and Chapter 6 on the Applied Research Methods. Both of these chapters will give you an insight into how psychologists conduct research.

In the core studies chapter, you will look in detail at ten well known studies in psychology. For each study this book follows the same pattern:
- Spread 1: aims, context and procedures.
- Spread 2: findings and conclusions.
- Spread 3: evaluating the methodology, alternative evidence and student answers to exam questions.

Other features are also included such as 'Meet the researcher' boxes, activities and 'Can You' questions.

In Chapter 6 (Applied Research Methods) you will study the methods and techniques that psychologists use when studying behaviour, as well as considering the advantages of disadvantages of these methods/techniques.

PY2 Core studies and applied research methods

The exam is divided into three sections. Sections A and B relate to the core studies. You can see an example of Section C on page 133.

---

90 minutes (1 hour 45 minutes)

SECTION A

Answer all questions in this section.
You are reminded that the focus of your response must be the skill of knowledge and understanding.

1. Summarise the aims **and** context of Milgram's (1963) research 'Behavioural study of obedience'. [12]
2. Outline the procedures of Gibson and Walk's (1960) research 'The visual cliff'. [12]
3. Describe the findings **and** conclusions of Loftus and Palmer's (1974) research 'Reconstruction of automobile destruction: an example of the interaction between language and memory'. [12]

SECTION B

Answer all questions in this section.
You are reminded that the focus of your response must be the skill of analysis and evaluation.

4. Evaluate the methodology of Asch's (1955) research 'Opinions and Social Pressure'. [12]
5. With reference to alternative evidence, critically assess Gibson and Walk's (1960) research 'The visual cliff'. [12]
6. With reference to alternative evidence, critically assess Rosenhan's (1973) research 'On being sane in insane places'. [12]

Academic psychologists in universities or other research institutions conduct studies to test psychological theories and explanations. For example, in Chapter 1 we saw that Hans Selye conducted studies with rats to test his **General Adaptation Syndrome (GAS)** model, and in Chapter 2 we looked at Bandura's study with the Bobo doll that demonstrated **Social Learning Theory (SLT)**. These are examples of research studies. Other psychologists want to read about such research in order to develop their own ideas and theories, so psychologists (and all scientists) publish reports of their research in academic journals (see right).

A core study is an article originally published in an academic journal that has achieved lasting fame – mainly because the findings have been central to the development of psychological ideas.

Journal articles

Journal articles follow a fairly standard format, as outlined below. In fact, the exam questions follow this same format – context and aims, procedures, findings and conclusions (see facing page). So we have also followed the same format when presenting each of the core studies in this chapter.

Below we have explained each of the key features of a journal article, illustrated by the first page of the Loftus and Palmer (1974) core study.

Abstract A summary of the study.

Aims and context Articles usually begin with a review of previous research (theories and studies), leading up to the aims for this particular study. The researchers outline the aims for this study and may also state their research predictions and/or a **hypothesis**/es.

Procedures A detailed description of what the researchers did, such as providing details about the participants and the methods used to collect data. The main point is to give enough detail for someone else to **replicate** (repeat) the study.

Findings (sometimes called 'results') This section contains what the researchers found, and includes **quantitative** data in tables and graphs to illustrate what participants did. It also may include **qualitative** data, where participants offer comments on their behaviour or experience.

Conclusions (sometimes called the 'discussion') The researchers offer interpretations of the findings, such as making generalisations about people based on how the participants behaved in the study. They might propose explanations of the behaviours observed, and might also consider the implications of the results and make suggestions for future research.

Core study 1: Loftus and Palmer (1974). This is the first page of the original article.

Reprinted from Loftus & Palmer (1974). 'Reconstruction of automobile destruction: an example of the interaction between language and memory.' *Journal of Verbal Learning and Verbal Behavior, 13*, 585–589, © 1974 with permission from Elsevier.

SCHOLARLY JOURNALS

There are thousands of scholarly journals publishing more than 1 million research papers each year. They differ from 'popular' magazines because they contain in-depth reports of research. The articles are written by academics and are *peer reviewed*. This means that the articles are read by other academic experts who decide whether the research is worthy of publication (i.e. honest and valid).

Several hundred such journals relate specifically to psychology, e.g. *The Psychologist, Archives of Sexual Behaviour, Journal of Early Adolescence* and *The British Journal of Psychology*.

These journals can be published weekly, monthly or less frequently. Academic textbooks are based on such articles, and link research claims to scholarly reports – as you can see by looking in the references at the back of this book.

Read the originals

We have provided fairly detailed accounts of each core study, but it is a good idea to look at the original articles. In many cases these can be found on the internet, and we have given the links in the text. If the original report is not on the web, then you can give the full reference for the study to your local library, and it will obtain photocopies through the British inter-library loan service, for a small fee.

There are many such core studies and, if you are interested, you can read about them (as well as some of the WJEC core studies) in the following books:

Banyard, P. and Grayson, A. (2007). Introducing Psychological Research, 3rd edn. London: Palgrave.

Hock, R.R. (2008). Forty Studies That Changed Psychology. *London: Pearson Educational.*

Rolls, G. (2005). Classic Case Studies in Psychology. *London: Hodder and Stoughton.*

Slater, L. (2004). Opening Skinner's Box: Great Psychological Experiments of the Twentieth Century. *New York: Norton.*

Asch (1955) Opinions and social pressure

Social influence is the study of how our thoughts, feelings and behaviour are affected by other people. In the 1950s, Solomon Asch was one of a number of social psychologists who sought to understand the processes involved in social influence. The sociologist Gabriel Tarde commented: *'Social man is a somnambulist'*, in other words much of our behaviour is performed as if we were sleep walking. People's opinions and attitudes are formed to a considerable extent by the opinions and attitudes of those around them, and much of this takes place without conscious effort.

You may dispute this – you may think you uphold your own beliefs and opinions, and that your opinions are your own rather than blind conformity. However, Asch's research shows us otherwise, and has certainly astonished people.

"Louise, everyone is wearing that this year ...
don't be such a sheep to fashion."

www.cartoonstock.com

WHAT IS CONFORMITY?

An individual is said to *conform* if they choose a course of action that is favoured by the majority of other group members or is considered socially acceptable. In contrast, an individual is described as *deviating* if they choose to behave in a way that is not socially acceptable or that the majority of group members do not appear to favour. Because the individual is clearly influenced by how the *majority* of people think or behave, this form of social influence is sometimes referred to as *majority influence*. The fact that an individual goes along with the majority in *public*, does not, however, indicate that they have changed their *private* attitudes or beliefs. Therefore most majority influence is characterised by **public compliance** rather than **private acceptance**.

Conformity is an important process for psychologists to understand as it is thought to have a significant impact on many of our behaviours and the decisions we make in many situations, for example, how juries make decisions, and student behaviour in classrooms.

CONTEXT AND AIMS

A number of earlier studies looked at the way people in groups formed their own opinions. For example, Jenness (1932) asked students to guess how many beans there were in a jar. Then they were given an opportunity to discuss their estimates and, finally, they were asked individually to give their estimates again. Jenness found that individual estimates tended to converge to a group norm. It seems reasonable that, in an *ambiguous* situation (such as trying to work out how many beans there are in a jar), one looks to others to get some ideas about a reasonable answer. However, Jenness's research is thought to be limited by the fact that he specifically asked them to produce a group estimate, rather than just observing whether they would produce similar estimates.

Sherif (1935) conducted a similar investigation into responses to an ambiguous stimulus using the *autokinetic effect* (this is where a stationary spot of light is projected on to a screen in an otherwise dark room and it appears to move about). Sherif told participants he was going to move the light, and asked them to estimate by how far the spot of light had moved. All participants were initially tested individually, and were then asked to work with three others who had given quite different estimates of movement. After their discussion, each was asked to provide individual answers again. These had become quite similar to those of the others in their group, demonstrating a tendency to establish and conform to group norms.

Sherif's research is considered to be an improvement over Jenness's because he did not specifically inform participants that they had to produce a group estimate, his participants arrived at a group norm under their own volition.

However, Asch thought that the research of both Jenness and Sherif was limited because it did not really measure **conformity** – it measured the formation of group norms rather than whether people conformed to the behaviour and opinion of others. Asch also believed that the research lacked impact because conformity is quite likely in ambiguous situations where there are no clear answers. So Asch devised a new way to test conformity.

Aims

In *ambiguous* situations, it makes sense for us to look to others to help us determine our behaviour and attitudes, such as deciding which TV programmes are best or which knife to use in a restaurant. If you're not sure what to think or do, then you look to see what everyone else is doing. But if there is a clearly right answer, are people still influenced by the behaviour of others?

Asch aimed to investigate the effects of group pressure on individuals in an *un*ambiguous situation. He wanted to find out if, when confronted with an obviously incorrect answer, individuals would give an answer that perpetuated this error (conformed) or would give an independent response.

PROCEDURES

The baseline study

Asch asked student volunteers to take part in a 'vision' test, although, unbeknown to these volunteers, all but one of the participants were really confederates (i.e. colleagues) of the experimenter. The real purpose of the experiment was to see how the lone 'naïve' participant would react to the behaviour of the **confederates**.

In total, 123 male undergraduates from three different US colleges were tested. In each session there was one naïve participant and a group of six to eight confederates. The participants (the real one and the confederates) were seated in a room, with the naïve participant always seated last or second to last (to ensure that he heard the others' answers before giving his own).

The participants were shown two large white cards (such as those on the right). On one card is a single vertical black line – the standard line whose length is to be matched. On the other card are three vertical lines of various lengths. The participants were asked to select the line that is the same length as the standard line. One of the comparison lines is the same length, the other two are substantially different (a difference of about 2cm or more).

The experiment began uneventfully, with all the confederates identifying the correct line, but after a few trials all of the confederates make an erroneous selection. In total, the confederates were instructed to give the same *incorrect* answer in 12 out of the 18 trials with each participant.

After completing the trials, Asch revealed the true nature of the research and interviewed the naïve participants about their responses and behaviour.

Additional procedures

Asch questioned whether the size of the majority or its unanimity was more important in determining conformity. He therefore tried a number of variations to discover the effect of certain factors on conformity levels.

- **The size of the group** This was varied from 1–15 people.
- **A truthful partner** One of the group answered truthfully. This role was played by a confederate or another naïve participant.
- **A dissenting, inaccurate partner** A confederate was introduced who disagreed with the majority but also disagreed with the naïve participant.
- **A partner who changes his mind** In the previous studies, the naïve participant was observed in a single setting. What would happen if the situation changed? In this variation, the confederate partner starts by giving correct responses for the first six critical trials, but then joined the majority for the remaining six critical trials.
- **A partner who leaves** The partner starts by giving correct responses for the first six critical trials, and then has to leave because of an important appointment.

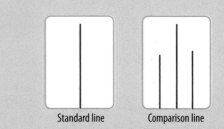

Standard line   Comparison line

▲ Examples of the cards used in Asch's experiment to test conformity in an unambiguous situation.

▼ The experimenter shows the lines to a group of participants, who are all confederates of the experimenter except the one naïve participant, who is seated second to last in the group.

You can watch videos of the Asch experiment on YouTube.

Original article

Asch's article was published in the journal *Scientific American*. The full reference is: Asch, S.E. (1955). Opinions and social pressure. *Scientific American*, *193*(5), 31–35. Copies of this article can be found on the internet, e.g. at www.columbia.edu/cu/psychology/terrace/w1001/readings/asch.pdf.

Other resources

- The Asch effect and politics (the Obama effect): mbd.scout.com/mb.aspx?s=176&f=3586&t=3294461.
- The Asch phenomenon and consumer behaviour: frontpage.wiu.edu/~mfjtd/asch.htm.
- The Asch song – *Asch Followed Sherif* (sung to the tune of *I Shot the Sheriff* by Bob Marley): socialpsychlyrics.blogspot.com/2007/10/solomon-aschs-1951-1955-conformity.html.

Asch (1955) Opinions and social pressure

FINDINGS

The baseline study

When faced with unanimous wrong answers from confederates, the naïve participants also gave wrong answers 36.8% of the time, i.e. on the critical trials, 36.8% of the responses made by naïve participants were incorrect.

Control trials Just to confirm that the stimulus lines were unambiguous, Asch conducted a control trial with no confederates giving wrong answers. In ordinary circumstances, Asch found that people made mistakes less than 1% of the time.

Individual differences There was a considerable range in conformity levels. One quarter (25%) of the participants never gave a wrong (conforming) answer. At the other extreme, some individuals went with the majority nearly all the time, and 75% conformed at least once.

Participant behaviour (independent or compliant) over the critical trials tended to be consistent: *'those who strike out on the path of independence do not, as a rule, succumb to the majority … those who choose the path of compliance are unable to free themselves and the ordeal is prolonged'*.

- Those who were independent had staunch confidence in their own judgement' and felt it was *'their obligation to call the play as they saw it'*, even though they regarded the majority as correct
- Those who were extremely yielding underestimated the frequency with which they conformed. They explained their behaviour in various ways; for example, they said they yielded in order not to spoil the results. Some thought they were 'deficient' in comparison with the rest of the group, and this 'deficiency' needed to be hidden at all costs.

▲ The photograph shows participants 5, 6 and 7; number 6 is the naïve participant. He is leaning forward in order to re-examine the stimulus cards because he can't believe what he is seeing – the confederates have unanimously identified the wrong standard line. In fact, this naïve participant disagreed with the majority on all 12 critical trials.

Additional findings

As we have seen, Asch varied key features of the group to observe the effects on conformity levels. The findings of these variations were as follows.

- **The size of the group** He found that with only one confederate, the naïve participant was swayed very little. With two confederates, the naïve participant accepted the wrong answer 13.6% of the time. With three confederates, this rose to 31.8%. The addition of further confederates made very little difference.
- **A truthful partner** This reduced the pressure to conform; participants answered incorrectly only 25% as often as in the baseline investigation.
- **A dissenting, inaccurate partner** The effect was again to reduce the pressure to conform – the presence of a dissenter increased independence.
- **A partner who changes his mind** When the confederate partner started by being independent, but then conformed to the majority, the naïve participant also behaved independently for the first six critical trials but then submitted to the majority's wrong answers, following his partner. Thus his initial independent behaviour had no lasting effect.
- **A partner who leaves** If the independent partner had to leave the investigation after the first six critical trials (for a pre-arranged appointment), then the naïve participant also reverted to being influenced by the majority, but less so than if the partner had deserted for 'no good reason'.

MEET THE RESEARCHER

▲ Solomon Asch (1920–1996).

Solomon Asch was born in Warsaw and emigrated to the USA as a teenager. He studied psychology at Columbia University in New York, and influenced a generation of social psychologists, including Stanley Milgram (see next core study), whose PhD he supervised.

In the 1950s, behaviourism dominated psychology. Asch played an important role in establishing a more balanced and productive blend of natural and social science, masterminding some inventive and enduring research studies.

He is probably best known for his studies of conformity in the 1950s, and his name is synonymous with the topic to the extent that the finding that individuals will frequently acquiesce to the majority is known as the *Asch effect*.

CONCLUSIONS

This study shows that there is a surprisingly strong tendency to conform to group pressures in a situation where the answer is clear. Asch pointed out: *'Life in society requires consensus as an indispensable condition. But ... when consensus comes under the dominance of conformity, the social process is polluted and the individual ... surrenders the powers on which his functioning as a feeling and thinking being depends.'* In other words, group agreement is a necessary aspect of social life, but it is psychologically unhealthy to be dominated by majority pressure.

Factors that affected conformity

The pressure of the majority was reduced when there was only a small majority, and was also reduced by the presence of a dissenter, even when the dissenter gave a different incorrect answer. This shows that the effect of the majority depends to a considerable extent on the majority being unanimous. Even when the dissenter started by behaving independently, his movement back to the majority view was enough to reduce the naïve participant's ability to remain independent.

Resisting conformity

For Asch, the important finding was that there was any conformity at all. Asch pointed out that, on two-thirds of the trials, his participants had remained independent. This is clear evidence of how people can *resist* the pressure to conform. This study is represented in most social psychology textbooks as resounding evidence of people's tendency to conform when faced with a unanimous majority. It is, however, also evidence of conditions under which people resist conformity. Asch said: *'That we have found the tendency to conformity in our society so strong that reasonably intelligent and well meaning young people are willing to call white black is a matter of concern. It raises questions about our ways of education and about the values that guide our conduct. Yet anyone inclined to draw too pessimistic conclusions from this report would do well to remind himself that the capacities for independence are not to be underestimated ... those who participated in this challenging experiment agreed nearly without exception that independence was preferable to conformity.'*

▲ **Independent behaviour or conformity?** True independence or non-conformity means that you are not following the norms of any social group.

CAN YOU...?

1... Explain what is meant by conformity.

2... Identify **two** studies that were conducted prior to Asch's study and explain the conclusions from each of these studies.

3... Briefly outline the aims of this study.

4... How many participants were there in the baseline study?

5... Describe **three** key characteristics of the participants.

6... Identify **six** key aspects of the baseline procedures (e.g. the participants were deceived and told the study was a vision test).

7... Describe **two** of the additional procedures.

8... Identify **six** findings from this study.

9... For each finding, state a conclusion that could be drawn from it. Try to make each conclusion different.

10... What evidence leads you to conclude that this study supports the view that people are surprisingly conformist?

11... What evidence leads you to conclude that this study supports the view that people are surprisingly independent in their behaviour?

EXAM QUESTIONS

SECTION A

Summarise the aims **and** context of Asch's (1955) research 'Opinions and Social Pressure'. [12]

Outline the procedures of Asch's (1955) research 'Opinions and Social Pressure'. [12]

Describe the findings **and** conclusions of Asch's (1955) research 'Opinions and Social Pressure'. [12]

Notes *In Section A of the Unit 2 exam, you might be asked any of the questions above. Each question will be worth 12 marks. In order to gain the full 12 marks, your answer should:*

▶ *Be accurate and well detailed.*

▶ *Display a depth and range of knowledge, though not necessarily in equal measure; this means that you can either cover a few points in considerable detail (i.e. depth) or cover a number of points in less detail (range).*

▶ *Be well structured and coherent.*

▶ *Have accurate grammar, punctuation and spelling.*

▶ *Be about 200–250 words in length, which is shorter than the requirement for other 12-mark questions, but the emphasis is on accuracy.*

DO IT YOURSELF

No. 5.4

At the beginning of this chapter, we outlined the format of a journal article (see page 67). Each of the core studies in this chapter is based on such a journal article and follows the same plan as such articles – context and aims, procedures, findings and conclusions. However, one element has been omitted – the abstract. This is something you could now write: a summary of the context and aims, procedures, findings and conclusions of Asch's study. Limit yourself to 200 words.

Asch (1955) Opinions and social pressure

On this spread we are going to evaluate the core study by looking at issues related to its methodology and comparing the study to alternative evidence. When it comes to evaluation, you can make up your own mind. We have presented some evidence and statements, and invite you to use this to construct your own view of the core study.

EVALUATING THE METHODOLOGY

See Chapter 6 (Applied research methods) for an explanation of these concepts.

Method

Asch's study was not an **experiment**, but it was conducted in a lab environment. *What advantages does this offer? What disadvantages are there to using this method?*

Reliability

Larsen repeated Asch's research in 1974. He found conformity levels were a lot lower than those found by Asch. Some think this means Asch's findings lack **reliability**. *What might have been responsible for the lower rates of conformity found by Larsen?*

Validity

Asch conducted his conformity research by observing participants' responses using a 'line comparison' task. *Give* **two** *reasons why this task might not have been a valid measure of conformity?*

The naïve participants didn't know the other 'participants'. *How might have this affected the conformity rates?*

The naïve participants had to answer out loud. *To what extent might this affect levels of conformity?*

Sampling

Asch collected his findings using a **sample** of male college students. This sample was both gender-biased and culture-biased. *Explain how the sample used by Asch might have affected the results.* (It may help you to read some of the alternative evidence presented on this page.)

Ethical issues

Asch's study involved both active and passive **deception**. *Explain whether these are acceptable or not.*

The photograph on the previous spread shows that the true participant may have found the experience quite distressing. Bogdonoff *et al.* (1961) tested the autonomic arousal of participants in an Asch-like task and found that they were aroused (high blood pressure, etc.), indicating the anxiety they were experiencing. *To what extent do you think that the participants in this study experienced psychological harm?*

Do you think that Asch could have discovered what he did without deceiving his participants?

DO IT YOURSELF

No. 5.5

Some people are more conformist than others. Burger and Cooper (1979) showed that people who have a high desire for personal control (internals) were less likely to conform. In this experiment, participants were shown a series of cartoons and asked to rate them in terms of funniness. A confederate sat by their side, giving his ratings out loud for some of the cartoons. Participants with a low desire for control were more likely to agree with the confederate's ratings than those with a high desire for control.

You could try to repeat this experiment yourself, using Rotter's scale for *locus of control* (see page 104) to measure individual desire for control.

Ethics warning: All the participants you use must be aged over 16, and you must debrief them carefully.

ALTERNATIVE EVIDENCE

Previous research

Look back at the findings and conclusions of Jenness (1932) and Sherif (1935) on page 68. *Do Asch's findings support, contradict or develop their findings and conclusions?*

A child of its time

Perrin and Spencer (1980) suggested that Asch's high conformity rates might be due to the fact that the research was conducted in the USA in the 1950s – the era of McCarthyism and a highly conformist society. Perrin and Spencer repeated Asch's study in England in the late 1970s. They found that only one student conformed in 396 trials. *Why do you think Perrin and Spencer's results were so different to Asch's?*

Doms and Avermaet (1981) believed that Asch's results may be more realistic than those of Perrin and Spencer, because Perrin and Spencer used science students who may have felt more confident about their ability to estimate line length. Another study by Perrin and Spencer (1981) used youths on probation, and found similar levels of conformity to Asch. However, there were other factors in this later study that may have been important, namely that the participants were youths on probation and the confederates were probation officers – so conformity may have been influenced by a desire to please probation officers! *What conclusions can you draw from this evidence in relation to Asch's research?*

Gender bias

Some studies have found that women are actually *more* conformist than men (e.g. Neto, 1995). This may be explained in terms of the fact that women are more concerned with social relationships then men are, which means that, in the experimental situation, they have different short-term goals. The result is that women *appear* to be more conformist than they are in the real world (Eagly, 1978). *Explain how these findings support, contradict or develop Asch's findings.*

Culture bias

The original sample consisted of US students, members of an **individualist** society. Individualist societies emphasise the importance of individual needs and goals. In contrast, some societies (e.g. Japan and Israel) are described as **collectivist** because they share possessions and even identity. The individual is defined more in terms of the group than individual needs and characteristics. Smith and Bond (1988) reviewed 133 studies carried out in 17 countries, and concluded that collectivist societies were more conformist than individualist ones. *Explain how these findings support, contradict or develop Asch's findings.*

Individual differences

Some people are more conformist than others. On the facing page, we have already considered gender and cultural differences. In addition, there are personality differences. For example, some people are classed as 'externals', i.e. they have a more external **locus of control** than 'internals'. Externals tend to believe that they have little control over their lives and that things frequently happen because of luck. Externals are more likely to rely on the opinions of others (see the study by Burger and Cooper in the Do It Yourself activity on this spread). *Explain how these findings support, contradict or develop Asch's findings.*

Compliance or internalisation

A key question about Asch's study was whether participants were just going along with the answers so they wouldn't sound foolish (called 'compliance'), or whether majority influence actually changed their perceptions (i.e. internalised the majority view).

A recent study by Berns *et al.* (2005) used brain-scanning techniques **fMRI** to observe which parts of the brain were active while participants were engaged in an Asch-like task. They found that, on the critical trials (where confederates were given incorrect answers) the most active areas of the brain were the perceptual circuits rather than brain regions involved with making judgements. This suggests that the Asch task actually changes the way people see the world, although it is possible that activity in this part of the brain was caused because participants were double-checking what they thought they saw.

The area of the brain related to fear was activated when participants were behaving independently, supporting the view that participants conform out of fear of being rejected by the group. *Explain how these findings support, contradict or develop Asch's findings.*

Conclusion

There have been numerous attempts to replicate the so-called *Asch effect*. Some studies have found support for Asch. For example, Nicholson *et al.* (1985) repeated the study with British and US students and found that 32% and 38%, respectively, conformed at least once. On the other hand, some studies have found no effect. For example, Lalancette and Standing (1990) found no conformity, even though they made the task more ambiguous (which should increase conformity). They concluded that the Asch effect appears to be an unpredictable phenomenon rather than a stable tendency of human behaviour. *What do you think they mean by this?*

What is your own overall conclusion about the Asch effect? Explain the evidence that supports your conclusion.

EXAM QUESTIONS

SECTION B

Evaluate the methodology of Asch's (1955) research 'Opinions and social pressure'. [12]

With reference to alternative evidence, critically assess Asch's (1955) research 'Opinions and social pressure'. [12]

Notes *In Section B of the Unit 2 exam, you could be asked either of the questions above. In order to gain the full 12 marks for each question, your answer should:*

▶ *Present clearly structured evaluation.*

▶ *Present a coherent elaboration of each point.*

▶ *Display a depth and range of analysis, though not necessarily in equal measure; this means that you can either cover a few points in considerable detail (i.e. depth) or cover a number of points in less detail (range).*

▶ *Be about 300–350 words in length; the focus is on a sufficient breadth of material but also sufficient detail for each point made, i.e. depth and breadth.*

You may find it useful to look at the student answers at the end of the other core studies to identify and avoid the typical mistakes that students make when answering Section B questions.

Example exam question with student answers

Examiner's comments on these answers can be found on page 176.

EXAMPLE OF QUESTION 2

> **Outline the procedures of Asch's (1955) research 'Opinions and social pressure'.** [12]

Megan's answer

Asch's aim was to find out if people conformed in unambiguous situations. He put a naïve participant with a group of confederates and they all had to do a line test. On most of the trials the confederates would give a wrong answer on purpose and Asch waited to see if the naïve participant who was sat near the end of the group would give right answer or not. He found that ¾ of the real participants went along with the fake participants at least once.

Tomas's answer

In groups of seven to nine, male students are told that they will be taking part in a 'psychological experiment in visual judgement'. The experimenter shows the group two cards. On card 1 there is a 'standard' line. On card 2 there are three lines of various lengths. They have to choose the line on the second card that is the same length as the standard line (the answer is obvious).

A 'naïve' participant is sat in the last but one seat to ensure that he has heard the unanimous replies of the other participants when they verbally report their answers on 18 trials. The naïve participant does not know that the other 'participants' in the group are actually 'confederates' of the experimenter and have been told to give the same obviously wrong answer on 12 of the 18 trials, called 'critical' trials.

Asch wanted to see on the 12 critical trials if the naïve participant would verbally report the same answer as the other participants (a conforming response) or if the naïve participant would verbally report a different answer to the rest of the participants (a non-conforming response). After completing the trials, Asch revealed the true nature of the research and interviewed the naïve participants about their responses and behaviour.

Milgram (1963) Behavioural study of obedience

Like Asch's study, Milgram's also relates to social influence. However, whereas Asch's study was about *indirect* social influence, this study is concerned with *direct* social influence – **obedience** to unjust authority. The study focuses on *unjust* authority rather than simply on 'authority' because who would refuse to obey a just authority? Therefore, in order to understand obedience and resistance, it is necessary to look at unjust authority.

The study we are going to consider is probably the best known and most intriguing study in psychology. You can make up your own mind about why it provides such enduring fascination.

CONTEXT AND AIMS

WHAT IS OBEDIENCE?

Obedience refers to a type of social influence that causes a person to act in response to a direct order from a figure with perceived authority. There is also the implication that the person receiving the order is being made to do something that they would not have done without the order.

In this form of social influence, the individual is faced with the choice of whether to *comply* with a direct order from a person with higher status (for example, a soldier obeying an order from his or her superior officer) or whether to *defy* the order. Because of the hierarchical superiority of the authority figure, the individual must also consider the *consequences* of his or her *dis*obedience.

▲ Eichmann on trial in Jerusalem, Israel, in 1961. He was found guilty and hanged for his crimes. The presiding judge commented: 'Even if we had found that the Accused acted out of blind obedience, as he argued, we would still have said that a man who took part in crimes of such magnitude as these over years must pay the maximum penalty known to the law, and he cannot rely on any order even in mitigation of his punishment.'

Throughout human history, there have been atrocities involving human inhumanity to other humans. Arguably the most infamous was the murder of millions of Jews in the Holocaust during the Second World War. At Auschwitz, one of the most efficient of the Nazis' death camps, there were up to 12 000 deaths a day. In August 1944, Adolf Eichmann reported to Heinreich Himmler that his unit had overseen the deaths of approximately four million Jews in death camps and that an estimated two million had been killed by mobile units.

Was such brutality simply a product of evil and sadistic minds, or was this *extraordinary* behaviour performed by *ordinary* people? Adolf Eichmann, who had been in charge of implementing the 'Final Solution', was captured in 1960. He was put on trial in Jerusalem, Israel, in 1961. His demeanour during the trial was hardly that of the vicious war criminal many had expected. Hannah Arendt (1963) wrote: *'It would have been comforting indeed to believe that Eichmann was a monster … The trouble with Eichmann was precisely that so many were like him, and that the many were neither perverted nor sadistic, that they were, and still are, terribly and terrifyingly normal.'*

The disturbing implication was that *'in certain circumstances the most ordinary decent person can become a criminal'* (Arendt, 1963). At his trial, Eichmann like many other war criminals when brought to justice, claimed he had been 'only obeying orders'.

Many researchers believed that the obedience required to perpetuate the Holocaust was due to the fact that 'Germans are different'. They believed that Germans tended to have a particular 'type' of personality – the **authoritarian personality**. This concept was proposed by Adorno *et al.* (1950), describing individuals who are typically hostile to people of inferior status while being 'servile' to those who they perceive to be of a higher status than themselves. Such individuals tend to uphold the norms of the society in which they live, and are intolerant of alternative ways of life. Adorno *et al.* suggested that authoritarian personalities are likely to become prejudiced against minority groups as a result of unconscious hostility arising from a harsh disciplinarian upbringing, and that this is displaced on to minority groups, such as Jews or black people (a **psychodynamic** explanation).

▲ Adolf Eichmann was head of the Gestapo's Department for Jewish Affairs between 1941 and 1945.

Aims

At the same time as Eichmann was being tried in Israel, Milgram was starting his studies at Yale University. He wished to test the 'Germans are different' hypothesis – the belief that obedience can be explained in terms of internal, **dispositional** factors.

Milgram recognised that obedience is an indispensable part of social life. In order to live in communities, some system of authority is required. The issue of obedience is particularly relevant to understanding the atrocities of the Second World War: *'the inhumane policies [of the Second World War] may have originated in the mind of a single person, but they could only be carried out on a massive scale if a very large number of persons obeyed orders'.*

Milgram aimed to create a situation that allowed him to measure the process of obedience, even when the command requires destructive behaviour.

PROCEDURES

Participants

Milgram placed an advertisement in a New Haven newspaper (see right). From the people who responded, he selected 40 males aged between 20 and 50 years. The advertisement led the participants to believe that they would be taking part in research about memory and learning. The men in the sample had a range of jobs, from postal clerks to engineers, and they varied in educational level from one who hadn't finished primary school to one with a doctorate. Each man was paid $4.50 for his participation in the study. He was told he would receive this simply for coming to the lab – payment did not depend on remaining in the study.

Method

The study took place in a lab at Yale University. When participants arrived they were greeted by the 'experimenter', a 31-year-old man dressed in a grey technician's coat. Another 'participant' was at the lab, a mild-mannered and likeable 47-year-old accountant, Mr Wallace. In fact both of these men were accomplices of Milgram (called **confederates**).

The participants drew slips of paper to decide which of them would play the role of teacher or learner. The selection was rigged – the naïve participant was always assigned to the teacher role and the accomplice was always assigned the learner role.

Both learner and teacher were then taken to the experimental room where the learner was strapped into an 'electric chair' apparatus to prevent excessive movement. An electrode was placed on the learner's wrist, linked to a shock generator in the adjoining room.

The shock machine The teacher was taken to the adjoining room and seated in front of the shock generator. This large machine had 30 switches on it, each showing an incremental rise in voltage starting at 15 volts and going up to 450 volts. For every four switches, there were 'shock' labels, starting at 'slight shock' at 15 volts to 'intense shock' at 255 volts and finally 'XXX' at 450 volts, a potentially fatal shock. The experimenter gave the teacher a 'sample' shock to demonstrate that the machine was real.

The learning task Once the study began, the teacher was told to administer a shock when the learner gave a wrong answer, and to escalate to a higher level of shock each time, announcing the shock level each time.

Feedback from learner The learner was told to give approximately three wrong answers to every correct one. The learner was also told to make no comment or protest until the shock level of 300 volts was reached. At this point he should pound on the wall but thereafter make no further comment.

Feedback from experimenter The experimenter was trained to give a sequence of four standard 'prods' if the teacher hesitated about delivering the shock or asked for guidance:
- 'Please continue.'
- 'The experiment requires that you continue.'
- 'It is absolutely essential that you continue.'
- 'You have no other choice, you must go on.'

There were also special prods such as: 'Although the shocks may be painful, there is no permanent tissue damage, so go on.'

Dehoax After the research was completed, the teacher was thoroughly 'dehoaxed' and the experimenter reunited the teacher and learner. They were then interviewed about their experience in this study.

DO IT YOURSELF

No. 5.7

1. Construct your own step-by-step guide to the procedures of this study. Number each step.
2. Produce your own re-enactment of the study, including a replica of the shock machine. Perhaps even film it for YouTube!

Re-enactments There are many re-enactments of the study on YouTube, especially one made by the BBC, and also Derren Brown's fascinating recreation of the Milgram experiment ('*The Heist*').

Milgram song Have a listen at: www.wjh.harvard.edu/~wegner/shock.mp3.

Original article
The full reference for Milgram's article is Milgram, S. (1963). Behavioral study of obedience. *Journal of Abnormal and Social Psychology, 67,* 371–378. A copy can be found at: www.garfield.library.upenn.edu/classics1981/A1981LC33300001.pdf.

Other resources
- All you ever wanted to know about Stanley Milgram at www.stanleymilgram.com.
- Milgram published the results of all of his obedience studies in a book entitled *Obedience to Authority: An Experimental View* (Milgram, 1974). This includes interviews with many of the participants.
- There is an excellent biography of Stanley Milgram by Thomas Blass: *The Man Who Shocked the World: The Life and Legacy of Stanley Milgram* (Blass, 2004).

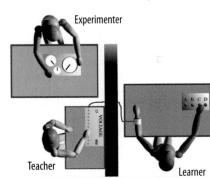

Experimenter

Teacher

Learner

◀ The 'learner' is strapped into a chair in a separate room. The 'teacher' sits next door to deliver shocks whenever the learner makes a mistake. The experimenter delivers 'prods' to encourage the 'teacher' to continue.

◀ The experimenter (in the lab coat) was Milgram's assistant. The picture shows him testing the shock on a 'teacher'. © Stanley Milgram, reproduced courtesy of Alexandra Milgram.

FINDINGS

Prior to the study

Milgram surveyed 14 Yale psychology students. They estimated that 0–3% of the participants would administer 450 volts.

Experimental results

- At 300 volts, five (12.5%) of the participants refused to continue. This was the point at which the learner made the only protest. All the participants had continued to this point.
- A total of 26 of the 40 participants (65%) administered the full 450 volts.
- This means that 35% of the participants defied the experimenter's authority.

Signs of extreme tension

Many subjects showed nervousness, and a large number showed extreme tension: *'subjects were observed to sweat, tremble, stutter, bite their lips, groan and dig their finger-nails into their flesh'*.

Fourteen participants displayed 'nervous laughter and smiling'. Their remarks and outward behaviour indicated that they were acting against their own values in punishing the learner. In the post-experimental interview (the 'dehoax'), these participants explained that they were not sadistic and that their laughter had not meant that they were enjoying shocking the learner.

Three participants had 'full-blown uncontrollable seizures'. One participant had such a violent convulsion that the research session had to be stopped.

After the study

Participants were sent a follow-up questionnaire. Of the 92% of participants' who responded:

- 84% were 'glad/very glad' to have taken part.
- 15% were 'neutral' about having taken part.
- 2% were 'sorry/very sorry' to have taken part.
- 80% said more experiments like this should be carried out.
- 74% felt they had learned something of personal importance.

▼ *The graph shows the number of participants who dropped out at different shock levels. Five participants (12.5%) stopped at 300 volts, which is when the learner protested and banged on the wall. Twenty-six participants (65%) continued to 450 volts (marked XXX on the shock generator).*

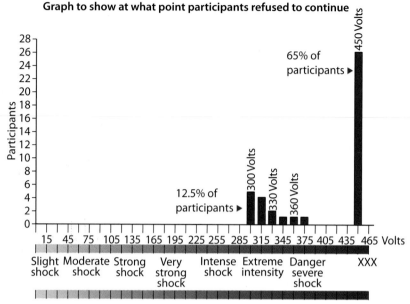

Graph to show at what point participants refused to continue

Responses from participants

- *'I think he's trying to communicate, he's knocking … Well it's not fair to shock the guy … these are terrific volts. I don't think this is very humane … Oh, I can't go on with this.'*
- *'He's banging in there. I'm gonna chicken out. I'd like to continue, but I can't do that to a man … I'm sorry, I can't do that to a man. I'll hurt his heart. You take your [money].'*

Some participants simply got up and left, without saying anything. Those who continued to the end often heaved a sigh of relief, mopped their brows, some shook their heads apparently in regret, some remained calm throughout.

MEET THE RESEARCHER

▲ Stanley Milgram (1933–1984).

Stanley Milgram grew up in a working class Jewish family in New York, and was a classmate of Philip Zimbardo's (see page 134). When Zimbardo was asked if it was a coincidence that both of them developed an interest in social influence his response was:

'We were both interested in situational influences because growing up poor, one sees failure and evil in your midst and you don't want to believe it is the dispositions of your family and friends, but rather in situational forces imposed on them.'
(Zimbardo personal communication)

Although Milgram is best known for his study of obedience, he was a prodigious researcher in other areas too. In 1967, he found a way to test what was known as the 'small world problem'. He randomly selected people to send packages to a stranger located in Massachusetts, USA. The senders were given only the recipient's name, occupation, and general location. They were instructed to send the package to someone they knew on a first-name basis who they thought most likely to know the target personally. That person would do the same, and so on, until the package was personally delivered to its target recipient. Amazingly, it took (on average) only about six intermediaries to get each package delivered, leading to the 'six degrees of separation' claim that each person in the world is separated from everyone else by just six steps! Try it out yourself on Facebook where there is a 'Six degrees of separation' group (www.facebook.com/group.php?gid=2215880552).

CONCLUSIONS

Milgram concluded that *'the phenomenon of obedience must rest on the analysis of the particular conditions in which it occurs'*. In other words, he concluded that it is the circumstances in which the participants found themselves that amalgamated to create a situation in which it proved difficult to disobey.

Milgram concluded that there were 13 elements in this situation that had contributed to these levels of obedience.

1. The location of the study at a prestigious university provided authority.
2. Participants assumed that the experimenter knew what he was doing and had a worthy purpose, so should be followed.
3. Participants assumed that the learner had voluntarily consented to take part.
4. The participant didn't wish to disrupt the experiment because he felt under obligation to the experimenter due to his voluntary consent to take part.
5. This sense of obligation was reinforced because the participant was being paid (although he had been told he could leave).
6. Participants believed that the role of learner was determined by chance; therefore the learner can't really complain.
7. It was a novel situation for the participant, who therefore didn't know how to behave. If it had been possible to discuss the situation with others the participant might have behaved differently.
8. The participant assumed that the discomfort caused was minimal and temporary, and that the scientific gains were important.
9. Since the learner 'played the game' up to shock level 20 (300 volts), the participant assumed the learner was willing to continue with the experiment.
10. The participant was torn between meeting the demands of the victim and those of the experimenter.
11. The two demands were not equally pressing and legitimate.
12. The participant had very little time to resolve the conflict at 300 volts, and he didn't know that the victim would remain silent for the rest of the experiment.
13. The conflict was between two deeply ingrained tendencies – not to harm someone, and to obey those whom we perceive to be legitimate authorities.

DO IT YOURSELF   No. 5.8

1. Once again, you could write an abstract for this study, as you did for Asch's study. This abstract should contain brief details of the context and aims, procedures, findings and conclusions of Milgram's study – in a total of about 200 words. (Try not to cheat by looking at our summary at the end of this chapter – we used 160 words.)
2. See who can write the shortest summary that still covers all the key points.

One observer related: *'I observed a mature and initially poised businessman enter the laboratory smiling and confident. Within 20 minutes he was reduced to a twitching, stuttering wreck, who was rapidly approaching a point of nervous collapse. He constantly pulled on his earlobe, and twisted his hands. At one point he pushed his fist into his forehead and muttered, "Oh God, let's stop it". And yet he continued to respond to every word of the experimenter, and obeyed to the end.'*

(Milgram, 1963)

In Chapter 4, we looked at **attribution theory** (see page 46). Heider proposed that we explain our own and other people's behaviour in terms of internal (**dispositional**) or external (**situational**) factors, and that we tend to prefer dispositional rather than situational explanations (the **fundamental attribution error – FAE**). Milgram's findings can be explained in terms of the FAE . He found that participants' behaviour was quite different from what people had predicted beforehand. People 'prefer' a dispositional explanation (someone would only give strong shocks if they were inhuman) rather than a situational one (in a lab people may feel they have to obey).

CAN YOU...?   No.5.3

1... Explain what is meant by obedience.
2... Explain the link between Adorno's concept of the authoritarian personality and the 'Germans are different' hypothesis.
3... Briefly outline the aims of this study.
4... How many participants were there in the study?
5... Describe **three** key characteristics of the participants.
6... Identify **three** features of the procedures designed to increase a participant's anxiety.
7... Identify **eight** key aspects of the procedures.
8... Identify and explain **six** findings from this study.
9... For each finding, state a conclusion that could be drawn from this. Try to make each conclusion different.
10...Outline **three** explanations that Milgram provided for his results.
11...What evidence leads you to conclude that this study supports the view that people are surprisingly obedient?
12...What evidence leads you to conclude that this study supports the view that people resist obedience?

EXAM QUESTIONS

SECTION A

Summarise the aims **and** context of Milgram's (1963) research 'Behavioural study of obedience'. [12]

Outline the procedures of Milgram's (1963) research 'Behavioural study of obedience'. [12]

Describe the findings **and** conclusions of Milgram's (1963) research 'Behavioural study of obedience'. [12]

Notes *In Section A of the Unit 2 exam, you might be asked any of the above questions. Each question will be worth 12 marks. In order to gain the full 12 marks your answer should:*

▶ *Be accurate and well detailed.*

▶ *Display a depth and range of knowledge, though not necessarily in equal measure; this means that you can either cover a few points in considerable detail (i.e. depth) or cover a number of points in less detail (range).*

▶ *Be well structured and coherent.*

▶ *Have accurate grammar, punctuation and spelling.*

▶ *Be about 200–250 words in length; this is shorter than the answers for other 12-mark questions, but the emphasis is on accuracy.*

On this spread we are going to evaluate the core study by looking at issues related to its methodology and comparing the study to alternative evidence. Despite the significance of Milgram's research in social psychology, it has been the subject of a great deal of criticism. Some critics have focused on the questionable **ethics** of this study, others have questioned its **validity** as a representation of real-life obedience. Philip Zimbardo claims that the reason Milgram's research has attracted so much hostile criticism was because of *what* he discovered about human nature rather than the way he discovered it.

EVALUATING THE METHODOLOGY

See Chapter 6 (Applied Research Methods) for an explanation of these concepts.

Method

Milgram conducted his research in a lab environment. *What advantages and disadvantages does this offer?*

Experimental validity

Orne and Holland (1968) claim that this research lacks **experimental validity** as the participants did not believe the electric shocks were real. It simply wouldn't have made sense that someone in a learning experiment would receive fatal shocks. Therefore participant's simply behaved as they were expected to behave due to the **demand characteristics** of the study. In particular, because they were paid, they felt obliged to go along with the situation as they had entered a social contract.

On the other hand, Milgram (1974) later reported that 75% of the participants strongly believed they were giving electric shocks, 22.6% had some doubts, and 2.4% were certain the shocks were not real. *What do you conclude about the experimental validity of Milgram's study?*

Ecological validity

A further issue concerns the extent to which it is reasonable to generalise the findings of this study to the 'real' world. The study was conducted in a highly contrived, sterile situation. *Would people behave in the same way in everyday life? Provide evidence to support your views.*

In one way, this criticism is groundless because the fact that the study is in a lab is irrelevant. Milgram set out to test obedience to authority, and he could have done this in any situation where there is a clear authority figure that people think they ought to obey. On the other hand, you might argue that obedience to authority does not occur in real life in such overt ways, nor is it so extreme. *What do you conclude about the **ecological validity** of Milgram's study?*

There is other evidence that can be considered, such as the replication in different cultural settings. Smith and Bond (1998) reviewed studies in eight countries and found generally higher levels of obedience, including 92% in Holland. *What do you conclude about the ecological validity of Milgram's study?*

Sampling

Milgram selected his participants via a newspaper advertisement. *Why might this **volunteer sample** be a limitation?*

Although Milgram did select a sample that reflected a variety of backgrounds, all of his initial sample was male. *Why might that be a limitation? Why might men be more or less obedient?*

In fact, in subsequent experiments, Milgram and others found an identical rate of obedience in male and female groups (65%), although obedient women consistently reported more stress than men.

Ethical issues

Baumrind (1964) claimed that Milgram caused psychological damage to his participants that could not be justified. Milgram defended himself in several ways. First, he did not know, prior to the study, that such high levels of distress would be caused. Second, he did consider ending the study when he observed the participants' behaviour, but decided that there was no indication of injurious effects (Milgram, 1974). Third, 84% of the participants did say afterwards that they were glad to have participated. Finally, the potential damage to participants should be weighed against the importance of the findings. *Did Milgram expose his participants to unnecessary psychological harm?*

What about other ethical issues? For example, did participants have the **right to withdraw**? Do you think that Milgram could have found out what he did without deceiving his participants?

ALTERNATIVE EVIDENCE

Using real shocks

Sheridan and King (1972) found similarly high levels of obedience using real shocks. A small puppy was used as the 'victim' to whom real electric shocks of increasing severity were administered. Even though the puppy was in the same room and could be seen yelping as the shocks were given, 75% of participants delivered the maximum shock. Rather surprisingly, the women obeyed more than the men did. *What conclusions can you draw from this evidence in relation to Milgram's study?*

Replication

Burger (2009) conducted a partial replication of Milgram's study using a similar set-up to some of the later variations, but he did not allow the volunteers to carry on beyond 150 volts once they had shown their willingness to do so. He found that 70% of participants taking part were willing to push the 150 volts button knowing it would cause pain to another human. *Explain how these findings develop Milgram's findings.*

DO IT YOURSELF No. 5.9

When researchers propose new research, it must be approved by an **ethical committee**. Elect members of your class to serve as an ethical committee and nominate a person to play the role of Milgram, arguing why his research study should be allowed.

You could also conduct a class debate on the ethics of Milgram's research.

Read about other real life stories of obedience, such as the My Lai massacre or the 'Hoax most cruel' (search Google).

Field studies

Hofling *et al.* (1966) investigated obedience in a hospital setting. Nurses were telephoned by a 'Dr Smith', who asked that they give 20mg of a drug called *Astroten* to a patient. This order contravened hospital regulations in a number of ways – nurses were not supposed to take instructions over the telephone, nor from an unknown doctor, and the dosage was twice that advised on the bottle. Nevertheless, 21 out of 22 (95%) nurses did as requested. As in Milgram's study, when nurses were asked beforehand whether their colleagues would obey, they all said no nurse would. When the nurses involved in the study were interviewed afterwards, they said in their defence that they had obeyed because that's what doctors expect nurses to do.

This study shows that obedience does occur in real-life settings … or does it? Rank and Jacobson (1977) also asked nurses to carry out an irregular order. This time 16 out of 18 (89%) *refused*. The difference was that on this occasion the drug was familiar (*Valium*) and the nurses were allowed to consult with peers – a more realistic representation of actual hospital practices. *Explain how these findings support, contradict or develop Milgram's findings.*

Milgram's variations

Milgram (1974) conducted 18 variations of his original obedience study, systematically manipulating features of the situation to observe the effects on participants' obedience. For example, in the *experimenter absent* variation, the experimenter left the room after giving his instructions and gave subsequent orders over the phone. In this study, obedience levels fell to 21%. In the *presence of allies* variation, there were two further 'teachers' (confederates) who refused to carry on; obedience dropped to 10%. In the *proximity* study, the learner was in the same room as the teacher; obedience levels fell to 40%. *What conclusions can you draw from this evidence?*

Real life events

David Mandel (1998) has argued that Milgram's conclusions about the situational determinants of obedience are not borne out by real life events. He based this on historian Christopher Browning's detailed analysis of Reserve Police Battalion 101. In Poland in 1942, Major Wilhelm Trapp, commander of Reserve Police Battalion 101, received orders to carry out a mass killing of Jews in a small town. Trapp offered to assign men to other duties if they felt uneasy about the killing, but most nevertheless obeyed, despite the presence of factors that, according to Milgram, should increase defiance: the authority figure said they didn't have to obey; he was not present when they committed the murders; they were face-to-face with their victims; and there were some disobedient peers. Mandel has argued that Milgram provided an obedience alibi. *Does Milgram's research explain real-life obedience, or does it simply provide an alibi? Explain your answer.*

CAN YOU...? No.5.4

EXAM QUESTIONS

SECTION B

Evaluate the methodology of Milgram's (1963) research 'Behavioural study of obedience'. [12]

With reference to alternative evidence, critically assess Milgram's (1963) research 'Behavioural study of obedience'. [12]

Notes *In Section B of the Unit 2 exam, you might be asked either of the above questions. In order to gain the full 12 marks for each question, your answer should:*

▶ *Present clearly structured evaluation.*

▶ *Present a coherent elaboration of each point.*

▶ *Display a depth and range of analysis, though not necessarily in equal measure; this means that you can either cover a few points in considerable detail (i.e. depth) or cover a number of points in less detail (range).*

▶ *Be about 300–350 words in length (the focus is on a sufficient breadth of material, but also sufficient detail for each point made, i.e. depth and breadth).*

You may find it useful to look at the student answers at the end of other core studies to identify and avoid the typical mistakes that students make when answering Section B questions.

Example exam question with student answers

Examiner's comments on these answers can be found on page 176.

EXAMPLE OF QUESTION 1

Summarise the aims and context of Milgram's (1963) research 'Behavioural study of obedience'. [12]

Megan's answer

Obedience is when people do what they are told to do. Milgram wanted to do his research because millions of people died in the holocaust and because people thought that the Holocaust had happened because 'Germans were different'.

Tomas's answer

Obedience is a form of social influence where an individual acts in response to an order from another individual, usually an authority figure. Although 'obedience' has negative connotations, it can also be considered a virtue and is a necessary part of society e.g. if people did not obey speed limits on roads there would be a lot more accidents.

Adorno et al. (1950) believed that the Holocaust happened because the Germans had 'authoritarian' personalities (AP). AP are hostile to people they think are inferior to them, act like servants to those who they think are better than them and are intolerant to alternative ways of life. Adorno suggested those with AP are likely to have been brought up by disciplined, harsh parents and that as adults they displace unconscious hostility as prejudices against minority groups, hence the holocaust could happen. Many researchers believed that 'Germans are different'; they believed the German population consisted of many individuals who demonstrated the AP and that because of that it couldn't happen in other countries. The AP explanation suggests a dispositional explanation for obedience.

Adolf Eichmann explained his role in the Holocaust at his trial by claiming that when he was a high-ranking member of the Gestapo he 'obeyed orders without thinking, I just did as I was told'. Eichmann was found guilty and hanged in 1962.

Rahe, Mahan and Arthur (1970) Prediction of near-future health-change from subjects' preceding life changes

The first two core studies we studied were grouped together as examples of social psychology – an approach where behaviour and experience are understood in terms of our relationships with other people. We now turn to physiological psychology, an approach to understanding behaviour that emphasises bodily processes such as hormones and nerves. In Chapter 1, we considered the **biological approach** in general and, within that, a typical theory – Selye's **GAS model** of stress. We are now going to consider the relationship between stress and health again.

WHAT ARE LIFE CHANGES?

Life changes are those events – such as getting married, retiring or dealing with bereavement – that necessitate a major transition in some aspect of our life. Because they have such an impact on us, they are sometimes referred to as *critical* life changes to reflect this. There is, of course, considerable variation in the impact of these 'critical' life changes. What may be profoundly stressful for one person (such as the death of a spouse), may be a blessed relief for another. Likewise, something as minor as the death of a much-loved pet or changing schools, may be devastatingly stressful to some people. Although the term 'life change' suggests that something must happen in order to cause a person such stress, the same reaction can be found when something *doesn't* happen. For example, *not* being promoted, or *not* getting to university are extremely stressful life 'not-changes' for many people.

MEET THE RESEARCHERS

Dr Thomas Holmes (1919–1989), a medical doctor, allegedly became interested in the link between illness and stress when he noticed that he usually developed a cold when his mother-in-law came to stay. In the 1950s, Holmes conducted research with patients with tuberculosis (TB), linking stress with the onset of the illness, and valuing the **idiographic** approach insofar as he believed we need to understand each individual's story.

As a medical student, **Dr Richard Rahe** came to work with Dr Holmes. His subsequent career has focused on research into stress and coping, working largely for the US Navy. He currently consults with military and National Guard medical commands to improve recovery from stress for services personnel returning from Afghanistan and Iraq. In 1997, Rahe received the *Hans Selye Award* for making a significant contribution to our understanding of stress.

▲ Dr Richard Rahe (1936–).

CONTEXT AND AIMS

Hans Selye's research in the 1930s (see pages 4–5) suggested a causal link between the *psychological* state of stress and *physical* illness, creating the field of **psychosomatic** research. Dr Thomas Holmes was one of a number of researchers to investigate this link further. Working in a TB sanatorium, Holmes and co-worker Norman Hawkins observed that this infectious illness was more common among poor people. They suggested that it was not poverty *per se*, but the emotional effects of poverty, that increased vulnerability to the illness.

This was supported in a study by Hawkins *et al.* (1957) comparing TB patients with non-TB workers at the sanatorium (matched for age, sex, race, income). They found an increase in 'disturbing occurrences' in the two years prior to admission in TB patients, and noted that this was considerably more in the TB patients than the controls.

In the 1960s, this work was further developed by Dr Richard Rahe working with Dr Thomas Holmes. They recognised that a standard measurement tool was needed in order to be able to assess stress-related life changes. In order to develop such a measure, they analysed the case histories of more than 5000 patients, producing a list of 43 critical life events. They established the stressfulness of each event by asking 400 people (of different ages, gender, education, etc.) to score each event in terms of how much readjustment would be required by the average person. The participants were asked to provide a numerical figure for this readjustment, taking marriage as an arbitrary baseline value of 500. If an event would take longer to readjust

to than marriage, then they should give the event a larger score. Scores for all participants were totalled and averaged to produce *life change units* (LCUs) for each life event. Together, the 43 life events and associated LCUs were used to construct the *Schedule of Recent Experience* (SRE) (Rahe *et al.*, 1964) and later the *Social Readjustment Rating Scale* (SRRS, see facing page) (Holmes and Rahe, 1967).

The SRE/SRRS gave researchers a means of collecting a quantifiable score for 'stress', and thus enabled them to investigate the relationship between stress caused by change from an existing steady state (i.e. life changes) and illness.

However, ethical constraints mean it is unfair to expose individuals to specific life events just to see if they develop an illness. So researchers conducted *retrospective* studies: they assessed the LCU scores of participants who had been ill and compared them with the LCU scores of people who had not been ill (as in the study by Hawkins *et al.* above). However, there are problems with retrospective methods, such as individuals having to be able to recall information from their past that is possibly subject to memory distortions. There are also likely to be investigation effects – the perception of their illness by many participants may be affected by wanting 'to please' the researcher, making the process quite subjective.

A further issue with previous research is that it has involved groups of people who are already ill and in hospital. This means that the conclusions may not apply to the normal population.

Aims

Rahe *et al.* (1970) aimed to conduct a *prospective* study using a normal population to investigate if there is a relationship between life events/changes and illness. A prospective study is one where a group of participants is identified at the start of the study (in this case a normal population), and followed forward in time.

▲ The participants in this study were serving aboard US Navy cruisers. Rahe, Mahan and Arthur suggest that a ship presents a natural unit in which to conduct a study of the distribution of diseases because all the crew are exposed as a whole to common work stresses, climatic change and infectious agents. Illness among crew members is therefore likely to be due to constitutional vulnerabilities rather than environmental factors.

DO IT YOURSELF

No. 5.10

Don't forget to construct your own step-by-step guide to the procedures of this study. Number each step.

PROCEDURES

The study involved 2684 men who were naval and marine personnel serving aboard three US Navy cruisers: two were aircraft carriers involved in military operations off the coast of Vietnam, and the other aircraft carrier was based in the Mediterranean.

The mean age of participants across the three cruisers was 22.3 years, and participants came from a range of backgrounds in terms of education, rank and maritime experience. Of the initial sample, 10% of were 'lost' as a result of men being transferred off the ships.

Participants were required to fill in the military version of the SRE. This is a pen and paper self-administered questionnaire documenting significant changes in a person's life relating to: personal, family, community, social, religious, economic, occupational, residential and health experiences. Each sailor completed the SRE every six months over a period of two years prior to a six to eight-month tour of duty at sea.

Each life change on the SRE was assigned a *life change unit* LCU. This value reflects the severity and adjustment needed for that particular event, and was formulated by a sample of US civilians (as described on the facing page). This process of assigning values was repeated with a number of different samples to ensure the reliability of the LCUs.

As each ship returned from the overseas assignments, a research physician went aboard and reviewed all of the sailors' health records. Each ship had a medical facility where records were kept of even the most minor health changes reported by crew members, thus enhancing reliability. Sick room visits that were thought to be motivated by a desire to be excused from work were excluded from the final analysis.

Neither the participants nor the medical departments on the ships were aware of the research aims of this project, i.e. they were not aware that the shipboard illness record would be used to make a link with the SRE questionnaire results.

DO IT YOURSELF

No. 5.11

Do your own investigation into the relationship between stress and illness.

1. You need a method to assess stress. There are many variations of the SRRS available on the internet. Use the scale above with adults, or try a youth version, such as the one at: www.thekentcenter.org/ stressscale.htm. You could use Rahe's revised SRE (see, for example, www.mindtools.com/stress/ps/ScheduleofRecentExperience.htm), or you could construct your own.
2. You then need to consider how you will measure the covariable 'illness'. For example, you might note how many absences a student has over a period of one month (excluding absence for reasons other than illness).
3. You could plot your results in a scattergraph, or use the Excel method (see page 148) to calculate the correlation coefficient.

The Social Readjustment Rating Scale

The SRE used in this study was similar to the SRRS below, further adapted so that it was specifically relevant to military experiences, such as including a life event for being selected for a promotion.

Rank	Life event	LCU
1	Death of a spouse	100
2	Divorce	73
3	Marital separation	65
4	Jail term	63
5	Death of a close family member	63
6	Personal injury or illness	50
7	Marriage	53
8	Fired at work	47
9	Marital reconciliation	45
10	Retirement	45
11	Change in the health of a family member	44
12	Pregnancy	40
13	Sex difficulties	39
14	Gain new family member	39
15	Business readjustment	39
16	Change in financial state	38
17	Death of a close friend	37
18	Change to a different line of work	36
19	Change in number of arguments with spouse	35
20	Mortgage bigger than $10 000	31
21	Foreclosure on mortgage or loan	30
22	Change in responsibilities at work	29
23	Son or daughter leaving home	29
24	Trouble with in-laws	29
25	Outstanding personal achievement	28
26	Wife begins or stops work	26
27	Begin or end school	26
28	Change in living conditions	25
29	Revision of personal habits	24
30	Trouble with boss	23
31	Change in work hours/conditions	20
32	Change in residence	20
33	Change in schools	20
34	Change in recreation	19
35	Change in church activities	19
36	Change in social activities	18
37	Mortgage or loan smaller than $10 000	17
38	Change in sleeping habits	16
39	Change in number of family get-togethers	15
40	Change in eating habits	15
41	Holiday	13
42	Christmas	12
43	Minor violations of the law	11

FINDINGS

Relationship between TLCUs and illness

The relationship between the pre-cruise *total life change units* (TLCUs) and cruise period illness was examined. The covariables were (a) the two-year period prior to the cruise and (b) cruise-period illness. The correlation between these covariables produced no **significant** correlation. However, there was a significant **positive correlation** between (a) the six-month period prior to the cruise and (b) cruise-period illness. A **correlation coefficient** was calculated to be .118, which may sound a weak correlation, but given the number of participants involved was actually highly significant (there was a probability of less than 1% that this result could have occurred by chance – this is written as *p* (probability) <0.01). The relationship was strongest for Cruiser One and Cruiser Three.

Decile groups

Crew members were divided into 10 groups (deciles) according to the TLCUs. Decile 1 contained the 10% of the ship's crew with the lowest TLCU scores during the six-month period prior to the cruise, decile 2 contained the 10% of sailors with the next lowest TLCU scores, and so on. Table 1 (see right) shows the mean number of cruise-period illnesses for each decile group. The only significant difference between groups in terms of mean illness rate occurred between deciles 2 and 3, demarcating the low illness group.

Sailors that fell into the low TLCU groups (decile 1 and 2) represented a definite low illness group (see Table 2, right). Conversely, sailors with a high TLCU score (decile 9 and 10) represented a high illness group. There was a significant difference in mean scores between the low illness group and deciles 6–8, and between deciles 3–5 and the high illness group.

Regrouping the scores

The decile groups produced a rather uneven distribution. The range of TLCUs in deciles 1–6 was 1–194, whereas the range in deciles 7–10 was 195–1000. In order to consider the linearity of the scores, they were regrouped into ranges of 0–99, 100–199, 200–299, and so on. The final four divisions were grouped together because fewer than 3% of the men fell within this group. The **scattergraph** on the right shows a clear linear (i.e. straight line), positive correlation of this data.

> **DO IT YOURSELF**
>
> No. 5.12
>
> - Find a good way to represent graphically the data in the tables above, e.g. using a bar chart.
> - Convert the data in the scattergraph to a table of data.

www Original article

The full reference for this study is Rahe, R.H., Mahan, J.L. and Arthur, R.J. (1970). Prediction of near-future health-change from subjects' preceding life changes. *Journal of Psychosomatic Research*, *14*, 401–406. You can obtain a copy of this article by giving the full reference to your local library.

Other resources

On the internet you can access another piece of research using the SRE conducted by Ransom Arthur and his research team: Rubin, R.T., Gunderson, E.K.E. and Arthur, R.J. (1972). Life stress and illness patterns in the US Navy. *Psychosomatic Medicine, 34*, 533–547. See www.psychosomaticmedicine.org/cgi/reprint/34/6/533.pdf.

▼ **Table 1 Mean illness rates during the cruise period for each decile group**

Decile groups were determined by ordering the crew in terms of TLCUs and dividing them into 10 groups.

Decile group	Number of sailors	Mean illness rate for each decile group
1	258	1.434
2	268	1.377
3	266	1.583
4	258	1.543
5	273	1.498
6	260	1.685
7	269	1.651
8	274	1.693
9	277	2.083
10	261	2.049

▼ **Table 2 Mean illness rates for low and high decile groups**

Illness group	Decile group	Number of sailors	Mean illness rate for each decile group
Low	1–2	526	1.405
	3–5	797	1.784
	6–8	803	1.676
High	9–10	538	2.066

▼ **Scattergraph showing positive linear correlation between LCUs and mean illness scores.**

The crew members were regrouped so that the range of TLCU scores for each group was the same, i.e. 0–99 (plotted at the **median** for the group i.e. 44.5), 100–199, and so on. At the top, the scores 600–999 were grouped together at the median of 800 for the group.

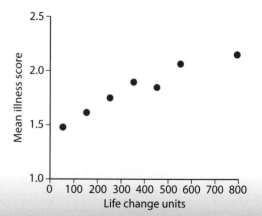

Both the other authors of this core study, Jack Mahan and Ransom Arthur, were also in the Navy. Captain Ransom J. Arthur retired from the Navy in 1974 and then served as Professor of Psychiatry at the University of California at Los Angeles (UCLA). He was a champion swimmer, and both he and Richard Rahe represented the Navy in swimming competitions.

◄ Stress can trigger psychological as well as physical illnesses. US singer Mariah Carey's well publicised bout of depression in 2001 was blamed on the chronic stress of a punishing work schedule.

CONCLUSIONS

The results of this prospective study support the notion of a linear relationship between participants' TLCU score and their subsequent illness rate.

It is important to note that the illnesses experienced by the men were generally minor in degree, and their pre-cruise life changes were often few and of low significance. This made it more difficult to detect the relationships between TLCUs and illness. In populations with greater illness variability, a stronger relationship might be demonstrated.

The fact that a significant relationship was detected under such conditions makes the findings more impressive, and they are supported by the fact of being consistent with other prospective/retrospective studies.

Cruiser Two experienced the most arduous cruise of the three ships. This may explain why the relationship between TLCUs and illness was not as strong for the Cruiser Two data, and suggested that, in stressful environments, life changes will have less effect on illness as their effects are overwhelmed by environmental factors.

Further analysis of the data suggested that the life-change information predicted illness better in the older participants (over 21 years) and the married enlisted men than in the group of young, single sailors.

CAN YOU...?

No. 5.5

1... Explain what is meant by life changes.

2... Explain the link between Selye's research and the study by Rahe, Mahan and Arthur.

3... This research was published in the *Journal of Psychosomatic Research*. Explain what 'psychosomatic' means.

4... Briefly outline the aims of this study.

5... Explain what LCUs are and how they were calculated.

6... How many participants were there in the study?

7... Describe **three** key characteristics of the participants.

8... Identify **six** key aspects of the procedures.

9... To what extent do you think the SRE was a suitable measure to use with the participants in this study?

10... What is a correlation coefficient?

11... Explain what the decile groups were.

12... Explain why it was necessary to regroup the data in order to demonstrate a linear correlation.

13... Identify **six** findings from this study.

14... For each finding, state a conclusion that could be drawn from this. Try to make each conclusion different.

15... What evidence leads you to conclude that these results were especially impressive?

16... Can you suggest why the correlation between life changes and illness might be stronger in the older, married sailors than in the younger, single group?

EXAM QUESTIONS

SECTION A

Summarise the aims **and** context of Rahe, Mahan and Arthur's (1970) research 'Prediction of near-future health-change from subjects' preceding life changes'. [12]

Outline the procedures of Rahe, Mahan and Arthur's (1970) research 'Prediction of near-future health-change from subjects' preceding life changes'. [12]

Describe the findings **and** conclusions of Rahe, Mahan and Arthur's (1970) research 'Prediction of near-future health-change from subjects' preceding life changes'. [12]

Notes *In Section A of the Unit 2 exam, you may be asked any of the questions above. Each question will be worth 12 marks. In order to gain the full 12 marks, your answer should:*

▶ *Be accurate and well detailed.*

▶ *Display a depth and range of knowledge, though not necessarily in equal measure; this means that you can either cover a few points in considerable detail (i.e. depth) or cover a number of points in less detail (range).*

▶ *Be well structured and coherent.*

▶ *Have accurate grammar, punctuation and spelling.*

▶ *Be about 200–250 words in length (this is fewer words than for other 12-mark questions but the emphasis is on accuracy).*

On this spread we are going to evaluate the core study by looking at issues related to its methodology, and comparing the study to alternative evidence. When it comes to evaluation, you can make up your own mind. We have presented some evidence and statements and invite you to use this to construct your own view of the core study.

EVALUATING THE METHODOLOGY

See Chapter 6 (Applied Research Methods) for an explanation of the methodological concepts.

Method

Rahe *et al.* analysed their data using a **correlation**. There are certain disadvantages of using such methods. *Explain the implications of using this methodology for the conclusions that can be drawn from the study.*

One problem with correlational research is that there may be **intervening variables**. It is possible that people with high levels of anxiety would be more likely to report negative life events and would also be more prone to illness. *Explain how this could be used to evaluate the study by Rahe* et al.

Reliability

Stress was measured using the SRE. *How was the* **reliability** *of this scale assessed?*

Participants had to recall events from the past two years. *How reliable would this data be?*

Validity

There are significant problems with the SRE as a method of assessing stress levels. For example, it doesn't distinguish between desirable and undesirable stressors, nor does it take account of the social/psychological resources that a person may have available. Also, a lot of the events noted on the scale are unusual; some participants might not actually experience many or even any of the events listed. A number of other scales have been developed for assessing stress (see right). *What do you conclude about the* **validity** *of the SRE as a method of assessing stress, especially in a group of sailors with a mean age of 22.3 years?*

There are also issues related to the measurement of illness. *Were illnesses being measured by Rahe* et al. *really stress-induced? Can you think of other reasons why the participants might have become ill?*

The validity of the findings can also be assessed by comparing the findings from this core study to other research (see right). *What do you conclude about the validity of the findings?*

Sampling

Rahe *et al.*'s sample consisted of 2664 males from the US Navy with an average age of 22.3 years. *How might these characteristics have influenced the overall results?*

Ethical issues

Issues such as lack of fully **informed consent**, **confidentiality**, **right to withdraw** and final **debriefing** might concern us. *To what extent to you think that Rahe* et al. *dealt appropriately with ethical issues?*

DO IT YOURSELF

No. 5.14

The participants in this study clearly knew they were involved in a project, because they filled in the SRE. However, their illness record was made available to the researchers probably without their direct consent because such a record would simply be available to senior naval personnel. To what extent does this count as fully informed consent? Discuss the ethics of this study with your class.

ALTERNATIVE EVIDENCE

Research using the SRE

Arthur conducted a further study using the SRE (Rubin *et al.*, 1972). This study examined patterns of illness in naval aviators flying combat missions from an aircraft carrier during a six-month deployment to Vietnam. They found that there was a predictive relationship between their SRE scores and subsequent illness in their sample. *Explain how these findings support, contradict or develop Rahe* et al.'s *findings.*

Research using the SRRS

Cohen *et al.* (1991, 1993) asked participants to complete the SRRS to assess their current level of stress in terms of LCUs. The participants were then given nasal drops. The **experimental group** were given nasal drops containing a virus that causes the common cold, whereas the control group had non-infectious nasal drops. Participants were quarantined and monitored for approximately seven days. The results of these studies showed that participants with higher reported levels of stress were more likely to be infected with the cold virus. *Explain how these findings support, contradict or develop Rahe* et al.'s *findings.*

Other methods of measuring stress

Research using the SRRS appears to suggest that any life-changing event has the potential to damage health because of the significant readjustment it entails. However, some critics now suggest that it is the *quality* of the event that is crucial, with undesired, unexpected and uncontrolled changes being the most harmful.

Daily hassles Lazarus (1990) further suggested that as major life changes are relatively rare in the lives of most people, it is the minor daily stressors (i.e. hassles) of life that are the more significant source of stress for most people. For example, DeLongis *et al.* (1988) studied stress in 75 married couples. They gave the participants a life events questionnaire and a hassles and uplifts scale. They found no relationship between life events and health, but did find a significant positive correlation of +.59 between hassles and next-day health problems such as flu, sore throats, headaches and backaches. *Explain how these findings support, contradict or develop Rahe* et al.'s *findings.*

Acknowledging social resources Moos and Swindle (1990) produced the LISRES (*Life Stressors and Social Resources Inventory*). They identified eight areas of ongoing life stressors: health, home, finance, work, partner, child, extended family, friends. The LISRES also includes an assessment of social resources available to the individual as these moderate the effect of stressors.

▲ In Chapter 1, we referred to the **immune system**. This consists of cells such as *white blood cells*, *natural killer (NK) cells* and *macrophages*, which attack invading *antigens* (i.e. bacteria, viruses, toxins and parasites). Some immune system cells are tuned in to particular antigens (such as a measles virus), and when that antigen enters the body they produce millions of specialised immune proteins called *antibodies* to eliminate the antigen.

Link between stress and the immune system

More recent research has sought to explain the link between stress and illness in terms of depressed functioning of the **immune system**. When individuals are stressed, the cells in the immune system are reduced, which decreases an individual's ability to fight infection. In one classic study, Kiecolt-Glaser *et al.* (1984) measured immune system activity in students taking important medical exams. Blood samples were taken one month before exams (low stress) and during the exam period itself (high stress). Immune system functioning was assessed by measuring 'natural killer' (NK) cell activity in the blood samples. NK cell activity was significantly reduced in the second blood sample taken during the exams compared with the sample taken one month before. This suggests that short-term, predictable stressors reduce immune system functioning, increasing vulnerability to illness and infection. *Explain how these findings support, contradict or develop Rahe* et al.'s *findings.*

There is also evidence that short-term stress may have a beneficial effect on the immune system (up-regulation). Evans *et al.* (1994) looked at the activity of one particular *antibody*, secretory IgA (sIgA), which coats the mucous surfaces of the mouth, lungs and stomach, and helps protect against infection. The researchers arranged for students to give talks to other students (mild but acute stress). These students showed an increase in sIgA, whereas levels of sIgA decreased during examination periods that stretched over several weeks. Evans *et al.* (1997) propose that stress appears to have two effects on the immune system: up-regulation for very short-term stress and down-regulation for long-term stress. *Explain how these findings support, contradict or develop Rahe* et al.'s *findings.*

CAN YOU...? No.5.6

EXAM QUESTIONS
SECTION B

Evaluate the methodology of Rahe, Mahan and Arthur's (1970) research 'Prediction of near-future health-change from subjects' preceding life changes'. [12]

With reference to alternative evidence, critically assess Rahe, Mahan and Arthur's (1970) research 'Prediction of near-future health-change from subjects' preceding life changes'. [12]

Notes *In Section B of the Unit 2 exam, you may be asked either of the questions above. In order to gain the full 12 marks for each question, your answer should:*

▸ *Present a clearly structured evaluation.*

▸ *Present a coherent elaboration of each point.*

▸ *Display a depth and range of analysis, though not necessarily in equal measure; this means that you can either cover a few points in considerable detail (i.e. depth) or cover a number of points in less detail (range).*

▸ *Be about 300–350 words in length (the focus is on a sufficient breadth of material but also sufficient detail for each point made, i.e. depth and breadth).*

You may find it useful to look at the student answers at the end of other core studies to identify and avoid the typical mistakes that students make when answering Section B questions.

Example exam question with student answers

Examiner's comments on these answers can be found on page 176.

EXAMPLE OF QUESTION 3

> **Describe the findings and conclusions of Rahe, Mahan and Arthur's (1970) research 'Prediction of near-future health-change from subjects' preceding life changes'.** [12]

Megan's answer

Rahe et al. found a significant positive correlation coefficient of .118 between the TLCUs for the six months prior to the cruise and illness. Rahe found a positive linear relationship between the life changes recorded by a participant over a 2 year period and his likelihood of developing major health change. Rahe found that the relationship between TLCUs for the 6 month period immediately prior to their 6–8 month deployment and illness was most apparent in the married enlisted men category, compared to non-married sailors. Rahe found that sailors that fell into the low TLCU groups (labelled decile 1 and 2) represented a definite low illness group, decile 1 had a mean illness of 1.434. Conversely sailors with a high TLCU score (labelled decile 9 and 10) represented a high illness group, decile 10 had a mean illness of 2.049. Rahe concluded that the results of this prospective study support the notion of a linear relationship between participants' TLCU score and illness rate. Rahe concluded that although the number of illnesses experienced were few and the life events measured by the SRE were generally rare amongst the sample, the findings were still impressive.

Tomas's answer

Rahe found a correlation between the life event scores and illness. Married sailors were likely to be more sick then unmarried ones. The sailors that were really stressed were likely to have loads of illnesses, whereas the sailors that weren't stressed had hardly any. Rahe concluded this was the same as other research.

Bennett-Levy and Marteau (1984) Fear of animals: what is prepared?

Our next core study is again an example of the physiological/**biological approach** in psychology. It focuses on the suggestion that a predisposition to acquire certain fears is inherited because it enhances an individual's survival and reproduction. This is an example of the **evolutionary approach** to understanding behaviour. The evolutionary approach offers explanations in terms of **genetic** inheritance and is thus part of the physiological/biological approach.

THE EVOLUTIONARY APPROACH

Darwin's theory of evolution by **natural selection** is based on three main assumptions. First, only a small proportion of each generation survives to reproduce. Second, offspring are not identical to their parents, and so each generation exhibits a degree of variation, and at least some of this variation is heritable. Third, some characteristics give the animal that possesses them an advantage over others in the 'survive and reproduce' stakes.

Some variations, or traits, are *naturally selected* because they are **adaptive**. A trait is adaptive if it increases an individual's chances of survival and reproduction. For example, if an animal is afraid of certain dangerous animals, such as poisonous snakes, this is likely to enhance survival and thus reproduction. If this fearfulness is inherited by the animal's offspring, the individual's genetic line is likely to thrive, whereas a genetic group without this trait is less likely to survive. The trait of fearfulness towards certain objects enables the animal to adapt to its environment and is naturally selected.

One important thing to understand is that none of this is conscious. Behaviour and traits are only naturally selected if (a) they are heritable and (b) they enhance survival and reproduction.

▲ Evolutionary psychologists suggest that such selection took place largely in the **environment of evolutionary adaptation** (EEA), a period of time when humans lived on the African plains. Early humans such as Homo ergaster, depicted here, lived nearly 2 million years ago in the eastern Rift Valley of Africa. The dangers they faced on a daily basis led to the evolution of our fear response.

CONTEXT AND AIMS

Evolutionary psychology suggests certain fears are adaptive behaviours that helped our distant ancestors to survive. If we are extremely fearful of an animal and we try to get away from it, we are unlikely to be hurt by it. The fears that were important to the survival of our ancestors may lie dormant in our brains.

Seligman (1971) proposed the concept of **biological preparedness** – an inherited predisposition to fear certain classes of animals, such as snakes. Three observations support this belief.

1. The distribution of animal phobias is non-random, i.e. certain animals, such as spiders, are often the object of fears, whereas others, such as flies, are not.
2. Fears of these animals is not matched by traumatic experience, i.e. people may fear spiders despite there having been no actual contact to have triggered this fear.
3. Fears often appear very early in life, reaching a peak at around the age of four years old.

The concept of biological preparedness is further supported by research with wild- and lab-reared monkeys. Mineka *et al.* (1980) found that wild-reared monkeys showed considerable fear of real, model and toy snakes, whereas lab-reared monkeys showed only a mild response to the snakes. This could be explained in terms of the direct experiences that wild monkeys might have had that created a fear response (**operant conditioning** or **observational learning**).

However Bennett-Levy and Marteau noted that the lab monkeys *did* demonstrate a fear response when the 'snake' showed a significant amount of movement. Therefore they suggested that monkeys (and humans) may not have a 'prepared template' to fear snakes *per se*, but they may be prepared to fear 'snake-like movements'.

Hinde (1974) also suggested that certain other characteristics evoke a fear response, namely novelty and strangeness. Hinde further suggested that a large discrepancy between a stimulus (such as a snake) and the organism's model of the world is the basis for this response.

This was supported by Bennett-Levy and Marteau's experience of treating patients with phobias. They found that patients' descriptions of what they feared about animals invariably focused on what the animals looked and felt like.

Aims

Seligman's concept of biological preparedness offered no suggestion about the mechanism by which such preparedness would operate. Bennett-Levy and Marteau aimed to investigate the underlying mechanism – human beings are 'biologically prepared' to fear certain stimulus configurations in animals, such as rapid or abrupt movement and discrepancies from the human form. They predicted that the perceptual characteristics of small, harmless animals should be related to the distribution of ratings of fear and avoidance of these animals.

PROCEDURES

Two questionnaires were handed out to 113 participants who were attending a British health centre. The questionnaires were distributed in a random order.

- Group 1, which completed questionnaire 1, comprised 34 females and 30 males. The **mean** age of group 1 was 35.5 years, **SD** = 16.9.
- Group 2, which completed questionnaire 2, comprised 25 females and 24 males. The mean age of group 2 was 35.1 years, SD = 16.4.

The questionnaires concerned 29 small harmless animals and insects. The reason for studying 'harmless' animals was because, it was argued, the same perceptual characteristics that create fear in harmful animals should create fear in harmless animals even though they are of no biological significance to the survival of humans.

In the case of animals that might have been considered to be harmful (e.g. grass snakes or jellyfish) participants were asked to rate them as harmless in order that harmfulness was not a factor in the ratings made.

Questionnaire 1 This was designed to measure self-reported fear and avoidance of the animals and insects. Participants rated the animals on two scales.

1. **Fear scale** Participants were asked to rate their fear of the animal on a three-point scale.
2. **Nearness scale** Participants rated their avoidance by completing a five-point scale of nearness. Participants were instructed that '*as some animals and insects are difficult to pick up in the wild, imagine that they have been injured in some way. For instance, the birds have a broken wing, or the squirrel a broken foot, etc.*'.

Questionnaire 2 This was designed to measure self-reported ratings of the same 29 animals and insects as used in questionnaire 1 but specifically along four perceptual dimensions. The following instructions were given: '*We would like you to consider how UGLY, SLIMY and SPEEDY the animals are, and how SUDDENLY they appear to MOVE*'. A three-point scale was used.

Questionnaire 1 and 2 combined

- **Fear** is rated on a three-point scale, where 1 = not afraid, 2 = quite afraid, 3 = very afraid.
- **Nearness** is rated on a five-point scale, where 1 = enjoy picking it up, 2 = would pick it up, but unpleasant, 3 = touch it or go within 15cm, 4 = stand 30–180cm away, 5 = move further than 180cm away.
- **Ugly, slimy, speedy and moves suddenly** are rated on a three-point scale, where 1 = not, 2 = quite, 3 = very.

	Questionnaire 1		Questionnaire 2			
	Fear	Nearness	Ugly	Slimy	Speedy	Moves suddenly
Ant						
Baby chimpanzee						
Baby seal						
Beetle						
Blackbird						
Butterfly						
Cat						
Caterpillar						
Cockroach						
Crow						
Frog						
Grass snake						
Grasshopper						
Hamster						
Jellyfish						
Ladybird						
Lamb						
Lizard						
Moth						
Mouse						
Rabbit						
Rat						
Robin						
Slug						
Spaniel (dog)						
Spider						
Squirrel						
Tortoise						
Worm						

MEET THE RESEARCHERS

James Bennett-Levy recently took up the post of Associate Professor at the Northern Rivers University Department of Rural Health, Sydney University, Australia. Prior to that, he worked as a consultant clinical psychologist with the Oxford Cognitive Therapy Centre, specialising in cognitive behavioural therapy.

Theresa Marteau trained and worked as a clinical psychologist, which is where she met James. She then moved into health psychology, researching emotional, cognitive and behavioural responses to health risk information. She is currently Professor of Health Psychology at King's College, London.

When asked what led them to conduct this study, they told us: '*Theresa had recently been treating someone with a phobia of insects. She and James had dinner together one evening under the silver ceiling, when the conversation turned to the topic of animal phobias. "I wonder why some insects and animals are more feared than others?", they mused. "Wouldn't it be interesting to find out?"*' (personal communication).

▲ James Bennett-Levy and Theresa Marteau.

Bennett-Levy and Marteau (1984) Fear of animals: what is prepared?

▼ Table 1 Mean ratings of animal characteristics

The table below shows mean scores for all 29 animals on the six dimensions rated by groups 1 and 2. Animals appear in order of their nearness rating.

	Fear	Nearness	Ugly	Slimy	Speedy	Moves suddenly
Rat	2.08	3.90	2.24	1.10	2.35	2.53
Cockroach	1.58	3.25	2.53	1.20	1.96	2.04
Jellyfish	1.81	2.95	2.00	2.47	1.39	1.51
Spider	1.64	2.88	2.43	1.06	2.25	2.52
Slug	1.19	2.84	2.63	2.90	1.04	1.02
Grass snake	1.55	2.78	1.80	1.78	2.12	2.42
Beetle	1.33	2.50	2.10	1.18	1.55	1.57
Lizard	1.25	2.45	1.88	1.54	2.53	2.78
Worm	1.16	2.39	2.18	2.45	1.14	1.20
Frog	1.17	2.28	1.88	2.24	1.80	2.31
Moth	1.25	2.27	1.53	1.09	2.04	2.32
Ant	1.14	2.22	1.86	1.04	2.04	2.14
Crow	1.22	2.14	1.67	1.02	2.02	2.08
Mouse	1.27	2.13	1.35	1.02	2.35	2.56
Grasshopper	1.16	2.06	1.76	1.12	2.48	2.77
Squirrel	1.11	2.03	1.02	1.02	2.44	2.71
Caterpillar	1.05	1.84	1.65	1.24	1.14	1.12
Baby Seal	1.03	1.63	1.06	1.42	1.50	1.48
Blackbird	1.08	1.59	1.10	1.00	2.04	2.20
Hamster	1.00	1.50	1.02	1.00	1.98	2.23
Baby Chimpanzee	1.09	1.48	1.33	1.00	1.63	1.73
Butterfly	1.00	1.33	1.06	1.02	2.08	2.36
Spaniel (dog)	1.08	1.31	1.08	1.02	2.06	1.84
Tortoise	1.00	1.31	1.41	1.08	1.08	1.06
Robin	1.00	1.31	1.02	1.00	2.10	2.29
Lamb	1.00	1.16	1.02	1.00	1.61	1.90
Cat	1.03	1.14	1.02	1.00	2.17	2.31
Ladybird	1.02	1.14	1.10	1.00	1.71	1.88
Rabbit	1.02	1.13	1.04	1.00	2.35	2.65

▼ Table 2 Correlation matrix of animal characteristics, fear and nearness measures

	Ugly	Slimy	Speedy	Moves suddenly	Fear	Nearness
Ugly		.75	−.20	−.16	.82	.87
Slimy	.75		−.29	−.21	.61	.77
Speedy	−.20	−.29		.95	.17	−.02
Moves suddenly	−.16	−.21	.95		.02	.05
Fear	.82	.61	.17	.02		.90
Nearness	.87	.77	−.02	.05	.90	

DO IT YOURSELF

No. 5.16

Table 1 contains a large amount of information. It may make things clearer if you identify the top three animals in each of the categories listed. You could also identify the bottom three animals in each of the categories.

FINDINGS

Table 1 shows the mean scores for all 29 animals on the six dimensions rated by groups 1 and 2.

Rats were feared considerably more than any other animal. Informal questioning suggested that it was because they were perceived as potentially harmful.

Sex differences

In the ratings for nearness, females were found to be less willing to approach or pick up 10 of the animals than males. These animals were (in descending order) jellyfish, cockroach, ant moth, crow, worm, beetle slug, mouse and spider.

Similar differences were found in the fear ratings. However, there were no notable sex differences in ratings of ugliness, sliminess, speediness and suddenness of movement.

The men in group 1 rated themselves as less fearful than the women, but were nevertheless apparently just as responsive to the animal characteristics. For example, there was an extremely close correlation in the nearness ratings of men and women (**correlation coefficient** (r) = +.96).

Correlation matrix

Table 2 shows the correlations between the different ratings. You can see that:
- Speediness and sudden movement are highly correlated (r = +.95).
- The correlation between nearness and sudden movement is +.05, but when the effect of ugliness is removed this rose to +.61.
- Similarly partial correlations were determined for fear and speediness and nearness and speediness, which were significant.

Thus, as expected, all four ratings of perceptual characteristics (ugliness, sliminess, speediness and suddenness) are related to both fear and nearness.

*A number of findings in this study are reported as correlation coefficients. These are explained fully on page 148. A correlation of +.36 or more is significant at the 5% level (i.e. there is a 5% chance that this result is in fact due to chance). A correlation of −.36 is also significant, the minus sign indicates that as one variable increases, the other decreases (i.e. **negative correlation**).*

CONCLUSIONS

'The results of this study suggest that the perceptual characteristics of animals are of some importance in determining their positive or negative appraisal by humans.'

Animals that have the four perceptual characteristics (ugly, slimy, speedy or sudden-moving) are experienced as less approachable and more fear-provoking than other animals.

Despite the effort to remove the effect of anticipated harm by instructing participants to rate certain animals as harmless, this is obviously an important characteristic when it comes to rating the fearfulness and other perceptual characteristics of animals.

Clinical phobias

Bennett-Levy and Marteau were interested in whether the **biological preparedness** explanation might be implicated in the development of clinical **phobias**. The term 'clinical phobia' refers to an excessive fear that has been diagnosed by a health professional as a mental disorder. The key characteristic that distinguishes a clinical phobia from an everyday phobia is the degree to which an individual's functioning is impaired by the disorder.

However, it is not possible to study clinical patients because the fact that they have developed an excessive fear of certain animals would distort their responses. The alternative is to study fear ratings from a normal population (as in this study), and relate this to the occurrence of clinical phobias. There should be a strong correspondence between the two.

The findings of this study might be applied to help patients with clinical phobias by dealing with their fear of key perceptual characteristics, such as sliminess.

Biological preparedness

There are two possible mechanisms by which fears are inherited.

1. **The discrepancy principle** (Hinde, 1974) can explain the strong relationship between ratings of ugliness and sliminess, and the fear and nearness ratings. Participants said that their judgment of ugliness was based on sliminess, hairiness, the colour of the animal, the number of limbs and antennae, and the relation of its eyes to its head. All of these characteristics fit with the discrepancy principle that what is feared is the discrepancy from the human form.

2. **Aversive stimulus configurations** (Schneirla, 1965) were all significantly correlated with fear once the effects of other variables were removed. In addition, participants reported other tactile and auditory cues that contributed to the fearfulness of certain animals, such as the feel of a spider and the hissing of a snake. 'The results from the study indicated that humans are probably not prepared specifically to fear animals of biological significance to the species. Rather, the degree to which humans are prepared to approach or fear an animal depends not only on its objective harmfulness, but also on the presence of certain fear-evoking perceptual properties, and its discrepancy from the human form.'

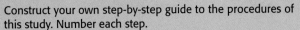

DO IT YOURSELF

No. 5.17

- Construct your own step-by-step guide to the procedures of this study. Number each step.
- Find a good way to represent the data in the tables opposite graphically, e.g. using a bar chart or a **scattergraph**.
- Write an abstract for this study, as you have done before. This abstract should contain brief details of the context and aims, procedures, findings and conclusions of this study – all in about 200 words.

CAN YOU...?
No. 5.7

1... Explain the concept of biological preparedness.
2... Explain in what way fear of certain animals would be adaptive.
3... Identify **one** study that was conducted prior to Bennett-Levy and Marteau's study and explain the conclusions that can be drawn from this study.
4... Briefly outline the aims of Bennett-Levy and Marteau's study.
5... How many participants were there in the study?
6... Why were participants instructed to rate certain animals/insects as harmless?
7... Group 1 were described as 'mean age 35.5, SD = 16.9'. Explain what this means
8... Describe **three** key characteristics of the participants.
9... Explain the difference between groups 1 and 2 in this study.
10...Describe the questionnaire that each group was asked to complete.
11...Explain the difference between the two questionnaires that were used.
12...Identify **six** findings from this study.
13...State a conclusion that could be drawn from each finding. Try to make each conclusion different.
14...Outline the **two** mechanisms that can explain how fear is inherited.
15...Provide some evidence from this study that supports each of these mechanisms.

EXAM QUESTIONS

SECTION A

Summarise the aims **and** context of Bennett-Levy and Marteau's (1984) research 'Fear of animals: what is prepared?'. [12]

Outline the procedures of Bennett-Levy and Marteau's (1984) research 'Fear of animals: what is prepared?'. [12]

Describe the findings **and** conclusions of Bennett-Levy and Marteau's (1984) research 'Fear of animals: what is prepared?'. [12]

Notes In Section A of the Unit 2 exam, you may be asked any of the questions above. Each question will be worth 12 marks. In order to gain the full 12 marks, your answer should:

▶ *Be accurate and well detailed.*

▶ *Display a depth and range of knowledge, though not necessarily in equal measure; this means that you can either cover a few points in considerable detail (i.e. depth) or cover a number of points in less detail (range).*

▶ *Be well structured and coherent.*

▶ *Have accurate grammar, punctuation and spelling.*

▶ *Be about 200–250 words in length, which is fewer words than for other 12-mark questions but the emphasis is on accuracy.*

Bennett-Levy and Marteau (1984) Fear of animals: what is prepared?

On this spread we are going to evaluate the core study by looking at issues related to its methodology, and comparing the study to alternative evidence. When it comes to evaluation, you can make up your own mind. We have presented some evidence and statements, and invite you to use this to construct your own view of the core study.

EVALUATING THE METHODOLOGY

See Chapter 6 (Applied Research Methods) for an explanation of these concepts.

Method

Bennett-Levy and Marteau collected their data using **questionnaires**. *Explain at least **one** advantage and **one** disadvantage of using questionnaires in this research.*

Bennett-Levy and Marteau analysed their data using **mean** scores. *Explain **one** advantage and **one** disadvantage of using the mean scores in this research.*

Bennett-Levy and Marteau analysed their data using **correlations**. *Explain at least **one** advantage and **one** disadvantage of using a correlational analysis in this research.*

The participants who completed questionnaire 1 (fear and avoidance) were different from the participants who answered questionnaire 2 (ugly, slimy, speedy, sudden movement). *Why might this affect the results?*

Reliability

A questionnaire is **reliable** if the same results are obtained when the same person answers the questionnaire on two separate occasions. *Do you think the questionnaires used in this study would be reliable?*

Validity

Merckelbach *et al.* (1987) repeated Bennett-Levy and Marteau's research and found similar associations between fear and avoidance of an animal and its perceived characteristics. *Does this suggest that Bennett-Levy and Marteau's findings are reliable or valid? Explain your answer.*

Two measurements were used in this study – two questionnaires that assessed aspects of fear. In the case of both questionnaires, we might ask how realistic they are – is real fearfulness the same as *asking* people about how they would respond to a particular animal? One way to assess **validity** is to consider the extent to which these measures did measure what they intended to measure. *To what extent do you think the measurements were valid?*

Sampling

There were 113 participants in the **sample**, 59 females and 55 males. The genders were also fairly evenly split over the two questionnaires. *Why is this important?*

The **target population** studied was British. *How might this affect the extent to which the findings can be generalised to a wider population?*

Ethical issues

Are there any ethical issues evident in this research?

DO IT YOURSELF

No. 5.18

You might construct a more realistic scale by including photographs of the animals on the scale. To assess whether this would make a difference, give some people the original scale and give other people the scale with photographs. Alternatively, you could go to a zoo and ask people who are viewing certain animals.

ALTERNATIVE EVIDENCE

The essence of the concept of biological preparedness is that an animal will have an innate readiness to learn to associate certain classes of stimuli with an avoidance response. These stimuli would be things that would have been dangerous to our distant ancestors in the **environment of evolutionary adaptation (EEA)**, and thus avoidance would be adaptive. Such stimuli are described as *'fear-relevant'* (FR) stimuli, as distinct from *'fear-irrelevant'* (FI) stimuli. A spider is an FR stimulus, whereas a flower is an FI one.

Biological preparedness

A number of predictions arise from the concept of **biological preparedness**:

- An avoidance/fear response should be learned more rapidly to stimuli that would have been dangerous in the EEA (FR stimuli).
- Such fears, once acquired, would be more difficult to 'unlearn' (i.e. it would be difficult to extinguish the **conditioned response**).
- We should observe **'contrapreparedness'** – a *decreased* likelihood that associations will be learned between FR stimuli and responses that would not be adaptive.

Rapid learning Seligman (1971) found that two to four small electric shocks were enough to induce a **phobia** to pictures of spiders or snakes, although a larger series of shocks was required to induce the same sort of phobic response to pictures of flowers. *Do these findings support, contradict or develop Bennett-Levy and Marteau's findings?*

Extinction Öhman (2000) noted that conditioned fear responses to stimuli such as houses and flowers became extinct as soon as the unconditioned aversive shock (a mild shock) was no longer paired with these stimuli. A fear response still persisted, however, with stimuli such as snakes and spiders. *Do these findings support, contradict or develop Bennett-Levy and Marteau's findings?*

Contrapreparedness McNally and Reiss (1982) found that certain associations with FR stimuli are less likely to be learned. The researchers sought to condition human participants to associate FR stimuli (a picture of a snake) or FI stimuli (a picture of a flower) with a safety signal (the absence of a shock). If conditioning was successful, the person, when viewing a picture, should experience a sense of relief because they have learned to associate the picture with no shock. The results provided marginal support for the notion of contrapreparedness. *Do these findings support, contradict or develop Bennett-Levy and Marteau's findings?*

In Chapter 2 (page 20), we told Seligman's story about acquiring an aversion to sauce béarnaise but not to the music of Wagner when he became very sick after eating the one and listening to the other. This experience led him to suggest that we are biologically prepared to learn connections to certain stimuli more readily than others.

Observational learning in animals

Cook and Mineka (1990) conducted a series of studies where observer monkeys watched videotapes of other monkeys behaving fearfully with either a toy snake or toy crocodile. The result was that the observer monkeys later displayed a fearful response to these stimuli, whereas the same learning tended not to occur if observer monkeys were shown identical videos but this time with artificial flowers or toy rabbits.

Mineka and Cook (1986) also demonstrated that observation could 'inoculate' a monkey against acquisition of a fear. If a monkey was first exposed to other monkeys behaving non-fearfully with a snake, they did not then acquire a fear when shown the videos. *Do these findings support, contradict or develop Bennett-Levy and Marteau's findings?*

Studies with humans

In general, FR conditioning has been less successful with human participants, although some researchers have had positive results. For example, Regan and Howard (1995) conditioned human participants by showing slides of FR or FI stimuli followed by a white noise (the NS). Later, when the noise was played the humans were more likely to demonstrate a fear response when the white noise had been associated with a fear-relevant stimulus (e.g. small animal) than a fear-irrelevant stimulus (e.g. landscape). *Do these findings support, contradict or develop Bennett-Levy and Marteau's findings?*

Expectancy bias

A review of lab studies by McNally (1987) concluded that although there was firm evidence for enhanced resistance to extinction of fear responses conditioned by FR stimuli, evidence for rapid acquisition was, at best, equivocal.

This led Davey (1995) to propose a simpler explanation – *expectancy biases*. An expectancy bias is an expectation that FR stimuli (such as dangerous situations, past experience of unpleasantness) will produce negative consequences in the future. There is no need to invoke past evolutionary history. This explains certain inconsistent data, such as some modern phobias (e.g. a phobia of hypodermic needles). *Do these findings support, contradict or develop Bennett-Levy and Marteau's findings?*

EXAM QUESTIONS
SECTION B

Evaluate the methodology of Bennett-Levy and Marteau's (1984) research 'Fear of animals: what is prepared?'. [12]

With reference to alternative evidence, critically assess Bennett-Levy and Marteau's (1984) research 'Fear of animals: what is prepared?'. [12]

Notes In Section B of the Unit 2 exam, you may be asked either of the questions above. In order to gain the full 12 marks for each question, your answer should:

▶ *Present clearly structured evaluation.*

▶ *Present a coherent elaboration of each point.*

▶ *Display a depth and range of analysis, though not necessarily in equal measure; this means that you can either cover a few points in considerable detail (i.e. depth) or cover a number of points in less detail (range).*

▶ *Be about 300–350 words in length (the focus is on a sufficient breadth of material, but also on sufficient detail for each point made, i.e. depth and breadth).*

Example exam question with student answers

Examiner's comments on these answers can be found on page 176.

EXAMPLE OF QUESTION 4

> **Evaluate the methodology of Bennett-Levy and Marteau's (1984) research 'Fear of animals: what is prepared?'.** [12]

Megan's answer

Bennett-Levy and Marteau used a questionnaire to collect data. The advantage of this is you can collect data easily from lots of people, and the disadvantage is that people may not tell you what they really think. They may lie to seem more socially accepting.

Another issue is whether people would have been psychologically harmed by doing this questionnaire because they had to think about things that scared them.

Finally we could ask whether this study is valid – other studies such as Merkelbach's, suggest it is.

Tomas's answer

Bennet-Levy and Marteau (BL&M) collected their data using questionnaires. An advantage of questionnaires is that it allows lots of information to be collected from many participants (Ps) in a comparatively short time. A disadvantage is that Ps may not tell the truth about their fears and avoidance of animals. BL&M analysed their data using correlations. An advantage of using correlations is that it tells us how strong the relationship is between fear or avoidance and the perceptual characteristics of the animal. A disadvantage is that we cannot prove that the perceptual characteristics caused the fear or avoidance of the animal.

BL&M asked Ps in questionnaire 2 to rate the 'sliminess' and the 'ugliness' of the 29 animals. These terms have negative connotations and may influence how the Ps respond to the questionnaire. Also, Ps were asked how near the animal they would be prepared to be, as a measure of avoidance. An advantage of asking Ps is that it avoids the potential ethical issue of exposing Ps to psychological harm by putting them close to animals which they are afraid of. A disadvantage is that the Ps are only being asked how they would behave, they may over or underestimate how close they would be willing to get to the animals.

The Ps who completed questionnaire 1 were different to the Ps who answered questionnaire 2. The results may be affected by intergroup differences even though BL&M randomly allocated the questionnaires to the Ps.

Loftus and Palmer (1974) Reconstruction of automobile destruction: an example of the interaction between language and memory

The core study by Loftus and Palmer is an example of the **cognitive approach** in psychology, which we studied in Chapter 4 of this book. The cognitive approach emphasises the role of thinking on our behaviour. Loftus and Palmer's research is concerned with the accuracy of **eyewitness testimony** (EWT), seeking to explain *why* it may be inaccurate by looking at the effect of **leading questions**.

CONTEXT AND AIMS

When eyewitnesses give evidence to a court in the UK they must take an oath or swear the following affirmation: '*I do solemnly, sincerely and truly declare and affirm that the evidence I shall give shall be the truth, the whole truth, and nothing but the truth*'. However, what happens if the eyewitness believes that they are telling the truth, but in reality that testimony is not 100% accurate? The witness is, after all, having to rely on their memory, and, if mistaken, is the witness really telling the truth?

The inaccuracy of EWT is a matter of major concern. Research in the USA has shown that inaccurate eyewitness memory is the main factor leading to false convictions. The *Innocence Project* claims that eyewitness misidentification is the single greatest cause of wrongful convictions in the USA, playing a role in more than 75% of convictions that were subsequently overturned through DNA testing (find out more at: www.innocenceproject.org/understand/Eyewitness-Misidentification.php).

One explanation offered for the inaccuracy of EWT is that questioning by the police or other officials after a crime may alter witnesses' perception of the events and thus affect what they subsequently recall. Some questions are more 'suggestive' than others. In legal terms, such questions are called *leading questions* – a question that '*either by its form or content, suggests to the witness what answer is desired or leads him to the desired answer*' (Loftus and Palmer, 1974, page 585).

Leading questions may affect eyewitnesses' ability to judge the speed of vehicles, because people are quite poor at judging the numerical details of traffic accidents, such as time, speed and distance. Marshall (1969) found that when Air Force personnel, who knew in advance that they would be asked to estimate the speed of a vehicle, observed a car travelling at 12mph, their estimates ranged from 10–50mph.

Such estimates may be influenced by certain variables, such as the phrasing of a question to elicit a speed judgment. Fillmore (1971) suggests that using the words 'smashed' and 'hit' implies differential rates of movement. Such words also lead the listener to assume different consequences for the impacts to which they are referring, with 'hit' being perceived as *gentler* than smashed.

DO IT YOURSELF

No. 5.19

Elizabeth Loftus investigated leading questions by asking people the question: '*Do you get headaches frequently?*' People who were asked this question reported an average of 2.2 headaches per week, whereas those who were asked 'Do you get headaches occasionally, and if so, how often?' reported an average of 0.7 headaches! The *way* the question was asked had a significant effect on the answer given. Try it out for yourself.

Aims

Loftus and Palmer's aim was to investigate the accuracy, or inaccuracy, of memory. In particular, they wished to investigate the effect of leading questions on the estimate of speed.

The aim of the first experiment was to see if the estimates given by participants about the speed of vehicles in a traffic accident would be influenced by the wording of the question asked. For example, participants who were asked about how fast the cars were travelling when they *hit* each other would give different speed estimates and have different expectations from participants asked the same question with the word '*smashed*' instead.

The second experiment investigated whether leading questions simply bias a person's response or actually alter the memory that is stored.

▲ Participants were shown film clips of different traffic accidents and asked to estimate the speed the cars had been travelling at before the accident. The form of the question varied, so that some participants were asked how fast the cars were travelling when they hit each other, whereas others were asked the same question using the word smashed, collided, bumped or contacted.

PROCEDURES

Experiment 1

There were 45 student participants in the study. They were shown seven film clips of different traffic accidents. The length of the film segments ranged from 5–30 seconds. The clips were originally made as part of a driver safety film.

After each clip, participants received a questionnaire in which they were asked to give an account of the accident they had just seen, and were also asked a series of specific questions about the accident. Among these questions was one 'critical' question which asked the participants: 'About how fast were the cars going when they ____ each other?' The word used in the blank space varied from group to group. In total there were five groups with nine participants in each. The questions were:

- About how fast were the cars going when they *hit* each other?
- About how fast were the cars going when they *smashed* each other?
- About how fast were the cars going when they *collided* with each other?
- About how fast were the cars going when they *bumped* into each other?
- About how fast were the cars going when they *contacted* with each other?

Participant estimates of speed in each group were recorded in miles per hour.

Experiment 2

This study involved a new set of 150 student participants.

Part 1 Participants were shown a film of a multiple car crash. The actual accident lasted less than four seconds. The participants were then asked a set of questions including the critical question about speed. The participants were divided into three groups, each of 50 participants.
- **Group 1** was asked: 'How fast were the cars going when they *smashed* into each other?'
- **Group 2** was asked: 'How fast were the cars going when they *hit* each other?'
- **Group 3** This was the **control group** and its members were not exposed to any question.

Part 2 One week later the participants were asked to return to the psychology lab and were asked further questions about the filmed accident. The critical question that all participants were asked was: 'Did you see any broken glass?' There was no broken glass in the film but, presumably, those who thought the car was travelling faster might expect there to have been broken glass.

This is a great video on YouTube about the accuracy of memory 'False memory and eyewitness testimony' at: www.youtube.com/watch?v=bfhIuaD183I&feature=PlayList&p=743ADEA06B23C9A7&index=0&playnext=1.

Original article
The full reference for this core study is Loftus, E.F. and Palmer, J.C. (1974). Reconstruction of automobile destruction: an example of the interaction between language and memory. *Journal of Verbal Learning and Verbal Behavior*, *13*, 585–589. You can read this article in full at: http://www.homepages.utoledo.edu/mcaruso/social/loftus.pdf.

Other resources
A classic book by Elizabeth Loftus is *Eyewitness Testimony* (1996, a revision of her 1979 book).

She has also written two books with Katherine Ketcham:
- *The Myth of Repressed Memory: False Memories and Allegations of Sexual Abuse* (1996)
- *Witness for the Defense: The Accused, the Eyewitness and the Expert Who Puts Memory on Trial* (1992).

Research by Elizabeth Loftus is discussed in a chapter of *Opening Skinner's Box: Great Psychological Experiments of the Twentieth Century* by Lauren Slater (2004), a book that contains the background to a number of key studies in psychology, although it has received some serious criticism (search Google).

"Do the words 'huff and puff' mean anything to you, Mr Wolf?"

www.cartoonstock.com

Loftus and Palmer (1974) Reconstruction of automobile destruction: an example of the interaction between language and memory

FINDINGS

Experiment 1

The mean speed estimate was calculated for each **experimental group**, as shown in the table and graph below. The group given the word 'smashed' estimated a higher speed than the other groups (40.8 mph). The group given the word 'contacted' estimated the lowest speed (31.8 mph).

▼ **Table 1 Speed estimates for different verbs in experiment 1**

Verb	Mean speed estimate (mph)
Smashed	40.8
Collided	39.3
Bumped	38.1
Hit	34.0
Contacted	31.8

▼ **Graph 1 Showing data in Table 1**

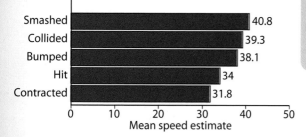

Experiment 2

Part 1 The findings of experiment 2 are shown in Table 2 on the right. Participants gave higher speed estimates in the 'smashed' condition, just like the participants in experiment 1.

Part 2 Participants returned a week later and answered further questions about the filmed accident. The findings are shown in the bar chart on the right. Participants in the 'smashed' condition were more than twice as likely to report seeing broken glass than those in the group given the word 'hit' or in the control condition.

- **'Smashed' condition:** 16 reported having seen broken glass; 34 reported not having seen broken glass.
- **'Hit' condition:** 7 reported having seen broken glass; 43 reported not having seen broken glass.
- **Control condition:** 6 reported having seen broken glass; 44 reported not having seen broken glass.

CONCLUSIONS

The findings indicate that the form of a question (in this case, changes in a single word) can markedly and systematically affect a witness's answer to that question.

Loftus and Palmer propose two explanations for this result.

1. **Response-bias factors** The different speed estimates occur because the critical word (e.g. 'smashed' or 'hit') influences or biases a person's response.
2. **The memory representation is altered** The critical word changes a person's memory so that their perception of the accident is affected. Some critical words would lead someone to have a perception of the accident having been more serious.

If the second conclusion is true, we would expect participants to 'remember' other details that are not true. Loftus and Palmer tested this in their second experiment. In the 'smashed' condition, the two pieces of information combine to form a memory of an accident that appears quite severe and therefore generates certain expectations, for example that there is likely to be broken glass.

The findings from experiment 2 suggest that the effect of leading questions is not the result of response-bias but because leading questions actually alter the memory a person has for the event.

These findings can be understood in relation to research on the effects of verbal labels on to-be-remembered forms, such as in the classic study by Carmichael *et al.* (1932) (see facing page). Verbal labels cause a shift in the way information is represented in memory in the direction of being more similar to the suggestion given by the verbal label.

▼ **Table 2 Speed estimates for different verbs in experiment 2**

Verb condition	Speed estimate (mph)			
	1–5	6–10	11–15	16–20
Smashed	0.09	0.27	0.41	0.62
Hit	0.06	0.09	0.25	0.50

▼ **Graph 2 Yes' and 'No' responses to the question about broken glass in experiment 2**

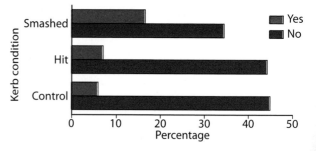

DO IT YOURSELF

No. 5.21

Construct your own step-by-step guide to the procedures of this study. Number each step.

Write an abstract for this study, as you have done before.

MEET THE RESEARCHERS

Elizabeth Loftus is Distinguished Professor at the University of California, Irvine. She is probably one of the best known living psychologists, famous for her extensive research on **eyewitness testimony** and, more recently, **false memory**. She is often called as an expert witness in court cases to testify about the unreliability of memory, such as in the Michael Jackson case, and she has received countless awards such as the 2001 William James Fellow Award from the American Psychological Society (for 'ingeniously and rigorously designed research studies … that yielded clear objective evidence on difficult and controversial questions').

John Palmer was a student studying psychology when he was given the chance to work with Elizabeth Loftus on this study. He has gone on to focus on visual attention and is a Research Professor at the University of Washington, USA.

▲ Elizabeth Loftus (1944–).

▲ John Palmer (1954–).

DO IT YOURSELF
No. 5.22

You could replicate the study by Carmichael *et al.* on the left. In order to do this, you will need to use an **independent groups design**, i.e. half of the participants will get the words on the left and half will get the words on the right. Later you will ask participants to redraw the original figure.

In order to decide whether participants were influenced by the word they were given, you will need to ask independent judges to judge the pictures. For example, for the first figure you would ask the judge to decide whether the picture produced is more like a curtain or a diamond. Then for each participant and each picture you can score whether they were or were not influenced by the verbal label. Finally, you should decide how to summarise this data in a table and/or graph.

STUDY BY CARMICHAEL *ET AL.* (1932)

This study by Carmichael *et al.* provided evidence for the effect of verbal labels. Participants were shown a set of drawings (central column) and then provided with a verbal description (either the column on the left or the one on the right). When participants were later asked to redraw the image, the resulting object was typically affected by the verbal label.website that she died at home surrounded by family and friends. There is a page of tributes from hundreds of people inspired by her.

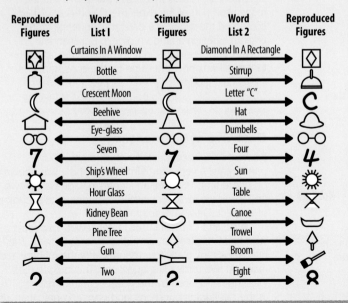

Reproduced Figures	Word List I	Stimulus Figures	Word List 2	Reproduced Figures
	Curtains In A Window		Diamond In A Rectangle	
	Bottle		Stirrup	
	Crescent Moon		Letter "C"	
	Beehive		Hat	
	Eye-glass		Dumbells	
	Seven		Four	
	Ship's Wheel		Sun	
	Hour Glass		Table	
	Kidney Bean		Canoe	
	Pine Tree		Trowel	
	Gun		Broom	
	Two		Eight	

CAN YOU...?
No. 5.9

1... Explain what is meant by eyewitness testimony.

2... Explain what is meant by leading questions and how these distort memory.

3... Identify **two** studies that were conducted prior to Loftus and Palmer's study. Explain the conclusions from each of these studies and how these relate to the study by Loftus and Palmer.

4... The study involves two separate experiments. Explain the aims of each of these experiments.

5... How many participants were there in each experiment?

6... Explain why the participants should not know the true aims of this study.

7... For each experiment, identify **three** key features of the procedures.

8... Why was it a good idea to ask a series of questions rather than just the critical question alone?

9... Why is it a good idea to have a control group in the second experiment?

10...Identify **six** findings from this study.

11... State a conclusion that could be drawn from each finding. Try to make each conclusion different.

12...What evidence leads you to conclude that leading questions affect memory rather than simply biasing a person's responses?

EXAM QUESTIONS

SECTION A

Summarise the aims **and** context of Loftus and Palmer's (1974) research 'Reconstruction of automobile destruction: an example of the interaction between language and memory'. [12]

Outline the procedures of Loftus and Palmer's (1974) research 'Reconstruction of automobile destruction: an example of the interaction between language and memory'. [12]

Describe the findings **and** conclusions of Loftus and Palmer's (1974) research 'Reconstruction of automobile destruction: an example of the interaction between language and memory'. [12]

Notes *In Section A of the Unit 2 exam, you could be asked any of the questions above. In order to gain the full 12 marks for each question, your answer should follow the guidelines given on page 101.*

CORE STUDY 5 continued

Loftus and Palmer (1974) Reconstruction of automobile destruction: an example of the interaction between language and memory

On this spread we are going to evaluate the core study by looking at issues related to its methodology, and comparing the study to alternative evidence. When it comes to evaluation, you can make up your own mind. We have presented some evidence and statements, and invite you to use this to construct your own view of the core study.

EVALUATING THE METHODOLOGY

See Chapter 6 (Applied Research Methods) for an explanation of these concepts.

Method

Loftus and Palmer conducted their research using **lab experiments**. *Outline **two** advantages of using this method in this research.*

In experiment 1, Loftus and Palmer calculated the mean estimated speeds for each of the different verbs. However, each verb contained only nine participants. *What limitation might there be in using the mean score in this way in Loftus and Palmer's research?*

Reliability

A number of other studies have produced similar findings (such as the study by Loftus and Zanni, see right). *In what way does this demonstrate that the findings from this study are reliable?*

Validity

Loftus and Palmer's research is frequently criticised for lacking **ecological validity**. How might the following aspects contribute to this criticism?

- The study took place in a lab.
- Participants observed film clips of car accidents rather than a real accident, where observers might feel scared or anxious.
- Participants were aware that they were in an experiment and may have suspected that they would be questioned about the film clips.

To what extent do you think the findings of this study can be generalised to everyday life?

Sampling

The participants in this study were US college students. *In what way is this group of participants unique? How would the unique characteristics of the **sample** in this study affect the conclusions drawn?*

Ethical issues

Loftus and Palmer did not gain fully **informed consent** from their participants. *In this study, is **deception** acceptable? Would Loftus and Palmer have produced the same findings if the participants had been fully informed?*

DO IT YOURSELF

No. 5.23

What do you conclude about the ecological validity of the study by Loftus and Palmer? Hold a 'mock trial'. One team has the task of arguing that this study has ecological validity and another team has to present the opposite case. You might do some extra research first. What does your class conclude?

ALTERNATIVE EVIDENCE

Other lab studies

Loftus and Zanni (1975) showed participants a film of a car accident. They then asked some participants 'Did you see *a* broken headlight?' and others 'Did you see *the* broken headlight?'. Of those asked about *a* broken headlight, 7% reported seeing one (although there wasn't one in the film), compared with 17% of people asked about *the* broken headlight. The use of 'a' and 'the' was a form of leading question. ***Does this research support, develop or contradict Loftus and Palmer's research?***

Loftus (1979) showed participants a series of pictures of a man stealing a red wallet from a woman's bag. Later, 98% identified the colour correctly. Furthermore, despite later being given an erroneous description of the wallet as brown, participants persisted in describing the wallet as red. ***Does this research support, develop or contradict Loftus and Palmer's research?***

Loftus *et al.* (1978) showed slides of events leading up to a car accident. One group was shown a red Datsun stopping at a junction with a 'STOP' sign. The other group was shown a 'YIELD' sign. Later, all participants were given a set of questions. Half of each group had the question 'Did another car pass the red Datsun while it was at the YIELD sign', and the other half of each group had a question saying 'STOP sign'. Finally, they were shown pairs of slides and had to identify which slides were in the original sequence. Of the participants who had had consistent questions (e.g. saw a stop sign and were then asked about a stop sign), 75% picked the correct slide, whereas this was picked by only 41% of those had had a misleading question (e.g. saw a stop sign but were then asked about a yield sign). ***Does this research support, develop or contradict Loftus and Palmer's research?***

Bekerian and Bowers (1983) replicated the stop sign/yield sign study by Loftus *et al.* (1978). In the recognition part of the experiment, Loftus *et al.* had presented the slides in a different sequence to the original order (in a random order). Bekerian and Bowers gave the slides in the original order, and found that recall was now the same for the consistent and misleading groups. ***What do you conclude from this study? Does this research support, develop or contradict Loftus and Palmer's research?***

Real-life eyewitnesses

Buckout (1980) conducted a study with 2000 participants. A very short film (13 seconds) was shown on prime-time TV. Later, an identity parade was shown on TV and viewers were invited to phone in their choice of suspect. Only 14% got it right!

Yuille and Cutshall (1986) interviewed 13 people who had witnessed an armed robbery in Canada. The interviews took place four months after the robbery and included two misleading questions. The interviewees were not influenced by the post-event information in the misleading questions, and gave accounts that were very similar to those in their initial witness statements. *What do you conclude from these studies? Does this research support, develop or contradict Loftus and Palmer's research?*

False memories

Loftus's research interest has moved from EWT to **false memories**. A false memory is a memory of something that did not happen but feels as if it were a true memory. Her research has focused on seeing whether this could be demonstrated experimentally. Loftus and Pickrell (1995) conducted a study referred to as 'lost in the mall'. They interviewed participants about childhood events, implanting a memory about having been lost in a shopping mall when younger (participants were told a close relative had reported the incident). About 20% of the participants came to believe in their false memories to such an extent that they still clung to them even after being debriefed. *In what way does this support the research on EWT?*

Braun *et al.* (2002) told 120 participants that they were going to evaluate advertising copy and answer questions about a trip to Disneyland. Group 1 read a generic Disneyland advertisement that mentioned no cartoon characters. Group 2 was given the same copy, but an adult-sized tall cardboard Bugs Bunny was propped in a corner of the interview room. Group 3 read a fake Disneyland advertisement featuring Bugs Bunny, and group 4 read both the fake advertisement *and* saw the cardboard Bugs Bunny. Of the people in group 2, 30% later said they remembered meeting or knew they had met Bugs Bunny when they'd visited Disneyland during their childhood, and 40% of the participants in group 4 reported the same thing (they couldn't have seen Bugs

Bunny at Disneyland because he isn't a Disney character). *Does this research support, develop or contradict Loftus and Palmer's research?*

EXAM QUESTIONS

SECTION B

Evaluate the methodology of Loftus and Palmer's (1974) research 'Reconstruction of automobile destruction: an example of the interaction between language and memory'. [12]

With reference to alternative evidence, critically assess Loftus and Palmer's (1974) research 'Reconstruction of automobile destruction: an example of the interaction between language and memory'. [12]

Notes *In Section B of the Unit 2 exam, you might be asked either of the questions above. In order to gain the full 12 marks for each question, your answer should follow the guidelines given on page 91.*

Example exam question with student answers

Examiner's comments on these answers can be found on page 177.

EXAMPLE OF QUESTION 5

Example of question 5 With reference to alternative evidence, critically assess Loftus and Palmer's (1974) research 'Reconstruction of automobile destruction'. **[12]**

Megan's answer

Loftus asked some people 'Did you see a broken headlight?' and then asked other people 'Did you see the broken headlight?'. More people asked about the broken headlight reported seeing one. But when some Canadian researchers asked real eyewitnesses they found that they were not affected by questions that were misleading. This research was better than Loftus and Palmer's because it was not done in a lab. People were asked about what they could remember from childhood trips to Disneyland after they had seen ads with Bugs Bunny on them. The researchers found that lots of them could remember meeting Bugs, which couldn't have happened because he isn't a Disney character.

Tomas's answer

Loftus (1979) showed the theft of a red purse from a bag and participants were later exposed to information containing errors, but 98% of participants correctly remembered the purse as red. This research seems to contradict Loftus and Palmer's (L&P) research as it found eyewitness recollection is not as easily corrupted as L&P's research would suggest, but is there more accuracy in this research because the colour of the purse is quite a basic feature, whereas speed is a more complex estimation?

Yuille and Cutshall (1986) interviewed 13 people who had witnessed a real-life armed robbery. The interviews took place 4 months after the robbery and included 2 misleading questions. Interviewees were not influenced by post-event information and gave accounts that were very similar to their initial witness statements. This research contradicts L&P as it suggests that EWT is not as inaccurate as L&P would suggest; this is especially important as Y&C's research uses real life witnesses rather than relying on research in a lab (like L&Ps).

Braun et al. (2002) told 120 participants they were going to evaluate Disneyland ads and answer questions about childhood trips to Disneyland. There were four groups – (1) ad with no cartoon characters, (2) same ad with cardboard Bugs Bunny in corner of room, (3) ad with Bugs Bunny, (4) ad and cardboard Bugs Bunny. Later, 30% of Group two and 40% of Group four said they remembered meeting Bugs Bunny when they'd visited Disneyland during their childhood. This would have been impossible as Bugs Bunny is a Warner Bros. character. This research develops L&P's because it demonstrates that the misinformation doesn't even need to be verbal for it to have an effect on our recall; false memories can also be established with more subtle non-verbal misinformation.

Gardner and Gardner (1969) Teaching sign language to a chimpanzee

The second **cognitive** psychology core study is concerned with language, the system of signs and symbols that humans use to communicate with each other. People try to communicate with animals in many different ways – using commands to direct their dogs, teaching parrots to utter interesting words and, famously, Dr Dolittle learned to talk to them. However, there is a more serious side to teaching human language to animals. If it can be shown that some animals are capable of using sign language then the clear division between animals and humans no longer exists. Over the past 60 years, a number of researchers have tried to teach human language to animals, including parrots, chimpanzees and gorillas, with the aim of trying to determine an answer. On another level, such projects have simply provided a fascinating window into the minds of other animals.

WHAT IS LANGUAGE?

All animals communicate and some animals have highly complex systems for this, such as the dance of the honey bee. But many argue that none of this is the same as 'language'. The US linguist Charles Hockett (1960) produced what he called the 'design features of language', 13 characteristics that distinguish human language from animal communication. Many of the features are found in animal communication, but only human language displays all of the features.

- **Interchangeability** The ability to send and receive messages.
- **Semanticity** The use of symbols to stand for or refer to objects, situations or events.
- **Displacement** Communication about things not currently present.
- **Productivity** The creation of an infinite variety of new messages.
- **Learning and transmission** The acquisition of language and its transference to the next generation.

You can read the full list plus see further details at: people. exeter.ac.uk/bosthaus/ Lecture/hockett1.htm.

CONTEXT AND AIMS

To what extent are humans qualitatively different from all other animals? This is a question that challenges scientific and religious beliefs. It has been suggested that one crucial difference that distinguishes humans from animals is that we have language. However, a number of researchers have tried to demonstrate that, in fact, some animals can acquire human language, which would challenge this distinction.

Noam Chomsky (1957) argued that humans have a special part of their brain (the *'language acquisition device'* or LAD) that means that we are biologically 'programmed' to acquire language. This explains why human cultures all over the world have language, no matter how primitive they are, and why children acquire it so rapidly and naturally. According to this view, other animals should not be able to acquire language.

Hayes and Hayes (1952) worked extensively with a chimpanzee called Vicki. They aimed to teach her to produce a vocal language, but in their six years of working with Vicki, she was only able to make four sounds that approximated to English words – *mama, papa, cup* and *up*.

Premack and Premack (1966) raised a chimpanzee, Sarah, and taught her to use different coloured and shaped chips to represent words. She placed these on a board to make sentences. First she learned the symbol for an object (*apple*), then to string symbols together to form sentences (first *Mary + apple*, next *Mary + give + apple*, and finally *Sarah + give + apple + Mary*). By the end, she had acquired 130 signs and could make sentences of up to eight units long. However, Sarah did not spontaneously ask questions, although she would practise sentences on her own.

Bryan (1963) reports that the vocal apparatus of the chimpanzee is very different from that of humans. Even though chimpanzees are capable of making many different sounds, vocalisation tends to occur in situations of high stress or excitement; when undisturbed, chimpanzees are normally silent. Gardner and Gardner therefore concluded that a vocal language was not appropriate for this species.

Yerkes (1943) does, however, note that laboratory chimpanzees are capable of spontaneously developing begging and similar behaviours, and that the use of their hands to help solve manipulatory, mechanical problems is a particular skill of the chimpanzee, which would make them suited to using sign language.

DO IT YOURSELF

No. 5.24

Teach your monkey classmate to sign. Work silently in pairs, one person (the teacher) teaches another classmate (the learner) a sentence in sign language by signing the individual letters. Find the hand signals on the internet, for example at: www. bsu.edu/aslclub/history.htm. The learner then presents the sentence they have learned to the rest of the class, who have to decode what the learner is signing.

Aims

Gardner and Gardner aimed to investigate if they could teach a chimpanzee to communicate using a human language, specifically *American Sign Language* (ASL). Their intention was to raise the chimpanzee in the same way that a child is raised, so that language would be acquired naturally.

They decided to use a chimpanzee because the species is highly intelligent, very sociable and known for its strong attachments to humans. Sociability is especially important because it is probably a prime motivator in the development of language. It is therefore best to use an animal interested in socialising.

There were several reasons for deciding to use a chimpanzee in this study. First of all, previous evidence suggested that chimpanzees would have difficulty using their vocal apparatus. Secondly, chimpanzees are good with their hands, which meant they should cope well with the mechanics of signing.

PROCEDURES

Washoe was a wild-caught female infant chimpanzee who was approximately 8–14 months old when she arrived at the Gardners' lab. Chimpanzees are completely dependent until the age of about two years.

During the first few months, the focus of the research was on building a daily routine and relationships between Washoe and her several human 'companions', who cared for her in shifts.

The Gardners reasoned that Washoe would only be likely to learn language if she interacted with others in the same way that a child does. Therefore, during her waking hours, Washoe was always with at least one of her companions. Her human companions were to be friends and playmates, and they were to introduce games and activities that would be likely to result in maximum interaction with Washoe. All the companions were able to use American Sign Language (ASL), and all communication was restricted to signing, 'chattering' with Washoe extensively as one does with an infant. ASL consists of a set of manual gestures that correspond to particular symbols but also words or concepts. The words can be arbitrary or iconic (image-based).

Training methods

The training methods used by Washoe's human companions included the following.

- **Imitation** of signs using the 'Do this' game, where the trainer says 'do this' and then the chimpanzee is meant to imitate the specified act for the reward of being tickled. Unfortunately, this didn't prove very successful with Washoe, who readily imitated gestures but not on command.
- **Prompting** Imitation was also used as a method of prompting. For example, sometimes Washoe would lapse into poor 'diction' – using a sign rather sloppily. Then she would be shown the correct sign and would imitate this.
- **Using signs** During games and everyday routines (feeding, dressing, bathing and so on), all objects and activities were named with the appropriate signs so that she would associate the signs with the objects/activities. In this way, Washoe came to have an *understanding* of a large vocabulary of signs.
- **Babbling** is an important stage in the development of human speech, when infants practise the elements of speech, so it was important for Washoe to 'babble' in sign language (i.e. manual babbling). This was encouraged by repeating the babble back, and linking it to actual signs in the same way that a human parent might say 'mummy' when the infant babbles 'mamama'.
- **Instrumental (operant) conditioning**, i.e. using rewards to increase the likelihood that a behaviour would be repeated. Tickling was the most effective reward to use with Washoe.
- **Shaping** Washoe was initially rewarded for producing a sign that was similar to the actual sign, but gradually she would only be rewarded for closer and closer approximations.
- **Direct tuition** A tutor would form her hands into the right gestures, and then she would repeat this, a much quicker method of acquiring new words.

Recording the observations

The core study article covers a 22-month period during which a record was kept of Washoe's language acquisition. Each new sign that Washoe acquired had to fulfil certain criteria before it would count as a new sign for Washoe:

- Three different observers had to report seeing Washoe use the sign spontaneously and appropriately (except if she was asked 'What do you want?' or similar).
- The sign had to be recorded every day over a 15-day period.

BIOGRAPHICAL NOTES ON WASHOE

▲ Washoe was a female chimpanzee similar to the one pictured here.

Washoe Pan Satyrus (*Pan satyrus* is an old taxonomic classification used for chimpanzees) was born in West Africa, around September 1965. She was wild-captured and brought to the USA to work for the US Air Force. Details of her military service are unknown.

She was then adopted by Drs Allen and Beatrix Gardner for their research. She was named Washoe after the county in Nevada where they lived. Washoe is a Native American word from the Washoe tribe meaning 'people'.

In 1970, at the age of five, she moved with Roger and Deborah Fouts to the University of Oklahoma and, in 1980, went with them to Central Washington University, where she was housed at the *Chimpanzee and Human Communication Institute* (CHCI), along with a group of other chimpanzees.

Washoe died in October 2007, aged about 42. It is reported on her website that she died at home surrounded by family and friends. There is a page of tributes from hundreds of people inspired by her.

American Sign Language (ASL or Ameslan)

ASL is the main sign language used in the USA and parts of Canada and Mexico. British Sign Language (BSL) is quite different from ASL, and the two sign languages are not mutually intelligible. In ASL, there are signs for each letter of the alphabet and each digit, and also signs for individual words. For example, to sign 'shoes' you form the symbol for the letter 'S' (see below) with both hands, and strike both closed hands together a few times. ASL also includes signs for abstract words. For example, the sign for 'please' is made by placing your flat right hand over the centre of your chest and moving it in a clockwise motion (from the observer's point of view) a few times. Such signs are arbitrary rather than image-based, a key feature of language.

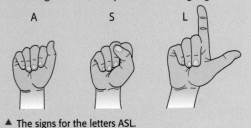

A   S   L

▲ The signs for the letters ASL.

- Find out about Washoe and her companions at: www. friendsofwashoe.org/.
- Other speaking apes include Koko (www.koko.org/friends/) and Kanzi (www.greatapetrust.org).
- There are lots of videos on YouTube of all of these apes, including Koko signing with ASL.

Original article

The full reference for the original article is Gardner, R.A. and Gardner, B.T. (1969). Teaching sign language to a chimpanzee. *Science*, *165*, 664–672. You can access the first page online (www.sciencemag.org/ cgi/pdf_extract/165/3894/664) or hand the reference in to your local library.

Other resources

The Gardners gave a full account of their research with Washoe and other chimpanzees in their book *Teaching Sign Language to Chimpanzees* (Gardner *et al.*, 1989).

Roger Fouts wrote about Washoe in his book *Next of Kin: My Conversations with Chimpanzees* (Fouts and Mills, 1997).

MEET THE RESEARCHERS

Beatrix (Trixie) Tugendhat Gardner was born in Austria in 1933, and at the age of six fled the Nazis, going first to Brazil and then to the USA, where she attended school and university. She completed her graduate studies at Oxford University, working with the famous **ethologist** Niko Tinbergen. When she returned to the USA, she went to Wellesley College in Massachusetts, where she met her husband Allen Gardner. Their marriage has been described as 'made in heaven' (Van Cantfort, 2002) because it brought together Trixie's ethological approach (observing animals in a natural habitat) with Allen's experimental approach and interest in cognitive psychology.

In 1963, the Gardners moved to the University of Nevada where, three years later, they first met up with Washoe and started the signing project. Trixie Gardner continued to work on this and similar projects at the University of Nevada until her sudden death while on a lecture tour in Italy at the age of 61.

In total, Allen and Trixie Gardner taught four chimpanzees to use sign language: Washoe, Moja, Tatu and Dar. The report presented here is only a small slice of the total work they did and gives a biased picture – this is one of the problems with the 'core study' approach. Such classic studies are often the beginning rather than the end of a line of research, as is the case for this core study.

R. Allen Gardner began his psychology studies at Northwestern University with Benton Underwood, one of the leaders in the post-war development of cognitive research on the acquisition and retention of verbal materials.

Allen Gardner continues his lifelong interest in chimpanzee communication and is Professor of Cognitive and Brain Sciences at the University of Reno in Nevada.

FINDINGS

At the end of the project, 30 words met the criteria set by Gardner and Gardner. The speed of acquisition is shown in the table below.

	Months of training		
	7	14	21
Number of signs Washoe could use	4	13	30

The 30 words are shown below in order of acquisition. The earliest signs were simple demands, the later ones were mainly the names of objects.

> *come-gimme, more, up, sweet, open, tickle, go, out, hurry, hear-listen, toothbrush, drink, hurt, sorry, funny, please, food-eat, flower, cover-blanket, you, napkin-bib, in, brush, hat, shoes, pants, clothes, cat, key, baby.*

Four other words, (*dog*, *smell*, *me* and *clean*) were judged to be stable, but had not met the specified criteria. Some examples of the specific ways that Washoe used words are as follows.

- *More* When asking to continue or repeat an activity, e.g. more tickling or a second helping of food.
- *Drink* When asking for water. To indicate pop, Washoe often combined *drink* with *sweet*.
- *Sorry* After biting someone, or when someone was hurt in another way (not necessarily by Washoe). Also used when told to apologise for mischief.
- *Baby* For dolls (both human and animals).
- *Please* When asking for an object or activity. Often combined with *go*, *out*, *drink*.

Washoe's language acquisition resembled the process that occurs in human children in three ways.

1. **Differentiating** Washoe came to use the sign *flower* to include reference to odours, for example when smelling cooking or opening a tobacco pouch. The Gardners taught Washoe a new sign for *smell* using passive shaping and prompting. Washoe learned to discriminate between the two signs, although she did continue occasionally to misuse *flower* in a 'smell' context.

2. **Transfer** Another aspect of learning language is learning to generalise from one particular thing to a general class of objects. Washoe showed this ability early on in being able to apply words like 'flower' to different kinds of flowers, and also to use the sign for 'dog' when she heard a dog barking, not just when she saw a dog.

3. **Combining signs** Like human children, once she had about eight signs in her repertoire, Washoe started to combine two or three signs to represent more complex meanings, such as *listen dog* (to refer to a barking dog). This may have happened because the researchers combined signs themselves, so in a sense Washoe was therefore imitating them. She did, however, produce her own novel combinations such as *open food drink* (open the fridge) and *go sweet* (to be carried to the raspberry bush). Most famously, she signed *baby in my drink* when a doll was in her cup.

CONCLUSIONS

The Gardners were wary of answering the question of whether Washoe had acquired language because they felt it was against the spirit of their research. They argued that the question can only be answered if there is a clear way to distinguish between one class of communicative behaviour that can be called language, and another class that cannot.

The study did show that chimpanzees can be taught more than a few words (in previous studies chimpanzees had learned only up to four words). The study also showed that sign language is an appropriate medium of communication for the chimpanzee. Furthermore, the study did suggest that more could be accomplished – Washoe's ability spontaneously to transfer the use of signs from specific things to general ones and her ability to combine two or three words both suggested that significantly more could be accomplished in further phases of this project.

One of the challenges was to develop a reliable way of demonstrating that Washoe was using language in a meaningful way. The Gardners suggested that one way to do this would be to place an object in a box with a window. A researcher, who didn't know what the object was, could ask Washoe to say what she sees. However, this would only work for items small enough to fit in a box. The Gardners did this successfully in later work.

DO IT YOURSELF

No. 5.25

- Construct your own step-by-step guide to the procedures of this study. Number each step.
- Find a good way to represent the data in the tables on the facing page graphically, such as a bar chart.
- Write an abstract for this study, as you have done before. This abstract should contain brief details of the context and aims, procedures, findings and conclusions of this study – all in about 200 words.

CAN YOU...? (No. 5.11)

1... Explain how (and if) we can distinguish between human language and the natural system of communication used by chimpanzees.

2... Identify **two** studies that were conducted prior to Gardner and Gardner's study, and explain the conclusions from each of these studies.

3... Briefly outline the aims of this study.

4... Describe **three** key characteristics of the participant in this case study.

5... Explain what ASL is.

6... Why do you think it was important, for this project, that ASL involves arbitrary as well as iconic symbols?

7... Outline the different methods used to teach Washoe to use ASL.

8... Explain the process of **instrumental learning** (**operant conditioning**, see page 17).

9... Suggest the reward that a child might get when they utter their first word.

10. Identify **six** findings from this study.

11... For each finding, state a conclusion that could be drawn from it. Try to make each conclusion different.

12... Why were there such strict criteria for the signs?

13... What do you think the main difficulty would be in recording sign language in a chimpanzee?

14... In what way did Washoe's language acquisition resemble the way human children acquire language?

15... What evidence is there to support the view that Washoe did learn to use language?

16... What evidence is there against this view?

EXAM QUESTIONS

SECTION A

Summarise the aims **and** context of Gardner and Gardner's (1969) research 'Teaching sign language to a chimpanzee'. [12]

Outline the procedures of Gardner and Gardner's (1969) research 'Teaching sign language to a chimpanzee'. [12]

Describe the findings **and** conclusions of Gardner and Gardner's (1969) research 'Teaching sign language to a chimpanzee'. [12]

Notes In Section A of the Unit 2 exam, you might be asked any of the questions above. Each question will be worth 12 marks. In order to gain the full 12 marks, your answer should:

▶ Be accurate and well detailed.

▶ Display a depth and range of knowledge, though not necessarily in equal measure; this means that you can either cover a few points in considerable detail (i.e. depth) or cover a number of points in less detail (range).

▶ Be well structured and coherent.

▶ Have accurate grammar, punctuation and spelling.

▶ Be about 200–250 words in length, which is fewer words than for other 12-mark questions but the emphasis is on accuracy.

Gardner and Gardner (1969) Teaching sign language to a chimpanzee

On this spread, we are going to evaluate the core study by looking at issues related to its methodology, and comparing the study to alternative evidence. When it comes to evaluation, you can make up your own mind. We have presented some evidence and statements, and invite you to use this to construct your own view of the core study.

EVALUATING THE METHODOLOGY

See Chapter 6 (Applied Research Methods) for an explanation of these concepts.

Method

This study was a **case study**. *What are the advantages and disadvantages of this research method in the context of this study?*

Reliability

The Gardners were aware that clear criteria needed to be established in order to verify Washoe's acquisition of vocabulary. In order to do this, three observers had to report seeing Washoe sign spontaneously and appropriately. *How else did they ensure **reliability**? In what way does this demonstrate that the findings from the study are reliable?*

Validity

The record of Washoe's achievements was made by the researchers who knew her well, which means that their expectations might have biased their recordings (**observer bias**). *To what extent do you think the findings of this study can be considered to be valid?*

The case of Clever Hans is described on page 140 – Hans's apparent mathematical abilities were shown to be no more than a response to his trainer's cues. *Was Washoe spontaneously producing language, or was she just responding to cues from her trainers?*

The Gardners and others have continued to conduct research with chimpanzees and other apes (see studies on the right). *To what extent can the results of this study be generalised to other chimpanzees?*

Ethical issues

Dawkins (1990) notes that morally questionable research using non-human animals might be acceptable if the goal is the relief of human suffering, but might not be acceptable if the goal is simply the satisfaction of intellectual curiosity. Was it ethical to use Washoe in this way?

Part of the process of teaching language to an animal is to enculturate them into the human world. *Is it ethical to teach human language to animals?*

Although Washoe was treated well by the Gardners and her other companions, Washoe was a 'wild-born' chimpanzee. *Is what we've learned from this research of such importance that it justifies her removal from her natural environment and her having to live her life in captivity, completing tasks that are not 'natural' to her species?*

DO IT YOURSELF

No. 5.26

How ethically acceptable is this study? Divide your class into groups with some groups preparing arguments for the benefits of this research and some groups preparing arguments for the costs.

ALTERNATIVE EVIDENCE

More research with Washoe and friends

It was claimed that Washoe was the first chimpanzee to learn to use human language. After the research reported in this core study, Washoe lived for another 38 years. When she died, her caretakers claimed that she had a vocabulary of 250 signs and provided many reports of everyday conversations with her.

The Gardners (Gardner *et al.*, 1989) went on to cross-foster (i.e. raise animals of another species) other chimpanzees. Moja, Tatu and Dar were raised in a similar way to Washoe, although there were some improvements in the method. First, the new chimpanzees were all newborns when they arrived. Second, their arrival was staggered so that they grew up like 'siblings', providing company and role models for each other, and making the environment more naturalistic. Third, they recognised that **operant conditioning** merely taught the chimps to make requests and therefore aimed to use language mainly as a means of dialogue, in the same way that human children enjoy language for its own sake and not just as a means of getting what they want. All three chimpanzees ultimately joined Washoe at the *Chimpanzee and Human Communication Institute* (CHCI).

Gardner (personal communication) argues that evolution is a continuous process, which means there would be no reason to believe that there is a sudden jump in abilities from one species to another. It would be reasonable to believe that our closest relatives have the capacity to develop language.

What do you conclude from this evidence? Does this evidence support, develop or contradict Gardner and Gardner's research?

Loulis

Washoe became pregnant several times, but none of her pregnancies was successful. In the 1970s, she was given an adoptive son, Loulis. The researchers at CHCI decided that none of the caretakers would sign when Loulis was there except to use the key seven signs *who, which, want, where, name, that*, and *sign*. This meant that Loulis would only be able to acquire language if it was taught to him by the other chimpanzees. Remarkably, Loulis nonetheless acquired more than 50 signs just by watching the other chimps, mirroring the manner in which human children acquire language. *What do you conclude from this evidence? How does this evidence support, develop or contradict Gardner and Gardner's research?*

Other apes
Nim Chimpsky

Another study on animal language was carried out by Terrace (1979) on a chimpanzee called Nim Chimpsky (named after the linguistics expert Noam Chomsky). Nim learnt 125 different signs and put them together in combinations. Terrace recorded more than 20 000 communications from Nim during a two-year period. When he looked at the data, he was disappointed to find a marked difference between Nim's communication and child language, and concluded that Nim was not using the equivalent of human language.

Kanzi and Mulika

Kanzi and his sister Mulika are two bonobo chimpanzees. They were taught to use language through the use of lexigrams.

▲ A lexigram panel is a visual symbol system that consists of geometric symbols (lexigrams) that stand for words. The chimpanzees' companions carried a lexigram panel everywhere so that the chimpanzees could indicate what they wished to say.

Kanzi first learned to use lexigrams through interactions with his mother, Matata. Neither Kanzi nor Mulika were specifically taught to use lexigrams. It appeared that they acquired their knowledge through an interest in communicating with their human companions. By the age of 17 months, Kanzi was able to produce more than 2500 non-imitative combinations. This was fewer than Nim but, unlike Nim, all of Kanzi's communications were other-focused (i.e. not about himself) and were more often about games than food. Savage-Rumbaugh *et al.* (1986) compared this word acquisition to the progress made by two 'common' chimpanzees who were much less successful, concluding that some chimpanzees may have a greater propensity for language than others. *How does this evidence support, develop or contradict Gardner and Gardner's research?*

Computer language: ELIZA

For 30 years, computers have been able to simulate conversation. For example, in the 1960s, Weizenbaum created a programme called ELIZA that was able to respond to a user's input as if it were a non-directive psychotherapist. Expert judges were not always able to tell the difference between ELIZA's responses and those of a real therapist (see Boden, 1977). This suggests that there is a difference between being able to produce language and actually understanding it. *What do you conclude from this evidence? Does this evidence support, develop or contradict Gardner and Gardner's research?*

CAN YOU...? No.5.12

EXAM QUESTIONS

SECTION B

Evaluate the methodology of Gardner and Gardner's (1969) research 'Teaching sign language to a chimpanzee'. [12]

With reference to alternative evidence, critically assess Gardner and Gardner's (1969) research 'Teaching sign language to a chimpanzee'. [12]

Notes *In Section B of the Unit 2 exam, you might be asked either of the questions above. In order to gain the full 12 marks for each question, your answer should:*

▶ *Present clearly structured evaluation.*

▶ *Present a coherent elaboration of each point.*

▶ *Display a depth and range of analysis, though not necessarily in equal measure; this means that you can either cover a few points in considerable detail (i.e. depth) or cover a number of points in less detail (range).*

▶ *Be about 300–350 words in length (the focus is on a sufficient breadth of material but also sufficient detail for each point made, i.e. depth and breadth).*

You may find it useful to look at the student answers at the end of other core studies to identify and avoid the typical mistakes that students make when answering Section B questions.

Example exam question with student answers

Examiner's comments on these answers can be found on page 177.

EXAMPLE OF QUESTION 1

> Summarise the aims and context of Gardner and Gardner's (1969) research 'Teaching sign language to a chimpanzee'. [12]

Megan's answer

Hockett produced the 'Design features of Language' and he believed that animal and human communications had some features which were similar, but that human languages were more complex than animal communication. Hockett believed that animals demonstrated some features of language e.g. displacement and productivity, but they did not demonstrate all of his identified features.

Hayes and Hayes had a chimp called Vicki for 6 years, aiming to teach her to produce a vocal language, however she was only able to make four sounds which were like English words.

Bryan later claimed that chimps don't have the necessary vocal chords for speech. So Gardner and Gardener concluded that a vocal language was not appropriate for this species, but previous researchers had noted that lab chimps were able to beg and use their hands to help solve manipulative problems.

Gardner and Gardner aimed to teach a chimpanzee (chosen because they are intelligent and sociable animals) to communicate using American Sign Language.

Tomas's answer

Studying animal language may help us to understand how humans are different to animals. Chomsky suggested that only humans have language because they are born with a special device which animals don't have.

Vicki the chimp was worked with for 6 years but she could only say 4 words. Perhaps Vicki couldn't talk because she didn't have a voice box. So Gardner and Gardner aimed to teach Washoe how to communicate by using sign language.

Langer and Rodin (1976) The effects of choice and enhanced personal responsibility for the aged

Developmental psychology is concerned with the way people change as they age, and also with behaviour at different stages in their lives. The next two developmental core studies look at behaviour at both ends of the spectrum – first a way to increase healthiness in the aged, and then the development of perception in infants.

DO IT YOURSELF

No. 5.27

You could assess you own sense of control using a scale developed by Julian Rotter – *Rotter's Locus of Control Scale* (Rotter, 1966). The scale determines whether you are more controlled by your own choice (an 'internal' type) or by external influences (an 'external'). There are online versions; see, for example: www.ucalgary. ca/~lapoffen/tasha/rotter.htm.

You might correlate your score with some measure of physical illness, as the context to this core study suggests that people with a low sense of control are more likely to become ill.

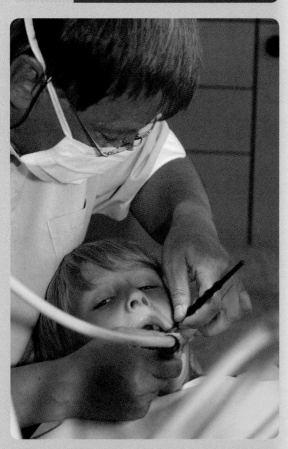

▲ This understanding of the role of control can be applied to situations where individuals receive painful treatments, such as at the dentist's. Some dentists offer you the opportunity to give a signal if the pain gets too much (like raising your hand or pressing a button). Patients in such situations appear to be able to tolerate more pain (Brown, 1986).

WHAT IS 'CONTROL'?

Control refers to the extent to which an individual feels able to direct or regulate his or her own behaviour. An individual may feel controlled by other forces (internal bodily processes or external agents), or may feel in control, i.e. self-directing and responsible. Perceived control may be more important than actual control.

CONTEXT AND AIMS

It is possible that some of the physical changes that occur as people move into old age are not biologically determined, but are instead due to a loss of a sense of personal control. As a person becomes old, they experience a loss of roles, which leads to a loss of perceived competence and a decreased sense of responsibility. A person with an increased sense of purpose may benefit in terms of decreased mortality.

Adler (1930) described the need to control one's personal environment as *'an intrinsic necessity of life itself'*. deCharms (1968) notes: '*Man's primary motivation propensity is to be effective in producing changes in his environment. Man strives to be a causal agent, to be the primary locus of causation for, or the origin of his own behaviour; he strives for personal causation.*'

Several lab studies have demonstrated that an increased sense of control reduces stress and pain. For example, Langer *et al*. (1975) found that hospital patients who felt a greater sense of control requested fewer pain relievers and were judged by nurses to show less anxiety. In another study, Stotland and Blumenthal (1964) showed that students who were allowed to choose the order in which to take a series of ability tests were less anxious (as measured by sweatiness, an indicator of activity of the **autonomic nervous system**) than those given the tests in a predetermined order.

Martin Seligman (1975) linked lack of control to depression. He described a syndrome of **learned helplessness** that develops when an individual persistently feels unable to control events in their life, and which leads to permanent feelings of helplessness and ultimately depression.

The effects of helplessness are graphically illustrated by Bettleheim's (1943) description of the *Muselmänner*, the walking corpses in the concentration camps. He noted that many of these prisoners: '*… came to believe the repeated statements of the guards – that there was no hope for them, that they would never leave the camp except as a corpse … [survival] depended on the ability to arrange to preserve some areas of independent action, to keep control of some important aspects of one's life despite an environment that seemed overwhelming and total.*'

Ferrare (1962) presented some startling data from his observations of geriatric patients. He questioned a number of individuals, and found 17 who said they did not have any alternative other than to move to a specific old people's home. Of these individuals, eight had died within four weeks of taking up residence, and a further eight had died within 10 weeks' residence. All of these deaths were classified as unexpected.

Aims

Langer and Rodin aimed to investigate the effects of enhanced personal responsibility and choice in a group of nursing home patients. They specifically wanted to see whether increased control has generalised beneficial effects, and whether physical and mental alertness, activity, sociability and general satisfaction are all affected.

They also wished to see whether the direct experience of personal responsibility would be generalised such that those participants who had greater control in specific situations generalised this to other aspects of their lives.

Original article

The full reference for the original article is: Langer, E J. and Rodin, J. (1976). The effects of choice and enhanced personal responsibility for the aged. A field experiment in an institutional setting. *Journal of Personality and Social Psychology*, 34, 191–198. You can obtain this article through your local library.

The follow-up study (Rodin and Langer, 1977) can be read at: capital2.capital.edu/faculty/jfournie/documents/Rodin_Judith.pdf.

Other resources

More recently, Ellen Langer has researched mindfulness. Read about it here: www.teachersmind.com/pdfdirectory/Mindful.PDF.

Listen to Ellen Langer speaking about this core study and on mindfulness on BBC's *Mindchangers* – copy available at www.psychblog.co.uk (search 'Mind Changes').

PROCEDURES

The study was conducted in a nursing home in Connecticut, USA, that was rated as one of the finest. It offered medical and recreational facilities to its residents and was modern, cheerful, clean and comfortable.

Participants

There were four floors in the home, of which two were selected for this study because the residents on each of these floors were similar in terms of their physical and psychological health; they had been at the home for similar lengths of time and were of a similar **socioeconomic** background (a measure of a person's education, occupation and income). There was not much communication between floors.

One floor was randomly assigned to be the **experimental group** (responsibility induced group, RIG), while the other floor was to act as a **control group** (comparison group, CG). The details of each group are described on the right.

In the RIG, there were 8 males and 39 females. In the CG, there were 9 males and 35 females. Some of the residents who lived on these floors were omitted from the research because they were of a different age, bedridden or non-communicative.

Briefing

To introduce the experimental treatment, the nursing home administrator, an outgoing 33-year-old male, called a meeting in the lounge of each of the floors and made an announcement to each set of residents separately. He explained that the meeting was to tell them about some of the things that were available to them.

The RIG group was told: *'Many of you don't realise the influence you have over your own lives here. Take a minute to think of the decisions you can, and should be, making. For example, you have the responsibility of caring for yourselves, of deciding … how you want your rooms arranged … You should be deciding how you want to spend your time … I wanted to take this opportunity to give you a present … the plant is yours to keep and take care of as you'd like.'*

The CG groups was told: *'Many of you don't realise all you're allowed to do here. Take a minute to think of all the options that we've provided for you in order for your life to be fuller and more interesting. For example, … we want your rooms to be as nice as they can be, and we've tried to make them that way for you … We feel that it's our responsibility to make this a home you can be proud of and happy in. … I wanted to take this opportunity to give you a present … the plants are yours to keep. The nurses will water and care for them for you.'*

Three days later, all participants were visited by the administrator and he reiterated the message.

- RIG: *'Remember what I said last Thursday. We want you to be happy. Treat this like your home and make all the decisions you used to make. How's your plant coming along?'*
- CG: *'Remember what I said last Thursday. We want you to be happy. How's your plant coming along?'*

There were two groups of participants in this study.

- **RIG**
  - Emphasis on residents being responsible for themselves.
  - Asked to give their opinions about how complaints are handled.
  - Allowed to select their own plant to be taken care of by themselves.
  - Allowed to choose which night was to be 'film night'.
- **CG**
  - Emphasis on staff being responsible for residents.
  - Told that all complaints would be handled by staff.
  - Given a plant that was to be taken care of by someone else.
  - Told which night was to be 'film night'.

Questionnaires

Two questionnaires were used, designed to assess the effect of induced responsibility. Each questionnaire was administered one week before the briefing (at the start of the study to establish a baseline), and then again three weeks after the briefing (to assess the effects of the increased sense of personal control).

- The first questionnaire was administered by a research assistant. The assistant was unaware of the experimental hypothesis. It assessed how much control the residents felt over general events in their lives, and how happy and active they felt. It included an eight-point scale ranging from 0 (none) to 8 (total). After each interview, the research assistant also rated the residents' alertness (0–8).
- A second questionnaire was completed by the two nurses who worked on both floors (one the day nurse and the other the night nurse). The nurses were unaware of the experimental **hypothesis**. They rated each resident's happiness, alertness, dependency, sociability and activity levels. They made notes on eating and sleeping habits, and on how much time had been spent doing various activities such as reading, watching television, visiting other patients, watching the staff, talking to the staff, sitting alone doing nothing among others.

Behavioural measures

Residents were also assessed on behavioural measures, such as attendance at the film night, participation in competitions (such as guessing the number of jelly beans in a jar), and use of wheelchairs.

Langer and Rodin (1976) The effects of choice and enhanced personal responsibility for the aged

▼ Table 1 Mean scores for self-report, interviewer ratings and nurses' ratings for experiment and comparison groups

Questionnaire responses	Responsibility-induced (RIG)			Comparison group (CG)			Probability ($p<$)
	Pre	Post	Diff.	Pre	Post	Diff.	
Self report							
Happy	5.16	5.44	.28	4.90	4.78	−.12	.05
Active	4.07	4.27	.20	3.90	2.62	−1.28	.01
Perceived control							
Have	3.26	3.42	.16	3.62	4.03	.41	
Want	3.85	3.80	−.05	4.40	4.57	.17	
Interviewer rating							
Alertness	5.02	5.31	.29	5.75	5.38	−.37	.025
Nurses' ratings							
General improvement	41.67	45.64	3.97	42.69	40.32	−2.39	.005
Time spent visiting patients	13.03	19.81	6.78	7.94	4.65	−3.30	.005
Visiting others	11.50	13.75	2.14	12.38	8.21	−4.16	.05
Talking to staff	8.21	16.43	8.21	9.11	10.71	1.61	.01
Watching staff	6.78	4.64	−2.14	6.96	11.60	4.64	.05

DO IT YOURSELF
No. 5.29

Feed your friend In pairs, get a friend to feed you your lunch/snack. You cannot assist them in any way apart from opening your mouth, chewing and swallowing. How does this activity make you feel in terms of control?

DO IT YOURSELF
No. 5.28

You could represent the data above in a graph – using bar charts or pie charts, or any visual means. Try out a variety of different methods for different aspects of the data.

FINDINGS

Questionnaires

Two questionnaires were given out in this experiment to assess the feelings and behaviour of the residents.

First, the pre-test assessment of the residents showed the two groups were very similar prior to the start of the study. None of the differences were significant. This was an important baseline measure.

Second, the pre-test and post-test scores were compared between the two groups, as shown in Table 1. The following key differences were noted.

Self-report

- Residents in the RIG reported significantly greater increases in happiness after the experimental treatment than CG residents (significance level $p<0.05$, which means that there was only a 5% chance that this result could have occurred due to chance).
- In the RIG, 48% of the residents reported feeling happier, compared with only 25% of the residents in the CG.
- Residents in the RIG reported themselves to be significantly more active after the experimental treatment than did residents in the CG ($p<0.01$).

Interviewer rating

- Residents in the RIG were rated as having greater increases in their levels of alertness than were residents in the CG ($p<0.025$).

Perceived control

- Questions that were related to perceived control showed no significantly greater increase for the RIG.
- However, 20% indicated that they didn't understand what 'control' meant, and these answers were therefore not very meaningful.

Nurses' ratings

- The correlation between the ratings made by the two nurses of the same patient was .61 (for the RIG) and .68 (for the CG) (both significant at $p<.005$).
- The RIG showed increases in the proportion of time spent visiting other patients, visiting people from outside the home, and talking to the staff. They spent less time engaging in 'passive' activities, such as watching the staff, reading and watching television.
- When analysing the nurses' ratings for each patient (the total pre-test score from the total post-test score), a positive average total change score of 3.97 for the RIG was found, compared with a negative average total change score of −2.39 for the CG. The difference between these mean scores is highly significant ($p<0.005$).
- The only measure where improvement was greater for the CG than the RIG was watching staff – a passive activity.
- Of the residents in the RIG, 93% were considered to have improved (i.e. all but one resident), compared with only 21% of the CG (six residents).

Behavioural measures

As with the questionnaires, the behavioural measures showed the same pattern of differences between the RIG and CG:

- Film night attendance was significantly higher in the RIG ($p<.05$). A similar attendance check taken one month before the briefing revealed no differences in the attendance of the residents on the two floors.
- In the jelly bean guessing competition, 10 residents from the RIG and only one resident from the CG participated, a significant difference ($p<.01$).

DO IT YOURSELF

You can write an abstract for this study, as you have done before. This abstract should contain brief details of the context and aims, procedures, findings and conclusions of this study – all in about 200 words. You might also produce a step-by-step guide to the procedures.

CONCLUSIONS

The findings clearly support the view that *'inducing a greater sense of personal responsibility in people who may have virtually relinquished decision making, either by choice or necessity, produces improvement'.*

Despite the fact that residents in the CG group were told that staff members were there to make them happy, and that residents were treated in a sympathetic manner, 71% of the CG were actually rated as having become more debilitated over the short three-week period of this study.

It is not clear from this study whether the behavioural improvements shown (e.g. the attendance at the film night) were a direct consequence of increased perception of choice and decision-making opportunities, or whether they were an indirect consequence. It could be that the increased sense of control led to increased happiness, and that this in turn caused the behavioural improvements.

One thing worth noting is that the improvements in the behavioural measures were quite small, though significant. Bigger improvements might be achieved by more individually administered treatments, and treatments that are repeated on several occasions.

The findings of this study certainly suggest that mechanisms can and should be developed to increase the sense of personal responsibility of people in care homes. Such treatments could slow down or even reverse the apparently inevitable negative consequences of ageing.

CAN YOU...?

1... Explain what is meant by control.
2... Identify **two** studies that were conducted prior to Langer and Rodin's study and explain the conclusions from each of these studies.
3... Briefly outline the aims of this study.
4... Write a suitable experimental **hypothesis** for this study. (A hypothesis is a statement of what the researcher believes to be true. It should identify the **independent** and **dependent variables**.)
5... Why was it important that the interviewer did not know which group each resident belong to.
6... Why was it important that the nurses did not know the experimental hypothesis? How might such knowledge have biased the nurses' ratings?
7... How many participants were there in the study?
8... Describe **three** key characteristics of the participants.
9... Identify **six** key aspects of the procedures.
10...Identify **six** findings from this study.
11... State a conclusion that could be drawn from each finding. Try to make each conclusion different.
12...What evidence leads you to conclude that this study supports the experimental hypothesis?

EXAM QUESTIONS

SECTION A

Summarise the aims **and** context of Langer and Rodin's (1976) research 'The effects of choice and enhanced personal responsibility for the aged'. [12]

Outline the procedures of Langer and Rodin's (1976) research 'The effects of choice and enhanced personal responsibility for the aged'. [12]

Describe the findings **and** conclusions of Langer and Rodin's (1976) research 'The effects of choice and enhanced personal responsibility for the aged'. [12]

Notes In Section A of the Unit 2 exam, you could be asked any of the questions above. Each question will be worth 12 marks. In order to gain the full 12 marks for each question, your answer should follow the guidelines given on page 101.

MEET THE RESEARCHERS

Ellen Langer has continued to conduct research related to the topic of this study, extending her interests to study the illusion of control, ageing, decision-making, and mindfulness theory. In the late 1970s, she became the first woman ever to be tenured in psychology at Harvard University, and continues as a psychology professor there. You can read about her research and view her artwork at www.ellenlanger.com. When asked about her recollections of this study, Ellen said:

'Initially we weren't sure we should publish the findings. We were confident we had done everything properly, but since there was nothing like it in the literature we wo0rried a bit about how extreme the findings were. An increase in longevity was quite different from scores on a scale, which was the norm for the field at the time.'
Personal communication

Judith Rodin went on to help pioneer the fields of behavioural medicine and health psychology as a Yale University faculty member for 22 years. She subsequently became provost of Yale, president of the University of Pennsylvania, the first woman to lead an Ivy League institution, and then president of the Rockefeller Foundation. Dr. Rodin remains widely recognised for her ground-breaking research in obesity, eating disorders, aging and women's health – work which earned her both the American Psychological Association's Distinguished Early Career Award in 1977 and its Distinguished Lifetime Contribution Award in 2005.

▲ Ellen Langer (1947–) (top) and Judith Rodin (1944–).

On this spread we are going to evaluate the core study by looking at issues related to its methodology, and comparing the study to alternative evidence. When it comes to evaluation, you can make up your own mind. We have presented some evidence and statements, and invite you to use this to construct your own view of the core study.

EVALUATING THE METHODOLOGY

See Chapter 6 (Applied Research Methods) for an explanation of these concepts.

Method

Langer and Rodin called their research a **field experiment**. *What advantage does this offer? What disadvantage does it pose?*

One floor was randomly assigned to be RIG, while the other floor was to act as the CG. *Why was this random assignment necessary?*

Reliability

The correlation between the ratings made by the two nurses of the same patient was .61 (for the RIG) and .68 (for the CG) (both significant at $p<.005$). *In what way does this demonstrate that the findings from the study are* **reliable**?

Validity

In order to ensure validity of observations, two nurses were asked to provide these ratings. *How did Langer and Rodin ensure that these were unbiased and therefore valid?*

The nursing home in Connecticut, USA, offered medical and recreational facilities to its residents and was modern, cheerful, clean and comfortable. *Why might this pose* **validity** *issues?*

Sampling

The RIG group consisted of 8 males and 39 females; the CG consisted of 9 males and 35 females. The two groups were similar in terms of their physical and psychological health, lengths of time in the home and **socioeconomic** background. *Why was it important to have two similar groups?*

Ethical issues

Langer and Rodin did not have the fully **informed consent** of the participants in their research. *Is this a significant* **ethical issue**? *Explain your answer.*

The residents in the CG were subsequently found to be twice as likely to die than the RIG residents. *Is it ethical to place some participants in a* **control group** *where a beneficial treatment has been withheld from them? Explain your answer.*

This study showed significant, although small, improvements in those residents who were given an increased sense of control. *Is Langer and Rodin's research of such importance that it negates the ethical issues it induced?*

ALTERNATIVE EVIDENCE

Follow up study

Rodin and Langer (1977) re-evaluated the residents in this core study 18 months later. Nurses' ratings were again used to assess differences along with health measures. Both suggested that the experimental treatment and/or the processes that it set in motion had had sustained beneficial effects. The most striking data came from mortality rates. The average mortality rate for the 18 months before the study was 25%. In the following 18 months, 15% of the residents in the RIG died compared with 30% of those in the CG. *What do you conclude from this evidence?*

General studies on the effects of perceived control

Suls and Mullen (1981) used the SRRS to assess life changes, noting which changes were controllable and which were not. They found that it was the uncontrollable life changes that were associated with subsequent illness, whereas controllable ones were not. *How does this evidence support, develop or contradict Langer and Rodin's research?*

Cohen *et al.* (1993) used the *viral-challenge technique* to study the effects of stress on more than 400 volunteers. Individuals were divided into an **experimental group** (who were given nasal drops containing the common cold virus) and a control group (who received harmless nasal drops). All participants completed a questionnaire to assess their levels of perceived stress.

Cohen *et al.* found a **positive correlation** between levels of stress and the likelihood of catching a cold. In particular, those participants who felt their lives were unpredictable and uncontrollable were twice as likely to develop colds as those suffering low stress. *How does this evidence support, develop or contradict Langer and Rodin's research?*

DO IT YOURSELF

No. 5.31

You could have a class debate about the ethics of this study. Randomly assign some class members to argue in favour of the ethical acceptability of this study, and another group to argue against it. Alternatively, students could prepare a research proposal for this study, which could be considered by a student **ethical committee**.

DO IT YOURSELF

No. 5.32

Do a quick survey of where elderly relatives live – alone in own home, with other relatives, nursing home, sheltered accommodation, and so on. Then think about the impact that those different living arrangements might have on their sense of control.

Or arrange to visit a local nursing home. What sort of facilities do the residents have? Do you think you would be happy in this sort of environment? (If you do this, think carefully about ethical issues.)

Field experiments

Schulz (1976) randomly assigned institutionalised elderly people to one of four conditions. Participants in the first group could determine both the frequency and duration of visits by college students. Those in group 2 were informed when they would be visited and how long the visitor would stay for, but had no control over these details. Group 3 participants were visited on a random schedule, and those in group 4 were not visited, serving as a control group. Schulz found a positive impact on the well-being of the institutionalised aged when they could predict (group 2) and control (group 1) the visits. *How does this evidence support, develop or contradict Langer and Rodin's research?*

Savell (1991) exposed 43 institutionalised older adults to differential opportunities for choice. This study found no significant difference between the choice and no choice groups in terms of physical well-being, subjective well-being or leisure satisfaction. One possible explanation for these contrasting findings is that the choice of activities did not give individuals a significantly enhanced sense of personal control. *How does this evidence support, develop or contradict Langer and Rodin's research?*

Natural experiments

Some studies have not directly manipulated control but have instead studied the elderly over time to see if those who had a greater sense of control were more likely to remain healthy. For example, Kunzmann *et al.* (2000) used data from the *Berlin Aging Study* (age range 70–103 years). Overall, they found a positive relationship between perceived control and emotional well-being.

Wurm *et al.* (2007) used longitudinal data from the *German Aging Survey* (more than 1000 participants, aged 40–85 years at the start). Participants were assessed at the beginning of the study and again six years later. As expected, there was a negative correlation between the perceived sense of control and physical illness. However, they identified a further factor of importance – individuals who held negative attitudes towards ageing also experienced more physical illness. Wurm *et al.* suggest that a range of cognitive factors (such as a sense of control and stereotypes about ageing) is important in predicting the physical health of the elderly. *What do you conclude from this evidence? Does this evidence support, develop or contradict Langer and Rodin's research?*

EXAM QUESTIONS

SECTION B
Evaluate the methodology of Langer and Rodin's (1976) research 'The effects of choice and enhanced personal responsibility for the aged'. [12]

With reference to alternative evidence, critically assess Langer and Rodin's (1976) research 'The effects of choice and enhanced personal responsibility for the aged'. [12]

Notes In Section B of the Unit 2 exam, you could be asked either of the questions above. In order to gain the full 12 marks for each question, your answer should:

▶ *Present clearly structured evaluation.*

▶ *Present a coherent elaboration of each point.*

▶ *Display a depth and range of analysis, though not necessarily in equal measure; this means that you can either cover a few points in considerable detail (i.e. depth) or a number of points in less detail (range).*

▶ *Be about 300–350 words in length (the focus is on a sufficient breadth of material but also sufficient detail for each point made, i.e. depth and breadth).*

You may find it useful to look at the student answers at the end of other core studies to identify and avoid the typical mistakes that students make when answering Section B questions.

Example exam question with student answers

Examiner's comments on these answers can be found on page 177.

EXAMPLE OF QUESTION 3

> **Describe the findings and conclusions of Langer and Rodin's (1976) research 'The effects of choice and enhanced personal responsibility for the aged'.** [12]

Megan's answer

They found that the old people that were given plants to look after were happier than those old people who did not have plants. They concluded that having plants makes you feel happy.

Tomas's answer

Langer and Rodin (L&R) found that in pretests the two groups were very similar. They found the Responsibility Induced Group (RIG) reported greater increases in happiness after the experimental treatment than residents in the Comparison Group (CG). In fact 48% of the residents in the RIG reported feeling happier, compared to only 25% of the residents of the CG.

L&R found that the RIG reported themselves to be significantly more active after the experimental treatment than residents in the CG. The RIG showed increases in the proportion of time spent visiting other patients, visiting people from outside the home and talking to the staff. They spent less time engaging in 'passive' activities such as watching staff, reading and watching television.

L&R found the nurses rated residents in the RIG as having greater increases in alertness than residents in the CG.

The average total change for the RIG was 3.97 compared to −2.39 for the CG. In fact, 93% of the residents in the RIG were considered to have improved, compared to only 21% of the CG and 71% of the CG were rated as having debilitated over the 3 week period.

L&R found that more of the RIG went to film night and took part in competitions than the CG.

L&R concluded that giving people a greater sense of personal responsibility produces improvement. They also concluded that it might be possible to reverse/prevent elderly people suffering the negative effects of ageing by giving them the ability to make decisions and making them feel competent.

Gibson and Walk (1960) The visual cliff

This developmental core study is concerned with the **nature–nurture** debate, an issue that lies at the heart of developmental psychology. What aspects of our behaviour are inherited (i.e. **nature**), and what aspects are mainly determined by experience (i.e. **nurture**)? Psychologists who are interested in topics such as intelligence, aggression, gender, mental illness and personality all ask the question: is a person's behaviour best explained by **genetic** predispositions, or by the environment that they grew up in? Another topic area that is concerned with the nature–nurture question is perception. This core study marked a landmark in understanding perceptual development.

What is perception?

There is a difference between perception and sensation. The senses (eyes, ears and so on) receive and register physical data (light, sound and so on). These sensations are altered through interpretation and elaboration, so that what is 'seen' or 'heard' has meaning. Perception is the process of understanding sensory information.

▲ A healthy fear of heights is likely to be **innate** because it is **adaptive**. To perceive heights, we use depth perception, so this is also likely to be innate.

DEPTH PERCEPTION

The perception of distance (or depth perception) refers to our ability to comprehend that some objects are more distant than others despite the fact that the visual image received by the **retina** is actually two-dimensional, just like a picture. To some extent, depth is perceived using *binocular cues* (cues from both eyes), for example *retinal disparity* (the closer an object is to the viewer, the more disparate the images from the two eyes will be). However, most depth perception is based on *monocular cues* (cues from one eye), which are also called 'pictorial cues' because they are the same cues used by artists when producing three-dimensional pictures. These cues include *relative size* (smaller objects appear further away), *texture gradient* (there is more detail in objects that are closer), *occlusion* (if one object partially blocks another it appears to be closer), *linear perspective* (parallel lines appear to converge in the distance) and *motion parallax* (as we move, objects that are closer to us appear to move more quickly across our field of view than do objects that are in the distance).

CONTEXT AND AIMS

Depth perception is our ability to perceive how close or far an object is from us. It is just one element of our visual capabilities, but it is an essential perceptual ability to possess for negotiating our way around our world. If we had no depth perception, we would probably not survive very long – just think about everyday activities like descending stairs or walking along the pavement without falling into the road.

Nativists believe that we are born with the capacity to perceive depth. They believe these abilities may not all be functioning properly when we are born, but that the process of maturation, rather than learning, determines the development of these capacities. **Empiricists** believe that we acquire our abilities through our experiences. **Interactionists** believe that our abilities are the product of both – innate abilities interacting with environmental factors.

When we are born, the nervous system has all the appropriate components, although it is immature – about half the size of that of an adult. The **optic nerve**, for example, is obviously shorter than it will be when it is adult sized, but it is also narrower as it does not have the necessary **myelin sheath** that ensures good transmission of information.

Nativists would assume that depth perception would be an innate characteristic. Empiricists would assume that depth perception is acquired in response to environmental demands, i.e. after we start to become mobile. Interactionists would assume that depth perception is the product of the developing visual system (e.g. the myelin sheath around the optic nerve is thought to be fully developed by the age of four months) and experience (i.e. from the time we are born we are exposed to various complex and intriguing stimuli such as faces, which have subtle cues about depth, such as shadowing).

Although most infants start to demonstrate some independent locomotion by the age of six months, many species are able to demonstrate movement from the time that they are born. Such animals belong to species described as *precocial* (the young are relatively mature and mobile from the moment of birth or hatching). If depth perception is innate, we would expect it to be apparent by the time a young animal is mobile because this would be **adaptive** – a young animal that does not have this ability at this critical time is less likely to survive, and therefore an innate ability to perceive depth would be adaptive.

Aims

Gibson and Walk aimed to investigate if the ability to perceive depth is learned through experience or whether it is part of a child's 'original endowment'. They reasoned that, if the ability is innate, it should be apparent by the time infants were able to move independently.

Gibson and Walk decided to use not only human infants in their research, because using human infants alone would mean the outcome was inconclusive as to whether nativist, empiricist or interactionist arguments were correct. By using a range of non-human animals, such as kids (infant goats), lambs, chicks and kittens, they were able to investigate if cliff avoidance behaviours (depth perception) were evident from the time such young animals were mobile. This further research could then demonstrate that depth perception is an innate ability.

PROCEDURES

Apparatus

At Cornell University in the USA, Gibson and Walk designed a simple experimental set-up – the *'visual cliff'* – to investigate depth perception in babies and other young animals. The apparatus enabled the researchers to control optical, auditory and tactile stimuli, and also to protect participants. The visual cliff consisted of a large glass sheet that was supported 30cm or more above the floor. On one side, a sheet of patterned material was placed directly beneath the glass. On the other side, the patterned material was laid on the floor; this side of the apparatus formed the visual cliff. The patterns on the material underneath the glass gave visual cues that one side was 'shallow' and the other was 'deep' (the **retinal image** of more distant patterns is smaller and this information provides depth cues).

The participants (infants or young animals) were placed on the centre board that lay between the shallow and deep sides, and then encouraged to move across the shallow and the deep sides in order to observe whether they would refuse to crawl over the drop.

Human infants

A total of 36 infants aged 6–14 months were tested. All the infants were able to crawl (independent locomotion).

Non-human animals

The non-human animals tested on the visual cliff included:
- Chicks, lambs and kids (infant goats): mobile at one day old.
- Kittens: mobile at four weeks old.
- Kittens that had been reared in the dark for 27 days were also tested; such 'dark-rearing' prevented the cats from learning any depth cues before they were tested.
- Rats: mobile at four weeks old; some wore hoods so they were using their whiskers (touch) rather than visual cues; a further group of rats was reared in the dark before being tested.
- Pigs, dogs and aquatic turtles were also tested.

Controls

A number of control experiments were conducted to eliminate possible **extraneous variables**. For example, it is possible that reflections from the glass affected participants' behaviour, so they lit the patterned surfaces from below the glass.

Testing depth cues

There are two possible cues that the young animals may have used to perceive depth. First, the size/spacing of the pattern would indicate depth (on the shallow side the squares would appear larger and more widely spaced apart). A second cue was motion parallax – the patterned elements on the shallow side move more rapidly across the field of vision when an animal moves its position or head.

To remove the depth cue of size/spacing, the pattern on the depth size was increased so the retinal image for both sides was identical. To remove the depth cue of **motion parallax**, the patterned material was placed directly beneath the glass on both sides, but the pattern size was adjusted so that the squares on the 'shallow' side were bigger, giving the illusion of being closer.

DO IT YOURSELF No. 5.33

Try this experiment for yourself. Obviously, it would be unethical to use human infants because of the potential distress it may cause. However, you could simply role play the study, taking turns being the infant. This may sound very silly, but enactive experience helps understanding and enhances your memory. You will need two clear sheets of strong Perspex and four tables to rest these on. You will also need some chequered fabric.

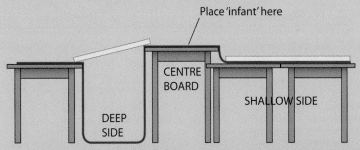

▲ The red line is the chequered fabric, and the blue lines are the Perspex.

▲ In the left hand photograph, the infant has been placed on the centre board by her mother. The shallow side of the 'visual cliff' apparatus is on the left and the deep side is on the right. In the right hand photograph, the mother has moved to one end of the apparatus and is encouraging her baby to move towards her.

You can watch some relevant videos at the following websites:
- Babies in the visual cliff experiment at: vimeo.com/77934.
- Great illusions based on depth perception at: www.richardgregory. org/experiments/index.htm.
- Motion parallax at: blog.trevorboyle.com/?p=30.
- Using parallax to measure distances in space at: www.youtube.com/ watch?v=2RelG0npptl.

Original article

The full reference for this article is Gibson, E.J. and Walk, R.D. (1960). The 'visual cliff'. *Scientific American*, 202 (4), 64–71. You can read the original article at: www.scribd.com/doc/3956434/The-Visual-Cliff.

Other resources

This is a great book on visual illusions (many using depth perception): Seckel, A.L. (2004). *Incredible Visual Illusions: You Won't Believe your Eyes!*

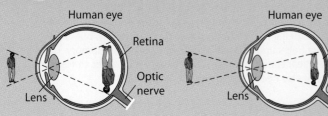

▲ The same object projects a different size retinal image depending on whether it is seen close to you (top picture) or further away (bottom picture). Our brain uses a range of depth cues, such as the converging lines that indicate that the top person is further away.

▶ In the picture on right, both images are the same size, but because of the depth perspective we 'see' the top one as further away and make an adjustment so it appears to be larger.

MEET THE RESEARCHERS

Eleanor Jack Gibson was married to James J. Gibson, whose theory of perception has had a major influence on the field of perception. He was partly the inspiration for this study, as he maintained that their young children would be able to detect a hazardous cliff edge and remain safe while Eleanor wasn't sure that they would stay away from the edge. Husband and wife also developed a theory of perceptual development, *differentiation theory* (Gibson and Gibson, 1955). They claimed that all perceptual abilities are innate and that a baby merely learns to differentiate between classes of object.

Richard D. Walk remains most famous for the visual cliff experiment and cross-species studies on the development of vision and movement. He also conducted research on learning and social relations, and was renowned for his original approaches and his ingenious experiments.

▲ Eleanor J. Gibson (1910–2002) and Richard D. Walk (1920–1999).

FINDINGS

Human infants

All 27 of the infants who moved off the centre board crawled out on to the shallow side at least once. Only three attempted to crawl on to the 'deep' side (cliff side). Many of the infants crawled away from their mothers when they called to them from the 'deep' side, others cried when their mothers stood there because they could not get to them without crossing the 'deep' side.

The infants often patted the glass with their hands, so they knew that there was a solid surface, and yet the appearance of a drop was enough to prevent them from venturing any further.

Non-human animals

The chicks, kids and lambs never hopped or stepped on to the 'deep' side, even at one day old. If a kid or lamb was placed on the deep side it froze in a posture of defence: front legs rigid and hind legs limp.

Rats depend upon their whiskers to navigate, rather than using visual cues. This explains why hooded rats were equally content to explore either side as long as they could feel the glass with their whiskers. However, when the centre board was placed higher so that the glass surface was out of reach of their whiskers, they nearly always descended from the centre board on to the shallow side (95–100% of the time).

Kittens at four weeks old showed preference for the shallow side, and 'froze' when placed on to the 'deep' side, or circled back to the centre board. However, the kittens that had been reared in darkness for their first 27 days of life crawled on to the shallow and deep side equally. When placed on the deep side, they demonstrated similar behaviours to when they were placed on the shallow side, and they did not 'freeze' like the normal kittens. After this initial research, these kittens were kept in 'normal' lighting conditions. They were tested daily on the visual cliff and by the end of one week the 'dark-reared' kittens demonstrated similar behaviours to kittens that had been reared in the light, i.e. almost unanimous preference for the shallow side.

The turtles preferred the shallow side. It was expected that they might select the deep side because it looked like the surface of water but, in fact, 76% crawled towards the shallow rather than the deep side.

Depth cues

With only the cue of **motion parallax**, the rats still preferred the shallow size, as did the chicks. When both patterns were placed directly under the glass (making size/spacing then the only depth cue) both young and hooded rats preferred the side with the larger pattern (the apparently 'shallow' side). The chicks showed no preference for the larger pattern (apparently nearer) over the less detailed pattern (apparently further away).

The dark-reared rats showed a preference for the shallow side when using only motion parallax. However, when given information about size/spacing alone (i.e. chequered pattern placed directly beneath the glass and size adjusted to 'look' shallow and deep), they showed no preference for the apparently shallow or deep sides.

CONCLUSIONS

The findings of this study demonstrated that most human infants can discriminate depth as soon as they can crawl. Some of them backed on to the 'cliff side' accidentally when negotiating their movement on the centre board, which suggests that infants should not be left close to a cliff edge even though they may be able to discriminate depth.

However, the evidence cannot *prove* that human depth perception is **innate**, although it does support the **nativist** view. This is further supported by the studies of non-human animals. All the findings fit with the life history and ecological niche of the animals studied. They all showed discrimination of depth by the time they were mobile – the chick and goat discriminated depth at the age of one day, and the cat and rat at the age of four. The poor performance of the turtles suggested that they have poorer depth discrimination, which may be because their natural habitat involves less danger from falling off cliffs so depth perception would not **adaptive** value.

The preference shown by rats for the shallow side when only size/shape cues were available could be explained in terms of learning. They were older at the time of testing than the chicks, and may therefore have learned to use these depth cues. This was supported by the fact that the dark-reared rats showed no preference.

The research with rats suggests that motion parallax is an innate cue, whereas size/spacing is a learned depth cue. *'The survival of a species requires that its members develop discrimination of depth by the time they take up independent locomotion, whether it be at 1 day (the chick and goat), 4 weeks (the rat and cat), or 6–14 months (the human infant). That such a vital capacity does not depend on possibly fatal accidents of learning in the lives of individuals is consistent with evolutionary theory.'*

CAN YOU...? No. 5.15

1... Explain what is meant by depth perception.

2... Explain how we perceive depth.

3... Outline the **three** possible explanations for how perception develops (nature, nurture and interactionist).

4... Briefly outline the aims of this study.

5... List the different groups of participants that were involved in this study.

6... Provide at least **one** key characteristic for each group of participants.

7... Identify **six** key aspects of the baseline procedure.

8... Identify **six** findings from this study.

9... For each finding, state a conclusion that could be drawn from it. Try to make each conclusion different.

10... What evidence leads you to conclude that this study supports the nativist view that perception is innate?

11... What evidence leads you to conclude that this study supports the empiricist view that perception is entirely learned?

12... What evidence leads you to conclude that this study supports the interactionist view that perception is a mixture of nature and nurture?

EXAM QUESTIONS

SECTION A

Summarise the aims **and** context of Gibson and Walk's (1960) research 'The visual cliff' '. [12]

Outline the procedures of Gibson and Walk's (1960) research 'The visual cliff' '. [12]

Describe the findings **and** conclusions of Gibson and Walk's (1960) research 'The visual cliff' '. [12]

Notes *In Section A of the Unit 2 exam, you might be asked any of the questions above. Each question will be worth 12 marks. In order to gain the full 12 marks your answer should:*

▶ *Be accurate and well detailed.*

▶ *Display a depth and range of knowledge, though not necessarily in equal measure; this means that you can either cover a few points in considerable detail (i.e. depth) or cover a number of points in less detail (range).*

▶ *Be well structured and coherent.*

▶ *Have accurate grammar, punctuation and spelling.*

▶ *Be about 200–250 words in length, which is fewer than for other 12-mark questions, but the emphasis is on accuracy.*

DO IT YOURSELF No. 5.34

You can again produce a step-by-step guide to the procedures, to help you remember them.

Also, write an abstract for this study, as you have done before. This abstract should contain brief details of the context and aims, procedures, findings and conclusions of this study – all in about 200 words.

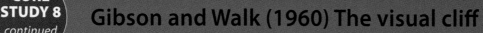

Gibson and Walk (1960) The visual cliff

On this spread we are going to evaluate the core study by looking at issues related to its methodology, and comparing the study to alternative evidence. When it comes to evaluation, you can make up your own mind. We have presented some evidence and statements, and invite you to use this to construct your own view of the core study.

EVALUATING THE METHODOLOGY

See Chapter 6 (Applied Research Methods) for an explanation of these concepts.

Method

Gibson and Walk conducted their research with infants in a lab environment. *What advantages did this offer for this core study? What disadvantages does this pose?*

Validity

One validity issue is concerning whether Gibson and Walk's research with infants is actually capable of assessing whether depth perception is innate or learned. The age of the human infants was 6–14 months. *Why might this have been a limitation? Why would this affect the validity of this study?*

More recent research (see right) has tested younger infants than those used by Gibson and Walk. *How does this enhance or otherwise the **validity** of this core study?*

In this study, depth perception was measured using the visual cliff apparatus. One problem is that infants very quickly learned that if they did slip off the centre board, they did not fall, i.e. they learned that the safety glass was safe (Adolph and Berger, 2006). *How valid was this form of measurement?*

Sampling

The human sample was limited to infants available to the researchers at Cornell University. *What might be unique about this **sample** and how might this affect the findings?*

Humans are 'socially dependent' animals. Most of the non-human animals tested by Gibson and Walk were not 'socially dependant' animals, i.e. they are not dependent on their mother for survival and nurturing. *Why is this a limitation of Gibson and Walk's research?*

Ethical issues

During the research, some of the infants demonstrated distress about not being able to get to their mother. *What ethical issues does this pose?*

Dawkins (1990) notes that morally questionable research using non-human animals might be acceptable if the goal is the alleviation of human suffering, but may not be acceptable if the goal is the satisfaction of intellectual curiosity. *Do you think it was ethical for Gibson and Walk to use non-human animals in this research?*

DO IT YOURSELF

No. 5.35

Try this to demonstrate binocular depth perception. Hold two pencils horizontally, one in each hand, at arm's-length from your body. With one eye closed, try to touch the ends of the pencils together. Now try with two eyes – it should be much easier. This is because each eye looks at the image from a different angle. This experiment can also be done with your fingers, but pencils make the effect a bit more dramatic.

You can read this and other activities related to perception at Neuroscience for Kids: faculty.washington.edu/chudler/chvision.html.

ALTERNATIVE EVIDENCE

Research using the visual cliff

In the study by Gibson and Walk, the infants were required to move across the two sides of the apparatus, which meant it was impossible to test infants who could not crawl, a limiting factor of this study. Schwartz *et al.* (1973) got round this by placing infants on the deep and shallow sides of the visual cliff apparatus and measuring their heart rate. Presumably if they sensed the drop their heart rate would increase. Schwartz *et al.* tested infants aged between five and nine months. When placed over the glass 'drop', the five month olds typically showed no increase in heart rate, whereas infants aged nine months did. *How does this research support, contradict or develop the findings proposed by Gibson and Walk?*

However, it is still possible that the young infants did perceive depth but simply had not yet understood the implications for their own safety (and so their heart rate did not increase), thus 'wariness' is not an appropriate measure. It is also possible that, by five months, infants have had the opportunity to learn about depth cues despite not yet crawling. *What can you conclude from this?*

Sorce *et al.* (1985) conducted the same visual cliff research, but this time the mother was instructed to maintain an expression of fear or happiness on the other side of the 'cliff'. When the mother expressed a happy face, the babies checked the cliff and crossed. When the mother showed an expression of fear, the babies were very reluctant to cross. *How does this research support, contradict or develop the findings proposed by Gibson and Walk?*

Recent research

A recent study has challenged whether the visual cliff is actually measuring depth perception. Witherington *et al.* (2005) noticed in the film footage of earlier experiments that even the youngest infants would brace themselves before touching the shallow end (suggesting they already had depth perception). In their own study, Witherington *et al.* found that the infants with the strongest aversion to the cliff were those with the most experience of walking/crawling. What they believe is really happening is that the infant is learning to associate the physical experience with the visual environment.

In this study, there were two groups of 20 infants. Those in group 1 were experienced at crawling but were not yet walking; those in group 2 had just begun to walk. The infants in group 2 were more wary of the 'cliff' than the younger infants in group 1. Thus it appears that new learning has to take place when the world is viewed from a new perspective (i.e. when walking). *How does this research support, contradict or develop the findings proposed by Gibson and Walk?*

Other methods of testing infant depth perception

Bower *et al*. (1970) obtained convincing evidence that infants as young as six days old have some depth perception. The infants were shown two objects: a large disc that approached to within 20 cm of them, and a smaller disc that came to within 8 cm of them. If the infants had no depth perception, their response to a large disc stopping further away should be the same as their response to a smaller, closer one because they both create the same retinal image. In fact, the infants were so upset by the smaller, closer one that the experiment was abandoned early, without testing all the infants. *How does this research develop the findings proposed by Gibson and Walk?*

Hofsten *et al*. (1992) demonstrated the use of motion parallax in three-month-old infants using the *habituation method*, which means showing an infant a display until the infant gets used to it (habituates). If the same display is shown again, the infant should show less interest than when looking at a novel display. In this study, the infants habituated to a display of three rods while being moved about in a chair. The three rods were at the same distance, but the middle one was moved in synchrony with each infant so as to create a motion parallax effect. The infant was then shown two further displays – one of three rods at the same distance from the infant, and the other with the middle rod further away (matching the effect of the motion parallax). The infants showed more interest in the three equidistant rods (a new display as far as they were concerned), demonstrating that they had the ability to use motion parallax. *How does this research develop the findings proposed by Gibson and Walk?*

A range of other cues contributes to depth perception. Yonas *et al*. (1986) showed that infants' ability to respond to depth cues in pictures emerges rather late. The ability to respond to overlap emerged at about six months, and responsiveness to texture gradient and linear perspective was only apparent by about seven months. Bremner (1994) concluded that the ability to interpret dynamic cues (e.g. as in the study by Bower *et al*.) appears earlier than the ability to use static pictorial depth cues. *How does this research develop the findings proposed by Gibson and Walk?*

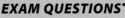

CAN YOU...?

EXAM QUESTIONS

SECTION B

Evaluate the methodology of Gibson and Walk's (1960) research 'The visual cliff'. [12]

With reference to alternative evidence, critically assess Gibson and Walk's (1960) research 'The visual cliff'. [12]

Notes *In Section B of the Unit 2 exam, you could be asked either of the questions above. In order to gain the full 12 marks for each question, your answer should follow the guidelines given on page 109.*

Example exam question with student answers

Examiner's comments on these answers can be found on page 177.

EXAMPLE OF QUESTION 2

> **Outline the procedures of Gibson and Walk's (1960) research 'The Visual Cliff'.** [12]

Megan's answer

At Cornell University, the researchers assembled the 'visual cliff' apparatus in a lab. The visual cliff consisted of a large glass sheet that is supported a foot or more above the floor with patterned material directly beneath the glass on one side, and several feet below it on the other. Chequered patterns on the material underneath the glass gave visual cues that one side was 'shallow', the other side was 'deep'. 36 infants from the age of 6–14 months were placed on the centre board of the visual cliff. All the infants were able to crawl (independent locomotion). Each child was then observed to see if it would crawl to the mother (cross onto the deep side) or if it would crawl onto the shallow side (away from the beckoning mother). Non-human animals (e.g. cats, rats, chicks, goats and aquatic turtles) were also tested on the visual cliff. They were also tested at the age at which they demonstrate locomotion. Chicks, lambs and kids (infant goats) were 1 day old. They also assessed two groups of kittens, both were 4 weeks old. One group had been 'reared normally' but the other had been reared in the dark for 27 days.

Tomas's answer

The visual cliff was a large glass sheet that was supported above the floor with patterned material directly beneath the glass on one side, and several feet below it on the other. The pattern on the material underneath the glass gave visual cues that one side was 'shallow', the other side was 'deep'. 36 infants from the age of 6-14 months were placed on the centre board of the visual cliff. Their mother then called to them to see if they would cross the 'visual cliff' to get to their mum. All of the 27 infants who moved off the centre board crawled out on to the shallow side at least once. Only 3 attempted to crawl on to the 'deep' side. Many infants crawled away from the mother when she called to them from the 'deep' side; others cried when she stood there because they could not get to her without crossing the 'deep' side. Chicks, at an age of less than 24 hours would always hop off the centre board on to the shallow side, rather than the 'deep' side. Kids and lambs never stepped on to the 'deep' side, even at 1 day old. Rats (who depend upon their whiskers to navigate, rather than visual cues), showed little preference for the shallow side, so long as they could feel the glass with their whiskers. When the centre board was placed higher than their whiskers, they nearly always descended onto the shallow side.

Buss (1989) Sex differences in human mate preferences

◀ Large eyes, rosy cheeks and red lips are all signs of youthfulness and therefore of fertility. Men who select partners with such features are more likely to be reproductively successful – so such signals become seen as attractive and are copied by older women.

The final two core studies are related to the topic of **individual differences**. There are many dimensions along which we all vary, such as intelligence and personality. Another dimension across which people vary is gender, and this core study looks at the differences between men and women when selecting a mate.

SEXUAL SELECTION

An important feature of most sexually reproducing species is that males are more brightly coloured than their female counterparts. The classic example of this is the peacock's tail – but *why* did the gaudy and cumbersome plumage of the peacock evolve? One would expect such disadvantageous traits not to be **naturally selected** – unless they enhanced reproductive success in some way. Charles Darwin suggested the answer lay in female *choice*. If a particular characteristic becomes established as a universal preference among females, then males who possess the best examples of that characteristic will have greater reproductive success. As a result, among peacocks there is selective pressure on males to produce brighter and more dramatic tails. This is the basic premise of the theory of sexual selection – any trait that increases the reproductive success of an individual will be selected and become more and more exaggerated over evolutionary time.

CONTEXT AND AIMS

Current mate preferences are of interest to evolutionary psychologists because they reflect prior selection pressures, thus providing important clues about a species' past reproductive history. They also demonstrate the current direction of **sexual selection**, by letting us know who is likely to be selected as a mate. Those mate characteristics that are heritable will appear more frequently in subsequent generations, whereas individuals lacking preferred characteristics will not be selected to mate and therefore their genes will not be perpetuated.

Despite the importance of mate preferences, little is known about which characteristics are valued by human males and females. There are three possible arguments that predict particular sex differences in mate preferences.

1. **Predictions based on parental investment and sexual selection theory (Trivers, 1972)** Sexual selection is driven in part by the different levels of investment males and females make in their offspring. In mammals, males make less investment because the female carries the baby. This greater investment means that females are likely to be choosier when selecting a partner. In particular, they might choose a partner who can offer resources (e.g. food, shelter, territory, protection) that will enhance the females' reproductive success. In modern times, this might translate into a preference for men with greater earning capacity, ambition and industriousness.

2. **Predictions based on reproductive value (Symons, 1979) and fertility (Williams, 1975)** A 13-year-old girl has high reproductive value (her future reproductive possibilities are high), whereas a 23-year-old would have lower reproductive value but higher fertility (her current probability of reproducing is higher). Youthfulness would be an indicator of both fertility and reproductive value. This could be signalled by physical characteristics (such as smooth skin, good muscle tone, lustrous hair and full lips) and by behavioural indicators (such as high energy level and sprightly gait). Males who fail to select females with such characteristics would, on average, leave fewer offspring than males who select females with such characteristics. It is less easy to judge male fertility from appearance, since age and fertility are less closely associated. This suggests that males more than females will value youth and physical attractiveness in potential mates.

3. **Prediction based on paternity probability (Daly et al., 1982)** In species where males invest parentally, then selection should favour those males who ensure that any effort is directed towards their own offspring rather than those of another male. Sexual jealousy is a means of increasing paternity probability. It functions to 'guard' their mate and dissuade male competitors. Preference for chastity in a potential mate is another mechanism of paternity probability. Males who preferred chaste females in our **Environment of Evolutionary Adaptation (EEA)** presumably enjoyed greater reproductive success. Females have less need for chastity because they can be certain of their own parenthood. However, it is possible that male sexual experience may signal that the male might have to share resources between a number of females and therefore chastity may also be an important signal for females.

Aims

Buss aimed to investigate if evolutionary explanations for sex differences in human mate preferences are found in cultures with varying ecologies, locations, ethnic compositions, religious orientations and political inclinations. **Cross-cultural studies** offer an opportunity for testing evolution-based hypotheses because we would expect behaviours that are innate to be the same in all cultures.

PROCEDURES

Samples

Buss analysed responses from 37 samples from 33 countries, located on six continents and five islands, creating a total number of participants equal to 10 047. The samples are listed on the right.

The **samples** varied in size from 55 in Iran, to 1491 in the US mainland sample. Apart from the Iranian sample, all samples exceeded 100 participants. The mean sample size was 272 participants. The age of participants in the sample groups ranged from 16.96 years in New Zealand, to 28.71 in West Germany. The mean age of the overall sample was 23.05 years.

- The **sampling techniques** varied widely across countries.
- In Estonia, one sub-sample consisted of couples applying for a marriage licence.
- In Venezuela, the sample consisted of every fifth household in a series of neighbourhoods that varied in **socioeconomic** class.
- In South Africa, the Zulu sample consisted of a rural population, some of which had the questions read aloud to them.
- In West Germany, the sample was selected through newspaper ads.
- In New Zealand, the sample consisted of high school students taken from three schools.

Data collection

The research data was collected in most cases by native residents of each country and mailed to the USA for analysis. Research collaborators were unaware of the central **hypotheses** of the investigation.

The questionnaire

Buss used two instruments to assess respondents' views on mating preferences.

Instrument 1: Rating

- **Part 1 Biographical data**, e.g. age, sex, religion, marital status, number of brothers and sisters.
- **Part 2 Mate preferences**, e.g. questions about the age at which respondents preferred to marry, age difference between respondent and spouse, how many children were desired.
- **Part 3 Rating scale** Participants had to rate 18 characteristics on a four-point rating scale from 3 (indispensable) to 0 (unimportant) – see right. Interspersed among these 18 were the four target variables: good financial prospects; good looks; chastity: no previous sexual intercourse; and ambition and industriousness.

Instrument 2: Ranking Participants were asked to place 13 characteristics in rank order based on their desirability in someone they might want to marry. Rank '1' was given to the most desirable characteristic, '13' to the least desirable characteristic in a potential mate. Among these 13 characteristics were the two target variables: good earning capacity; and physical attractiveness. Other variables included being religious, kind and understanding, and having an exciting personality.

Translations Research collaborations had the task of employing three bilingual speakers: one translated the questionnaire from English into their native language; the second translated the answers back into English; and the third resolved any discrepancies.

The translators were instructed to make sure all the terms were 'neutral' rather than using words that might be linked to a specific sex. For example, 'physically attractive' is sex neutral whereas 'handsome' and 'beautiful' are sex-linked.

Occasionally, questionnaires needed to be amended to reflect the cultural differences. In Sweden, many couples do not get married but just live together, so the questions had to be modified to reflect this cultural difference. In Nigeria, polygyny (a man having more than one wife) is practised, so questions had to be added to reflect the possibility of multiple wives.

SAMPLES USED IN THE STUDY

Nigeria, S. African (whites), S. African (Zulu), Zambia, China, India, Indonesia, Iran, Israel (Jewish), Israel (Palestinian), Japan, Taiwan, Bulgaria, Estonian S.S.R., Poland, Yugoslavia, Belgium, France, Finland, Germany – West, Great Britain, Greece, Ireland, Italy, Netherlands, Norway, Spain, Sweden, Canada (English), Canada (French), USA (Mainland), USA (Hawaii), Australia, New Zealand, Brazil, Columbia, Venezuela.

Rating scale

Respondents were asked to rate each characteristic on a four-point scale (see text).

	3	2	1	0
Good cook and housekeeper				
Pleasing disposition				
Sociability				
Similar educational background				
Refinement, neatness				
Good financial prospects				
Chastity: no previous sexual intercourse				
Dependable character				
Emotional stability and maturity				
Desire for home and children				
Favourable social status				
Good looks				
Similar religious background				
Ambition and industriousness				
Similar political background				
Mutual attraction – love				
Good health				
Education and intelligence				

DO IT YOURSELF

No. 5.36

Conduct some research yourself using the rating scale above. Compare male and female answers on the four target variables (good financial prospects, good looks, chastity, and ambition and industriousness). Decide on a suitable method to present your key findings. (The questionnaire Buss used can be found on: homepage.psy.utexas.edu/homepage/Group/BussLAB/measures.htm.)

David Buss's homepage, with links to articles and interviews, is at: homepage.psy.utexas.edu/HomePage/Group/BussLAB/publications.htm.

The mating game: see Robin Dunbar's research at: www.bbc.co.uk/science/humanbody/mind/articles/emotions/lonelyhearts.shtml.

Original article
The full reference for this core study is: Buss, D.M. (1989). Sex differences in human mate preferences: Evolutionary hypotheses tested in 37 cultures. *Behavioural and Brain Sciences*, 12, 1–49. You can read the article in full at: homepage.psy.utexas.edu/HomePage/Group/BussLAB/pdffiles/SexDifferencesinHuman.PDF.

Buss (1989) Sex differences in human mate preferences

FINDINGS

Good financial prospects

In 36 of the 37 samples (97%), females valued 'good financial prospects' in a mate more highly than did males. The sole exception was Spain, where there was a difference in the predicted direction, but it was not **significant**.

There was considerable variation in how much this mate characteristic was valued. In general, Western European samples valued earning capacity less than South American, North American, Asian, and African samples, although there were variations among samples within continents.

Ambition and industriousness

In 34 of the 37 samples (92%), females expressed a higher valuation for 'ambition and industriousness' in a mate than did males. In 29 samples (78%) this difference was significant at the .05 level (i.e. a possibility of 5% that these results occured by chance), providing moderate support for this hypothesised sex difference.

In three samples – those from Colombia, Spain and South African Zulus – the opposite sex difference was found (i.e. males rated 'ambition and industriousness' more highly than females did), although it was only significant in the South African Zulu sample. The research collaborator for the Zulu sample suggested that this may be because physical tasks, such as building the house, are considered to be women's work. Males in this culture usually commute from rural to urban centres to work.

Both sexes in the Nigerian, Zulu, Chinese, Taiwanese, Estonian, Palestinian, Colombian and Venezuelan samples placed a high value on this mate characteristic. This characteristic was not rated low in any sample, although samples in The Netherlands, Great Britain, West Germany and Finland expressed the least amount of preference for it.

Age differences

In all 37 samples, males preferred mates who were younger. The mean age difference preferred by males was 2.66 years, and the mean age at which males prefer to marry is 27.49 years. This therefore suggests an ideal age for females of 24.83 years, which is closer to peak female *fertility* than peak female *reproductive value*.

Across all countries, females preferred mates who were older. The mean desirable age difference was 3.42 years, and the mean age that females prefer to marry is 25.39, therefore ideal mate age is 28.81 years.

In cultures where polygyny was substantial (Nigeria and Zambia), male preference for being older was at it largest, 6.45 and 7.38 years, respectively. This could be because males tend to be older when they acquire wives in polygynous systems compared with monogamous (one partner) mating systems.

Good looks

All of the 37 samples showed that males rated 'good looks' in their mate more than females did. This difference was significant at the .05 level in 34 (92%) of the samples.

'Good looks' were particularly important to males in the Bulgarian, Palestinian, Nigerian and Zambian samples.

Chastity

Samples varied tremendously in the value placed on this characteristic. In 23 (62%) of the samples, males preferred chastity in their mates, whereas there was no significance in the remaining 14 samples. Samples from China, India, Indonesia, Iran, Taiwan and Israel (Palestinians) attached a high value to chastity in a potential mate. Chastity was viewed as 'irrelevant or unimportant' in most of the Western European samples.

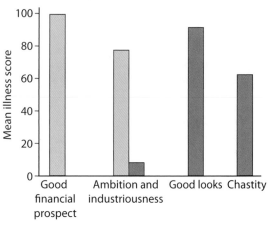

▼ Graph 1 showing the sex differences

☐ % samples where significantly more females valued this characteristic

▨ % samples where significantly more males valued this characteristic

A validity check

Two important questions needed to be answered:

1. Do self-reported preferences accurately reflect actual preferences?
2. Do mate preferences accurately reflect actual mating decisions?

In 27 of the 33 countries sampled, demographic data were obtained. The mean age difference was found to be 2.99 years, which is very close to the mean preferred age difference found in this study (2.66 for males and 3.42 for females, mean is 3.04 years).

The preferred age for marriage given in the study also closely matched actual age. For example, males in this study suggested the mean age for marriage would be 27.5, and the actual mean age was 28.2. For females, the mean preferred age was 25.4 and the actual mean age was 25.3.

MEET THE RESEARCHER

David M. Buss is Professor of Psychology at the University of Texas, at Austin. He is the author of more than 200 articles and books on the topic of evolutionary psychology, covering mating strategies, prestige, jealousy, homicide and, most recently, stalking. He has won many prestigious awards, including the American Psychological Society Distinguished Scientific Award for Early Career Contribution to Psychology in 1988. In his spare time he enjoys tennis, squash and films. He sent us the following anecdote about the study.

'The collection of data from the Zulu of South Africa proved especially difficult. My Zulu research collaborator said that many of the women were reluctant to divulge their mate preferences, because they feared that if men had this knowledge, they might use it to their advantage (presumably in deceiving women by feigning the possession of the desired characteristics). Nonetheless, he eventually managed to persuade the sample of Zulu women to express their preferences on the Zulu translations of our research instruments.'

(Personal communication)

CONCLUSIONS

Five evolution-based predictions received support from the data.

1. Females valued the financial capacity of potential mates more than males did, supporting the hypothesis that women seek cues related to resources.
2. Females valued ambition and industriousness more than males did, again supporting the hypothesis that women seek cues related to resources.
3. Males valued physical attractiveness and relative youth more than females did, supporting the hypothesis that males seek cues related to high reproductive capacity. The fact that males sought partners around the age of 25 suggests they look for cues related to fertility rather than reproductive value, falsifying Symond's view that reproductive value was more important. However, the fact that the age preference was several years beyond peak fertility suggests that other non-evolutionary factors may also be involved, such as compatibility and maturity.
4. Females preferred somewhat older mates. This was not specifically predicted at the outset, but supports the importance of resources because older men would be likely to have greater resources.
5. Males valued chastity more than females did, supporting the importance of paternity probability – although only modestly, as a large number of samples showed no difference. These less impressive results could be because chastity is less directly observable.

Buss concluded that his findings support evolutionary explanations of human behaviour; specifically that mating behaviour should differ according to gender, reflecting the differences in the reproductive capacities of males and females.

Buss also concluded that these findings show that mate preferences are not simply about female choosiness. Human males and females both express preferences and there are selective advantages for doing so.

At the same time, there are also cultural influences in play, as shown, for example, by the variability in chastity as a factor in mate choice.

DO IT YOURSELF
No. 5.37

- Construct your own step-by-step guide to the procedures of this study. Number each step.
- Find a good way to represent the results on the facing page graphically, for example using a bar chart.
- Write an abstract for this study, as you have done before. This abstract should contain brief details of the context and aims, procedures, findings and conclusions of this study – all in about 200 words.

▲ David Buss (1953–).

CAN YOU...?
No.5.17

1... Explain the process of sexual selection.
2... Outline **three or more** basic predictions about mate preferences that arise from evolutionary theory.
3... Briefly outline the aims of this study.
4... How many participants were there in the study?
5... Describe **three** key aspects of the sample.
6... Outline how **three** of the samples were obtained.
7... Describe the questionnaire that was used with the participants, identifying **six** key features.
8... Outline **six** findings from this study.
9... What was the purpose of the validity check and what did it show?
10... For each finding, state a conclusion that could be drawn from it. Try to make each conclusion different.
11... State the main conclusion that can be drawn from this study.
12... Outline **three** other conclusions.
13... What evidence leads you to conclude that this study supports evolutionary explanations of mate preference?
14... What evidence leads you to conclude that this study supports other explanations of mate preference?

EXAM QUESTIONS
SECTION A
Summarise the aims **and** context of Buss's (1989) research 'Sex differences in human mate preferences'. [12]

Outline the procedures of Buss's (1989) research 'Sex differences in human mate preferences'. [12]

Describe the findings **and** conclusions of Buss's (1989) research 'Sex differences in human mate preferences'. [12]

Notes *In Section A of the Unit 2 exam, you could be asked any of the questions above. Each question will be worth 12 marks. In order to gain the full 12 marks, your answer should:*

- ▶ *Be accurate and well detailed.*
- ▶ *Display a depth and range of knowledge, although not necessarily in equal measure; this means that you can either cover a few points in considerable detail (i.e. depth) or cover a number of points in less detail (range).*
- ▶ *Be well structured and coherent.*
- ▶ *Have accurate grammar, punctuation and spelling.*
- ▶ *Be about 200–250 words in length, which is fewer words than for other 12-mark questions, but the emphasis is on accuracy.*

On this spread we are going to evaluate the core study by looking at issues related to its methodology, and comparing the study to alternative evidence. When it comes to evaluation, you can make up your own mind. We have presented some evidence and statements, and invite you to use this to construct your own view of the core study.

EVALUATING THE METHODOLOGY

See Chapter 6 (Applied research methods) for an explanation of these concepts.

Method

Buss used a **questionnaire** to collect his data. *What advantage does this offer? What disadvantage does this pose?*

Reliability

The questionnaires were given to participants just once. *How **reliable** do you think their answers were?*

Validity

Extensive efforts were made to ensure that all respondents understood the questions – the questionnaire was translated into local languages, the questionnaire was read out to those who could not read, and questions were adapted to match local customs (such as adding questions related to multiple wives for cultures where polygyny was practised). *To what extent do you think that the answers provided accurately reflected what the respondents really felt and thought?*

The truthfulness of respondents' answers might have been affected by **social desirability bias**. *To what extent do you think that the answers provided accurately reflected what the respondents really felt and thought?*

One questionnaire asked respondents to rank order certain characteristics sought in potential mates. *How might the use of rank ordering affect the **validity** of Buss' findings?*

Sampling

The **mean** age of male participants was 23.49, and 22.52 for female participants. *How might this mean age have affected Buss's findings?*

The **sampling** strategies in the different cultures varied dramatically. Buss noted that many of the samples were 'samples of convenience (e.g. university students) and cannot be viewed as representative'. *How might the use of widely differing sampling techniques have affected Buss's findings?*

Buss also argued that the wide variety of sampling techniques used would tend to increase the consistency of findings because it minimises the biasing effects of any particular sampling technique. *How might the use of widely differing sampling techniques have affected Buss's findings?*

Buss acknowledges that the samples used were not representative, in particular rural and less educated people were underrepresented. *How might this issue affect the validity of Buss's results?*

Buss surveyed 10 047 individuals from 37 different cultures, but the 'cultures' are dominated by 'westernised, industrialised nations' (26 of the 37), which contributed 7749 (77%) of the participants in the whole sample group. *How might this issue affect the validity of Buss's results?*

Ethical issues

Psychologists are concerned about 'socially sensitive research', i.e. research that might have direct social consequences for the participants involved. *Are there any **ethical issues** evident in Buss's research?*

ALTERNATIVE EVIDENCE

Other cross-cultural studies

Cunningham *et al.* (1995) found very close agreement across cultural groups when rating female physical attractiveness. In this study, recently arrived native Asian and Hispanic students and white Americans rated the attractiveness of Asian, Hispanic, black, and white women in photographs. The mean correlation between groups in attractiveness ratings was +.93. *How do these findings support Buss's findings?*

Singh (1993) found that waist-to-hip ratio (WHR) was related to attractiveness across many cultures. Men prefer women who have a low WHR. The ideal is about 0.7. A woman with this WHR is likely to have a large bottom, indicating good fat reserves for pregnancy, and a narrow waist, indicating that she is not pregnant. Thus the reason that a low WHR would be attractive is that it is a sign of youthfulness and fertility. *How do these findings support or develop Buss's findings?*

Little *et al.* (2007) provided evidence of another indicator of fertility – facial symmetry. It has been proposed that symmetry is a sign of **genetic** robustness, which would be a desirable characteristic in a mate because it would be linked to more successful reproduction. Little *et al.* examined preferences for symmetry in both the UK and the Hadza, a 'primitive' hunter–gatherer society in Tanzania. Both groups preferred symmetrical faces, and this was strongest in the Hadza. *How do these findings support or develop Buss's findings?*

Lonely hearts advertisements

Waynforth and Dunbar (1995) recognised that personal ads were an easy-to-access source of quantifiable data on human mate choice. Such ads are particularly interesting because they represent the writer's initial or ideal bid in the lengthy process of mate selection. In contrast, actual partners represent the compromises that inevitably have to be made.

Waynforth and Dunbar analysed nearly 900 ads from four American newspapers. The ads were sorted into 10-year-age groups (20–29, 30–39, etc.) and scored for the frequency with which they mentioned certain key terms related to the following categories: physical attractiveness; wealth/status/family commitment; sexual fidelity; tolerance of children; and age requirements. They found the following differences in the ads posted by men and women:

- More men than women sought a youthful mate.
- More men sought a physically attractive mate.
- More women used 'physically attractive' terms to describe themselves.
- More men reported their economic status/earning power when describing themselves.

How do these findings support or develop Buss's findings?

DO IT YOURSELF
No. 5.38

Conduct your own research on mate preferences.
1. Ask people to identify (in rank order) their top five characteristics in an ideal mate. Then identify which of these relate to physical attractiveness, resources, etc.
2. Is there a difference between males and females? Is there a difference in different age groups?
3. Analyse the contents of lonely hearts ads. For each ad, record
   - the sex of the advertiser
   - the age group
   - whether the person is seeking or offering resources, or both
   - whether they is seeking or offering physical attractiveness, or both.
4. Is there a difference between males and females? Is there a difference in different age groups?

CAN YOU...?
No. 5.18

EXAM QUESTIONS

SECTION B
Evaluate the methodology of Buss's (1989) research 'Sex differences in human mate preferences'. [12]

With reference to alternative evidence, critically assess Buss's (1989) research 'Sex differences in human mate preferences'. [12]

Notes *In Section B of the Unit 2 exam, you could be asked either of the questions above. In order to gain the full 12 marks for each question, your answer should follow the guidelines given on page 91.*

In a later study, Dunbar (1995) looked at gay personal ads and found that heterosexual women were three times more likely to seek resources and status than lesbians, whereas homosexual men offered resources about half as often as did heterosexual men. This supports the evolutionary explanation because we would not expect lesbian and gay mate choice to be related to reproductive criteria. *How do these findings support or develop Buss's findings?*

Dunbar also notes that times have changed, and today many women have economic security of their own and are less interested in a partner's resources. They therefore often seek a 'caring and sharing' partner rather than one with resources. This still makes evolutionary sense because that kind of partner should enhance reproductive success. Indeed, Berezckei *et al.* (1997) found that females advertised for men who were family-oriented as well as financially sound. *How do these findings support or develop Buss's findings?*

Alternative explanations

Universal ideals of beauty can be explained from another evolutionary perspective. The reason for universal agreement may not be due to the fact that such features indicate fertility – they also are associated with a 'baby face': a high forehead, big eyes, small nose and chin (think Kate Moss's face). Adults may well have evolved a preference for 'baby' features because this ensures that we care for our young, and for this reason such features elicit feelings of attraction. However, Cellerino (2003) suggests these same features are signs of high levels of **oestrogen**, i.e. fertility.

Other factors may affect our attraction to others. **Nurture** explanations for interpersonal attraction include the 'mere exposure effect' – the more often you see someone, the more you like him or her. For example, a cross-cultural study by Langlois and Roggman (1990) found that people preferred 'average faces', which has been explained in terms of the *mere exposure effect*, that is we like things that are familiar to us. However, Cellerino (2003) found that when 'average' faces were enhanced (using computer graphics) with features associated with high levels of oestrogen, they were regarded as more attractive. *How do these findings contradict, support or develop Buss's findings?*

Example exam question with student answers

Examiner's comments on these answers can be found on page 178.

EXAMPLE OF QUESTION 4

Evaluate the methodology of Buss's (1989) research 'Sex differences in human mate preferences'. [12]

Megan's answer
Buss's research is really good because he asked over 10 000 people to take part. This means his sample is representative. He also used a questionnaire, which allowed him to collect the data quickly. There are no ethical issues in Buss's research.

Tomas's answer
Buss used a questionnaire to collect his data. This allowed Buss to collect data from a large number of participants in a shorter space of time than if he had conducted interviews. However, participants may not tell the truth or may not know what they want in a potential mate or may give what they think are socially desirable responses.

Is ranking the characteristics of ideal potential mates really valid? Just because we may think we know what we want in a mate doesn't mean that is what we end up with! Also by rank ordering certain characteristics sought in potential mates we do not know how much more important the differences are as the rank order may not be of equal intervals. A rank order of characteristics sought in an ideal mate offers us only ordinal level data, when interval data would be preferable.

Buss surveyed about 10 000 individuals from 37 different cultures, however the 'cultures' are dominated by 'westernised, industrialised nations' (26 of the 37) and these samples contributed to nearly 8000 of the whole sample group. Although Buss' research initially seems impressive, if the sample is dominated by one type of particular culture then it is not representative of the different relationship styles. It might have been more valid to include more traditional cultures. Secondly, the mean age of male participants was 23.5 and was 22.5 for female participants. This is quite young and therefore may not reflect what older individuals would look for in a potential mate. Thirdly, the sampling strategies in the different cultures varied dramatically. Buss notes that many of the samples were 'samples of convenience' (e.g. university students) and cannot be viewed as representative. By not being representative it means that the individuals who took part in the research may not have been typical of everyone in that culture. Buss himself noted that 'rural, less educated and lower levels of socioeconomic status are underrepresented'.

Rosenhan (1973) On being sane in insane places

▲ As touch, taste, sight, smell and hearing boarded the chartered flight to Havana, Professor Fitzherbert knew in his heart that he had lost more than good friends, in fact, he had finally lost his senses.

We finish Chapter 5 with one of the all time classic studies in psychology. In Unit 1 you studied a number of different therapies used to treat mental illness, each representing a different approach in psychology. One approach, the **biological approach**, seeks to explain behaviour in terms of physical processes – such as **neurotransmitters**, **hormones**, and **genetic** factors. This means that psychological disorders are explained in the same way that physical illnesses are explained, i.e. in terms of physical factors. The biological approach is also referred to as the **'medical model'** because it aims to treat psychological disorders as if they were physical illnesses. Psychological *disorders* are called *illnesses* (mental illness). Cure is only possible by removing the root cause and returning the body to its 'normal' level of functioning. Because of its emphasis on *scientific* investigation and understanding, the medical model is the most widely respected model of abnormality. However, its representation of mental disorders as 'disease' states equivalent to physical illnesses also makes it one of the most controversial.

DIAGNOSING MENTAL ILLNESS

A key feature of the medical model of abnormality is that mental illnesses are diagnosed in the same way that physical illnesses are diagnosed – the doctor (psychiatrist) identifies a set of symptoms in the patient and uses these to identify the disorder. The doctor is helped by a set of diagnostic criteria such as the **Diagnostic and Statistical Manual (DSM)**, which lists all mental illnesses and their symptoms. The manual is revised regularly, with the current version being *DSM-IV-TR*.

In some circumstances, the medical model has proved very effective, for example in the case of **syphilis**. In the 19th century, the syndrome called *general paresis* was identified, which had psychological symptoms such as delusions of grandeur and progressive forgetfulness. Once it was recognised that all of the symptoms belonged to one disorder (called *general paresis*), systematic research found a common cause – the syphilis bacterium. Once the cause was known, a cure could be found, which happened in 1909 with the discovery of *arsphenamine* as a treatment for the disorder.

This demonstrates that:
- Mental illnesses might have physical causes.
- In order to discover such causes, one needs to diagnose a syndrome.
- Once a cause has been identified, a suitable treatment may be found.

CONTEXT AND AIMS

In the 1960s, psychiatrists such as Michel Foucault, Ronnie Laing and Thomas Szasz launched the '**anti-psychiatry**' movement, challenging the fundamental claims and practices of mainstream psychiatry, i.e. the medical model. Foucault (1961) described the development of the concept of mental illness in the 17th and 18th centuries, when 'unreasonable' members of the population were locked away, institutionalised and subjected to some quite inhuman treatments, such as using freezing showers and straightjackets. Foucault argued that the concepts of sanity and insanity were in fact social constructs, i.e. they were not 'real' but, instead, constructions made by a particular society.

Foucault's ideas had a strong influence on Laing in the UK and Szasz in the USA. Laing (1960) argued that **schizophrenia** (described on page 8) was best understood in terms of an individual's experience rather than as a set of symptoms. Szasz (1960) argued that the medical model is no more sophisticated than believing in demonology, and is unhelpful to our understanding of psychiatric conditions. He suggested that the concept of mental illness was simply a way of excluding non-conformists from society.

David Rosenhan was influenced by these ideas and, with regard to his interest in the law as well as psychology, asked: *'If sanity and insanity exist, how shall we know them?'*. We may be convinced that we can tell the normal from the abnormal, but the evidence for this ability is not quite as compelling.

- It is common to read about murder trials where the prosecution and defence each call their own psychiatrists who disagree on the defendant's sanity.
- There is much disagreement about the meaning of terms such as 'sanity', 'insanity', 'mental illness' and 'schizophrenia'.
- Conceptions of normality and abnormality are not universal; what is considered normal in one culture may be seen as quite aberrant in another.

Rosenhan did not suggest that there is no such thing as deviant or odd behaviours, nor that 'mental illness' is not associated with personal anguish. However, there is an important question about whether the *diagnosis* of insanity is based on characteristics of patients themselves or the context in which the patient is seen. Evidence suggests that the diagnosis of mental illness is *'useless at best and downright harmful, misleading, and pejorative at worst'* (Rosenhan, 1973).

Aims

Rosenhan aimed to investigate whether psychiatrists could distinguish between people who are genuinely mentally ill and those who are not. He argued that the question of personality versus situation can be investigated by getting 'normal' people (that is people who do not have, and have never had, serious psychiatric symptoms) to seek to be admitted to a psychiatric hospital. If such 'pseudopatients' were diagnosed as sane, this would show that the sane individual can be distinguished from the insane context in which he is found. On the other hand, if such pseudopatients were diagnosed as insane, then this suggests that it is the context rather than the individual's characteristics that determines the diagnosis, that the psychiatric diagnosis of 'insanity' has less to do with the patient and more about the (insane) environment in which they are found. In other words, do *'the salient characteristics that lead to diagnoses reside in the patients themselves or in the environments and contexts in which the observers find them?'* (Rosenhan, 1973).

PROCEDURES

Study 1

The pseudopatients were five men and three women of various ages and occupations (for example, graduate student, psychologist, paediatrician, psychiatrist, painter and housewife), including Rosenhan himself. They attempted to gain admission to 12 different hospitals in five different states in the USA. The hospitals represented a range of different kinds of psychiatric institutions – modern and old, well staffed and poorly staffed. Only one was a private hospital.

Gaining admission to hospital Each pseudopatient called a hospital and asked for an appointment. On arrival (s)he told the admissions officer that (s)he had been hearing voices saying words that included 'empty', 'hollow', and 'thud'. These symptoms were deliberately chosen because of their similarity to existential symptoms (the alleged meaninglessness of life) and their absence in the psychiatric literature. Beyond the description of auditory hallucinations, each pseudopatient described their life events accurately (both good and bad). None of them had any history of pathological (i.e. abnormal) behaviour.

Life in hospital The pseudopatients were instructed to behaviour normally once they were admitted to the psychiatric ward, and, other than some understandable nervousness and tension about being found out, the pseudopatients behaved perfectly normal.

They spent their time talking to the other patients, and making notes of observations of life on the ward. Initially the notes were made surreptitiously, but it soon became apparent that the staff did not really care. The pseudopatients secretly did not take their medication, but otherwise followed the ward routine.

The reports from the nurses showed that the patients were friendly, co-operative and 'exhibited no abnormal indications'. The pseudopatients did not know when they would be discharged; one of the conditions of taking part in the study was that they had to get out by their own devices.

Study 2

After the results of this research were publicised, staff in another hospital (that had not received any pseudopatients) challenged Rosenhan claiming that it could not happen in their hospital. So Rosenhan informed them that in the next three months, one or more pseudopatients would present themselves. The staff were asked to rate on a 10-point scale their confidence level that the person was genuinely ill (where 1 reflected high confidence that the patient was a pseudopatient). Judgements were obtained on 193 patients admitted for psychiatric treatment during this time.

Study 3

Rosenhan also included a mini-study of the way staff responded to pseudopatients. In four of the hospitals, pseudopatients approached a staff member with the following question: *'Pardon me, Mr/Mrs/Dr X, could you tell me when I will be eligible for grounds privileges?'* (or *'… when will I be presented at the staff meeting?'* or *'… when am I likely to be discharged?'*). The pseudopatient did this as normally as possible and avoided asking any particular person more than once in a day.

DO IT YOURSELF

No. 5.39

Divide your class into groups and secretly assign different 'approaches' to each group (biological, behaviourist, psychodynamic, cognitive – and you could include some others, such as humanist, evolutionary and social constructionist). Then have a class discussion about whether 'mental illnesses' exist and how best to diagnose or treat them – each group should argue from the point of view of the approach assigned to it.

---

www *The Birth of Modern Psychiatry* is a great video discussing anti-psychiatry and this core study, with commentary by David Rosenhan. See www.youtube.com/watch?v=McPnMQ31W_k for Part 1 and links to other parts.

Original article
The full reference for this core study is Rosenhan, D.L. (1973). On being sane in insane places. *Science, 179,* 250–258. You can read the full article at: psychrights.org/articles/rosenham.htm.

Other resources
- Read books by Foucault, Laing and Szasz.
- Read the book or see the film of *One Flew Over The Cuckoo's Nest.*
- *Buster's Fired a Wobbler* (Burrell, 1989) is a more recent book based on the author's experiences as a psychiatric nurse in the UK.
- Research by Rosenhan is discussed in a chapter in *Opening Skinner's Box: Great Psychological Experiments of the Twentieth Century* (Slater, 2004), including Slater's replication of this study.
- A somewhat related experiment involving the diagnosis of 10 people (five with previously diagnosed mental illness, and five without) by three mental health experts was undertaken by BBC TV's Horizon series and broadcast in 2008 as two programmes entitled *How Mad Are You?*
- An episode of the *Simpson's* called *Stark Raving Dad* covers many of the points in the article. See: www.holah.karoo.net/rosenhan.htm for the link.

▲ The absurdity of psychiatric diagnosis is dramatically captured in the book *One Flew Over The Cuckoo's Nest* (Kesey, 1962). The book was based on Kesey's experience of working in a mental hospital, where he spent long hours talking to mental patients. He did not believe that these patients were insane, rather that society had pushed them out because they did not fit the conventional ideas of how people were supposed to act and behave. The book was a major success, echoing the public concern in the 1960s about the involuntary medication, lobotomies and electroconvulsive treatments being used on mental patients. In 1975, it was made into a film starring Jack Nicholson as Randle McMurphy, the rebellious inmate of a psychiatric hospital who fights back against the authorities' cold attitudes of institutional superiority. It was one of the most successful films of the 1970s.

FINDINGS

Study 1

All the pseudopatients were admitted and all but one were diagnosed as schizophrenic. Each was eventually discharged with a diagnosis of schizophrenia 'in remission'. The length of hospitalisation varied from 7–52 days, with an average of 19 days.

Very limited contact between staff and patients was observed in this study. For example, the average amount of time that attendants spent 'out of the cage' (the glassed quarters where professional staff had their offices) was 11.3% of their total time at work, and much of this was spent on chores rather than mingling with patients. On average, the nurses emerged from the cage 11.5 times per shift. The physicians, especially psychiatrists, were even less available. They were rarely seen on the wards, appearing an average of 6.7 times per day, with the average daily contact between patients and psychiatrists being 6.8 minutes per day (based on data from six patients over 129 days of hospitalisation).

While the pseudopatients were at the hospital, the 'real' patients regularly voiced their suspicions, with 35 out of 118 patients making statements such as *'You're not crazy'*, *'You're a journalist'* or *'You're a professor checking up on the hospital'*.

During the research, the pseudopatients were given a total of 2100 tablets, including *Elavil* (amitriptyline), *Stelazine* (trifluoperazine) and *Compazine* (prochlorperazine).

Nursing records for three pseudopatients indicate that their writing was seen as an aspect of their pathological behaviour (*'patient engages in writing behaviour'*).

Study 2

Over the three months, 193 patients were admitted for treatment. None of them was actually pseudopatients but:

- 41 were judged to be pseudopatients by at least one staff member
- 23 were suspected of being pseudopatients by at least one psychiatrist
- 19 were suspected of being pseudopatients by a psychiatrist and one other staff member.

Study 3

The most common response was a brief reply as the member of staff continued walking past without pausing or making eye contact. Only 4% of the psychiatrists and 0.5% of the nurses stopped; 2% in each group paused and chatted.

In contrast, as a control, a young woman approached staff members on the Stanford University campus and asked them six questions. All of the staff members stopped and answered all questions, maintaining eye contact.

CONCLUSIONS

Type 1 and 2 errors

In study 1, the psychiatrists failed to detect the pseudopatients' sanity despite the fact that they were clearly sane. This failure may be because doctors have a strong bias towards a **Type 2 error** – they are more inclined to call a healthy person sick (a false positive) than a sick person healthy (a false negative, **Type 1 error**). It is clearly more dangerous to misdiagnose illness than health, and err on the side of caution.

In study 2, the hospital staff were now making more Type 1 errors (calling a sick person healthy), presumably because they were trying to avoid making Type 2 errors. *'One thing is certain: any diagnostic process that lends itself so readily to massive errors cannot be a very reliable one'* (Rosenhan, 1973).

Making Type 1 errors may be reasonable when dealing with physical illness, but is less necessary in psychiatry, and also considerably more dangerous because psychiatric diagnoses carry personal, legal and social stigmas.

Psychodiagnostic labels

The results show the profound effect of a 'label' on our perceptions of people. Many studies in psychology have demonstrated the same thing. For example, Asch (1946) showed that central personality traits (such as 'warm' and 'cold') have a powerful effect on how we perceive someone's total personality.

In the same way, once a person is labelled 'abnormal', this means that all subsequent data about him or her are interpreted in that light because such labels are 'sticky'. For example, the pseudopatients were released with the label 'schizophrenia *in remission'*, suggesting that they were still schizophrenic but temporarily sane. It is doubtful that people really regard mental illness in the same way as they regard physical illness. You can recover from a broken leg, but not from schizophrenia (you remain 'in remission').

MEET THE RESEARCHER

David L. Rosenhan is Emeritus Professor of Law and Psychology at Stanford University, a post he has held since 1970. This core study was an outcome of his combined and continuing interests in psychology and law – the legal issues around defining someone as insane. Slater (2004) reported that Rosenhan recruited his pseudopatients by phoning friends and asking if they were doing anything in October. This included his friend Martin Seligman, with whom he wrote the classic textbook *Abnormal Psychology*. Slater also reported that Rosenhan had recently been afflicted by a paralysing condition that was as yet undiagnosed: *'This renegade researcher, one who devoted the better part of his career to the dismantling of psychiatric diagnosis. Now here he was, a diagnostic question himself'* (Slater, 2004, page 65).

▲ David Rosenhan.

DO IT YOURSELF No. 5.40

This is a complex study, with many important themes. After you have read through the whole study (and you might also read the original), construct a mobile or some other work of art to illustrate the various strands. Present your work to the class, explaining what you selected to represent. This will help you to process the various different studies and themes within the report.

The central theme is this core study is personality versus situation. This theme was also central to Milgram's study and to Attribution Theory (see page 46).

Powerlessness and depersonalisation

The behaviour of the staff in study 3 served to show how the patients were depersonalised, because contact was avoided. In general, the staff treated the patients with little respect: punishing them for small incidents and beating them. Such treatment is depersonalising, and creates an overwhelming sense of powerlessness. This was further exacerbated by the living conditions in the psychiatric hospitals: personal privacy was minimal (e.g. no doors on toilets), anyone could read patients' files (e.g. volunteers on the wards), and physical examinations were conducted in semi-public rooms.

Another source of depersonalisation was the use of psychotropic drugs. Drugs convince staff that treatment is being conducted and therefore further patient contact is not necessary.

Rosenhan argued that we prefer to invent knowledge (e.g. labelling someone as 'schizophrenic') rather than admitting we don't know. This is not merely depressing, but frightening. How many people in our psychiatric institutions are sane, one wonders, but not recognised as such? Once hospitalised, the patient is socialised by the bizarre setting, a process Goffman (1961) called 'mortification'.

▲ Depersonalisation.

Summary and conclusion

It is clear that we cannot distinguish the sane from the insane. Hospitalisation for the mentally ill results in powerlessness, depersonalisation, mortification and self-labelling – all of which are counter-therapeutic.

One solution might be to use other approaches to the treatment of mental illness, such as community mental health facilities to avoid the effects of the institutional setting, or to use behaviour therapies that avoid psychiatric labels.

A second solution is to increase the sensitivity of mental health workers and recognise that their behaviour is also controlled by the situation.

DO IT YOURSELF
No. 5.41

You can write an abstract for this study, as you have done before. This abstract should contain brief details of the context and aims, procedures, findings and conclusions of this study – all in about 50 words for each.

You could also construct your own step-by-step guide to the procedures of this study. Number each step to help you remember the details.

CAN YOU...?
No. 5.19

1... Explain the medical model of abnormality.

2... Explain the views of the anti-psychiatry movement and how this led to Rosenhan's study.

3... Briefly outline the aims of this study.

4... The pseudopatients weren't the participants in this study – they were **confederates** of the researcher. Who were the participants in this study?

5... Why did Rosenhan decide to have the pseudopatients display 'existential' symptoms?

6... Identify **six** key aspects of the procedures for study 1.

7... Describe details of the procedures in the two additional studies.

8... Identify **six** findings from this study.

9... For each finding, state a conclusion that could be drawn from it. Try to make each conclusion different.

10... Describe a situation in which the label 'schizophrenia in remission' might be a handicap to an individual.

11... Explain the terms 'Type 1 error' and 'Type 2 error'.

12... When might it be reasonable to make a Type 1 error?

13... Explain what the term 'mortification' means in this context.

14... What evidence leads you to conclude that this study supports the view that we cannot distinguish the sane from the insane?

15... What evidence leads you to conclude that this study supports the view that situational factors rather than dispositional factors determine the diagnosis of mental illness?

EXAM QUESTIONS

SECTION A

Summarise the aims **and** context of Rosenhan's (1973) research 'On being sane in insane places'. [12]

Outline the procedures of Rosenhan's (1973) research 'On being sane in insane places'. [12]

Describe the findings **and** conclusions of Rosenhan's (1973) research 'On being sane in insane places'. [12]

Notes *In Section A of the Unit 2 exam, you could be asked any of the questions above. Each question will be worth 12 marks. In order to gain the full 12 marks, your answer should:*

▶ *Be accurate and well detailed.*

▶ *Display a depth and range of knowledge, though not necessarily in equal measure; this means that you can either cover a few points in considerable detail (i.e. depth) or cover a number of points in less detail (range).*

▶ *Be well structured and coherent.*

▶ *Have accurate grammar, punctuation and spelling.*

▶ *Be about 200–250 words in length, which is fewer words than for other 12-mark questions, but the emphasis is on accuracy.*

Rosenhan (1973) On being sane in insane places

On this spread we are going to evaluate the core study by looking at issues related to its methodology, and comparing the study to alternative evidence. When it comes to evaluation, you can make up your own mind. We have presented some evidence and statements, and invite you to use this to construct your own view of the core study.

EVALUATING THE METHODOLOGY

See Chapter 6 (Applied Research Methods) for an explanation of these concepts.

Method

Rosenhan conducted a **naturalistic observation**. *What advantages does this offer? What disadvantages does this offer?*

The observations were made by the pseudopatients, a kind of 'participant observation'. *What are the advantages and disadvantages of such observations in the context of this study?*

Study 3 was an experiment (a field experiment). *What advantages does this offer? What disadvantages does this offer?*

Reliability

The conclusions from the first study were based on the experience of eight pseudopatients in a number of different hospitals. In the second study, only one hospital was involved. *What do you conclude about the **reliability** of this data?*

Slater (2004) reported that she had presented herself at the emergency rooms of multiple hospitals with a single auditory hallucination (see right). She claimed she was given prescriptions for either **antipsychotics** or **antidepressants**. *Does this suggest that Rosenhan's findings are reliable?*

Validity

The willingness to commit a patient on flimsy evidence could be because the psychiatrist wouldn't suspect for a minute that someone might be pretending, and would therefore assume that anyone seeking admission must have a good reason to do so. *How might this affect the **validity** of this study?*

The hospitals selected by Rosenhan were in five different states on the east and west coasts of the USA, and included old and new hospitals with a variety of other differences. *Why is having such a variety of hospitals important to the validity of Rosenhan's research?*

Sampling

The participants in this study were the staff (nurses and doctors) in the hospitals studied. *In what way are the samples unique? How does this affect the conclusions drawn from the study?*

Ethical issues

The pseudopatients didn't inform the staff at the hospitals that they were being observed as part of research. *Why not? Does this pose any **ethical issues**?*

DO IT YOURSELF

No. 5.42

'There is nothing to be gained by a diagnosis of schizophrenia.'

Divide your class into groups and prepare a case for the prosecution or defence for this assertion. Each group should do some further research on the internet. Then conduct a class debate. Whichever view you support, make sure you are also prepared to answer the claims of the opposition.

ALTERNATIVE EVIDENCE

Replications

Slater (2004) attempted to replicate Rosenhan's study, although not as a piece of systematic research. Unlike Rosenhan's pseudopatients, Slater had previously been diagnosed with a mental disorder (clinical depression). She presented herself at nine psychiatric emergency rooms with the lone complaint of an isolated auditory hallucination (hearing the word 'thud'). In almost all cases, she claims that she was given a diagnosis of psychotic depression and was prescribed either antipsychotics or antidepressants. Slater concluded that psychiatric diagnoses are largely arbitrary and driven by a 'zeal to prescribe'. *How does this support, contradict or develop Rosenhan's conclusions?*

Spitzer *et al.* (2005) sought to challenge Slater's findings. They gave 74 emergency room psychiatrists a detailed case description derived from the clinical description in Slater's book, and asked them a series of questions regarding diagnosis and treatment recommendations. They found that only three psychiatrists offered a diagnosis of psychotic depression, and only one-third recommended medication. *How does this support, contradict or develop both Slater and Rosenhan's conclusions?*

Critics

Spitzer (1976) claimed that Rosenhan's findings do not invalidate psychological diagnostic systems. Spitzer argued that it is not surprising that the psychiatrists believed in the pseudopatients because:

- diagnosis does rely on verbal reports
- they wouldn't expect that someone would use to trickery to get into such a place.

If the same thing occurred in a medical emergency room, you'd get the same result – someone might complain of severe intestinal pain and could be admitted to the hospital with a diagnosis of gastritis. Even though the doctor was tricked, the diagnostic methods were not invalid. *In what way do such arguments challenge Rosehan's conclusions?*

Kety (1974) similarly claimed: *If I were to drink a quart of blood and, concealing what I had done, come to the emergency room of any hospital vomiting blood, the behaviour of the staff would be quite predictable. If they labelled and treated me as having a peptic ulcer, I doubt I could argue convincingly that medical science does not know how to diagnose that condition. In what way do such arguments challenge Rosehan's conclusions?*

Spitzer (1976) reports that after investigating the case histories of individuals with schizophrenia admitted to his own hospital and 12 other US hospitals, he found that the discharge diagnosis of 'schizophrenia in remission' (given to the pseudopatients) is given very rarely. *How does this support, contradict or develop Rosehan's conclusions?*

Diagnosis can be reliable

One answer to Rosenhan's research is that more recent versions of the **DSM** produce more reliable diagnoses. Sarbin and Mancuso (1980) note that a psychiatrist using the newer *DSM-III* (published in 1980) would not diagnose Rosenhan's pseudopatients with schizophrenia, since the 'hallucination' must be repeated on several occasions, whereas Rosenhan's pseudopatients reported only one occurrence. Carson (1991) claimed that *DSM-III* had fixed the problem of reliability once and for all. Psychiatrists now had a reliable classification system, so this should have led to much greater agreement over who did or did not have schizophrenia. *How does this support, contradict or develop Rosenhan's conclusions?*

Diagnosis is unreliable

Despite the claims (above) for increased reliability in *DSM-III* (and later revisions), there is still little evidence that the *DSM* is routinely used with high reliability by **clinicians** (mental health professionals such as psychiatrists and psychologists). Such reliability is established using **inter-rater reliability** – the extent to which different clinicians given the same diagnosis when dealing with the same patient. Research (e.g. Whaley, 2001) has found inter-rater reliability correlations in the diagnosis of mental illness as low as +.11. *How does this support, contradict or develop Rosenhan's conclusions?*

Langwieler and Linden (1993) sent a trained pseudopatient to four physicians, each with a different professional background. Although the pseudopatient exhibited the exact same symptoms to all the doctors, they proposed four different diagnoses and recommended four different methods of treatment. The researchers attributed the differing diagnoses to the situation, although, in contrast to Rosenhan's study, this time the situational factors were the varying backgrounds and attitudes of the physicians. *How does this support, contradict or develop Rosenhan's conclusions?*

Loring and Powell (1988) gave 290 psychiatrists a transcript of a patient interview and told half of them that the patient was black and the other half that the patient was white. They concluded: *'Clinicians appear to ascribe violence, suspiciousness, and dangerousness to black clients even though the case studies are the same as the case studies for the white clients'. How does this support, contradict or develop Rosenhan's conclusions?*

DO IT YOURSELF

No. 5.43

Invite someone who works with individuals with mental health issues to speak to your class about their views on diagnosis and treatment.

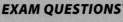
EXAM QUESTIONS

SECTION B
Evaluate the methodology of Rosenhan's (1973) research 'On being sane in insane places'.   [12]

With reference to alternative evidence, critically assess Rosenhan's (1973) research 'On being sane in insane places'.   [12]

Notes *In Section B of the Unit 2 exam, you could be asked either of the questions above. In order to gain the full 12 marks for each question, your answer should follow the guidelines given on page 91.*

Example exam question with student answers

Examiner's comments on these answers can be found on page 178.

EXAMPLE OF QUESTION 5

With reference to alternative evidence, critically assess Rosenhan's (1973) research 'On being sane in insane places'. [12]

Megan's answer

Kety's quart of blood scenario challenges Rosenhan's conclusions as Kety believes that by the pseudopatients admitting to hearing a voice it was only appropriate for them to be treated as if they had some form of psychiatric illness.

Sarbin and Mancuso (1980) note that a psychiatrist using DSM-III would not diagnose Rosenhan's pseudopatients with schizophrenia, since the 'hallucination' must be repeated on several occasions, whereas Rosenhan's pseudopatients only report one occurrence. Sarbin and Mancuso are contradicting Rosenhan's findings as they believe that if repeated, they wouldn't find the same results as Rosenhan using later versions of the DSM, but if Rosenhan were to repeat his research today he could also just update his research to reflect diagnostic criteria from the latest version of the DSM to 'feign' insanity.

Spitzer (1976) reported that after investigating the case histories of individuals admitted with schizophrenia in his own hospital and other hospitals, he found that the discharge diagnosis of 'schizophrenia in remission' (given to the pseudopatients) is given VERY rarely. This research contradicts Rosenhan's conclusions as Spitzer claims that this discharge diagnosis must have been a result of the pseudopatients' behaviours and not of the setting (the psychiatric hospital) where the diagnoses were made.

Tomas's answer

Slater conducted a repeat of Rosenhan's study by presenting herself to various emergency departments and telling them she was experiencing certain symptoms, like those reported by Rosenhan's pseudopatients. She was diagnosed with a kind of depression and given medication. This appears to support Rosenhan's findings and shows that clinicians are still making similar mistakes despite claims that DSM is more reliable. However Slater admits that this was not a rigorous study, and she had suffered mental illness in the past so the diagnoses were not totally inaccurate.

Chapter 5 summary

Core study 1 – Asch (1955)

Context
- Jenness (1932): participants estimated beans in a jar.
- Sherif (1935): used autokinetic effect (ambiguous).

Aims
To see if group pressure on an individual in an unambiguous situation would lead the individual to give a conforming or an independent response.

Procedures
- 123 male student volunteers for a vision test.
- Groups of seven to nine naïve participants plus confederates.
- Shown standard and three stimulus lines.
- 18 trials, of which 12 were 'critical'.
- Additional procedures, e.g. size of group, truthful partner.

Findings
- 36.8% conformity on critical trials.
- 25% of naïve participants never conformed.
- Some individuals conformed nearly all the time.
- Group size didn't matter if more than three confederates.
- Truthful partner dramatically reduced conformity.

Conclusions
Shows there is a strong tendency to conform, and also how people resist conformity (e.g. presence of dissenter).

Core study 3 – Rahe, Mahan and Arthur (1970)

Context
Previous research by Selye, Holmes, Hawkins and Rahe suggested a psychosomatic link between stress and illness.

Aims
To conduct a prospective study using a normal population.

Procedures
- 2664 men in the US Navy, mean age 22.3 years.
- Filled in military version of the SRE for four six-month periods over previous two years.
- Record of illnesses kept for six- to eight-month tour of duty.
- Non-sick calls excluded from illness record.
- Participants and medical staff not aware that illness record would be used.

Findings
- Significant positive correlation between SRE for six months prior to cruise and cruise period illness, +.118.
- Sailors in decile groups 1 and 2 formed low illness group (joint mean illness score 1.405).
- Sailors in decile groups 9 and 10 formed high illness group (joint mean illness score 2.066).
- Regrouped data showed linear correlation.

Conclusions
TLCU score and illness positively correlated, though this was strongest in older, married participants.

Core study 2 – Milgram (1963)

Context
Brutality of Nazis led to questions about obedience, could be explained by the authoritarian personality (Adorno et al., 1950).

Aims
(1) To investigate the power of legitimate authority even when a command requires destructive behaviour. (2) To test the dispositional hypothesis for obedience, 'Germans are different'.

Procedures
- 40 male volunteers, different education and occupations.
- Teacher (naïve), learner (confederate), experimenter.
- Ostensibly a learning experiment.
- Learner receives progressively stronger shocks for mistakes.
- At 300 volts, learner bangs on wall, no further comments.
- Experimenter delivers prods to naïve participant to continue.

Findings
- Students predicted 3% would fully obey.
- 12.5% stopped at 300 volts.
- 65% fully obeyed (full 450 volts).
- Many showed signs of extreme stress.
- 84% said they were glad to have taken part.

Conclusions
It was the circumstances that created a situation where it was difficult to disobey. Milgram proposed 13 situational factors, e.g. no time to think, obligation to experimenter.

Core study 4 – Bennett-Levy and Marteau (1984)

Context
The concept of biological preparedness suggests that humans may have an innate predisposition to inherit certain fears.

Aims
To investigate the mechanism by which preparedness would operate, i.e. perceptual characteristics of certain animals.

Procedures
- 113 male and female participants, average age about 36, standard deviation of about 16.
- Questionnaire listed 29 harmless animals and insects.
- Three-point fear scale and five-point nearness scale.
- Three-point scale for four perceptual dimensions: ugly, slimy, speedy, sudden movement.

Findings
- Rats feared considerably more than others.
- Sex differences, e.g. females less willing to deal with 10 of the animals, such as jellyfish, cockroach, ant, moth, crow, worm.
- Four ratings of perceptual characteristics (ugly, slimy, speedy, sudden movement) significantly correlated to both fear and nearness (as long as effect of ugliness partialled out).

Conclusions
The findings support both the discrepancy principle and the notion of aversive stimulus configurations.

Core study 5 – Loftus and Palmer (1974)

Context
EWT has been shown to be inaccurate, which may be due to leading questions. People are not good at estimating speed.

Aims
(1) To investigate effect of leading questions. (2) To see if effects are due to distortion of memory rather than response bias.

Procedures
- Experiment 1: film of car accident, set of questions included critical question about speed (smashed, collided, bumped, hit, contacted).
- Experiment 2: after film, three groups: smashed, hit and control group; one week later asked about broken glass.

Findings
- 'Smashed' led to highest speed estimate (40.8 mph); 'contacted' was lowest (31.8 mph).
- In experiment 2, 'smashed' group again reported higher speed estimates.
- 'Smashed' group twice as likely to report broken glass (16/50 did) than 'hit' group (7/50 did); control condition was 6/50.

Conclusions
Leading questions distort memory itself and don't simply bias an individual's response. Similar to the effect of verbal labels.

Core study 6 – Gardner and Gardner (1969)

Context
Chomsky had proposed that language is uniquely human. Attempts to teach language to chimpanzees had been unsuccessful (e.g. Vicki and Sarah).

Aims
(1) Use ASL to teach a chimpanzee language. (2) Teach the chimpanzee in the same manner as a child would acquire language.

Procedures
- Washoe exposed solely to intensive communication with ASL, cared for constantly by tutors.
- Training consisted of imitation, prompting, using signs in everyday routine, manual babbling, instrumental conditioning, shaping, direct instruction.

Findings
- After 22 months, 30 signs plus another four that were stable.
- Washoe's language resembled that of a child in three ways: could differentiate, transfer, combine signs.

Conclusions
Not clear whether it was language but:
- Chimps can be taught more than a few words.
- ASL is a suitable language for chimps.
- More could be accomplished with Washoe.

Core study 7 – Langer and Rodin (1976)

Context
Loss of control in old age might lead to a sense of helplessness. Research has linked a reduced sense of personal responsibility to higher anxiety and increased likelihood of death.

Aims
To see if enhanced personal responsibility and choice in a group of nursing home patients had beneficial effects.

Procedures
- Two floors in a US nursing home designated RIG and CG, respectively.
- RIG briefed about their self-responsibility, told to care for plant and to choose movie night.
- CG briefed about responsibility of staff for their happiness; staff would care for plant and tell them when movie night is.
- Residents and nurses given questionnaire one week before briefing and again three weeks later.

Findings
- Questionnaire type 1: RIG reported feeling happier (48% vs 25%) and more active.
- Questionnaire type 2: nurses' ratings showed greater general improvement in RIG; 93% had improved compared with 21% of CG.
- Behavioural measure: RIG more likely to enter jelly bean competition and go to movies.

Conclusions
Greater personal responsibility may slow down or even reverse the apparently inevitable negative consequences of ageing.

Core study 8 – Gibson and Walk (1960)

Context
Innate ability to perceive depth would be adaptive..

Aims
To test whether perceptual abilities are best explained in terms of nature or nurture.

Procedures
- Visual cliff; deep and shallow sides separated by centre board.
- Mother encouraged infant to crawl towards her.
- Patterned material provided depth cues.
- 36 infants aged 6–14 months tested.
- Chicks, lambs, kids tested (precocial).
- Kittens and rats (normal and dark-reared), mobile from four weeks.
- Rats tested on use of size/shading and motion parallax by placing patterned fabric immediately below glass.

Findings
- Humans: only three attempted the deep side.
- Chicks, lamb, kids froze on deep side.
- Rats: if they couldn't use their whiskers stayed off deep side.
- Turtles: 76% crawled on deep side.
- Dark-reared rats and kittens showed no depth discrimination when first shown the visual cliff.
- Chicks and rats relied on motion parallax.

Conclusions
- All animals show discrimination of depth by the time they are mobile.
- This depth perception appears to be learned through earlier perceptual experiences.

Core study 9 – Buss (1989)

Context
Evolutionary theory predicts particular sex differences in mate preferences related to parental investment, sexual selection, fertility and reproductive values, and paternity probability.

Aims
To see if consistent sex differences are found in different cultures.

Procedures
- 37 samples from 33 countries; total of 10 047 participants.
- Variety of types of sample (e.g. urban, rural, Western, non-Western) and variety of sampling techniques.
- Questionnaire 1 collected biographical data, data on mate preferences and rating scale (18 characteristics, four-point scale).
- Questionnaire 2 – ranking of 13 characteristics.

Findings
- In 36 of the 37 samples (97%), females valued 'good financial prospects' more highly than males did.
- In 34 samples (92%), females valued 'ambition and industriousness' more than males did; only 29 samples significant.
- In all 37 samples, males preferred mates who were younger; the ideal age for females was 24.83.
- In all 37 samples, males rated 'good looks' more than females.
- In 23 of the 37 samples, males preferred chastity in their mates.

Conclusions
The findings support evolutionary explanations of human behaviour, show that both men and women exercise choosiness, and provide some evidence for cultural influences.

Core study 10 – Rosenhan (1973)

Context
Anti-psychiatry movement challenged the medical model, and concepts of sanity and insanity.

Aims
To investigate the reliability of psychiatric diagnoses and consider whether abnormality is due to personality or situation.

Procedures
- Study 1: eight pseudopatients, 12 hospitals; said they heard voices (existential symptoms) otherwise behaviour normal.
- Study 2: staff in one psychiatric hospital told to expect pseudopatients over next three months.
- Study 3: pseudopatients asked staff a question as they walked past.

Findings
- Length of stay between seven and 52 days, average stay 19 days, discharged as 'schizophrenia in remission'.
- Limited staff contact, e.g. 6.8 minutes per day with psychiatrist.
- Real patients suspected the pseudopatients.
- Study 2: 41 real patients suspected by staff members and 23 by psychiatrists.
- Study 3: 4% of psychiatrists and 0.5% of nurses stopped.

Conclusions
- Not possible to distinguish the sane from the insane.
- Psychiatrists had a bias towards a type 2 error.
- Labels had a profound effect on perceptions.
- Patients depersonalised, leading them to behave in an insane manner.

Review activities

You have now completed all 10 core studies. This is a good time to review your knowledge. You can use many of the review activities described at the end of each of the chapters in Unit 1 (see pages 15, 29, 43 and 57) with the contents of this chapter. For example, you could try the following.

- **Rolling shows** Work in small groups, and each prepare a montage of illustrations and words related to one core study. Find further images for your study from the internet. In future lessons, you can begin with a look at one of the rolling shows. Alternatively, each group could produce a rolling show for all 10 studies. Decide which rolling show is best.
- **MCQs** Again, work in small groups or pairs. Each group/pair should produce two multiple-choice questions for each of the 10 core studies. Put them all together to form a big revision test.
- **Post-it fun** Students should have pile of small Post-its on which they should write anything they can remember about a named core study. Then the Post-its can be arranged on the wall in your classroom to produce a mind map.
- **Writing exam advice** Use the notes in this chapter to write advice for each of the five types of core study question. There is also advice on page vii.
- **The art of précis** You should have already written an abstract for each core study. Now try to write a 100-word version for each component (aims and context, procedures, findings and conclusions, methodology and alternative evidence).

Charades

On 25 slips of paper, write the names of all 15 researchers for the 10 core studies and a key word for each study (such as fear or obedience) = 25 slips of paper.

Place the slips of paper in a hat. Class members should take turns drawing a slip from the hat. They must act out the word on the paper. Award points for the time taken for the class to guess the word. The winner is the person (or team) with the lowest number of points. (Note: it might be more fun if the slip is returned to the hat each time.)

TV interview

Imagine that the results from a specific core study have just been published, and a local TV reporter wants to conduct a five-minute interview with the researcher about the research. Pairs of students can act as the interviewer (who needs to prepare some questions) and the researcher (who should know all the answers, e.g. what the research is about, why it was important).

Be creative, for example dress in suitable clothes for that era and act like the researcher you are playing. If you film the interviews, you could then edit them together into a programme.

Escape questions

Students should devise a set of questions with short answers for each core study – perhaps divide the class into 10 groups, with each group preparing a set of 30 questions for its core study.

When revising the core studies, focus on one specific core study each day; students should be warned in advance which study it will be. Students then line up five minutes before the end of the lesson and are asked a question in turn. If they get their question right, they get a couple of minutes free, if they get it wrong they go to the back of the line.

Making mind maps with the summaries

Copy each core study summary into the middle of an A3 sheet of paper in the form of a mind map (see page 15). Then add (and annotate) the methodological issues around the outside. This is a good way of developing/recapping the skills necessary for 'evaluate the methodology' type questions.

You could also add the alternative evidence to recap material for question 5.

Questions out of a hat

This is a way of practising exam questions. Write down all the possible questions that could be asked for the core studies: there are five question types and 10 core studies, so there will need to be a total of 50 slips of paper.

Draw one question out of the hat and give students five minutes' preparation time, and then 20 minutes to write their answers. (The exam is 105 minutes long and there are five questions, which gives about 20 minutes per question plus reading time.)

You could cut this down to 15 minutes per answer, then ask students to put their pens down and reread what they have written, then giving them a final few minutes' writing time.

Marking

Students should work with a partner and mark each other's work:
- Use the mark scheme on page vii to determine a mark.
- The partner should delete anything that is not relevant.
- Partners should produce a version that would be worth full marks.

Crossword

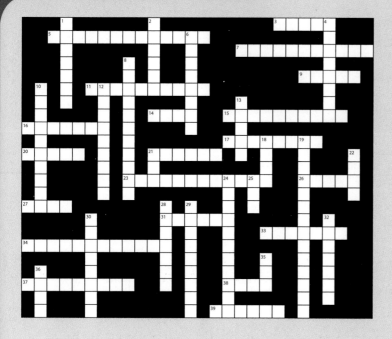

Answers on page 179.

There is a copy of the crossword template on the website at: www.folensblogs.com/psychcompanion/blog/.

Across

3. Gibson and Walk tested non-human animals such as kids, which are young _____. (5)
5. In Rosenhan's study, the symptoms reported by the pseudopatients. (7, 6)
7. In Gibson and Walk's study, the method used to assess babies' ability. (6, 5)
9. Number of pseudopatients in Rosenhan's study. (5)
11. Asch's study was investigating _____. (10)
14. In Milgram's study, number of participants who stopped at 300 volts. (4)
15. In Langer and Rodin's study, one of the tasks involved guessing the number of _____. (10)
16. In the study by Loftus and Palmer, this verb led to the highest speed estimates. (7)
17. In Asch's study, participants had to compare the length of three lines with a _____ line. (8)
20. Term used to describe the true participant in Asch's study. (5)
21. The number of critical trials in Asch's study. (6)
23. Buss's study is an example of this approach. (12)
26. In Langer and Rodin's experiment, participants were specifically asked about how well their _____ was doing. (5)
27. The IV in the experiment by Loftus and Palmer. (4)
31. Washoe's adopted baby. (6)
33. Rahe et al. separated participants into groups called _____ in order to analyse the findings. (7)
34. Washoe was taught to use _____ _____ language. (8, 4)
37. Loftus and Palmer asked about whether this had been broken. (9)
38. Two researchers who criticised Milgram were _____ and Holland. (4)
39. The IV in Buss's study. (6)

Down

1. Role taken by true participant in Milgram's experiment. (7)
2. In Gibson and Walk's study, infants were encouraged to crawl towards this person. (6)
4. Psychologist who proposed the concept of biological preparedness. (8)
6. In Buss's study, the number of characteristics that were rated by participants. (8)
8. Rahe et al. investigated this topic. (4, 7)
10. Washoe was a _____. (10)
12. Milgram investigated this kind of social influence. (9)
13. Gibson and Walk investigated _____ perception. (5)
18. Participants in study by Rahe et al. were mainly in the _____. (4)
19. In Langer and Rodin's experiment, the experimental condition (RIG) was the _____ induced group. (14)
21. Rosenhan concluded that doctors are more inclined to call a healthy person sick, an example of a Type ____ error. (3)
22. Buss investigated _____ preferences. (4)
24. Langer and Rodin investigated people living in a _____ _____. (7, 4)
25. In Bennet, Levy and Marteau's study, the most feared animal. (3)
28. Rahe et al. found a positive correlation between stress and _____. (7)
29. Marteau and Bennett-Levy concluded that people feared those animals that were most discrepant from the _____ _____. (5, 4)
30. A means of rewarding Washoe. (8)
32. Loftus and Palmer were investigating _____ questions. (7)
35. The number of hospitals used in the second part of Rosenhan's study. (3)
36. Bennett-Levy and Marteau investigated the biological origins of _____. (4)

Chapter 6 Applied research methods   INTRODUCTION

Your Unit 2 exam is divided into core studies and applied research methods (see details on page 66). For the applied research methods section, there will be two questions for you to choose between, each of which looks like the question on the right.

If you look at the question, you will see that it begins with a short piece of 'stimulus' material (a scenario) describing a psychological study, including a display of the results (in this case it's a graph). This is followed by six short questions that ask you about:

(a) the research method   (d) the sampling method
(b) reliability   (e) an ethical issue
(c) validity   (f) drawing a conclusion.

The questions always follow this pattern, which gives you an insight into what you have to know to do well in the exam.

There is one especially important feature to note: each of the questions requires you to relate your knowledge to the particular study *described in the scenario*. This is called *contextualisation*. You must contextualise all of your answers in order to gain high marks in the exam. In other words, you cannot, for example, simply describe one advantage of using a correlation – you must explain why it is an advantage *in the case of this particular study*. Throughout this chapter we will give you plenty of practice in contextualising your answers.

▼ Below is an example question about applied research methods, taken from the WJEC sample papers. In the exam, there are two questions like the one below, of which you will be required to answer one. The question below is about correlations, but you may be asked about any research method (e.g. an experiment or an observational study or any of the eight different research methods that you will study in this chapter).

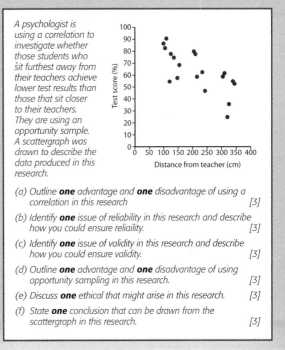

A psychologist is using a correlation to investigate whether those students who sit furthest away from their teachers achieve lower test results than those that sit closer to their teachers. They are using an opportunity sample. A scattergraph was drawn to describe the data produced in this research.

(a) Outline **one** advantage and **one** disadvantage of using a correlation in this research   [3]

(b) Identify **one** issue of reliability in this research and describe how you could ensure reliaility.   [3]

(c) Identify **one** issue of validity in this research and describe how you could ensure validity.   [3]

(d) Outline **one** advantage and **one** disadvantage of using opportunity sampling in this research.   [3]

(e) Discuss **one** ethical that might arise in this research.   [3]

(f) State **one** conclusion that can be drawn from the scattergraph in this research.   [3]

WHAT ARE RESEARCH METHODS?

Research methods are the techniques that psychologists (and all scientists) use to discover facts about the world. Psychologists use some methods that are common to all sciences, such as experiments and observations. But they also use other methods, such as interviews and questionnaires, which are less common in other scientific research. In addition, psychological research differs from other sciences because the objects of study are living, breathing, thinking human beings.

Overall this means there are some differences from, but also many similarities to, other sciences. One of the key similarities is the use of the **scientific method** – essentially this is how science works.

THE SCIENTIFIC METHOD

This is the method that underlies all scientific research.

1. Scientists *observe* things going on in the world about them.
2. They develop a tentative *explanation* for the things they observe, and produce a *hypothesis*.
3. In order to establish whether the hypothesis is true, they design a study to test it.
4. If the hypothesis is shown to be true, then *conclusions* can be drawn.
5. If the hypothesis is false then … think of a new explanation! Try again.

You will find that this method underlies much of what we have covered in this book. Like all scientists, psychologists seek to explain everyday phenomena and then to investigate their explanations in an objective and systematic way – although we should perhaps mention that not all psychologists believe that psychology is a science. But that's another story …

AN EXAMPLE OF THE SCIENTIFIC METHOD

Step 1 Observation

In the 1970s, there were a lot of prison riots in the USA, the most infamous was at Attica Prison in the state of New York in 1971. The prisoners felt they were being illegally denied certain rights and were being held under inhumane conditions, as illustrated by the fact that the prison was designed to hold 1200 inmates but actually housed 2225.

The riot was triggered when a rumour went round the prison that a prisoner was being held in his cell and was going to be tortured. A small group managed to gain control of part of the prison, and eventually took more than 40 officers and civilians hostage. They demanded that their needs be met before they would surrender.

This led to a four-day-long stand-off between the prisoners and the state police, during which time the prisoners gained support from various anti-government groups around the country. News crews were allowed inside the prison to interview the leaders, while preparations were being made on both sides for a major battle.

On 13 September 1971, 1500 police and national guardsmen stormed the prison with devastating consequences. The eventual death toll was 42, including 10 hostages.

… continued on the next spread

AN EXAMPLE OF THE SCIENTIFIC METHOD
(*continued from previous page*)

Step 2 A tentative explanation

The media speculated about the causes of the riot, and many newspapers at the time blamed the prisoners. They were, they said, 'bad apples', basically people who were 'evil' by nature, and would always end up causing trouble no matter what was done with them.

▲ Philip Zimbardo, Emeritus Professor at Stanford University, California.

Enter a young psychologist called Philip Zimbardo. He referred to the 'bad apple' account as a *dispositional* explanation – the belief that prison violence was due to the fact that both prisoners and guards have personalities that make conflict inevitable. Prisoners lack respect for law and order, and guards are domineering and aggressive. The dispositional explanation offers an account of behaviour in terms of the individual's disposition or personality.

Zimbardo argued that this dispositional explanation draws attention away from the complex matrix of social, economic and political forces that make prisons what they are, and thus prevents us from making them better places. In Zimbardo's view, prisoners and guards behave as they do because of the *situation* they are placed in. They display a lack of respect because of the social role conferred on them, because that's the kind of social role dictated by the prison. This is a *situational* explanation.

How can we tell which is the 'right' explanation – the dispositional or the situational hypothesis? The answer is 'by conducting a research study'. (These concepts of dispositional and situational explanations of behaviour were also used in Attribution Theory in Chapter 4.)

▲ The bodies of some of those killed in the Attica Prison riots. Philip Zimbardo offered an explanation for such riots and tested his explanation in the Stanford Prison Experiment (SPE).

Step 3 A study to test the hypothesis

Zimbardo designed a study to test the dispositional versus the situational explanation – the *Stanford Prison Experiment (SPE)* (Zimbardo *et al.*, 1973). His aim was to see how 'ordinary' people would behave if you placed them in a prison environment and arbitrarily designated some of them as guards and others as prisoners. If the guards and prisoners in this mock prison behaved in a non-aggressive manner, this would support the dispositional hypothesis. On the other hand, if these ordinary people came to behave in the same way as people in real prisons, then we would have to conclude that the environment plays a major part in the behaviour of guards and prisoners (the situational explanation).

Procedures An advertisement sought male volunteers for a psychological study of 'prison life', saying that they would be paid $15 a day. The 24 most stable (physically and mentally) men were selected, and randomly assigned to being a prisoner or a guard. There were two reserves and one dropped out, finally leaving 10 prisoners and 11 guards.

A mock prison was set up in the basement of the psychology department at Stanford University in California, USA. The 'prisoners' were unexpectedly 'arrested' at home. On entry to 'prison' they were put through a delousing procedure, searched, given a prison uniform with ID number, nylon stocking caps (to make their hair look short), and an ankle chain. They were in prison 24 hours a day, whereas the guards worked shifts.

The guards had uniforms, clubs, whistles, handcuffs and reflective sunglasses (to prevent eye contact). The aim was to reduce their sense of individuality so they would be more likely to act within their role rather than following their personal morals.

Findings Over the first few days, the guards grew increasingly tyrannical. They woke prisoners in the night and got them to clean the toilets with their bare hands. Some guards were so enthusiastic in their role that they even volunteered to do extra hours without pay.

The participants appeared at times to forget that they were only acting. Even when they were unaware of being watched, they still played their roles. When one prisoner had had enough he asked for parole – rather than saying he wanted to stop being part of the experiment. Had he come to think that he was actually a prisoner?

Five prisoners had to be released early because of their extreme reactions (crying, rage and acute anxiety), symptoms that had started to appear within two days of the beginning of the study. In fact, the whole experiment was ended after six days, despite the intention to continue for two weeks.

▲ A guard lining up the prisoners in the SPE.

Step 4 Drawing conclusions

In terms of the original aims of the experiment, we can conclude that situational factors seem to be more important than dispositional ones, because 'ordinary' students all too easily became brutal prison guards or subservient prisoners when placed in a conducive setting.

We say it 'seems' to demonstrate these conclusions – but there are important questions that must be asked. We need to *evaluate* the study – which means looking at its value. The findings of Zimbardo's study were plain for everyone to see, but if the techniques used in conducting the study were flawed, then the results may be meaningless.

You know this from studying science – as part of your science course you are likely to have conducted various investigations or case studies. For example, you may have been given data about the benefits and hazards of using mobile phones, and been asked to weigh up this evidence. This would have included an *evaluation* of the methods used to collect the data. An important part of the process of science is being critical about the results. So we now need to evaluate Zimbardo's study. Psychologists are particularly concerned with three main issues when evaluating research: **validity**, **reliability** and **ethical issues**.

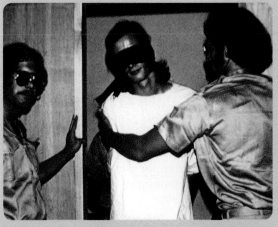

▼ The guards' treatment of the prisoners was often quite sadistic. After the study was finished guards and prisoners were introduced to each other in 'encounter sessions'. This was just one part of the thorough debriefing procedures that took place months and years after the study ended.

Was the study valid?

If we want to draw conclusions about 'real life', then the behaviour we study must match up to 'real life' behaviour. One of the questions raised about Zimbardo's study was whether the participants were behaving like *real* prisoners and guards, or were simply playing the roles assigned to them? In real life, people do act out roles, but they also have an individual sense of right and wrong. So if, for example, you were one of the guards in the study, you might order a 'prisoner' to clean the toilets with his bare hands because it was part of the 'game', whereas in real life you wouldn't do this because you would feel it to be wrong to treat a prisoner in such a dehumanising way.

In real life, a prison guard (or a prisoner) would be likely to adapt the role to suit his personal beliefs and the requirements of the situation. Most of the guards later claimed that they had simply been acting a role. This means the study might tell us very little about people's behaviour in real life, and would therefore mean that the findings are relatively *meaningless* – in scientific language, they would be seen as lacking validity.

However, there is an alternative view of the validity of this research. Zimbardo's analysis of the behaviour of his 'guards' showed that approximately 30% were 'cruel and tough'; about 50% were 'tough but fair'; and fewer than 20% were 'good guards' (i.e. generally helpful and kind to the 'prisoners'). This analysis matches a real life assessment of the behaviour of individuals in power. Historian Christopher Browning (1992) studied the actions of Reserve Police Battalion 101, a German mobile killing unit of 500 men who shot dead more than 38 000 Jews in just four months in 1942. These were not highly trained killers, but 'ordinary men', recruited because they were too old for the German army. Browning showed that, as with Zimbardo's guards, there was a nucleus of 'enthusiastic killers' who went out of their way to hunt Jews, a larger group who 'performed' only when assigned killing duties, and fewer than 20% who were classified as 'refusers and evaders'. Evidence such as this suggests that Zimbardo's findings do perhaps have some validity because they parallel events in the real world.

Was the study reliable?

An important aspect of any research finding is whether we can *rely* on it. Reliability can be determined by repeating the study to see if the same findings are produced. This is called **replication**. In the case of Zimbardo's study, there have never been any exact replications because of the distress caused to the participants.

However, Haslam and Reicher (2008) recently conducted a similar study that was televised and called *The Experiment*. A mock prison was created and filmed by the BBC. Fifteen volunteers were randomly assigned to the role of prisoners (10) and guards (5). Haslam and Reicher claimed that their study showed that Zimbardo's explanation was unsatisfactory, offering an alternative view that individuals identify with their social groups (i.e. being a prisoner), and when the social group breaks down the individuals are left vulnerable to being manipulated by those in power (in this case the guards). This is an explanation in terms of social identity.

Was the study ethical?

We said at the beginning of this chapter that psychological research is a little different from other scientific research because the objects of study are living, breathing, thinking human beings. We therefore have to think carefully about the effect of any study on the people who take part – the participants.

Participation in this study raised certain ethical issues, perhaps most importantly the issue of **psychological harm**. All participants experienced considerable emotional distress during the study. Five of the prisoners had to be released because of 'depression, crying, rage and acute anxiety', as well as one who had developed a 'psychosomatic rash'. The study was stopped after six days rather than being allowed to run the full two weeks. Zimbardo tried to make amends by conducting **debriefing** sessions for several years afterwards, and concluded that there were no lasting negative effects.

Such ethical issues don't affect the conclusions drawn from the research, but are an important factor to consider when designing and evaluating research.

You can read more about the SPE at www.prisonexp.org/, a website devoted to the Stanford Prison study, with a slide show, discussion questions, and links to other sites.

What is an experiment?

Doing research

Your study of psychology should be fun (!) and relevant to your life. So a good way to begin understanding the research process is to investigate something about human behaviour that interests you. However, before you get too excited, you can't study anything that would be unethical!

Observations of everyday life

You could think up your own idea, but here is one possibility. Many students do their homework in front of the TV. Cara's daughter thinks she does it just as well in front of the TV as working at a desk with no distractions. As you may imagine, Cara doesn't think this is true.

Research aim

To investigate whether people work just as well with the TV on, or whether their work will suffer as a result.

DO IT YOURSELF

No. 6.1

1. Work with a small group of other students and discuss the following questions.
   - How could you find out whether people can work just as well with the TV on as in a quiet room?
   - What will you need to measure?
   - Will you have two different conditions? What will you change across the two conditions?
   - How many participants will you need?
   - Will everyone take part in both conditions, or will you have two groups of participants?
   - What will you expect to find out?
   - What will the participants do?
   - What do you need to control?
2. When you have worked out what you will do, join with another group and explain your ideas to each other. The other group might ask useful questions that will help you refine your ideas.
3. Conduct your study. You might be able to do this in class, or each member of your group could go away and collect some data.
4. Pool the data collected by your group and prepare a poster to present your results and conclusions.

Ethical issues

Whenever you conduct research, you must always consider **ethical issues** carefully.

- Never use anyone under the age of 16 as a participant.
- Always obtain informed consent from all participants – tell your participants what they will be expected to do and allow them to refuse to take part.
- Debrief your participants after the study to tell them about any deception and to allow them to withdraw their data if, on reflection, they object to having taken part.

Before beginning any study, consult with others on the 'script' for the informed consent and the debrief.

RESEARCH DESIGN

If you designed the study on the left, you have just done what psychologists do: conducted a systematic study of human behaviour. You followed the scientific method: observation → explanation → state expectations → design a study → see if your expectations were correct.

Psychologists use special words to describe aspects of the research process. We have used some of the terms already, and most of them are probably familiar to you because you will have used them in science classes.

- *What did you expect to find out?*
  This is your **hypothesis**, a statement of what you believe to be true. Your hypothesis might have been something like: 'Students who do a memory task with the TV on produce work that is of lower quality than people who do the same task without the TV on.'
- *What did you measure?*
  This is called the **dependent variable** (**DV**). When you decided exactly what you would measure, you **operationalised** the DV. It isn't enough just to get people to do 'some work' and to see how well they did on that task – you should have made sure that all the participants were doing the same piece of work and should have specified what that piece of work was. The DV would have been something like their performance on a memory test, assessing the work they did.
- *What were your two conditions?*
  This is called the **independent variable** (**IV**). There are often two conditions of the IV, in this case having the TV on or having the TV off.
- *What will the participants do?*
  You worked out a set of standardised procedures – it is important to make sure that each participant did the exact same thing in each condition otherwise the results might vary because of changes in procedure rather then because of the IV.
- *What do you need to control?*
  You will have tried to control some **extraneous variables** (**EVs**) such as time of day (people might do better on a test in the morning than in the afternoon, so all participants should do the test at about the same time of day).

What is research? Anyone can have an opinion about human behaviour. You probably have lots of them, such as believing that if you eat less you will lose weight, or that girls have a better sense of humour than boys. But how do you know? Scientists aim to produce answers that are better than common sense. They do this by conducting well controlled studies. Throughout this book that is what you have studied.

EXPERIMENTAL DESIGN

If you designed the study on the facing page, you probably had two groups of participants – one group watched TV while working, whereas the other group watched no TV. Each group represented one condition of the IV. This is called an **independent groups design**.

On the other hand, you might have designed the experiment differently. You might have given the participants some material to study while watching TV and then tested their memory. The next day you might have given the same people some more material to study, this time in a silent room, and then tested their memory a second time and compared their performance in the two different conditions. This is called a **repeated measures design**.

There is a third possible kind of experimental design (i.e. design used when conducting an experiment). This is a **matched pairs design**, where there are two different groups of participants, but the participants in each group are matched or paired on key variables. For example, since we are testing memory, it would make sense to assess all participants on their memory ability. You would then pair together people with similar memory scores and place one member of each pair in Group A and his or her partner in group B. It is important to understand that the characteristics selected for matching must be relevant to the behaviour you are studying. For example, there would be little point in matching participants in terms of their memory ability if you were studying obedience.

AN EXPERIMENT IS ...

This study on the facing page is an **experiment**. The main characteristic of an experiment is that there is an IV that is changed or manipulated (TV on or not) to see if this has any effect on the DV (quality of work). This permits us to draw causal conclusions – we can make a statement about whether having the TV on or off *causes* a change in the work that is done.

You actually know a lot about experiments – you conduct them without thinking. For example, when you start a new class with a new teacher, you see how they respond to your behaviour – you might make a joke or hand your homework in on time (both of these are IVs) to see whether the teacher responds well (the DV). You are experimenting with cause and effect.

Different kinds of experiment

There are three different kinds of experiment. All experiments have one thing in common: they all have an IV and a DV.

- **Lab experiment** An experiment conducted in a *special environment* where variables can be *carefully controlled*. Participants are *aware* that they are taking part in an experiment, although they may not know the true aims of the study.
- **Field experiment** An experiment conducted in a more natural environment, i.e. in 'the field' (as distinct from a lab, 'the field' being anywhere outside a lab). As with the lab experiment, the IV is still deliberately manipulated by the researcher. Participants are often not aware that they are participating in an experiment.
- **Natural experiment** The environment is natural, as in a field experiment, but unlike a field experiment the change in the IV is also 'natural'. The experimenter makes use of a naturally varying IV instead of deliberately manipulating it, as happens in a field experiment.

Advantages and disadvantages

In order to understand the relative advantages and disadvantages of these three types of experiment, we are first going to have to look at the issue of validity, which we will do on the next spread.

DO IT YOURSELF

No. 6.2

Learning about research methods is a bit like learning a foreign language. When you learn a foreign language, you have to learn a new set of words and, more especially, what they mean. One of the best ways to do this is to speak the language – the same is true for research methods. Don't hold back, don't be scared – use the words.

To help you learn the language, you could create your own **Research Methods Vocabulary Book** to record all the terms used, their meanings and their advantages and disadvantages.

You can include a copy of the specification for applied research methods in your book, and tick off each term when you have recorded the details, again when you feel you understand it, and a third time when you feel you are now an expert!

Key term/ concept	Brief notes made	Good grasp	Expert under-standing
Lab experiment			
Field experiment			

And so on.

CAN YOU...?

No. 6.1

1... Produce a report of the study you conducted on noise and performance (or whatever other topic you chose). This report should include a pictorial representation of your results (e.g. a bar chart).

2... Explain the specific features of an experiment.

3... Identify the major advantage of the experimental method.

4... Decide on the relative advantages and disadvantages of each of the three kinds of experimental design described above.

Validity

What is *validity*?

The term 'validity' refers to how true or legitimate something is as an explanation of behaviour. It involves the issues of control, realism and generalisability.

Experimental control is a balancing act

Too little control means it is difficult to draw clear conclusions becuse of extraneous variables – variables other than the IV which may affect the DV.

Too much control means the behaviour we are studying isn't very much like everyday life (lacks mundane realism).

▲ Invariably, studies in psychology involve a balance between control and realism. The greatest control can be achieved in the lab. However, it is debatable to what extent findings from the lab can be generalised to other environments, especially the less controllable environments in which everyday life is lived.

Some psychologists argue that we can only discover things about behaviour if we uncover cause-and-effect relationships in highly controlled lab experiments. Others argue that studies in the natural environment are the only real option for psychologists that are interested in how life is actually lived.

CONTROL

Consider the following experiment (which is similar to the previous spread).

A class of psychology students conducted a study with the aim of finding out whether students could do their homework more effectively in silence or while in front of the TV. The study involved two conditions – doing a test in silence, and doing it with the TV on.

The **independent variable** (**IV**) was whether the TV was on or not. The **dependent variable** (**DV**) was the participants' score on the test. If TV is a distraction, the silence group should do better on the test.

But were there other things that might have affected their score on the test? What if all the participants in the silence group did the test in the morning and all the participants in the 'TV on' group did the test in the afternoon? It might be that people are more alert in the morning, and that is why they do better on the morning test. It might be that the students in one group were naturally more intelligent than those in the other group, and that would explain why one group did better. These are called **extraneous variables** (**EVs**).

If an experimenter fails to control such EVs, then the results of the study will be *meaningless*. The experimenter might claim that the IV caused a change in the DV, but in fact this might not be the case – changes in the DV could actually have been caused by something else – an EV. *Consequently, the experimenter might not have actually tested what they intended to test.* Instead, the influence of a different variable has been tested.

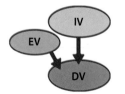

Control is therefore vital in experiments. An experimenter seeks to control as many *relevant* EVs as possible, i.e. those variables *extra* to the IV.

Sometimes the term 'confounding variable' is used instead of extraneous variable. The terms have different meanings, but at AS level it is acceptable for you to assume they are the same.

REALISM

The aim of any psychological study is to provide information about how people behave in 'real life'. If the set-up of a study is too artificial or contrived, then the participants will not act as they normally would.

For example, the study by Loftus and Palmer (see page 92) investigated eyewitness testimony by showing participants a film of a car accident and asking questions about the speed of a car. But how realistic is this? Is watching a film the same as seeing a real accident?

Many things affect the *realism* of a psychological study. The term **mundane realism** refers to how an experiment mirrors the real world. 'Mundane' means 'of the world' – commonplace, ordinary. Watching a car accident in a film in a lab lacks mundane realism, and this means that the results of the study might not be very useful in terms of understanding behaviour in the real world.

GENERALISABILITY

The point of realism in psychological research is to be able to *generalise* the results beyond the particular, unique research setting, especially to be able to understand behaviour in everyday life (the 'real world'). However a study can be very 'natural' or real (i.e. have a high degree of realism), but still lack **generalisability**. Consider the following examples.

- If all the participants in a study are US university students, it may not be reasonable to generalise the findings to the behaviour of all people because Americans (and students) have unique characteristics.
- If a study about obedience is conducted in a hospital with real nurses (see Hofling *et al.*, page 79), this might not tell us much about obedience in everyday life because part of a nurse's job is to obey doctors, which differs from other obedience relationships.

It is *very* important to remember this – just because a study is conducted in a natural environment (such as a hospital), doesn't mean the findings can be generalised to the real world.

Validity is...

...testing what you intended to test

...the certainty that changes in the IV were due to the DV

...the extent to which the test materials are 'real'

...being able to generalise from a research study to the real world/everyday situations.

Students often believe that validity is about 'being correct'. This is both right and wrong. It is right because a researcher seeks to find out whether the hypothesis is valid, i.e. correct, but it is wrong if you think that being correct means finding out that the predicted expectations have been confirmed. Validity is not about confirming your expectations.

This study was conducted by Craik and Tulving (1975). It is a good example of the cognitive approach to understanding human behaviour. The aim of the study was to show that memories are formed by processing the meaning of words (semantic processing).

Think about how you might apply this to inventing effective revision techniques.

Step 1: Answer the questions by ringing yes or no.

1. SPEECH — Is the word in capital letters? YES/NO
2. brush — Is the word a something used for cleaning? YES/NO
3. cheek — Does the word rhyme with 'teak'? YES/NO
4. FENCE — Is the word in small letters? YES/NO
5. FLAME — Does the word mean something hot? YES/NO
6. FLOUR — Is the word in capital letters? YES/NO
7. honey — Is the word in small letters? YES/NO
8. KNIFE — Does the word mean a type of furniture? YES/NO
9. SHEEP — Is the word a type of farm animal? YES/NO
10. copper — Is the word in capital letters? YES/NO
11. GLOVE — Does the word rhyme with 'shove'? YES/NO
12. MONK — Is the word in small letters? YES/NO
13. daisy — Does the word rhyme with 'teak'? YES/NO
14. miner — Is the word in small letters? YES/NO
15. cart — Does the word rhyme with 'start'? YES/NO
16. CLOVE — Is the word in capital letters? YES/NO
17. ROBBER — Does the word mean a type of flower? YES/NO
18. mast — Does the word rhyme with 'rove'? YES/NO
19. fiddle — Is the word in small letters? YES/NO
20. CHAPEL — Does the word rhyme with 'grapple'? YES/NO
21. SONNET — Does the word mean something to wear? YES/NO
22. WITCH — Does the word rhyme with 'rich'? YES/NO
23. sleet — Is the word a type of weather? YES/NO
24. brake — Is the word in small letters? YES/NO
25. twig — Does the word rhyme with 'coach'? YES/NO
26. grin — Does the word rhyme with 'school'? YES/NO
27. DRILL — Does the word mean a kind of fish? YES/NO
28. moan — Does the word mean a mode of travel? YES/NO
29. CLAW — Is the word part of an animal? YES/NO
30. singer — Does the word rhyme with 'ringer'? YES/NO

Step 2: Cover up the questions in step 1. Then look at the words below. Which of the following were in the list of 30 questions? Tick the right answers.

Brush	Lamp	Grin	Dance	Cart	Pond	Monk	Wool	Roach
Cheek	Cherry	Drill	Field	Clove	Lane	Chapel	Soap	Rice
Sonnet	Jade	Witch	Sleet	Sheep	Pail	Knife	Boat	Twig
Daisy	Clip	Miner	Juice	Speech	Bear	Brake	Tire	Child
Fence	Rock	Moan	Floor	Robber	Nurse	Fiddle	State	Boy
Flame	Earl	Claw	Glass	Mast	Lark	Honey	Week	Tree
Flour	Pool	Singer	Tribe	Copper	Trout	Glove	Gram	Orange

Step 3: From the table above on the right, tick each of the words you remembered.

Shallow	Speech	Fence	Flour	Honey	Copper	Monk	Miner	Clove	Fiddle	Brake
Rhyme	Cheek	Glove	Daisy	Cart	Mast	Chapel	Witch	Twig	Grin	Singer
Semantic	Brush	Flame	Knife	Sheep	Robber	Sonnet	Sleet	Drill	Moan	Claw

Step 4: Draw a bar chart to show your class findings.

Bar chart axes: Mean number of words recalled (0–100); categories Shallow, Rhyme, Semantic.

1... Consider the study on memory in the Do It Yourself box above (even if you haven't conducted it).

a) Describe the aim of this study, i.e. what was the study aiming to demonstrate about memory?

b) The task involved seeing how many words a participant remembered from the initial set of 30 questions – the expectation being that the words that were processed 'semantically' would be best remembered. However, participants might remember some words for other reasons. (This would be an EV.) Name **one** (or more) reason(s).

c) Suggest how this EV or EVs might be controlled.

d) One criticism of the cognitive approach is that the studies are not 'like real life'. Give **one** reason why this study is like everyday life, and **one** reason why it might be seen as artificial.

e) If the study is artificial, then we cannot generalise it to everyday life. Another issue relates to the participants in the study. If they are psychology students aged 16–17 years, explain how this might this affect the generalisability of the findings from this study.

f) If you conducted the study, describe what conclusions you would draw (i.e. what do you think the results demonstrate about memory?)

2... An area of study that has interested psychologists is massed versus distributed practice, i.e. whether learning is better if you practise something repeatedly (massed), or space your periods of practice (distributed). This topic has been studied in different settings.

▶ *Study 1: Participants were required to recall nonsense syllables on 12 occasions spread over either 3 or 12 days (Jost, 1897). Recall was higher when spread over 12 days. This finding has been supported by subsequent research.*

▶ *Study 2: Post office workers had to learn to type postcodes using either massed or distributed practice (Baddeley and Longman, 1978). Distributed practice was again found to be superior.*

Present arguments for why each of these studies could be viewed as having high and low validity.

More about validity

O n this spread, we look in more detail at the concept of **validity** – the key concept in understanding and evaluating research, and therefore worth spending time on. One issue is distinguishing between different types of validity – **experimental validity** and **ecological validity** (see below).

The main focus of this spread is to look at the situations that may reduce the validity of research, and how researchers can deal with this (see right).

EXPERIMENTAL AND ECOLOGICAL VALIDITY

Experiment validity

Experimental validity concerns what goes on *inside* a study. It is also called **internal validity**. It is concerned with things such as:

- Whether an **independent variable** (**IV**) produced the observed change in the **dependent variable** (**DV**) (or did something else affect the DV?).
- Whether the researcher tested what they intended to test; for example, if you want to find out whether watching TV affects the quality of homework, you cannot be certain you are doing this just by having the TV on (the person might not be listening to it).
- Whether the study possessed (or lacked) **mundane realism**.

To gain high experimental validity, you must design the research carefully, controlling **extraneous variables** (**EVs**) and ensuring that you are testing what you intended to test.

Ecological validity

Ecological validity is a form of **external validity**. It concerns being able to generalise the findings from one particular study to:

- Different places or settings.
- Different people or populations.
- Different historical periods (e.g. the 1950s or 2000s).

Ecological validity is affected by experimental validity – you cannot generalise the results of a study that was low in experimental validity, because the results have no real meaning for the behaviour in question.

CAN YOU...? No.6.3

Select two core studies from Chapter 5 and consider the ecological validity of these studies.

▶ *You might do this as a class debate, where one team argues in favour of, for example, high ecological validity, and one argues for low ecological validity.*

THREATS TO VALIDITY AND HOW TO DEAL WITH THEM

There are two main threats to the validity of any study:

1. The method used to measure variables is flawed (see below).
2. Changes in the DV are due to extraneous variables rather than the IV (see right).

1 Measuring variables

In an experiment, the DV needs to be measured, for example in our experiment on the effect of noise on performance we need to have some method of measuring 'performance' (such as performance of the task itself or a subsequent memory test).

Other variables are also measured or **operationalised**. For example, a researcher might be interested in seeing whether people who are hungry think that food looks more attractive. If you wanted to investigate this, you would need to decide how to define (operationalise) 'being hungry', and also how to measure (operationalise) attractiveness.

Threat to validity	How to deal with it
A researcher decides to test whether men or women are more stressed. In order to do this he decides to measure stress using a questionnaire. The threat to validity is whether the method of measuring stress is valid.	The validity of this measurement can be dealt with by considering **content validity**. This involves looking at your method of measurement and deciding whether it measures the intended content. You could ask an independent expert on the assessment of stress to evaluate the measurement to be used. The expert might suggest improvements, or might approve of the method, thus dealing with content validity.
	This could be dealt with by considering **concurrent validity**. This involves comparing the method of measurement used in the study with some other measurement of stress. We would expect people to be given similar scores on both measurements, thereby confirming concurrent validity.
	A third way to deal with measurement issues is to consider **construct validity**. This assesses the extent that a test measures the target construct. In the case of the stress measurement, we would look at a definition of stress and consider whether the questions were relevant to this construct.

'Ecological' refers to things being in the environment – the 'real' world or simply everyday life.

▲ **Clever Hans** (Hans von Osten) was an Arabian stallion owned by Wilhelm von Osten. Hans demonstrated an astonishing ability to perform arithmetic calculations. Someone would ask a simple arithmetic question, such as 'What are seven times four?', and would then start counting aloud. When the person reached 28, the horse would start stamping its hooves. However, rigorous testing showed that he was not adding, he was responding to subtle unconscious cues from his owner – Wilhelm was communicating expectations that acted as demand characteristics. The reason the horse did as expected was because of the cues, not his ability. Fulfilling expectations is the outcome of demand characteristics.

2 Extraneous variables

Threat to validity	How to deal with it
Situational variable Any environmental variable, such as time of day, temperature, or even noise levels at the time of testing, could act as an EV but only if it does affect performance on the behaviour tested, e.g. if the task is cognitive, time of day might be significant because people are more alert in the morning, but if the task is concerned with obedience, time of day might not matter.	The experimenter would control any potential EV through the use of **standardised procedures** to ensure that all participants are tested under the same conditions. In an **independent groups design**, the experimenter would make sure *both* groups are tested under the same conditions.
Participant variables can act as a kind of EV. Participants in one condition might perform better because they have certain characteristics in common, rather than because of the IV they receive. In the noise and performance experiment, it might be that the members of one group of participants were younger (and thus had better memories), or that they were more intelligent, more highly motivated, or more experienced at doing memory tests. These factors would act as EVs, making the results meaningless. It is important to realise that gender acts as an EV only in some circumstances. For example, we would not control gender in a memory experiment unless we had a reason to expect that it would matter.	This is only a problem when independent groups are used. The experimenter might test participants beforehand and use only participants with certain characteristics. Alternatively, participants might be matched (**matched pairs design**).
Investigator effects are any cues (other than the IV) from an investigator/experimenter that encourage certain behaviours in the participants, leading to a fulfilment of the investigator's expectations. Such cues act as an EV. The way in which an investigator asks a question might *lead* a participant to give the answer the investigator 'wants' (similar to **leading questions**, see page 92). Alternatively, the way the investigator responds to a participant might encourage some participants more than others. For example, research has found that male experimenters are more pleasant, friendly and encouraging with female participants than with other male participants (Rosenthal, 1966).	The person conducting the experiment should not be the person who designed it, so that they has no expectations about the content of the study. This is called a **double blind** technique, where neither the person conducting the study nor the participants are aware of the aims of the study.
A **demand characteristic** is an aspect of the research situation that triggers a predictable response in participants, causing most, if not all, of them to respond in a similar way. Particular cues in an experimental situation could communicate to participants what is expected of them (or 'demanded' of them), and what the investigator hopes to find. Participants respond to demand characteristics because they are actively searching for cues about how to behave. Demand characteristics might act as an alternative IV because they explain the change in the DV. The outcome is that the results are biased in favour of the research hypothesis, confirming the researcher's initial beliefs.	The solution lies in designing the research more carefully in order to eliminate such demand characteristics.

▲ Participants want to offer a helping hand. If they know they are in an experiment, they usually want to please the experimenter and be helpful, otherwise why are they there? This sometimes results in their being overly co-operative and behaving artificially. There is also the *'screw you' effect*, where a participant deliberately behaves in a way that spoils an experiment. Such effects are called **participant effects**.

CAN YOU...? No.6.4

In each of the studies listed near the bottom of the page, consider the problems that might arise in relation to validity, and answer the following questions.

1... Identify **at least one** issue of validity in this research.

2... Link each issue to the study by clearly explaining in what way this is an issue in the particular study (i.e. contextualisation).

3... Identify **at least one** method that could be used to deal with the issue of validity.

4... Link each method to the study by clearly explaining how the method would be used in the context of this particular study.

It might be useful to discuss your thoughts in small groups and then answer the questions yourself.

EXAM QUESTION

In the exam, you will be asked part (c) question, which says:

*'Identify **one** issue of validity in this research and describe how you could deal with this issue of validity. [3]'*

Examiner hint

In order to get full marks, you must do all four things listed above. Generic answers that make no link to the research will receive only one mark.

▶ **Study A:** Participants' memories were tested in the morning and in the afternoon, to see if there was any difference in their ability to recall numbers.

▶ **Study B:** Participants were given a list of adjectives describing Mr Smith. One group had positive adjectives first, followed by negative adjectives. The other group had the adjectives in reverse order. They were all then asked to describe Mr Smith.

▶ **Other studies** that you could consider are described on the next spread.

Ethical issues

What is an *issue*? It is a conflict between two points of view. In psychology, an **ethical issue** is a conflict between (1) what the researcher needs in order to conduct useful and meaningful research, and (2) the rights of participants. Ethical issues are conflicts about what is acceptable. On this spread, we consider various ethical issues that arise in psychological research.

ETHICAL ISSUES

Informed consent

From the researcher's point of view, **informed consent** means telling participants what is actually going to happen. This might cause participants to guess the aims of the study. For example, a psychologist might want to investigate whether people obey a male teacher more than a female teacher. If the participants are told the aim before the study takes place, it might change the way they behave – they might try to be equally obedient to both.

From the participants' point of view, they wish to be told what they will be required to do in the study so that they can make an informed decision about whether to participate.

Deception

From the researcher's point of view, it can be necessary to deceive participants about the true aims of a study otherwise participants might alter their behaviour which would make the study meaningless. A distinction, however, should be made between when a researcher simply withholds some of the details of the research aims, and when a researcher deliberately provides false information.

From the participants' point of view, **deception** is unethical – you should not deceive anyone without good cause. Perhaps more importantly, deception prevents participants from being able to give informed consent. They may agree to participate without really knowing what they have let themselves in for, and they might be quite distressed by the experience.

However, some people argue that deception is often relatively harmless, for example taking part in a memory study (no distress, quick experiment), and that the deception therefore may not be objectionable.

Right to withdraw

From the participants' point of view, they should have the **right to withdraw** from a study if they begin to feel uncomfortable or distressed. This is especially important if participants have been deceived about the aims and/or procedures. However, even if a participant has been fully informed, the actual experience of taking part could turn out to be rather different than they expected, so they should be able to withdraw.

From the researcher's point of view, if participants do leave during the study this will bias the results, because the participants who have stayed are likely to be more obedient or more resilient.

Protect from physical and psychological harm

From the researcher's point of view, studying some of the more important questions in psychology might involve a degree of distress to participants. It is also difficult to predict the outcome of certain procedures (such as in the *Stanford Prison Experiment*, page 134), and is therefore difficult to guarantee **protection from harm**.

From the participants' point of view, nothing should happen to them during a study that causes harm. It is considered acceptable if the risk of harm is no greater than in ordinary life. There are many ways harm can be caused to participants, some physical (e.g. getting them to smoke or drink coffee excessively) and some psychological (e.g. making them feel inadequate or embarrassing them). Participants should be in the same state after a study as they were before, unless they have given their informed consent to be treated otherwise.

Confidentiality

From the researcher's point of view it may be difficult to protect **confidentiality** because the researcher wishes to publish the findings. A researcher might guarantee *anonymity* (withholding the participants' names), but even then it might be obvious who has been involved in a study. For example, knowing that a study was conducted on the Isle of Wight could permit some people to be able to identify participants.

From the participants' point of view, the *Data Protection Act* makes confidentiality a legal right. It is only acceptable for personal data to be recorded if the data are not made available in a form that identifies the participants.

Privacy

From the researcher's point of view it might be difficult to avoid invasion of **privacy** when studying participants without their awareness.

From the participants' point of view, people do not expect to be observed by others in certain situations – such as within the privacy of their own homes – while they might expect it when they are out in public – sitting on a park bench, for example.

▲ **Confidentiality and privacy – what's the difference?**

The words 'confidentiality' and 'privacy' are sometimes used interchangeably, but there is a distinction between them. Confidentiality concerns the communication of personal information from one person to another, and the trust that this information will then be protected. Privacy refers to a zone of inaccessibility of mind or body, and the trust that this will not be 'invaded'. In other words, we have a right to privacy. If this is invaded, confidentiality should be respected.

DO IT YOURSELF

Have a look at the current versions of various ethical guidelines, and list the key points:
- The British Psychological Society (BPS) *Code of Ethics and Conduct* can be read at www.bps.org.uk/the-society/code-of-conduct/.
- Search Google for other codes of ethics.

DEALING WITH ETHICAL ISSUES

The most obvious way of dealing with ethical issues is through the use of guidelines produced by a professional organisation. All professionals (police officers, doctors, teachers, etc.) have a professional body whose job it is, among other things, to ensure that certain standards are maintained. In the UK, psychologists have the BPS, in the USA there is the *American Psychological Association* (APA), in Canada the *Canadian Psychological Association* (CPA), and so on. The intention of such guidelines is to tell psychologists what behaviours are not acceptable, and to give guidance on how to deal with ethical dilemmas.

How to deal with ethical issues	Limitations ☹
Informed consent Participants are asked formally to indicate their agreement to participate, and this should be based on comprehensive information concerning the nature and purpose of the research and their role in it.	If a participant is given information concerning the nature and purpose of a study, this might invalidate the purpose of the study. Even if researchers have sought and obtained informed consent, that does not guarantee that participants really do understand what they have let themselves in for.
Researchers offer the **right to withdraw**, so that participants know they can leave at any time.	Participants might feel they shouldn't withdraw because it will spoil the study. They might also feel they shouldn't withdraw because, in many studies, participants are paid or rewarded in some way (e.g. university students are often given course credits).
Deception Participants should be fully **debriefed** after the study and offered the opportunity to withhold their data.	Debriefing can't turn the clock back – a participant might still feel embarrassed or have lowered self-esteem.
Protection from harm Avoid any situation that could cause participants to experience psychological or physical damage.	Researchers are not always able accurately to predict the risks of taking part in a study.
Confidentiality Researchers should not record the names of any participants; they should use numbers or false names.	It is sometimes possible to work out who the participants were on the basis of the information that has been provided, for example the geographical location of a school. In practice, therefore, confidentiality might not be possible.
Privacy Do not observe anyone without their informed consent unless it is in a public place. Participants could be asked to give their retrospective consent.	There is no universal agreement about what constitutes a public place. Not everyone might agree about the acceptability of being observed in some conditions, such as lovers on a park bench.

All those conducting psychological research, including psychology students, are expected to be aware of their responsibility to ensure participants are treated in an ethically appropriate manner. Whenever you conduct any research, you must ensure that you deal properly with all the ethical issues.

CAN YOU...?

Ethical issues are *issues* because there are no easy answers. Below we have described various studies for your consideration. It might be useful to discuss your thoughts in small groups and then present your views to the class. You might want to investigate some of these studies more fully in order to decide about the associated ethical issues. A search on the internet should give further information. For each study:

1... Identify at least **one** ethical issues raised in it.

2... For each ethical issue, explain in what way it is an issue *in this study* (in other words, relate the issue to the context).

3... Suggest how the ethical issue might be dealt with.

EXAM QUESTION

In the exam, you will be asked a part (e) question, which says: Discuss **one** ethical issue that might arise in this research. [3]

Examiner hint

In order to get full marks, you could do all three things listed above. You are not required to 'deal' with the ethical issue, but it is a good way to produce a thorough answer.

▶ **Study A:** In the Stanford Prison Experiment (page 134), Zimbardo *et al.* (1973) took great care to inform the prospective participants about what would be involved in the study. However, the participants who were selected to be the prisoners were not informed that they would be arrested in their own homes, and did not know the amount of psychological distress that would be caused by participating.

▶ **Study B:** Craik and Tulving (1975, see page 139) conducted a study on memory where participants had to read 30 questions and respond 'yes' or 'no' to each. Afterwards, they were asked to recall as many of the words as they could. They were not informed of the true aims of the study (to compare deep with shallow processing), and were not told they would have to recall the words.

▶ **Study C:** Middlemist *et al.* (1976) investigated invasion of personal space by conducting a field experiment in a men's urinal. There were three conditions: a confederate (ally of the researcher) stands either immediately next to a participant, one urinal away, or is absent. An observer recorded the time for the onset of micturition (how long the men took before they started to urinate) as an indication of how comfortable the participant felt. Some psychologists regard this as an important study of personal space.

▶ **Study D:** Piliavin *et al.* (1969) investigated the behaviour of bystanders in an emergency situation to see how quickly they would offer help to someone (a confederate) who had collapsed on a New York underground train. The confederate acted either as if he were drunk (when he carried a bottle in a brown bag), or as if he were disabled (when he carried a black cane). Observers recorded how long it took for anyone to offer help. There was no opportunity to debrief participants.

▶ **Study E:** Orne (1962) observed that people behave in quite unusual ways if they think they are taking part in a psychology experiment. For example, in one experiment he asked participants to add up columns of numbers on a sheet of paper and then tear the paper up and repeat this again. If people believed this was part of a psychology experiment some were willing to continue the task for over 6 hours! This study led Orne to coin the term 'demand characteristics' – he claimed that the participants only tore the paper up because they were responding to the demand characteristics of the study. They would not do this in everyday life.

Lab and field experiments

On page 136, we considered **experiments**. On this spread, we will look in detail at **lab experiments** (an experiment conducted in a carefully controlled environment) and **field experiments** (experiments conducted in a more natural environment).

EVALUATING LAB AND FIELD EXPERIMENTS

Lab experiments are 'contrived'

- Participants know they are being studied, and this is likely to affect their behaviour. These are called **participant effects**.
- The setting is not like everyday life. This is described as being low in **mundane realism**. People behave more like they 'normally' do when a study is high in mundane realism.
- The IV or DV might be **operationalised** in such a way that it doesn't represent everyday experiences, e.g. using consonant syllables to test how memory works. This could, of course, happen in field experiments as well.

For all these reasons, participants in a lab experiment are *less* likely to behave as they would in everyday life.

Many of the problems outlined above for lab experiments could also arise in field experiments, for example the **independent variable** (**IV**) in a field experiment might lack realism. Therefore field experiments are not *necessarily* more like everyday life than lab experiments.

Field experiments are less controlled

Field experiments may be more natural, but it is more difficult to control **extraneous variables** (**EVs**). There is also a major **ethical issue** – if participants don't know they are being studied and it is difficult to debrief them, is it right to manipulate and record their behaviour?

Balancing act

Lab experiments tend to make control easier, but also tend to be less natural, especially because participants are aware they are being studied.

Field experiments tend to be more natural and more representative of everyday life, but this means less control and greater ethical problems.

An experiment permits us to study cause and effect. It differs from non-experimental methods in that it involves the manipulation of one variable (the IV), while trying to keep all other variables constant. If the IV is the only thing that is changed, then it must be responsible for any change in the **dependent variable** *(DV).*

Note that it is possible to do research in a lab that is not an experiment. For example, controlled observations are conducted in a lab (we will look at these on page 112).

Note also that there are field studies as well as field experiments. Any study that is conducted in a natural environment is called a **field study** *– it is only a field experiment if there is an IV that has been manipulated by an experimenter.*

▶ **Paying homage to formal terms***

People often focus too much on the words, and fail to really grasp the underlying meaning. This is the case with the terms 'field' and 'lab' experiment. It isn't always easy to decide whether a study is one or the other. What matters more are the underlying issues of validity and ethics. So don't get too hung up on the terms – focus on the meaning.

*An excellent phrase 'invented' by Hugh Coolican (2004a) to explain this problem.

Field or lab experiment?

Sometimes it isn't very easy to work out whether a study is a lab or field experiment. Consider the example below.

On page 54, we described the **weapon effect** study by Loftus *et al.* (1987). The study might seem, on the surface, to be a lab experiment – it was conducted under controlled conditions in a room unfamiliar to the participants. But the actual behaviour that was being measured (the participants' ability to identify the man running through the room) reflected natural behaviour. The participants were not aware that it was this behaviour that was being studied, and were therefore not primed to respond to participant effects or relevant **demand characteristics**.

Is this a lab or a field experiment?

IN DEFENCE OF ARTIFICIAL LAB EXPERIMENTS

Which drops faster – a kilogram of feathers or a kilogram of lead? Theoretically, they both drop at the same rate, because a kilogram of anything will drop at the same rate. However, if you try to test this, you will find that the kilogram of feathers drops more slowly because of air resistance. The air resistance is an EV. To test the proposition properly, the study would need to be done in a contrived set-up of a vacuum with no air to impede the feathers' fall.

Coolican (1996) argues in defence of contrived lab experiments that appear to lack realism. He points out that such settings are deliberately artificial in order to eliminate the EVs that are normally present in the real world. In fact, researchers do not always need to generalise from lab experiments to real life – the lab is intended as a place to test theory. If a study is successful here, then further studies might test the results in a more real-life, everyday context.

Sometimes, the contrived nature of the lab doesn't matter. For example, if you want to test the accuracy of **eyewitness testimony**, then doing this in a lab might be just like real life – you could arrange for participants to be doing a memory experiment in a lab, and while they are doing this a 'thief' comes into the room, steals a handbag and runs out. If you asked participants to try to identify the thief, how is this different from a real-life robbery? And remember that studies conducted in a natural environment might also lack validity because of a lack of control. **Think outside the box** – all studies have some validity, the question is how much and why.

Lab versus field experiments

It may help you to understand the difference between lab and field experiments by looking at the examples on this page and answering the questions on the right.

▶ **Study A:** *Bickman (1974) tested the effects of perceived authority on obedience. Confederates dressed in a sports jacket and tie, a milkman's uniform, or as a guard, and made requests to passers-by, such as asking them to pick up litter or give someone money for a parking meter. Participants obeyed most when the confederate was dressed as a guard. This study shows what most of us know – we are more likely to obey someone who looks like they have authority than someone who does not.*

▶ **Study B:** *Participants were asked to wait in a room before an experiment began. There was a radio playing either good or bad news, and a stranger was present. When participants were asked to rate the stranger, the degree of liking was related to the kind of news they had been listening to, showing that people like others who are associated with positive experiences (Veitch and Griffitt, 1976).*

▶ **Study C:** *Leventhal et al. (1967) wanted to investigate how to get people to stop smoking. Smokers were invited to the university and shown either a demonstration of smoke entering a mechanical 'smoking machine', or a short, fear-arousing film of an operation on the diseased lungs of a smoker (so disturbing that a number of participants walked out). Afterwards, both groups were asked about their intention to stop smoking. Smokers in the fear-arousal condition were much more likely to say they intended to give up.*

▶ **Study D:** *One group of school pupils was given information about how their peers had performed on a maths task. They were told either that their peers had done well or poorly on the test. The children were later given a maths test in class. Those who expected to do well did better than those led to expect to do poorly (Schunk, 1983).*

▶ **Study E:** *Researchers were asked to study what factors led to increased worker productivity at the Hawthorne Electrical factory. The study found that increased lighting led to increased productivity – but then also found that decreased lighting led to increased activity (Roethlisberger and Dickson, 1939). The researchers finally realised that the persistent increase in productivity was not related to lighting conditions at all (the IV), but because the workers were responding positively to the attention they were receiving, and that this was enhancing their performance. This outcome has been called the* Hawthorne effect *(after the study's location) – participant's behaviour in an experiment may be due to increased attention rather than the IV.*

▶ **Study F:** *Participants were tested in their teaching room and given nonsense trigrams (e.g. SXT) and then asked to count backwards until told to stop. Then participants were asked to recall the trigram. The counting interval was used to prevent the trigram being rehearsed. When the counting interval was three seconds, participants could recall most trigrams; when it was 18 seconds they couldn't recall many trigrams (Peterson and Peterson, 1959).*

▶ **Study G:** *Becklen and Cervone (1983) showed a video to participants. The video showed two teams of people passing a basketball, one team is wearing white and the other team are in black. Participants were asked to count the number of passes made by the black players. At the end they were asked if they had seen anything unusual during the film – in fact a woman holding an umbrella had walked through the room but most participants didn't notice this as they were attending to the passing of the ball. The video demonstrates that people don't see everything in their visual field because visual attention focuses on certain information. (You can see the video yourself on YouTube, type in 'visual attention basketball'.)*

CAN YOU...?   No. 6.6

Answer the questions below for the experiments A–G described on left.

1... Was the task required of the participants artificial (contrived)?

2... Was the study conducted in a natural setting?

3... Was the setting high or low in mundane realism?

4... Did the participants know they were being studied?

5... Were the participants brought into a special (contrived) situation, or did the experimenter go to them?

6... What relevant variables might not have been controlled?

7... Do you think this was a lab or field experiment?

Discuss: *What is the point of distinguishing between lab and field experiments?*

DO IT YOURSELF   No. 6.5

A field experiment on weapon focus

You can try to replicate the study by Loftus *et al.* (1987). Field experiments raise important ethical issues, so it will be possible to conduct this study only by using other students in your school or college, and they must be aged over 16 years.

You will need to conduct the study with **independent groups** – one group will see a **confederate** (someone who is not known to the group) come into the room either (a) holding a pen, or (b) holding something very unusual (but not a weapon!).

Both groups of participants will need to be engaged in a task that is interrupted by the entry of the confederate. You could arrange for the groups to be doing the study on page 139.
1. Things to consider:
   • Identify the conditions of the IV.
   • How would you measure the DV?
   • Are there any extraneous variables that should be controlled?
   • Why should the same person act as the stranger in both conditions?
   • Invent a set of dummy data that might be collected from this experiment and display this in a table and a graph; (it is useful to do this *before* conducting the study, using some dummy data, because it helps you to understand the design and might lead you to make some changes).
2. Record your intended procedures.
3. Approach a member of staff and ask if you can conduct a psychology experiment in two of their classes. Give them the full details of what you intend to do.
4. Conduct the study.
5. Produce a report of what happened and display your findings.

Natural (quasi-) experiments

The third kind of experiment is a **natural experiment**, where the experimenter makes use of a naturally varying **independent variable** (**IV**) instead of deliberately manipulating it. The reason for this is that there are some IVs that cannot be manipulated directly for practical or ethical reasons. For example, when studying the effects of day care, you couldn't deliberately put some children in day care, but you could study children who had already been placed in day care.

In a natural experiment, the effects of the IV on the **dependent variable** (**DV**) are observed by the experimenter, just as in field and lab experiments, but it is possible that some **extraneous variables** (**EVs**) are not controlled. For example, in a study comparing children who have experienced day care with those who have not, it might be that many of the children who were placed in day care also came from families that were less wealthy.

Strictly speaking an experiment involves the deliberate manipulation of an IV by an experimenter, therefore natural experiments are not 'true experiments' because no one has *deliberately* changed the IV to observe the effect this has on the DV. Such experiments are sometimes called **quasi-experiments**, meaning 'having some resemblance to experiments'.

The key thing to remember about lab, field and natural experiments is they all have an IV and a DV, and seek to demonstrate causal relationships. They differ in terms of factors such as control and realism.

GENERALISABILITY OF NATURAL EXPERIMENTS

Drawing valid conclusions from natural experiments is problematic for the following reasons.
- Participants are not **randomly allocated** to conditions, which means that there could be biases in the different groups of participants. For example, in the study on music and IQ (bottom of facing page), there are likely to have been other factors that differentiated between the music lesson and non-music lesson group (e.g. those in the music lesson group came from families with more money or were better motivated generally). These factors would act as an EV.
- The sample studied could have unique characteristics. For example, in the St Helena study (facing page), the people were part of a close-knit community, which means that the findings cannot be generalised to other cultures.

COMPARING LAB, FIELD AND NATURAL EXPERIMENTS

	Advantages ☺	Disadvantages ☹
Lab experiment To investigate causal relationships under controlled conditions	• Well controlled; EVs are minimised, thus higher **validity**. • Can be easily replicated (repeated) to check if the same results occur, which supports the validity of the results.	• Artificial, contrived situation where participants might not behave as they do in everyday life because of a lack of mundane realism, participant effects, **investigator effects** and **demand characteristics**. This reduces validity.
Field experiment To investigate causal relationships in more natural surroundings	• Less artificial, usually higher **mundane realism** and thus higher validity. • Avoids **participant effects** (because participants are not aware of the study), which may increase validity.	• EVs are less easy to control because the experiment is taking place in the real world, thus reducing validity. • There might still be demand characteristics, e.g. the way an IV is **operationalised** might convey the experimental hypothesis to participants.
Natural experiment To investigate potentially causal relationships in situations where the IV cannot be manipulated by an experimenter	• Allows research where IV cannot be manipulated for ethical or practical reasons, e.g. studies of deprivation. • Enables psychologists to study 'real' problems, such as the effects of disaster on health (increased mundane realism and validity).	• Cannot demonstrate causal relationships because IV not directly manipulated. • Inevitably many EVs (e.g. lack of random allocation), which are a threat to validity. • Can only be used where conditions vary naturally. • Participants might be aware of being studied, causing investigator effects and demand characteristics.

Examiner hint

*In question (a) in the AS Applied Research Methods exam, you will only ever be asked for **one** advantage and **one** disadvantage of the particular method used in the research example. However, at A2 level you might be asked for **two** advantages or **two** disadvantages of a particular method, so it helps to look at them now.*

Difference studies

Some people consider that **twin studies** (as discussed, for example, on page 13) are natural experiments. For example, a researcher might compare the similarity of identical twins (**MZ twins**) and non-identical twins (**DZ twins**) in terms of their intelligence. The IV is whether a twin pair is MZ or DZ, and the IQ score is the DV.

However the variable of genetic relatedness has not been manipulated (or changed). It is a naturally *occurring* variable not a naturally *manipulated* one. In any experiment, the IV has to have been, in some way, 'applied to someone' (Coolican, 2004a). Therefore 'relatedness' is not an IV.

The same is true of studies looking at gender (male and female), personality (extroverts and introverts), or age (younger versus older) – these conditions are not applied to the individual, they are an existing part of that person.

Such studies are **difference studies**. They are not experiments, but they could be called quasi-experiments. We cannot draw causal conclusions. We cannot, for example, say that gender caused an individual to have a higher IQ. We can only conclude that gender is related to IQ. An IV must be manipulated in some way in order to count as a true experiment; it cannot be an existing state of affairs.

EXAMPLES

A study was conducted on St Helena to see whether the introduction of TV would produce an increase in antisocial behaviour (Charlton *et al.*, 2000). The residents of this tiny island (122km²) received TV for the first time in 1995.

The majority of the measures used to assess antisocial behaviour showed no differences after the introduction of TV. This finding is in contrast to an earlier natural experiment by Williams (1985) in a Canadian town where TV was introduced for the first time. In this study, antisocial behaviour was found to increase.

The difference could be explained in terms of social norms. In St Helena, there was a community with a strong sense of identity and no major reason to be aggressive, whereas this was not true in the Canadian town.

Examiner hint

In the AS exam, when writing about advantages or disadvantages, you must remember to identify and contextualise. For example, identify one advantage and then contextualise it by linking the advantage to the particular piece of research. **Do not ever just describe a generic advantage.**

CAN YOU...? No. 6.7

1... Five studies are described below. Identify each study as a lab, field or natural experiment, and explain your decision.

▶ **Study A:** Two primary schools use different reading schemes. A psychological study compares the reading scores at the end of the year to see which scheme was more effective.

▶ **Study B:** Children take part in a trial to compare the success of a new maths programme. The children are placed in one of two groups – the new maths programme or the traditional one – and taught in these groups for a term.

▶ **Study C:** The value of using computers rather than books is investigated by requiring children to learn word lists, either using a computer or with a book.

▶ **Study D:** The effect of ads on gender stereotypes is studied by showing children ads with women doing feminine tasks or neutral tasks and then asking them about gender stereotypes.

▶ **Study E:** A study investigated the antisocial effects of TV by monitoring whether people who watch a lot of TV (more than five hours a day) are more aggressive than those who don't.

2... For each of the studies above (A–E), answer the following questions.

a) Outline **one** advantage of using the research method selected.

b) Explain why this advantage would be particularly important *for this particular study*.

c) Outline **one** disadvantage of using the research method selected.

d) Explain why this disadvantage would be particularly important *for this particular study*.

e) Identify **one** issue of validity in this research, and describe how you could deal with this issue of validity. Make sure that your answer is related to this specific study.

f) Discuss **one** ethical issue that might arise in this research. (Note that this question asks you to 'discuss' this issue. 'Discuss' means that you should do more than describe it – you could comment on why it is an issue, or consider how it could be dealt with.)

DO IT YOURSELF No. 6.6

You may of course think of your own natural experiment, but here is one you could try.

Music lessons can boost IQ

A recent study looked at the effects of music lessons on IQ (Schellenberg, 2004). The participants (aged six years old) had their IQs tested before the study began. They were allocated to one of four groups: two groups had 36 weeks of extracurricular music tuition (one had singing-based tuition, the other studied keyboard). A third group had extra drama lessons on top of normal school, and the **control group** simply attended school as usual. The children completed IQ and other tests at the end of the school year. Schellenberg found that the IQ performance of the two music groups increased significantly more than that of the drama and baseline groups.

You can conduct similar research making use of existing data – the fact that some people have had music lessons and others haven't. Thus you will be conducting a natural experiment. (Schellenberg's study is not a natural experiment – can you identify what kind of study it is?)

• **IV:** Divide your class into those who have received extra music lessons and those who have not. You must operationalise this IV, i.e. decide what constitutes 'having music lessons'. Would one week of lessons count, or one year?

• **DV:** For each member of your class, calculate a GCSE score as a rough measure of IQ. One way to do this is to assign a value to each grade, add all scores together and divide by the number of GSCE subjects taken. This gives you a final score for each student. You can use the table below to record your raw data.

• **Ethics:** Individuals may record their data anonymously.

• **Analysis:** Calculate a mean GCSE score for those in the group of pupils that have had music lessons and compare this with the mean GCSE score of those who have not had music lessons. Draw a graph to illustrate this data. What can you conclude?

GCSE SCORES Grade A*=9, A=8, B=7, C=6, D=5, E=4, F=3, G=2, U=1, X=0																							Total score (add white column numbers)	Final score (total score/ number of scores)	Music lessons (Y/N)
Participant	Grade	Score	Grade	Score	Grade	Score	Grade	Score	Grade	Score	Grade	Score	Grade	Score	Grade	Score	Grade	Score	Grade	Score	Grade	Score			
1																									
etc																									

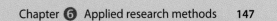

Correlations

The concept of a correlation should be familiar to you from GCSE maths. A **correlation** is a relationship between two variables.

Age and beauty covary. As people get older they become more beautiful. This is a **positive correlation** because the two variables *increase* together. You may disagree, and think that as people get older they become less attractive. You think age and beauty are correlated but it is a **negative correlation**. As one variable increases the other one decreases. Or you may simply feel that there is no relationship between age and beauty. This is called a **zero correlation**.

Linear and curvilinear

*The correlations we are looking at on this spread are all **linear** – in a perfect positive correlation, all the values would lie in a straight line from the bottom left to the top right.*

*However there is a different kind of correlation – a **curvilinear correlation**, where there is still a predictable relationship, but it is curved rather than linear. For example, stress and performance do not have a linear relationship. Performance on many tasks is depressed when stress is too high or too low; it is best when stress is moderate – as illustrated in the graph below. This is called the Yerkes-Dodson effect.*

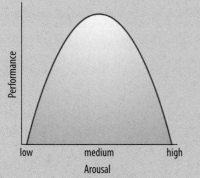

SCATTERGRAPHS

A correlation can be illustrated using a **scattergraph**. For each individual we obtain two scores, which are used to plot one dot for that individual – the *covariables* determine the *x* and *y* position of the dot. The scatter of the dots indicates the degree of correlation between the covariables.

Correlation coefficient

A statistical test is used to calculate the **correlation coefficient**, a measure of the extent of correlation that exists between the covariables.

- A correlation coefficient is a number.
- A correlation coefficient has a maximum value of 1 ($+1$ is a perfect positive correlation and -1 is a perfect negative correlation).
- Some correlation coefficients are written as $-.52$, whereas others are $+.52$. The plus or minus sign shows whether it is a positive or negative correlation.
- The coefficient (number) tells us how closely the covariables are related, $-.52$ is just as closely correlated as $+.52$, it's just that $-.52$ means that as one variable increases the other decreases (negative correlation), and $+.52$ means that both variables increase together (positive correlation).

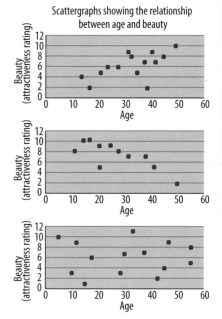

Scattergraphs showing the relationship between age and beauty

▲ The top scattergraph illustrates a positive correlation. The middle scattergraph shows a negative correlation. The bottom scattergraph is a zero correlation.

The correlation coefficients for all three graphs are: (1) $+.76$ (2) $-.76$ (3) $-.006$. The plus or minus sign shows whether it is a positive or negative correlation. The coefficient (number) tells us how closely the covariables are related. $-.76$ is just as closely correlated as $+.76$.

When conducting a study using a correlational analysis, you need to produce a correlational hypothesis. An experimental hypothesis states the expected relationship between an IV and a DV. A correlational hypothesis states the expected relationship between covariables. For example, age and beauty are positively correlated.

ADVANTAGES AND DISADVANTAGES OF STUDIES USING A CORRELATIONAL ANALYSIS

A correlation is not a research method. Therefore, strictly speaking, we shouldn't talk about a correlational study but a study using a correlational analysis.

Advantages ☺	Disadvantages ☹
• Can be used when it would be unethical or impractical to manipulate variables and can make use of existing data.	• People often misinterpret correlations and assume that a cause and effect have been found, whereas this is not possible.
• If a correlation is **significant**, then further investigation is justified.	• There may be other, unknown (**intervening**) variable(s) that can explain why the covariables being studied are linked.
• If the correlation is not significant, then you can rule out a causal relationship.	• As with experiments, could lack **internal/external validity**, for example the method used to measure IQ might lack validity
• As with experiments, the procedures can be repeated again, which means that the findings can be confirmed.	or the sample used might lack **generalisability**.

Significance

Significance is the extent to which something is particularly unusual.

When we look at a correlation coefficient, we need to know whether it is strong or weak. In order to do this, we use *tables of significance*, which tell us how big the coefficient needs to be in order for the correlation to count as significant (unusual).

The table on the right gives an approximate idea of the values needed. The more pairs of scores you have, the smaller the coefficient can be.

A coefficient of either −.45 or +.45 would be significant if there were 16 pairs of data, but not if there were 14 pairs.

The magnitude of the number informs us about significance, while the sign tells us which direction the correlation is in (positive or negative).

Significance table	
N=	
4	1.000
6	0.829
8	0.643
10	0.564
12	0.503
14	0.464
16	0.429
18	0.401
20	0.380
22	0.361
24	0.344
26	0.331
28	0.317

These values are for Spearman's test of correlation.

CAN YOU...?

No. 6.8

1... Identify **two** variables that are likely to be positively correlated (such as height and weight).

2... Identify **two** variables that are likely to be negatively correlated.

3... What does a correlation coefficient tell you about a set of data?

4... Give an example of a positive correlation coefficient and a negative correlation coefficient.

5... Explain what the following correlation coefficients mean:
   a) +1.00   **b)** −1.00   **c)** .00
   d) −.60   **e)** +.40   **f)** +.10

6... Consider the number +.36.

   a) Identify the magnitude and sign of this number.

   b) If this value were obtained after testing 20 people, would it be significant?

   c) Sketch a scattergraph to illustrate this correlation approximately.

   d) If you conducted a study with 30 participants, would a correlation of +.30 be significant?

7... A study investigates whether there is a negative correlation between age and liking for spicy foods. Participants are asked to rate their liking for spicy foods on a scale of 1–10, where 10 means they liked it a lot and 1 means not at all.

   a) What is meant by the term 'negative correlation' in this context?

   b) Why might you expect to find a negative correlation between these variables?

   c) Describe **one** advantage and **one** disadvantage of conducting a correlational analysis in this research.

   d) Describe **one** issue of validity in this research, and describe how you could deal with this issue of validity.

   e) Discuss **one** ethical issue that might arise in this research.

8... Guiseppe Gelato always liked statistics at school, and now that he has his own ice-cream business he keeps various records. To his surprise, he has found an interesting correlation between his ice cream sales and aggressive crimes. He has started to worry that he may be irresponsible in selling ice cream, because it appears to cause people to behave more aggressively. The table below shows his data.

All data rounded to 1000s	Jan	Feb	Mar	Apr	May	Jun	Jul	Aug	Sep	Oct	Nov	Dec
Ice-cream sales	10	8	7	21	32	56	130	141	84	32	11	6
Aggressive crimes	21	32	29	35	44	55	111	129	99	36	22	25

   a) Sketch a scattergraph of Guiseppe's data.

   b) What can you conclude from the data and the scattergraph?

   c) What intervening variable might better explain the relationship between ice cream and aggression?

   d) Describe how you would design a study to show Guiseppe that ice cream does (or does not) cause aggressive behaviour. (You need to **operationalise** your variables and decide on a suitable research design.)

   e) Describe **one** issue of validity in this research, and describe how you could deal with this issue of validity.

   f) Discuss **one** ethical issue that might arise in this research.

Representing data and drawing conclusions

The information collected in any study is called 'data' or, more precisely, a 'data set' (a set of items). Data are not necessarily numbers; they could be words used to describe how someone feels. Numerical data are described as **quantitative**, whereas data that are non-numerical are called **qualitative**. Once a researcher has collected data, it needs to be analysed in order to identify trends or to see the bigger picture. On this spread, we will look at methods of *quantitative* data analysis. Qualitative data analysis is discussed on page 162.

*Quantitative methods are sometimes referred to as **descriptive statistics** because they are methods of describing quantitative data.*

Levels of measurement

- **Nominal** The data are in separate categories, such as grouping people according to their favourite football team (e.g. Cardiff City, Neath Athletic, Llanelli, etc.).
- **Ordinal** Data are ordered in some way, for example asking people to put a list of football teams in order of liking. Llanelli might be first, followed by Neath Athletic and so on. The 'difference' between each item is not the same, i.e. the individual might like the first item a lot more than the second, but there might be only a small difference between the items ranked second and third.
- **Interval** Data are measured using units of equal intervals, such as when counting correct answers or using any 'public' unit of measurement.
- **Ratio** There is a true zero point, as in most measures of physical quantities.

NOIR This is an acronym to help you remember the four levels of data measurement: **n**ominal, **o**rdinal, **i**nterval and **r**atio.

QUANTITATIVE DATA ANALYSIS

Averages

Averages inform us about central or 'typical' values for a set of data, providing a useful *description* of a data set. An average can be calculated in different ways.

1. The **mean** is calculated by adding up all the numbers and dividing by the number of numbers. It can only be used with **interval** or **ratio** data (see left).
   + It makes use of the values of all the data.
   − It can be misrepresentative of the data as a whole if there are extreme values.
2. The **median** is the *middle* value in an *ordered* list, suitable for **ordinal** or interval data.
   + Not affected by extreme scores.
   − Not as 'sensitive' as the mean because not all values are reflected.
3. The **mode** is the value that is *most* common.
   + Useful when the data are in categories, i.e. **nominal** data.
   − Not a useful way of describing data when there are several modes (i.e. a multimodal set of data).

Range

Another method used to describe a data set is the **range**. Consider the data sets below:

3, 5, 8, 8, 9, 10, 12, 12, 13, 15 mean = 9.5 range = 12 (3–15)
1, 5, 8, 8, 9, 10, 12, 12, 13, 17 mean = 9.5 range = 16 (1–17)

The two sets of numbers have the same mean but a different range, so the range is helpful as a further method of describing the data. If we just used the mean, the data would appear to be the same. The range is the difference between the highest and the lowest number.

+ Easy to calculate, provides you with direct information.
− Affected by extreme values, doesn't take account of the number of observations in the data set.

DO IT YOURSELF

In the days when psychology students had to do coursework, this was a top choice. The study gives an interesting insight into how memory works. It was originally conducted by Bower *et al.* (1969) to show that our memories are improved by organising information – which explains why it is important to produce organised notes for revisions.

Your task is to design a study to test the hypothesis that memory is improved by organisation. You can use the words in the two lists on the right. Word list 1 is organised into categories, whereas word list 2 shows the same words in a random order.

1. Write your own list of the design decisions that need to be made, based on your experience of designing other studies. Ensure that you consider ethical issues carefully.
2. Write a fully operationalised hypothesis.
3. Conduct a **pilot study** to check your design, and make any alterations to the design that are necessary.
4. Now collect your data (or, if this is not possible, invent a set of data).
5. Present the data you have collected in a:
   - Table: show raw data, and *appropriate* measures of average and range
   - Graph: draw an *appropriate* bar chart and/or histogram.
6. What conclusions would you draw from your study?

EXTRA You could also correlate memory scores with GCSE scores (see method on page 147), and produce a **scattergraph** of your results.

No. 6.8

Word list 1		Word list 2	
Dogs	**Instruments**	Pear	Daffodil
Labrador	Harp	Beagle	Plum
Beagle	Piano	Clarinet	Nose
Boxer	Flute	Hail	Weather
Spaniel	Clarinet	Rain	Copper
Fruit	**Drinks**	Drinks	Labrador
Apple	Water	Rose	Water
Pear	Milk	Squash	Flowers
Plum	Squash	Hand	Brass
Orange	Coke	Boxer	Foot
Weather	**Body**	Iron	Tulip
Snow	Nose	Coke	Pansy
Rain	Foot	Gold	Dogs
Sleet	Toe	Harp	Sleet
Hail	Hand	Piano	Milk
Flowers	**Metal**	Metal	Orange
Daffodil	Brass	Apple	Toe
Rose	Gold	Body	Snow
Pansy	Copper	Fruit	Flute
Tulip	Iron	Instruments	Spaniel

DRAWING CONCLUSIONS

The main aim of any research study is to make some sense of the findings and use these to help explain human behaviour. This is what we mean when we 'draw conclusions'. What does the data show us about human behaviour?

Descriptive statistics are useful when it comes to drawing conclusions because they provide a *summary* of the data. They help us detect general patterns and trends.

Examples

From the Do It Yourself box on the facing page, you could write the following.
- People who studied the organised list were able to remember almost double the number of words compared with people in the random word list condition.
- The results showed a positive correlation between memory and GCSE score.

In other words, you are seeking to write a single sentence that succinctly describes the findings of a study.

You should not go beyond the data with your conclusions. For example, it would not be appropriate to assume from your study of memory and organised word lists that people remember more if they use organised lists. You can only draw an inference such as this if you use **inferential statistics**, which are covered as part of the A2 course.

VISUAL DISPLAY

A picture is worth a thousand words! Graphs provide a means of 'eyeballing' your data and seeing the findings at a glance.
- **Tables** The numbers you collect are referred to as 'raw data' – numbers that haven't been treated in any way. These data can be set out in a table or summarised using types of averages and/or range.
- **Bar chart** The height of each bar represents the frequency of that item. The categories are placed on the horizontal (*x*-axis) and frequency is on the vertical (*y*-axis). Bar charts are suitable for words and numbers (nominal or ordinal/ interval data).
- **Histogram** Similar to a bar chart except that the area within the bars must be proportional to the frequencies represented. In practice, this means that the vertical axis (frequency) must start at zero. In addition, the horizontal axis must be continuous (therefore you can't draw a histogram with nominal data). Finally there should be no gaps between the bars.
- **Scattergraphs** A kind of graph used when doing a correlational analysis (see page 148).

Examples of bar charts and histograms

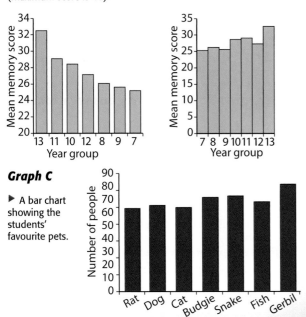

Graph A

▼ A bar chart showing the mean memory scores for each year group (maximum score is 40).

Graph B

▼ A histogram showing the same data as Graph A.

Graph C

▶ A bar chart showing the students' favourite pets.

CAN YOU...?   No.6.9

1... For each of the following data sets:
- **a)** Calculate the mean.
- **b)** Calculate the median.
- **c)** Calculate the mode.
- **d)** State which of the three measures would be most suitable to use and why.
- **e)** Calculate the range.

   Data set 1: 2, 3, 5, 6, 6, 8, 9, 12, 15, 21, 22

   Data set 2: 2, 3, 8, 10, 11, 13, 13, 14, 14, 29

   Data set 3: 2, 2, 4, 5, 5, 5, 7, 7, 8, 8, 8, 10

   Data set 4: cat, cat, dog, budgie, snake, gerbil.

2... Why is it better to know about the mean and range of a data set rather than just the mean?

3... There are three graphs on the left.
- **a)** Explain **two** key differences between the bar chart and the histogram.
- **b)** State **one** conclusion that could be drawn from the mean values in Graph A.
- **c)** What level of measurement is displayed in Graph C?

4... A psychologist has conducted a field experiment to see how long it takes people to offer help when someone falls down.
- **a)**

	Victim seems to be drunk	Victim has a cane
Median response time	35 seconds	23 seconds

   State **one** conclusion that could be drawn from median values in Graph A.
- **b)** Identify **one** issue of validity in this research, and describe how you could deal with this issue of validity.

5... It is thought that students born between September and December do better than children born in the summer months because they are older. Devise a study to test this hypothesis.
- **a)** Put your findings in a table.
- **b)** Draw a suitable graph for your findings.
- **c)** State **one** conclusion that could be drawn from your graph.
- **d)** Identify **one** issue of validity in this research, and describe how you could deal with this issue of validity.

Observations

In this chapter, we have examined various different methods used in research studies – **lab experiments**, **field experiments**, **natural (quasi-) experiments** and **correlations**. They have almost all been experiments. Many people use the word 'experiment' rather loosely when they actual just mean a 'study'. An experiment is a study where an **independent variable (IV)** has been manipulated so that the effect can be observed on a **dependent variable (DV)**. This enables us to draw causal conclusions that the IV *caused* any observed change in the DV. Correlations involve no such manipulation – and neither do observations. From now on in this chapter, we are looking at *non-experimental* research methods. However, such methods might be used in an experiment as a means to **operationalise** an IV or DV.

*In **controlled observations**, it is the participants' environment that is controlled, not the techniques used to obtain observational data. Systematic techniques are used in **naturalistic** and **controlled observations**.*

Bandura's Bobo doll study

*On page 26, we described the classic study by Bandura et al. (1961) that illustrates **social learning theory**. This is an example of an experiment with controlled observational techniques. The children's aggressiveness was observed at the end of the experiment to see if those exposed to the aggressive model behaved more aggressively. Each child was taken to a room that contained some aggressive toys (e.g. a mallet and a dart gun), some non-aggressive toys (e.g. dolls and farm animals) and a Bobo doll.*

The experimenter stayed with the child while they played for 20 minutes, during which time the child was observed through a one-way mirror. Every five seconds, the observers recorded what the child was doing, using the following measures.
- *Imitative physical aggression: any specific acts that were imitated.*
- *Imitative verbal aggression: any phrases that were imitated, such as 'POW'.*
- *Imitative non-aggressive verbal responses: such as 'He keeps coming back for more'.*
- *Non-imitative physical and verbal aggression: aggressive acts directed at toys other than Bobo, for example saying things that were not said by the model, or that were not demonstrated by the model playing with the gun.*

This is an example of an experiment that has used observational techniques to measure the DV.

DO IT YOURSELF
No. 6.9

Making observations

Work with a partner and take it in turns to observe each other. One of you will be Person A and the other will be Person B.

Person A should have a difficult task to do (e.g. answering one set of questions in this book). Person B should have a boring task to do (e.g. copying out an exam question). Each person should spend five minutes on his or her task, while the other person observes him or her, noting down any aspect of the partner's behaviour.

CAN YOU...?
No. 6.10

Answer the following questions about the observational study above (some of them could be answered without conducting the study).

1... Summarise your observations. You might use a graph or other descriptive statistic to help you.

2... Were the observations controlled or naturalistic?

3... Describe **one or more** difficulties that you encountered.

4... What uncontrolled factors might affect your findings? (These relate to validity.)

5... Describe **one** way you could deal with this issue of validity.

6... State **one** conclusion that could be drawn from this study.

OBSERVATIONAL RESEARCH

In an observational study, participants are observed engaging in whatever behaviour is being studied and the observations recorded.
- In a **naturalistic observation**, behaviour is studied in a natural situation where everything has been left as it normally is.
- In a **controlled observation**, some variables are controlled by the researcher, reducing the 'naturalness' of behaviour being studied. Participants are likely to know they are being studied, and the study might be conducted in a lab.
- Observation could also be used in an experiment, in which case observation is a research technique instead of a research method.

You might think that making observations is easy, but if you tried the Do It Yourself task on the left, you should now realise it is difficult for two main reasons:
- It is difficult to work out what to record and what not to record.
- It is difficult to record everything that is happening even if you do select what to record and what not to record.

Unstructured observations

The researcher records all relevant behaviour but has no system. This is likely to be because the behaviour to be studied is largely unpredictable.

The most obvious problem with recording unstructured observations is that there might be too much to record. Another problem is that the behaviours recorded will often be those that are most visible or eye-catching to the observer, but these may not necessarily be the most important or relevant behaviours.

Structured (systematic) observations

Like all research, observational research aims to be objective and rigorous. For this reason it is preferable to use **observational techniques**.

The researcher uses various 'systems' to organise observations. These include:
- **Coding system** to record the behaviour being observed.
- **Sampling procedures** to decide what to observe and when.

These are explained on the right.

Distinctions

- **Method and technique** All research involves making observations. In some research, the overall method is observational, where the emphasis is on observing a relatively unconstrained segment of a person's freely chosen behaviour. However, observational techniques are used in almost all studies, even experiments.
- **Controlled and naturalistic** Both kinds of observation use systematic methods to record observations, i.e. there is control over how the observations are made. Control over the environment is only true in a controlled observation, for example the setting may be moved from the person's normal environment or some of the items in the environment may be deliberately chosen.
- **Participant and non-participant** In many cases, the observer is merely watching the behaviour of others and acts as a non-participant. In some studies, observers also participate, which may affect their objectivity. Rosenhan's study (see page 122) is a classic example of a participant observation.
- **Overt and covert** One-way mirrors are used to prevent participants being aware that they are being observed. This is called **covert observation** (or undisclosed). Knowing that your behaviour is being observed is likely to alter your behaviour, and therefore observers often try to be as unobtrusive as possible, although this has ethical implications.
- **Naturalistic observation and natural experiment** Both involve naturally occurring variables that have not been manipulated by the researcher, although in a **natural experiment** there is an **independent variable (IV)** and its effect is observed on a **dependent variable (DV)** so that we can draw tentative causal conclusions. In a naturalistic observation, there is no IV.

CAN YOU...? No.6.11

1... A group of students has decided to study student behaviour in the school library.
- **a)** Suggest **one or more** hypotheses that you might investigate.
- **b)** List **five** behaviours you might include in a coding system.
- **c)** Identify a suitable sampling procedure and explain how you would do it.
- **d)** Discuss **one** ethical issue that might arise in this research.
- **e)** Explain in what way this would be a naturalistic observation.
- **f)** In this study, is observation a method or a technique?

2... For each of the following observations, state which sampling procedure would be most appropriate and explain how you would do it.
- **a)** Recording instances of aggressive behaviour in children playing in a school playground.
- **b)** Vocalisations (words, sounds) made by young children.
- **c)** Litter-dropping in a public park.
- **d)** Behaviour of dog owners when walking their dogs.

An example of a coding system

The Facial Action Coding System *(FACS) for observing facial expressions (Ekman and Friesen, 1978). Paul Ekman and others have developed the coding system below to code non-verbal behaviours. This can be used to investigate, for example, the expressions on people's faces when they are lying.*

▲ Outer brow raiser   ▲ Lip corner depressor

You can see illustrations of all the other codes at www-2.cs.cmu.edu/afs/cs/project/face/www/facs.htm.

Code	Description	Code	Description
1	Inner Brow Raiser	26	Jaw Drop
2	Outer Brow Raiser	27	Mouth Stretch
4	Brow Lowerer	28	Lip Suck
5	Upper Lid Raiser	41	Lid droop
6	Cheek Raiser	42	Slit
7	Lid Tightener	43	Eyes Closed
9	Nose Wrinkler	44	Squint
10	Upper Lip Raiser	45	Blink
11	Nasolabial Deepener	46	Wink
12	Lip Corner Puller	51	Head turn left
13	Cheek Puffer	52	Head turn right
14	Dimpler	53	Head up
15	Lip Corner Depressor	54	Head down
16	Lower Lip Depressor	55	Head tilt left
17	Chin Raiser	56	Head tilt right
18	Lip Puckerer	57	Head forward
20	Lip Stretcher	58	Head back
22	Lip Funneler	61	Eyes turn left
23	Lip Tightener	62	Eyes turn right
24	Lip Pressor	63	Eyes up
25	Lips part	64	Eyes down

Coding system

It is difficult to decide how different behaviours should be categorised. This is because our perception of behaviour is often seamless: when we watch somebody perform a particular action, we see a continuous stream of action rather than a series of separate behavioural components.

In order to conduct systematic observations, we need to break up this stream of behaviour into different *behavioural categories*. This is achieved through **operationalisation** – breaking up the behaviour being studied into a set of components. For example, when observing infant behaviour, you can have a list including things like smiling, crying and sleeping, etc., or, when observing facial expressions, a list of different expressions, such as is shown on the right.

Using a coding system means that a code is invented to represent each category of behaviour. Researchers might develop their own system of behavioural categories, or use something developed by other researchers.

Sampling techniques used in observations

When conducting a *continuous* observation, the observer should record every instance of the behaviour in as much detail as possible. However, continuous observation is not possible in many situations because there would be too much data to record, and there must therefore be a systematic method of **sampling** observations, such as the following.
- **Event sampling** Counting the number of times a certain behaviour (event) occurs in a target individual or individuals.
- **Time sampling** Recording behaviours at regular intervals. For example, noting what a target individual is doing every 30 seconds. At that time, the observer may tick one or more categories from a checklist/coding system.

More about observations

As with all research methods, there are advantages and disadvantages to observational techniques and methods. The main concerns are related to validity and ethical issues, plus a new concept, reliability.

VALIDITY OF OBSERVATIONS

Ecological (external) validity

Observational studies are likely to have high **ecological validity** because they involve more natural behaviours (but remember that naturalness doesn't always mean greater ecological validity).

However, **representativeness** may be a problem if, for example, children are only observed in middle-class homes, because we cannot generalise such findings to children from all classes.

Internal validity

Observations will not be valid if the **coding system** is flawed. For example, some observations might belong in more than one category, or some behaviours might not be codeable.

The validity of observations is also affected by **observer bias** – what someone observes is influenced by their expectations. This reduces the objectivity of observations.

Dealing with validity

A researcher can improve validity by conducting observations in varied settings with varied participants, which makes the findings more generalisable to other settings and other people.

The researcher can also use more than one observer to reduce observer bias, averaging data across observers (which balances out any biases).

RELIABILITY OF OBSERVATIONS

The concept of reliability is explained on the facing page. In observational research, the issue is that any observations should be consistent. If they are consistent, we would expect two observers to produce exactly the same observations. The extent to which two (or more) observers agree is called inter-rater or **inter-observer reliability**.

Dealing with reliability

Inter-observer reliability is measured by **correlating** the observations of two or more observers (we discussed correlation on page 150). A general rule is that if there is more than 80% agreement on the observations, the data have inter-observer reliability:

$$\frac{\text{Total agreement}}{\text{Total observations}} > 80\%$$

In order to improve reliability, observers should be trained in the use of a coding system/behaviour checklist. They should practise using it, and discuss their observations. The investigator can then check the reliability of their observations.

ETHICAL ISSUES

In studies where participants are observed without their knowledge, there are issues relating to **informed consent**.

Some observations might be regarded as an invasion of **privacy**, where case participant **confidentiality** should be respected. The use of one-way mirrors often involves **deception**.

In observations where participants *are* aware of being studied, there are still issues similar to those in all studies, such as informed consent, **right to withdraw** etc.

Examiner hint

*We pointed out earlier that in the Applied Research Methods part of the AS exam you will be required to describe only **one** advantage and **one** disadvantage of a research method in an exam question – yet we have provided several. These will be useful because it means you can select a criticism that is appropriate to the scenario, and should thus be better able to contextualise your advantage/disadvantage.*

ADVANTAGES AND DISADVANTAGES OF OBSERVATIONS

Advantages ☺	Disadvantages ☹
• What people say they do is often different from what they actually do, so observations might be more valid than, for example, questionnaires. • Give a more realistic picture of spontaneous behaviour, therefore high ecological validity. • Provide a means of conducting preliminary investigations in a new area of research, to produce hypotheses for future investigations.	• There can be little or no control of **extraneous variables (EVs)**, which might mean that something unknown to the observer could account for the behaviour observed. • The observer might 'see' what they expect to see. This is called observer bias. This bias could mean that different observers 'see' different things, which leads to low inter-observer reliability. • If participants don't know they are being observed, there are ethical problems such as deception and invasion of privacy. If participants do know they are being observed, they might alter their behaviour.

RELIABILITY

Reliability refers to whether something is consistent. If you use a ruler to measure the height of a chair today and check the measurement again tomorrow, you expect the ruler to be reliable (consistent) and provide the same measurement. You would assume that any fluctuation was because the dimensions of the chair had somehow changed. If the fluctuation was due to some change in the ruler, it would be pretty useless as a measuring instrument – not dependable, consistent or reliable.

Any tool used to measure something must be reliable, such as a psychological test assessing personality, or an interview about drinking habits, or observations made by two observers of a target individual.

If the 'tool' is measuring the same thing, it should produce the same result on every occasion. If the result is different, then we need to be sure that it is the thing (chair or personality) that has changed or is different, and not the measuring tool.

Validity and reliability

Different archers produce the following patterns of arrows.

| Reliable, but not valid | Not reliable, not valid | Reliable and valid |

Being reliable is being consistent, whereas being valid is being on target (related to what you are aiming to do).

A study that lacks reliability will therefore lack validity. For example, if an observer is inconsistent in the observations they make (e.g. recording some observations when they weren't sure what the target individual was doing), then the results are meaningless i.e. lack validity.

You can, however, have a study that is reliable but not valid. For example, if an observer uses a coding system that is not very thorough, and sometimes the target individual does things that can't be recorded, the observations may be perfectly reliable but lack validity, because the behaviour checklist was poor.

CAN YOU...? (No.6.12)

For each of the studies described below, answer the following questions.

1... Identify **two** behavioural categories that could be used to describe behaviour in this study.

2... How would you record the data in this observational study?

3... In this study, is observation a method or a technique?

4... Outline **one** advantage and **one** disadvantage of using observation in this study.

5... Identify **one** issue of reliability in this research, and describe how you could deal with this issue of reliability.

6... Identify **one** issue of validity in this research, and describe how you could deal with this issue of validity.

7... Discuss **one** ethical issue in this research.

Below is a list of observational studies to be used in conjunction with the questions above.

Examiner hint

In the exam, you will be asked questions about reliability and validity. Remember, when answering such questions, that you must do all four things listed on page 141 in order to get full marks. Generic answers that make no reference to the research will receive only 1 mark.

▶ **Study A:** *What distinguishes a successful teacher from an unsuccessful one? A group of students decide to observe various teachers while they are teaching.*

▶ **Study B:** *A psychologist decided to observe the non-verbal behaviours between two people having a conversation. (Non-verbal behaviours are those that don't involve language, such as smiling, touching, etc.)*

▶ **Study C:** *Imagine that you wished to investigate interpersonal deception to see if it was possible to use facial expressions to tell whether someone is lying or not.*

DO IT YOURSELF

 No. 6.10

Making systematic observations

The coding system below is adapted from one used by Fick (1993) in a study that looked at the effects of having a dog on the nature and frequency of social interactions in nursing home residents. You can use this shortened version below to make observations of other students in a common room or cafeteria.

- *Non-attentive behaviour (NAB):* participant is not engaged in group activity.
- *Attentive listening (AL):* participant maintains eye contact with other group members.
- *Verbal interaction (VI) with another person:* participant initiates or responds verbally to another person.
- *Non-verbal interaction with another person (NVI):* participant touches, gestures, smiles, nods, etc. to another person.

1. Decide on your research aims. For example, you could compare social interactions in the morning and afternoon, or differences between boys and girls, or between different environments (such as in class and in the cafeteria).
2. Draw up a grid to record your observations.
3. Decide on a sampling procedure.
4. Identify **one** issue of validity, and describe how you could deal with this issue of validity.
5. Identify **one** issue of reliability, and describe how you could deal with this issue of reliability.
6. When you have conducted the observation, present your findings using descriptive statistics, and state **one** conclusion that can be drawn.

Sampling methods

When making observations, a researcher usually uses some method of sampling, as we saw on page 153. However, sampling isn't used only in observational studies – researchers have to do this in all studies. For example, it would be impossible to conduct an experiment with all the schoolchildren in the UK, so if we wanted to find out about British schoolchildren, we would select a **sample** from this **target population**.

The most obvious way to do this is to use the people who happen to be around at the time (called an **opportunity sample**). This is probably the method you have been using up to now when doing your own experiments. Most psychologists use this method or a **self-selected sample**. The 'ideal' method is a **random sample** because it is the least biased. **Stratified** and **quota sampling** is the method most often used in questionnaires, and also the method students quite often want to use to get a representative sample.

▼ In any study, there is a target population, which is the group of individuals a researcher is interested in. The researcher aims to take a representative sample from this target population using a sampling method. The sample should be representative, so that generalisations about the target population can be made on the basis of the sample.

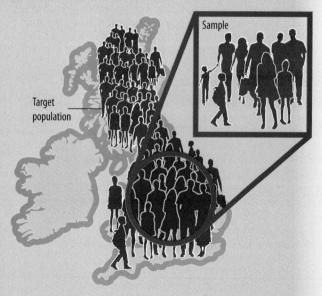

Target population

Sample

*A sampling method is about how participants are identified, NOT about who eventually takes part. Whatever the sampling method, some participants might refuse to take part, which then leaves the researcher with a biased sample – a sample of only those who are willing participants. However, this doesn't apply in most **field experiments** – when participants aren't aware that they are being studied, they can't refuse.*

All sampling methods aim to produce a representative sample, but are inevitably biased – bias means 'distorted' in some way. There are lots of biases, such as: experimenter bias, interviewer bias, observer bias, social desirability bias, sample bias, volunteer bias.

SAMPLING TECHNIQUES

Opportunity sample

How? Select those who are available, e.g. ask people walking by you in the street.
+ The easiest method because you just use the first participants you can find, which means it takes less time to locate your sample than if using one of the other techniques.
− Inevitably biased because the sample is drawn from a small part of the target population. For example, if you selected your sample from people walking around the centre of a town on a Monday morning, then it would be unlikely to include people from rural areas or professional people (because they are at work).

Self-selected (volunteer) sample

How? Advertise in a newspaper or on a notice board.
+ Access to a variety of participants (e.g. all the people who read that newspaper), which would make the sample more **representative** and less biased.
− Sample is biased because participants are likely to be more highly motivated and/or with extra time on their hands (= **volunteer bias**).

Random sample

How? See 'randomness' on facing page.
+ Potentially unbiased, all members of the target population have an equal chance of selection.
− The researcher could nevertheless end up with a biased sample (e.g. more boys than girls) because the sample is too small (see first Do It Yourself box on the facing page).

Systematic sample

How? Use a predetermined system to select participants, such as selecting every 10th person from the phone book.
+ Unbiased, as participants are selected using an objective system.
− Not truly random, unless you select a number using a random method and start with this person, and then you select every 10th person.

Stratified and quota sampling

How? Subgroups (or strata) within a population are identified (e.g. boys and girls, or age groups: 10–12 years, 13–15, etc.). Participants are obtained from each of the strata in proportion to their occurrence in the target population. Selection is done randomly (stratified sample) or by another method such as opportunity sampling (quota sampling).
+ More representative than an opportunity sample because there is equal representation of subgroups.
− Although the sample represents subgroups, each quota taken may be biased in other ways. For example, if you use opportunity sampling you have access to only certain sections of the target population.

Stratified sampling might be desirable when a target population has significant divisions that could have an effect on an individual's responses. For example, if a researcher was investigating school students' musical preferences, this might be affected by age and so, by just asking Year 7, a restricted sample would be tested. Therefore a researcher identifies key groups of people (or strata) so that a representative sample can be tested.

RANDOMNESS

'Random' means each member of the population having an equal chance of being selected. The easiest way to obtain a random selection is to draw numbers or names 'out of a hat'. This is sometimes called the 'lottery method'.

An alternative **random technique** is to give each participant a number and then select participants using a random number table or random function on a calculator or computer.

Random selection is used to obtain a random sample of participants, or for **random allocation** of participants to conditions when using an **independent groups design**.

▲ Each of the balls has an equal chance of being drawn, i.e. the draw is random.

CAN YOU...? No.6.13

1... Explain why it is desirable to obtain a representative sample.

2... Explain the difference between a random and a systematic sample.

3... Explain the difference between a quota and a stratified sample.

4... Identify the sampling method in each of the studies below.

  a) A researcher wished to study memory in children aged between 5 and 11 years. He contacted the headmaster of his local primary school and arranged to test the children in the school.

  b) A university department undertook a study of mobile phone use in adolescents, using a questionnaire. The questionnaire was given to a group of students in a local comprehensive school, selected by placing all the students' names in a container and drawing out 50 names.

  c) A group of psychology students decided to interview shoppers in a local shopping centre about attitudes towards dieting. They ensured that they identified townspeople from each age group.

  d) A class of psychology students conducted a study on memory. They put a notice on the notice board in the sixth form common room asking for participants who had an hour to spare.

  e) A researcher studied IQ in primary schoolchildren by selecting the first five names in each class register for every school he visited.

  f) A polling company employed a panel of people to consult about their opinions on political issues. They identified various subgroups in the population, and then randomly selected members from each subgroup.

5... For each of the studies above, state **one** advantage and **one** disadvantage of using that sampling method *in that particular study* (i.e.contextualise your answer).

6... A research study is conducted to compare the ability of boys and girls aged 5–12 to remember words. Their memories are tested by giving them 30 words to remember. The results are shown in the table below:

	Boys	Girls
Mean score	10.3 words	15.7 words
Range	15 words	22 words

  a) How would you describe the target population?

  b) Suggest a suitable sampling method.

  c) Describe **one** disadvantage with this method of selection.

  d) Identify **one** issue of reliability in this research, and describe how you could deal with this issue of reliability.

  e) Identify **one** issue of validity in this research and describe how you could deal with this issue of validity.

  f) Discuss **one** ethical issue in this research.

  g) State **one** conclusion that could be drawn from mean values in the table above.

  h) State **one** conclusion that could be drawn from the range of data shown in the table above.

Questionnaires and interviews

Psychologists aim to find out about behaviour. One way to do this is to conduct **experiments**, or to use non-experimental methods such as **correlations** and **observations**. Another non-experimental method or technique is to ask people questions about their experiences and/or beliefs. These are called *self-report* methods (because the person is reporting his or her own thoughts/feelings), and include questionnaires and interviews. A **questionnaire** can be given in a written form or it can be delivered in real-time (face-to-face or on the telephone), in which case it is called an **interview**.

A questionnaire or interview can be a research method or a research technique. For example:

- *The aims of a study might be to find out about smoking habits in young people. The researcher would design a questionnaire to collect data about what people do and why. In this case the questionnaire is the research method.*
- *The aims of a study might be to see if children who are exposed to an anti-smoking educational programme have different attitudes towards smoking from children not exposed to such a programme. The researcher would use a questionnaire to collect data about attitudes, but the analysis would involve a comparison between the two groups of children – an experimental study using a questionnaire as a research technique to assess the* **dependent variable** (**DV**).

1. QUESTIONNAIRES

A questionnaire is a set of questions. It is designed to collect information about a topic or topics. The two great strengths of questionnaires are:

1. You can collect the same information from a large number of people relatively easily (once you have designed the questionnaire, which is not so easy).
2. You can access what people think – observations and experiments rely on 'guessing' what people think and feel on the basis of how they behave. With a questionnaire you can ask people directly: whether they can, or do, give you truthful answers is another matter.

Open and closed questions

If you ask 'What do you like most about your job?', or 'What makes you feel stressed at work?', you may get 50 different answers from 50 people. These are called **open questions**, which tend to produce **qualitative data**.

Alternatively, a researcher can ask **closed questions**, for which there is a restricted range of answers. For example asking a person's age, or listing 10 things people usually like about their work and asking respondents to select two.

Closed questions

+ Produce **quantitative data**, which are easier to analyse.
− Respondents may be forced to select answers that don't represent their real thoughts or behaviour.

Open questions

+ Can provide unexpected answers and rich detail, thus allowing researchers to gain new insights.
− More difficult to summarise answers because there may be such a wide variety of different answers, which then makes it difficult to draw conclusions.

DO IT YOURSELF

No. 6.13

Design and use your own questionnaire

Select a suitable topic, e.g. 'Methods of exam revision', 'Places people go for a good night out', 'Why people choose to study psychology', or 'How emotional are you?'. Alternatively, you could choose a topic related to your studies, such as a questionnaire on obedience in everyday situations.

1. Steps in questionnaire design.
   a) Write the questions. Keep the questionnaire short, somewhere between 5 and 10 questions. Include a mixture of open and closed questions.
   b) Consider ethical issues and how to deal with them.
   c) Construct the questionnaire including standardised instructions.
   d) Pilot the questionnaire.
   e) Decide on a sampling technique.
2. Conduct the questionnaire.
3. Analyse the data. Just select a few questions for analysis. For quantitative data, you can use a bar chart. For qualitative data, you can identify some trends in the answers to open-ended questions and summarise these.
4. Write the report.

Examples of open questions

1 What factors contribute to making work stressful?
2 How do you feel when stressed?

Examples of closed questions

1 Which of the following makes you feel stressed? (You may tick as many answers as you like.)

☐ Noise at work   ☐ Lack of control
☐ Too much to do   ☐ Workmates
☐ No job satisfaction

2 How many hours a week do you work?

☐ 0 hours ☐ Between 11 and 20 hours
☐ Between 1 and 10 hours
☐ More than 20 hours

3 Likert scale

Work is stressful:
☐ Strongly agree ☐ Agree ☐ Not sure
☐ Disagree ☐ Strongly disagree

4 Rating scale

How much stress do you feel? (Circle the number that best describes how you feel.)

At work:
A lot of stress   5 4 3 2 1   No stress at all
At home:
A lot of stress   5 4 3 2 1   No stress at all
Travelling to work:
A lot of stress   5 4 3 2 1   No stress at all

5 Forced choice question
Select one answer

A   The worst social sin is to be rude
B   The worst social sin is to be a bore

2. INTERVIEWS

An interview can be structured or unstructured.

- A **structured interview** has pre-determined questions, i.e. a questionnaire that is delivered face-to-face with no deviation from the original questions.
- An **unstructured interview** has less structure! New questions are developed as you go along.

The semi-structured approach combines both structured and unstructured interviews, similar to the way your GP might talk to you when you are feeling ill. They start with some pre-determined questions, but further questions are developed as a response to your answers. For this reason, the semi-structured approach is also called the **clinical interview.**

CAN YOU...? No.6.14

1... Would you describe Kohlberg's and Gilligan's interviews (below) as structured, unstructured, or semi-structured (i.e. a mix of the structured and unstructured approach)? Explain your answer.

2... In the examples of interviews below, find an example of a closed question and an example of an open question.

3... On page 150, we explained the terms quantitative and qualitative. In the interviews below, find an example (not the same as for question 2) of a question that would produce quantitative data and one that would produce qualitative data.

4... A psychology student designed a questionnaire about attitudes to eating. Below are some questions from this questionnaire:

> i) Do you diet? Always Sometimes Never (Circle your answer)
>
> ii) Do you think dieting is a bad idea?
>
> iii) Explain your answer to (ii).

For each question (i–iii above):

a) State whether it is an open or closed question.

b) State whether the question would produce quantitative or qualitative data.

c) Give **one** disadvantage of this type of question.

d) Suggest **one** advantage of the type of question.

e) Write **one** further question, relevant to the topic of attitudes about eating, that would produce quantitative data, and one that would produce qualitative data.

EXAMPLES OF INTERVIEWS

Lawrence Kohlberg (1978) interviewed boys about their moral views in order to investigate the development of moral understanding. Interviewers gave the boys an imaginary situation and then asked a set of questions, such as the following moral dilemma.

In Europe, a woman was near death from a rare type of cancer. There was one drug that the doctors thought might save her. It was a form of radium that a druggist in the same town had recently discovered. The drug was expensive to make, but the druggist was charging 10 times what the drug cost him to make. He paid $400 for the radium and charged $4000 for a small dose of it. The sick woman's husband, Heinz, went to everyone he knew to borrow the money, but he could only get together about $2000 (half of what it cost). He told the druggist that his wife was dying, and asked him to sell it cheaper or let him pay later. But the druggist said: 'No. I discovered the drug and I'm going to make money from it.' Heinz got desperate and broke into the man's store to steal the drug for his wife.

- Should Heinz steal the drug?
- Why or why not?
- If the interviewee initially favours stealing, ask: 'If Heinz doesn't love his wife, should he steal the drug for her?'
- If the interviewee initially favours not stealing, ask: 'Does it make a difference whether or not he loves his wife?'
- Why or why not?
- Suppose the person dying is not his wife but a stranger. Should Heinz steal the drug for the stranger?
- Why or why not?

Carol Gilligan also investigated moral principles. In one study (Gilligan and Attanucci, 1988), participants were asked a set of questions about their own experiences of moral conflict and choice.

- Have you ever been in a situation of moral conflict where you had to make a decision but weren't sure what the right thing to do was?
- Could you describe the situation?
- What were the conflicts for you in that situation?
- What did you do?
- Do you think it was the right thing to do?
- How do you know?

The interviewer asked other questions to encourage the participants to elaborate and clarify their responses, such as saying, 'Anything else?'. A special focus was put on asking participants to explain the meaning of the words they used.

DO IT YOURSELF  No.6.14

Try your own interview

Try out the moral interviews with a partner in class. Take turns being the interviewer and interviewee for both kinds of interview. Discuss:

- What you found out.
- The differences in the information obtained.
- Which questions worked best and why.
- How truthful you were and why.

More about questionnaires and interviews

There are advantages and disadvantages to using **questionnaires** and **interviews**. The main concerns are related to **validity**, **reliability** and **ethical issues**.

VALIDITY

Ecological (external) validity

The **external validity** of questionnaires and interviews concerns the extent to which the findings can be generalised to other situations and other people. A major factor will be the **representativeness** of the sample used to collect data. For example, if a questionnaire collected data only from shoppers on a weekday morning in London, it would not be reasonable to generalise this to all people in the UK.

Internal validity

The **internal validity** of self-report techniques is related to the issue of whether the questionnaire or interview (or psychological test such as an IQ or personality test) really measures what it is intended to measure.

There are two main sources of bias in questionnaires/interviews. First, questions might be phrased in such a way that they 'lead' the respondent to be more likely to give a particular answer. This is called a **leading question** (as discussed in the study by Loftus and Palmer, see page 92).

The second source of bias is **social desirability bias**. Respondents prefer to select answers that portray them in a positive light rather than those that reflect the truth.

Both of these problems result in a lack of validity.

Dealing with external validity

External validity can be dealt with by using a more appropriate **sampling** method in order to improve **generalisability**. For example, a popular technique used with questionnaires is **quota sampling** (see page 156). This technique aims to provide a truly representative sample.

Dealing with internal validity

In order to assess whether a questionnaire/interview/test is measuring what it intended to measure, we can use one of the methods described on page 140, such as the following.

- **Concurrent validity** can be established by comparing the current questionnaire or test with a previously established test on the same topic. Participants take both tests and then the two test scores are compared.
- **Content validity**: Does the test *look* as if it is measuring what the researcher intended to measure? For example, are the questions obviously related to the topic? An expert might be asked to judge this.

If one or more measures of internal validity are low, then the items on the questionnaire/interview/test need to be revised in order to produce a better match between scores on the new test and an established one.

Leading questions These can be detected by running a **pilot study**. The questions can be tested on a small group of people. This means the questions can later be refined in response to any difficulties encountered.

Social desirability bias This can be assessed by using a **lie scale**. A number of questions are added to the questionnaire/interview/test as 'truth-detectors' – a person who is telling the truth should give a predictable answer. For example, the truthful answer to the question 'Are you always happy?' is 'no', but a person who wishes to present themselves in a positive light might be tempted to answer 'yes'. Respondents who lie on a high proportion of such items might not be giving truthful answers on the rest of the questionnaire.

RELIABILITY

Reliability refers to whether something is consistent (see page 155). **Internal reliability** is a measure of the extent to which something is consistent within itself. For example, all the questions on an IQ test (which is a kind of questionnaire) should be measuring the same thing. This may not be relevant to all questionnaires, because sometimes internal consistency is not important, for example a questionnaire about fear experiences might look at many different aspects of being fearful.

External reliability is a measure of consistency over several different occasions. For example, if an interviewer conducted an interview, and then conducted the same interview with the same interviewee a week later, the outcome should be the same – otherwise the interview is not reliable.

Reliability also concerns whether two interviewers produce the same outcome. This is called **inter-interviewer reliability**.

ADVANTAGES AND DISADVANTAGES OF QUESTIONNAIRES AND INTERVIEWS

	Advantages ☺
Questionnaires *Respondents record their own answers*	• Can be easily repeated so that data can be collected from a large number of people relatively cheaply and quickly. • Respondents might feel more willing to reveal personal/ confidential information than in an interview.
Structured interview *Predetermined questions*	• Can be easily repeated because the questions are standardised. • Requires less interviewing skill than unstructured interviews. • Easier to analyse than unstructured interviews because answers are more predictable.
Unstructured interview *Interviewer develops questions in response to respondent's answers*	• More detailed information can generally be obtained from each respondent than in a structured interview. • Can access information that might not be revealed by predetermined questions.

ETHICAL ISSUES

- **Deception** The true aims of the research might sometimes need to be concealed in order to collect truthful data.
- **Psychological harm** Respondents may feel distressed by certain questions or having to think about certain sensitive topics.
- **Privacy** Questions might be related to sensitive and personal issues, invading an individual's privacy.
- **Confidentiality** This must be respected; names and personal details should not be stored or revealed without permission.

Dealing with reliability

Internal reliability	**Split-half method** A group of participants is given a test once. The participants' answers to the test questions are divided in half. This is done by, for example, comparing all answers to odd number questions with all answers to even number questions. The individual's scores on both halves of the test should be very similar. The two scores can be compared by calculating a **correlation coefficient** (see page 148).
External reliability	**Test-retest method** A group of participants is given a test or questionnaire or interview once and then again sometime later (when the participants have had the chance to forget it). The answers can be compared and should be the same. If the tests produce scores, these can be compared by calculating a correlation coefficient. Note that the test must be given to the same person on the two separate occasions.

Examiner hint

In the exam, you will be asked questions about reliability, validity and ethical issues. Remember, when answering such questions, you must do the things listed on pages 141 and 143 in order to get full marks. Generic answers that make no link to the research will receive only 1 mark.

CAN YOU...?   No.6.15

1... A group of students wishes to study mobile phone use in people aged 14–18. Why might it be preferable to conduct an interview rather than a questionnaire?

2... Imagine instead that the students wished to find out about drug-taking. Why might it be preferable to conduct a questionnaire rather than an interview?

3. For both studies outlined above:

   a) Outline **one** advantage and **one** disadvantage of using a questionnaire/interview in the research.

   b) Identify **one** issue of reliability in this research, and describe how you would deal with this issue of reliability.

   c) Identify **one** issue of validity in this research and describe how you would deal with this issue of validity.

   d) Discuss **one** ethical issue that might arise in this research.

DO IT YOURSELF   No. 6.15

How daring are you?

Answer YES or NO to the questions below.

1 Do you get scared on fast roller coasters?
2 Are you scared of flying?
3 Would you rather read a good book than play a computer game?
4 Do you prefer staying in rather than going out?
5 Have you ever lied to your parents?
6 Do you use the internet every day?
7 Do you arrange your CDs in alphabetical order?
8 Have you ever played truth or dare?
9 Are you too shy to tell people what you really think?
10 Do you dislike answering questions in class?

If you answered yes to more than five of the questions in the questionnaire above, then you're a bit of a pussycat.

- Try assessing the internal and external reliability of the questionnaire above, as well as its content validity.
- To assess concurrent validity, you can compare the outcome with an established psychological test. For example, psychologists measure sensation-seeking using Zuckerman's (1994) sensation seeking scale (you can take the test and get your score at: www.bbc.co.uk/science/humanbody/mind/surveys/sensation/).

Rewrite the quiz to deal with your criticisms.

Disadvantages ☹

- Answers might not be truthful, for example because of leading questions and social desirability bias.
- The sample might be biased because only certain kinds of people fill in questionnaires – literate individuals who are also willing to spend time filling in a questionnaire and returning it.

- The interviewer's expectations might influence the answers the interviewee gives (called **interviewer bias**).
- Reliability might be affected by the same interviewer behaving differently on different occasions, or different interviewers asking different questions (low inter-interviewer reliability).

- More affected by interviewer bias than structured interviews because in an unstructured interview the interviewer is developing new questions on the spot, which might be less objective.
- Requires well-trained interviewers, which makes it more expensive to produce reliable interviews than structured interviews, which don't require specialist interviewers.

Examiner hint

When presenting an advantage or a disadvantage, students often write something like, 'The advantage of a questionnaire is that you can collect lots of data'. The problem with this is that it is not clear what 'lots of data' means. Compared with what? In fact, you can also collect lots of data in an experiment or an interview.

- *You need to provide clear detail. (What is 'lots of data'? Why is there 'lots of data'?)*
- *You need to offer a comparison. (Compared with what? e.g. compared with an interview.)*

A good answer would say, 'The advantage of a questionnaire is that you can collect data from more people than you would if using the interview method, which results in a large range of data to be analysed.' Of course, such an answer must also be contextualised.

Other research methods

Psychologists use many different methods in their research. On this spread we look at two further methods, but there are many others not covered in this chapter, such as **cross-cultural studies** (where behaviour in different cultural settings is compared), **longitudinal studies** (where people are followed over a long period of time to see how they develop), or **meta-analysis** (where a number of studies on the same topic are compared and conclusions drawn). In reality, many research projects involve the use of a variety of different methods. For example, Milgram's study of obedience (see page 74) was a lab investigation that also involved interviews with participants after the study.

CONTENT ANALYSIS

A **content analysis** is what it says – an analysis of the content of something. For example, a researcher might study the gender content of magazine advertisements and attempt to describe this content in some systematic way so that conclusions could be drawn. Content analysis is a form of indirect **observation**, indirect because you are not observing people directly but observing them through the artefacts they produce. These artefacts can be TV programmes, books, songs, paintings, etc. The process involved is similar to that of any observational study, the researcher has to make design decisions about the following.

- **Sampling method** What material to sample and how frequently (e.g. which TV channels to include, how many programmes, what length of time).
- **Behavioural categories** What categories can be used? These categories can be dealt with in two ways:
  - **Quantitative analysis** Examples in each category are counted. For example, when performing a content analysis of adolescent behaviour from letters in teen magazines, the researcher would decide on a set of topics (categories), and then count how many letters included those topics.
  - **Qualitative analysis** Examples in each category are described rather than counted. For example when performing a content analysis of adolescent behaviour from letters in teen magazines, the researcher would provide quotes from different letters to illustrate the category.

As with observations, if there is a team of researchers, it is important to ensure that they are applying criteria in the same way by calculating **inter-observer reliability**.

Example of a quantitative content analysis

Manstead and McCulloch (1981) analysed ads on British TV to look at gender stereotypes. They observed 170 ads over a one-week period, ignoring those that contained only children and animals. In each ads, they focused on the central adult figure and recorded frequencies in a table like the one on the right. For each ad, there might be no ticks, one tick or a number of ticks.

	Male	Female
Credibility basis of central character		
Product user	☐	☐
Product authority	☐	☐
Role of central character		
Dependent role	☐	☐
Independent role	☐	☐
Argument spoken by central character		
Factual	☐	☐
Opinion	☐	☐
Product type used by central character		
Food/drink	☐	☐
Alcohol	☐	☐
Body	☐	☐
Household	☐	☐

ADVANTAGES AND DISADVANTAGES OF CONTENT ANALYSIS

Advantages ☺
- Has high **ecological validity** because it is based on observations of what people actually do – real communications that are current and relevant, such as recent newspapers or children's books in print.
- When sources can be retained or accessed by others (e.g. back copies of magazines or videos of people giving speeches), findings can be **replicated** and so tested for **reliability**.

Disadvantages ☹
- **Observer bias** reduces the objectivity and validity of findings because different observers might interpret the meaning of the behavioural categories differently.
- Likely to be culture-biased because interpretation of verbal or written content will be affected by the language and culture of the observer and the behavioural categories used.

Quantitative data involves information that can be counted, whereas qualitative data is non-numerical and allows people to express themselves freely.

Example of a qualitative content analysis

Joronen and Åstedt-Kurki (2005) studied the role of the family in adolescents' peer and school experiences. They conducted **semi-structured interviews** with 19 adolescents aged 12–16, using questions such as 'What does your family know about your peers?' and 'How is your family involved in your school activities?' These interviews produced 234 pages of notes, which were analysed using a qualitative content analysis.

1. All answers to the same question were placed together. Each statement was compressed into a briefer statement.
2. These statements were compared with each other and categorised so that statements with similar content were placed together and a category (or theme) was identified.
3. The categories were grouped into larger units producing eight main categories, for example:
   - *Enablement*, e.g. 'Yeah, ever since my childhood we've always had lots of kids over visiting' (girl, 15 years).
   - *Support*, e.g. 'They [family members] help if I have a test by asking questions' (boy, 13 years).

One of the conclusions drawn from this study is that schools should pay more attention to the multiple relationships that determine an adolescent's behaviour.

CASE STUDY

A **case study** involves the detailed study of a single individual, institution or event. It uses information from a range of sources, such as from the person concerned and also from his or her family and friends. Many techniques can be used – the people might be interviewed, or they could be observed while engaged in daily life. Psychologists might use IQ tests or personality tests or some other kind of questionnaire to produce psychological data about the target person or group of people. They might use the experimental method to test what the target person/group can or cannot do. The findings are organised to represent the individual's thoughts, emotions, experiences and abilities. Case studies are generally longitudinal, in other words they follow the individual or group over an extended period of time.

We have examined several classic case studies in this book – such as the case of Little Hans (see pages 32 and 40) and the case of HM (see page 55).

ADVANTAGES AND DISADVANTAGES OF CASE STUDIES

Advantages ☺

- The method offers rich, in-depth data so information that might be overlooked using other methods is likely to be identified.
- Can be used to investigate instances of human behaviour and experience that are rare, such as investigating cases of children locked in a room throughout childhood to see what effects such deprivation has on emotional development.
- The complex interaction of many factors can be studied, in contrast with experiments where many variables are held constant.

Disadvantages ☹

- It is difficult to generalise from individual cases as each one has unique characteristics.
- It is often necessary to use recollection of past events as part of the case history and such evidence could be unreliable.
- Researchers might lack objectivity as they get to know the case, or theoretical bias might lead them to overlook aspects of the findings.
- There are important **ethical issues** such as **confidentiality** – many cases are easily identifiable because of their unique characteristics, even when real names are not given.

DO IT YOURSELF

No. 6.16

Sexism in the media

You could try to replicate the study by Manstead and McCulloch on the facing page.

1. You might try a pilot study to see if the categories work, and adapt them if necessary.
2. Decide on sampling methods. You can share the work with other class members.
3. Count the frequency of occurrences in each category.
4. Display your findings using one or more graphs.

An example of a case study: Phineas Gage

Phineas Gage is probably the most famous patient to have survived severe damage to the brain. In 1848, Phineas was working on the construction of a railway track in Vermont, USA, blasting rock with gunpowder. He would fill a hole with dynamite, then cover the dynamite with sand and insert a tamping iron that was 109cm long. This was then hammered into the hole to pack down the gunpowder. On one occasion he forgot to put in the sand, and as soon as he hammered the tamping iron in it exploded, driving the tamping iron right through his skull. Not only did he survive, but he also was still able to speak, despite massive bleeding and substantial loss of brain tissue. After a short spell in hospital, he went back to work, and lived for a further 12 years. Some years after he died, his body was exhumed (along with the tamping iron, which he had kept), and his skull placed on display at Harvard University.

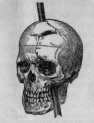

▲ *Phineas's skull on display and an artist's impression of how the tamping iron would have passed through his head.*

Phineas Gage was able to function fairly normally, showing that people can live despite losing large amounts of brain matter. However, the accident did affect Phineas's personality. Before the accident he was hard working, responsible and popular, whereas afterwards he became restless and indecisive, and swore a lot. His friends said he was no longer the same man.

This case was important in the development of brain surgery because it showed that parts of the brain could be removed without having a fatal effect. Thus surgeons started to remove brain tumours, no longer fearful that this would cause a patient's death. Phineas's injury also suggested that damage to the frontal lobe leads to personality change, which influenced the development of frontal lobotomies (see page 6).

CAN YOU...? No.6.16

1... Explain in what way a content analysis is a form of observation.

2... How might observer bias affect the findings of a content analysis?

3... A university department was given funding to investigate the stereotypes presented in children's books (age stereotypes, gender stereotypes, etc.). The study was to compare books that children read today with those from 20 years ago to see how, and if, stereotypes had changed.

    a) Suggest **three** items that could be used as behavioural categories in this study.

    b) Write *operationalised* definitions for these items.

    c) Identify **one** issue of reliability in this research, and describe how you could deal with this issue of reliability.

    d) Identify **one** issue of validity in this research and describe how you could deal with this issue of validity.

4... A hospital is interested in finding out why some patients with head injuries recover faster than others.

    a) Outline **one** advantage and **one** disadvantage of using a case study in this research.

    b) Identify **one** issue of reliability in this research, and describe how you could deal with this issue of reliability.

    c) Identify **one** issue of validity in this research, and describe how you could deal with this issue of validity.

Quantitative and qualitative data

On page 150, we identified the difference between **quantitative** and **qualitative** data.

- Quantitative data are expressed in numerical form – such as the number of items recalled, reaction times, or the number of aggressive acts observed.
- Qualitative data are in a non-numerical form – such as the answers that a respondent gives to an open-ended question or descriptions of what children were doing when observed in the playground.

It is sometimes said that qualitative data concerns 'thoughts and feelings' – but you can also have *quantitative* data about thoughts and feelings, for example a researcher could ask participants to rate their feelings about a film on a scale of 1–5. The result would be a number – a quantity. The difference between quantitative and qualitative research runs much deeper than 'thoughts and feelings'.

Qualitative research aims to produce an in-depth understanding of behaviour, and, because of the open-ended nature of the research, produce new explanations. The goal is to understand behaviour in a natural setting, to understand a phenomenon from the perspective of the research participant, and also to understand the *meanings* people give to their experiences. This means that the researcher is concerned with asking broad questions that allow respondents to answer in their own words, or the researcher might wish to observe people going about their everyday lives and could conduct an unstructured observation of behaviour.

ADVANTAGES AND DISADVANTAGES OF QUANTITATIVE AND QUALITATIVE DATA

	Advantages ☺	Disadvantages ☹
Quantitative data	• Easier to analyse because the data are given in numbers that can be summarised using measures such as **averages** and **range** as well as simple graphs. • Can produce neat conclusions because numerical data reduces the variety of possibilities.	• Oversimplifies reality and human experience (statistically **significant** but humanly insignificant).
Qualitative data	• Represents the true complexities of human behaviour. • Gains access to thoughts and feelings that may not be assessed using quantitative methods with **closed questions**. • Provides rich details of how people behave because participants are given a free rein to express themselves.	• More difficult to detect patterns and draw conclusions because of the large amount of data usually collected. • **Subjective** analysis can be affected by personal expectations and beliefs – however, quantitative methods are also affected by bias, they might simply *appear* to be objective.

What research techniques produce quantitative and qualitative data?

Quantitative and qualitative data can be produced in all kinds of studies.

- **Unstructured observations** generally produce *qualitative* data because the data that is collected is not placed in categories but, instead, everything that is observed is recorded.
- **Structured observations** produce numerical data in categories (*quantitative*). For example, Gardner and Gardner's study of Washoe counted how many times she produced certain words as she got older (see page 98).
- **Questionnaires** or **interviews** that use **open questions** produce *qualitative* data, whereas closed questions produce *quantitative* data (the frequency of different responses is recorded).
- **Unstructured interviews** are more likely to produce *qualitative* data because of the questions that develop (e.g. 'Why do you feel that?').
- **Content analysis** of TV programmes could produce *qualitative* data, and then the frequency of key themes could be counted, to produce *quantitative* data.
- **Case studies** can produce *quantitative* data, but tend to include details of an individual's life and quotes to highlight unique experiences, thus they are more *qualitative* than quantitative. For example, the case study of HM (on page 55) includes records of experiences and what he said.
- **Experiments** produce numerical data (*quantitative*), for example Loftus and Palmer's study (page 92) found out *how many* words were correctly recalled.
- In some experiments, participants are interviewed afterwards to find out if they have any important insights. For example, Asch interviewed participants after his conformity study (see page 68) and analysed their *qualitative* responses, to produce three broad categories that were the reasons why people conformed.

DO IT YOURSELF

No. 6.17

Conduct an interview where you collect qualitative data. For example, interview a friend about:

- What it is like to own a pet.
- What they thought about a film they saw recently.
- The best holiday they have ever had.

Present a summary of your interview by outlining key points with examples (this is a qualitative content analysis).

Reliability and validity revisited

Reliability and **validity** are the key issues that concern psychologists when designing and assessing research. It might be useful to review what we have covered in this chapter.

RELIABILITY

Reliability refers to consistency. Instruments such as rulers are usually very reliable, and it doesn't really matter who uses them as they give the same answer each time a particular line is measured. In psychology, reliability usually means the consistency of a test, a measuring instrument, or of different observers. A reasonable level of reliability should be reached or our results will be worthless.

Research method	Dealing with reliability
Observations	**Inter-observer reliability.**
Questionnaires and interviews	**Split-half** reliability (for **internal reliability**). **Test-retest** (for **external reliability**).
Experiments, correlations, case studies	Concerned with the reliability of any measurement you are using. For example, if you were measuring reaction time in an experiment, then reliability would concern the method used to time participants.
	Or, in a correlation, if you were measuring intelligence then you would be concerned with the reliability of the psychological test used. This is assessed in the same way that questionnaires and interviews are assessed – split-half reliability and test-retest.
	Repeat the study (**replication**), which can demonstrate that the finding is reliable, and also can demonstrate the finding is valid. If the same finding occurs again it is reliable, and this also demonstrates its 'trueness' (i.e. validity)

Students often get confused between reliability and validity. The following example about a car may help!

If a car is reliable the engine will start every time the key is turned in the ignition. If the car only starts sometimes it is not a reliable car.

If a car is valid it will have many features that we would expect in a car, such as an engine, steering wheel, tyres etc. and also it will be able to transport people from one place to another. A motorcyle is not a valid car as it doesn't have all the features expected from a car (e.g. no steering wheel). A toy car is not a valid car because it too lacks features (it can't transport people from one place to another).

VALIDITY

Validity refers to the legitimacy or 'trueness' of a result:
- **Internal validity** is whether a test or study has measured what it intended to measure.
- **External validity** is whether a study can be generalised beyond the particular setting/conditions in which it was conducted.

External validity is dealt with by using representative sampling methods.

Research method	Dealing with internal validity
Experiments	Control **extraneous variables** such as situational factors or **participant variables**.
Observations	Remove **observer bias**.
Questionnaires and interviews	Remove **interviewer bias**, **leading questions**, and/or **social desirability bias**. Check **content validity** and **concurrent validity**.
Experiments, correlations, case studies	Any measurement that is used can be assessed using content, concurrent and/or **construct validity**.

CAN YOU...?   No.**6.17**

For each of the 10 core studies in Chapter 5, answer the following questions. (These questions, a–f, are the same questions that appear in the AS Applied Research Methods exam).

   a) Outline **one** advantage and **one** disadvantage of using the named method in this research. [3]

   b) Identify **one** issue of reliability in this research, and describe how you could deal with this issue of reliability. [3]

   c) Identify **one** issue of validity in this research, and describe how you could deal with this issue of validity. [3]

   d) Outline **one** advantage and **one** disadvantage of using the sampling method in this research. [3]

   e) Discuss **one** ethical issue that might arise in this research. [3]

   f) State **one** conclusion that can be drawn from this research. [3]

AND FINALLY...

Let us end this chapter where we began – considering the value of science and the scientific approach. Research methods provide the systems for studying our world in an objective and systematic manner. They alert researchers to the potential biases and variables that may challenge the validity of any results. It is critical to understand that science is not perfect, but without a clear understanding of what counts as good and bad science, we are easily convinced, for example, to buy some new product, or believe in the value of the latest dieting programme, or pour our hard-earned money into a con-artist's pocket.

Chapter 6 summary

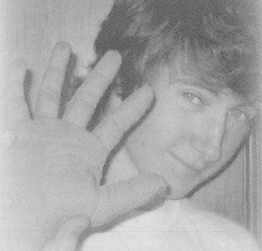

Experiment
- Experimenter manipulates an IV and observes the effect on the DV.
- Experimental design – repeated measures, independent groups, matched pairs.
- Lab – high control and easily replicated, but lack of mundane realism and investigator effects.
- Field – higher mundane realism and lack of investigator effects, but less control of EVs and could be demand characteristics.
- Natural (quasi) – only possibility for some behaviours, but the IV is not manipulated, so no causal effect demonstrated.

Correlation
- Positive, negative or zero correlation.
- Pairs of data for each individual plotted on a scattergraph.
- Strength of correlation shown by correlation coefficient.

Observation
- Unstructured – useful as preliminary study or when behaviours are rare.
- Structured – uses a coding system and sampling technique (event or time sampling).
- Method and technique, controlled and naturalistic, participant and non-participant, overt and covert, direct and indirect (content analysis).
- Validity affected by observer bias.
- Reliability dealt with by inter-observer reliability.
- Advantage/disadvantage – more realistic, but observer bias and ethical problems.

Questionnaire/ interview
- Questionnaires and interviews, structured and unstructured.
- Validity affected by social desirability bias and leading questions.
- Reliability – concerns about internal and external reliability.
- Can use rating scales, open questions (qualitative data) and closed questions (quantitative data).
- Questionnaire advantage/disadvantage – easily repeatable, but social desirability bias.
- Interview advantage/disadvantage – the questioning can respond to the answers given, but interviewer bias.

Other methods
- Content analysis – indirect observation, quantitative or qualitative.
- Case study – in-depth information but lacks generalisability.

VALIDITY

Validity concerns control versus realism ➔ generalisability:
- Experimental (internal) validity – measuring what you intend to measure.
- Ecological (external) validity – generalising to everyday situations.

Threats to validity:
- Measurement – validity dealt with through content, concurrent and construct validity.
- Extraneous variables – situational (can use standardised procedures), participant variables (can match participants), investigator effects (can use double blind), demand characteristics (needs better design).

ETHICAL ISSUES

- Informed consent, deception, right to withdraw, failure to protect from physical and psychological harm, confidentiality, privacy.
- Can be dealt with by debriefing.

RELIABILITY

- Reliability concerns consistency.
- Inter-observer, split-half and test-retest reliability.
- Internal (within the test) and external (over time).

SAMPLING

- Opportunity – easiest, but biased target population.
- Self-selected (volunteer) – good selection of participants, but biased because highly motivated, etc.
- Random – unbiased, but hard to do and could end up with a biased sample.
- Systematic – unbiased, but not truly random.
- Stratified and quota – represents subgroups, but still biased target population.

DATA

- Quantitative data e.g. answers to closed questions (numerical data), represented using mean, median, mode, range, tables, bar chart, histogram, scattergraph.
- Qualitative data e.g. answers to open questions (non-numerical data), participants freely expressing their thoughts and feelings.

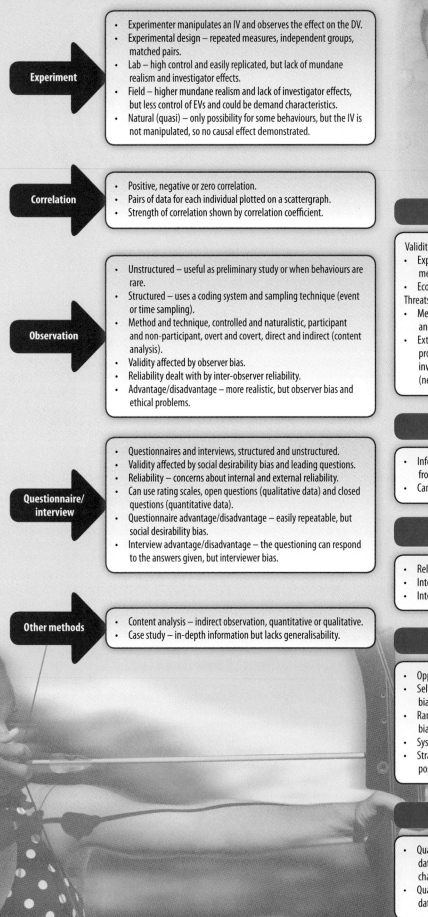

Crossword

Answers on page 180.

The template for this crossword can be found at www.folensblogs.com/companion/blog/.

Across

1. Data that focus on what people think and feel, and cannot be counted. (11)
5. Method of sampling where participants are selected using opportunity techniques from strata in proportion to the appearance of the groups in the target population. (5)
10. A kind of correlation where both variables increase together. (7)
11. Sampling method that uses newspaper advertisements to recruit participants. (9)
12. Level of measurement where data are in separate categories. (7)
15. The most common item in a data set. (4)
17. Establishing validity by considering to what extent the current measure measures the target concept. (9)
23. Process of ensuring that variables are in a form that can be easily tested. (18)
24. A correlation between two variables where, as the value of one variable increases, the other decreases. (8)
25. Type of correlation where there is no significant relationship between covariables. (4)
27. People wish to present themselves in a positive light when answering questionnaires, _____ desirability bias. (6)
29. In an experiment, the variable that is manipulated by the experimenter (initials). (2)
30. A type of graph that illustrates frequency, but the horizontal axis does not have to have any fixed order. (3, 5)
31. A method used to study individuals that provides rich insights but is difficult to generalise to the wider population. (4, 5)
33. Method to deal with validity by considering whether the current measure is assessing the intended behaviour. (7)

34. A sampling method where each member of the target population has an equal chance of being selected. (6)
35. A type of graph where the bars are proportional to the frequency of the events; cannot be used with nominal data. (9)
36. Type of question that encourages a respondent to give a particular answer. (7)
38. A small scale trial run of a study to test aspects of the design. (5, 5)
39. The extent to which measurements are consistent. (11)
40. A systematic distortion. (4)

Down

2. The extent to which a researcher has tested what they intended to test. (8, 8)
3. A systematic method for recording observations where individual behaviours are given a code for easy scoring. (6, 6)
4. Data that represents how much or how many there is/are of something i.e. a behaviour is measured in numbers. (12)
6. In a questionnaire, questions that invite a respondent to provide his/her own answer. (4)
7. The arithmetic average of a group of scores that takes all the values of the data into account. (4)
8. An experiment that takes place in an everyday environment, with the participants usually not being aware that they are being studied. (5)
9. In an experiment, the variable that is measured by the experimenter (initials). (2)
13. An investigative method that generally involves face-to-face interaction with another individual and results in the collection of data. (9)
14. A sampling method where the people that are most easily available are selected. (11)
16. Features of an experiment that a participant unconsciously responds to. (6, 15)
18. Level of measurement where data are ordered but the intervals between data are not known and are likely to be unequal. (7)
19. Type of question that provides a limited range of answers for a respondent to choose from. (6)
20. Kind of interview used by Freud that is semi-structured. (8)
21. Technique used to deal with a lack of informed consent or deception in a study. (10)
22. A kind of research design where neither the participant nor the experimenter is aware of the research aims. (6, 5)
26. Measurement of the distance between the lowest and the highest score. (5)
28. Validity is established by demonstrating a high correlation between the existing measure and another established measure of the same thing. (10)
32. Method of sampling where participants are randomly selected from different groups within the target population. (10)
37. A type of experiment where a researcher cannot vary the IV directly, but where it varies naturally – called a natural or _____-experiment. (5)

Review activities

In Unit 1, we suggested lots of ideas for review and revision (see pages 15, 29, 43, 57 and 62). You can use many of these ideas for reviewing and revising Chapter 6 – such as mind maps, writing your own multiple choice questions, and so on.

On this page we have provided a set of scenarios similar to those that will appear in the exam to help you revise. For each of them, you should answer the following exam-style questions.

> (a) Outline **one** advantage and one disadvantage of using [the named method] in this research. [3]
>
> (b) Identify **one** issue of reliability in this research, and describe how you could deal with this issue of reliability. [3]
>
> (c) Identify **one** issue of validity in this research, and describe how you could deal with this issue of validity. [3]
>
> (d) Outline **one** advantage and one disadvantage of using [the named sampling method] in this research. [3]
>
> (e) Discuss **one** ethical issue that might arise in this research. [3]
>
> (f) State **one** conclusion that can be drawn from the [the data in the table/graph] in this research. [3]

Scenario 1

A researcher is using a correlation to see whether students who sit further from their teachers achieve lower test results than those who sit closer to their teachers. She is using an opportunity sample of students from a local school. A scattergraph was drawn to describe the data produced in this research.

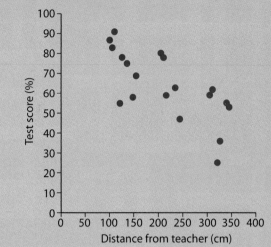

Examiner hint

*In all of the questions, you must remember that you will only gain full marks if you **contextualise** your answers, i.e. identify the issue and then link it to the specific research in the scenario.*

When you are practising answering these questions, highlight any link to the novel situation so you can clearly see where you are or are not making enough links.

Another technique is to read out your answer, and ask a partner to try to identify what the research is about just from using the links in your answers.

Scenario 2

A researcher is conducting an observation into whether there are differences in the games that boys and girls play when they are in the primary school playground. He has randomly selected the children he will observe from the school's register. A bar chart was drawn to describe the data produced in this study.

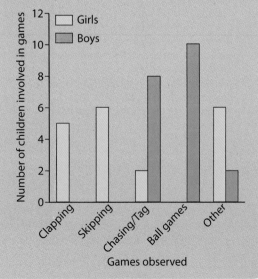

Scenario 3

A researcher is conducting a case study on whether having a dog as a pet has a beneficial impact on an individual's psychological and physical health. The researcher is using a self-selected sample. Below are some comments made by the person in the case study before getting a dog.

> *Physical health status:*
> * *My doctor says my blood pressure is a little high and that I should take some exercise and try to reduce my stress levels.*
> * *I'm a little overweight for my height.*
>
> *Psychological health status:*
> * *As I live by myself … I get a bit lonely sometimes.*

Below are some comments made by the person a year after getting a dog.

> *Physical health status:*
> * *My doctor says my blood pressure is in the normal range now.*
> * *I am still a little overweight…but I have lost some weight since getting Rover, my dog.*
>
> *Psychological health status:*
> * *I enjoy meeting and talking to other people walking their dogs. There are a couple of people that I see regularly who walk their dogs at the same time I walk Rover.*
> * *I sometimes feel guilty when I have to leave Rover alone in the house when I go to work.*

Scenario 4

Some researchers are conducting a questionnaire about what sort of holidays people enjoy, as measured on an 'enjoyment scale', where 0 is no enjoyment and 10 is most enjoyable. They are looking at activity holidays (e.g. skiing, hiking) or relaxing holidays (e.g. beach-based or pool-based) and using a quota sample of the bookings made at a travel agent. The range of scores is shown in the table below.

	Activity holiday	Relaxing holiday
Range of enjoyment scores	9	5

Scenario 5

A researcher is using a natural (quasi-) experiment to investigate if people with high IQ scores read more books than those with low IQ scores. The researchers are using a stratified sample (strata used include categories of IQ score: high IQ, mid-IQ, low IQ). The median scores are shown in the table below.

	High IQ scores	Low IQ scores
Median number of books read in the past six months	6	2

Scenario 6

A research team is conducting a lab experiment on the reaction times of individuals with blue eyes vs individuals with brown eyes to a visual stimulus. The researchers are using a self-selected (volunteer) sample of university students. A histogram was drawn to describe the data produced in this research.

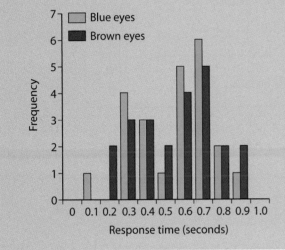

Scenario 7

A team of researchers is using a field experiment to investigate whether people are more likely to help an elderly person who has fallen over than a teenager in the same predicament. The researchers are using an opportunity sample of people in a high street on a Saturday afternoon. The mean scores are shown in the table below.

	Elderly person	Teenager
Number of people who helped in Trial 1	4	1
Number of people who helped in Trial 2	3	2
Number of people who helped in Trial 3	2	0
Number of people who helped in Trial 4	3	0
Number of people who helped in Trial 5	5	4
Number of people who helped in Trial 6	4	2
Number of people who helped in Trial 7	2	1
Mean score of the number of people who helped	**3.29**	**1.43**

Scenario 8

A team of researchers is conducting interviews with men and women from various cultural backgrounds about their preferences in an ideal mate. The researchers are using a systematic sample of households (every 5th home) in each culture. The modal results are shown in the table below. The question asked was:

'What do you think is the most important attribute in a potential mate?'
a) Attractiveness   b) Resources   c) Sense of humour   d) Good personality

	Female participants' choice	Male participants' choice
Participant 1	b) Resources	a) Attractiveness
Participant 2	c) Sense of humour	c) Sense of humour
Participant 3	d) Good personality	a) Attractiveness
Participant 4	a) Attractiveness	d) Good personality
Participant 5	b) Resources	d) Good personality
Participant 6	a) Attractiveness	a) Attractiveness
Participant 7	c) Sense of humour	d) Good personality
Participant 8	d) Good personality	b) Resources
Participant 9	c) Sense of humour	a) Attractiveness
Participant 10	d) Good personality	a) Attractiveness
Modal responses from participants	**c) Sense of humour AND d) Good personality**	**a) Attractiveness**

DO IT YOURSELF
No. 6.18

Questions (a)–(f) at the top left of the facing page are like the ones in the exam except that text has been left out from some of them. For example, in question (a) 'the named method' needs to be inserted. For Scenario 1 (see facing page), this would be 'a correlation'. For Scenario 2, it would be 'an observation'.

Write out question (a) in full for all the scenarios on this spread.

Do the same for questions (d) and (f), which also having missing text.

Example exam questions with student answers

Examiner's comments on these answers can be found on page 178.

Tomas has chosen to answer question 1, whereas Megan answered question 2.

QUESTION 1

A team of psychologists is conducting a field experiment at a local driving test centre. The researchers are investigating whether individuals who have high confidence make fewer errors on a driving test than those who have low confidence. Participants were asked to rate their confidence between 0 (no confidence) and 10 (very confident). A self-selecting (volunteer) sample of the learner drivers was used. The median scores of errors made on a driving test are noted in the table below.

	Median scores of errors made on a driving test
High confidence (confidence score of 6–10)	4
Low confidence (confidence score of 0–5)	6

(a) Outline **one** advantage and **one** disadvantage of using a field experiment in this research. [3]
(b) Identify **one** issue of reliability in this research, and describe how you could deal with this issue of reliability. [3]
(c) Identify **one** issue of validity in this research, and describe how you could deal with this issue of validity. [3]
(d) Outline **one** advantage and **one** disadvantage of self-selecting (volunteer) sampling in this research. [3]
(e) Discuss **one** ethical issue that might arise in this research. [3]
(f) State **one** conclusion that can be drawn from the median scores in this research. [3]

Tomas's answer

(a) An advantage of a field experiment is that it takes place in the real world, so it has more ecological validity. A disadvantage is that it is more difficult for the researcher to retain control over extraneous variables that may interfere with the IV and DV.

(b) One issue of reliability is whether the driving test examiners were all assessing driving errors in the same way. I would need to make sure that they did.

(c) One issue of validity is whether the 'confidence' rating is really measuring the confidence of the learner drivers. Some of the drivers might be giving lower confidence estimates as they might think that it is a 'socially desirable response' to be nervous before your driving test.

(d) An advantage is that they are a great deal easier for the researcher to select than other sampling techniques such as quota sampling. A disadvantage of self-selecting samples is that volunteers aren't necessarily representative of the general population, those with really low confidence in their driving skills may be feeling really nervous and therefore not want to participate in the study.

(e) Confidentiality might be an issue in this research as the participants may not want others to know how many errors they made on their driving test. If they made the research anonymous or used an alias so that only the learner driver would know the number of errors made on their driving test it might make the learner drivers more comfortable doing the research.

(f) The median values show that those learner drivers with high confidence ratings had a lower number of errors (2 errors less) than those learner drivers with low confidence ratings.

QUESTION 2

Psychologists are conducting research into the sports being played by men and women. They are giving out questionnaires to assess: (i) the gender of people playing sports and (ii) which sports are being played. The psychologists are using a systematic sample of the customers arriving at a local recreation centre. The results were compiled and can be seen in the bar chart below.

(a) Outline **one** advantage and **one** disadvantage of using a questionnaire in this research. [3]
(b) Identify **one** issue of reliability in this research, and describe how you could deal with issue of reliability. [3]
(c) Identify **one** issue of validity in this research, and describe how you could deal with issue of validity. [3]
(d) Outline **one** advantage and **one** disadvantage of systematic sampling in this research. [3]
(e) Discuss **one** ethical issue that might arise this research. [3]
(f) State **one** conclusion that can be drawn from the bar chart in this research. [3]

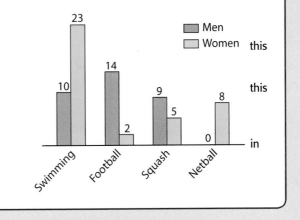

Megan's answer

(a) An advantage of questionnaires is that they allow us to easily collect both quantitative and qualitative data from a participant such as their gender and which sport they are playing at the Recreation Centre. A disadvantage is that participants may interpret the same question in different ways, one participant might think they have to note all the sports they play at the centre, whereas another may think they just note the activity they are doing on that visit.

(b) One issue would be whether the participants take part in the same activities every time they go to centre or whether they do different activities on different visits. The researcher could use the test re-test method to establish reliability by asking the same participants to complete an activities questionnaire the next time they went to the recreation centre, if they took part in the same activities on both trips the activity results would be reliable.

(c) As the data was selected using a systematic sampling technique the data from the participants at this recreation centre may not really accurately represent the number of men and women taking part in a variety of sporting activities.

The researchers could utilise a form of concurrent validity by asking instructors at the recreation centre to assess the gender profile of the activities that they supervise.

(d) An advantage of using systematic sampling is that it reduces any bias the researcher may have in identifying participants, they simply need to pick every nth customer arriving at the recreation centre. A disadvantage is that even though a recreation centre customer has been selected to be issued with a questionnaire, it does not mean that they have to take part or that they will complete the activities questionnaire.

(e) Informed consent may be an issue here as the participants have been selected rather than volunteering. Participants should be aware of the aim of the research 'sports played by men and women' and know exactly what is involved in the research, completing a questionnaire about 'participation in sport' BEFORE they make the choice about whether they take part or not.

(f) More men than women took part in Football and Squash; whereas more women than men took part in Netball and Swimming.

SECTION C MARKING SCHEME GRID

The questions on applied research methods are marked using the marking criteria below.

No. of marks	(a) and (d) Advantage and disadvantage ...	(b) and (c) Reliability/validity	(e) Ethical issue is ...	(f) Conclusion is ...
3	... Are noted. Both are linked to the novel situation.	Issue and way of dealing with it identified. Both are linked to the novel situation.	... Thoroughly discussed. Closely linked to the novel situation.	... Accurate and stated fully. Clearly linked to the novel situation.
2	... Are noted. There is some link to the novel situation.	Issue and way of dealing with it identified. Some link to the novel situation.	... Reasonably discussed. Some link to the novel situation.	... Accurate and stated. Some link to the novel situation.
1	... Are noted. There is no link to the novel situation.	Issue and way of dealing with it identified. No link to the novel situation.	... Discussed. No link to the novel situation.	... Accurate and stated. No link to the novel situation.
0	... Not appropriate.	Not appropriate OR the issue is not addressed.	... Not appropriate OR the issue is not discussed.	... Inaccurate or inappropriate.

You've reached the end of Unit 2 and you're ready to take the exam! Congratulations. On this spread we have provided lots of ideas that you can use in class and on your own to review and revise what you have learned.

Core studies bingo

1. Using the summaries at the end of Chapter 5 (pages 128–130), draw up a grid like the one below. In each square, write a 'fact' about the different parts of the core studies (i.e. context and aims, procedures, findings and conclusions). For example, for Asch's procedure you could write 'Used 123 male college students'.
2. When you have completed your grid, swap with another student.
3. Prepare slips of paper for the caller. For each core study there should be three slips, for example:
   • Asch – context and aims.
   • Asch – procedures.
   • Asch – findings and conclusions.
   You should end up with 30 slips of paper.
4. Put these slips of paper in a hat. Ask someone (the caller) to draw one slip at a time, reading out the researcher's name and the part of the study (for example, the caller might read out 'Asch –procedures' or 'Milgram – context and aims'). Each time the caller reveals a researcher name and part, see if you have the fact on your bingo card and cross it out. Have prizes for a line and a full house!
5. You could extend this to include methodology and alternative evidence for each study.

B	I	N	G	O
Used 123 male college students.	Could remember 30 words by the end of 22 months.	The shock generator had 30 switches on it.	In experiment 1 there were 45 students, in experiment 2, 150 students.	
Aimed to test the 'Germans are different' hypothesis.	Sample consisted of three women and five men.	Aimed to investigate differences in mate preference between males and females.	36 human infants aged 6–14 months were involved.	
Rats were feared the most, rabbits and ladybirds were feared the least.	Completed a military version of the Schedule of Recent Experiences	Questionnaires assessing happiness were administered by research assistants.	Accuracy for details of a complex event is distorted through leading questions.	
A greater sense of personal responsibility produces improvement.	Only three infants attempted to crawl on to the deep side.	Completed a questionnaire while attending a health centre.	Hospitalisation ranged from 7–52 days.	

Spot the mistakes – Milgram

Below is an answer to the question: Outline the procedures of Milgram's (1963) research 'Behavioural study of Obedience'. [12 marks]

1. Identify the errors in this answer.
2. Re-write the answer containing the correct information.

30 males were selected, via a newspaper advert. They had a variety of jobs and they varied in educational level. Each man was paid $45.00 for their participation in the experiment.

The research took place at Harvard University. Another 'participant' (accomplice of Milgram) is present, with an experimenter. The selection of roles was rigged. The real participant was always assigned to the learner role and the accomplice was always assigned the teacher role.

The teacher sees the learner strapped into an 'electric chair' apparatus. The teacher is told that this electrode is linked to a shock generator in the adjoining room. The teacher is sat down in front of the shock generator, a large machine had 25 switches on it, each showing a rise in voltage starting at 15 going to 350 volts. The teacher is to administer a shock when the learner gives an answer, moving up a switch each time the learner gets an answer wrong.

Eventually the learner starts to protest and scream after receiving the shocks. If the teacher hesitates about delivering the shock, the experimenter gives them a verbal prod such as 'the experiment requires that you continue'. Milgram wanted to know if the teachers, after hearing the protests of the learner, would continue to administer the shocks and if they obeyed, at what voltage would they stop. He also made detailed observations of the learner's behaviour.

After the research was completed the learner is thoroughly 'dehoaxed' and then interviewed about their experience.

You can make up your own 'spot the errors' for the other core studies. For each core study there are five possible exam questions (and answers) – so there's lots to do!

WRITE YOUR OWN EXAM QUESTIONS

At the end of Chapter 6 (page 168), we provided a set of research scenarios, one for each of the research methods identified in the specification (see page 66).

Now it's your turn. Work with a partner and write brief descriptions of different studies, one for each method. You can get ideas from all the studies we described in Chapter 1, and also look on the internet (type in a topic such as 'depth perception' and look at research studies). Each question must contain details of the method, the sampling technique used, and some display of the results.

Swap your questions with others in the class for them to complete. You can also mark each other's answers.

A GOOD TIP

when marking your classmates' answers is to highlight every word that directly links to the scenario. It quickly shows up whether there is none, some or lots of application in their answers.

Research methods: advantages and disadvantages

Draw up a table like the one below. Fill in one advantage and one disadvantage for each research method and sampling method.

		Advantage	Disadvantage
Research method	Lab experiment		
	Field experiment		
	Natural experiment		
	Correlation		
	Observation		
	Questionnaire		
	Interview		
	Case study		
Sampling method	Opportunity		
	Quota		
	Random		
	Self-selected (volunteer)		
	Stratified		
	Systematic		

Research methods vocabulary

Near the beginning of Chapter 6, we suggested that you keep a notebook with all the key words in it – a **Research Methods Vocabulary Book**.

You can use these words to make a revision game. Write a key word on one card and a very brief definition on another card. Various games can be played with these cards, such as those listed below.

- **Concentration** Place all the cards upside down in a random order. Turn two cards over. If they match (a word and its definition), then you keep the cards and have another go. If they don't match, turn them both back over and it is the next player's turn. The winner is the person with the most cards when they have all been paired.
- **Bingo** Deal out the definition cards to all class members (you could write the definitions on more than one card so that every class member has nine cards). The bingo caller has all the key words and reads them out one at a time. Turn your card over if the keyword on the card is called. Play continues until someone has turned over all their cards and calls BINGO!
- **Dominoes** Use the key words and definitions to make a set of dominoes.

| validity | Available participants | opportunity sample | Method of establishing reliability | Test-retest | Research method with IV and DV |

- **University challenge** Divide the class into teams. Start with two teams playing against each other. The quizmaster should read out a definition and team one must identify the key word. If the team gets it right, that team gets another go. The game is over when 30 cards have been read out. The definition cards are then reshuffled and a third team plays the winner of the first contest.

A very shy guy goes into a pub and sees a beautiful woman sitting at the bar. After an hour of gathering up his courage, he finally goes over to her and asks, tentatively, 'Um, would you mind if I chatted with you for a while?'

She responds by yelling, at the top of her voice, 'NO! I won't sleep with you tonight!' Everyone in the bar is now staring at them. Naturally, the guy is hopelessly embarrassed and slinks back to his table.

After a few minutes, the woman walks over to him and apologises. She smiles and says, 'I'm sorry if I embarrassed you. You see, I'm a psychology student, and I'm studying how people respond to embarrassing situations.'

To which he responds, at the top of his voice, 'What do you mean £200?!'

Examiner's comments

CHAPTER 1 THE BIOLOGICAL APPROACH (PAGE 16)

Example of Question 2

Comments on Megan's answer

As there is no evidence of any link between the approach and the therapy, this answer cannot be marked within the top two bands of the marking scheme (7 marks or above). The answer does display knowledge and understanding of how several therapies work, although the detail is limited. This answer would earn **5 out of 12 marks**.

Comments on Tomas's answer (below)

The link between the approach and the therapy is extremely clear at the start of this essay. Tomas has described the therapy accurately, and in detail. Although there is more breadth (range) than depth, descriptions of the different types of chemotherapy are coherently elaborated. This is a very good answer and would attract **12 out of 12 marks**.

Tomas's answer

The biological approach believes all behaviour is physiological in nature. One of the main assumptions of the biological approach is that our behaviour can be explained by chemical messengers in the brain, known as neurotransmitters. Chemotherapy is a therapy based on this approach, and, based on this assumption, aims to treat individuals by modifying the workings of the brain and altering neurotransmitter activity.

Chemotherapy is the term used to describe the use of psychoactive drugs to treat mental disorders. Antidepressant drugs, for example, work on the neurotransmitter serotonin, as it is believed that depression is due to insufficient amounts of this. These drugs generally work by reducing the rate at which certain neurotransmitters are re-absorbed into the nerve endings. For example, SSRI's (selective serotonin reuptake inhibitors) work by blocking the mechanism that re-absorbs serotonin into the synapse. The result of this is that more serotonin is left in the synapse, alleviating the feelings of depression (hopefully).

Antipsychotic drugs are used to treat disorders such as schizophrenia. Chlorpromazine, for example, is used to combat the positive symptoms of schizophrenia. This drug blocks the action of the neurotransmitter dopamine. The 'dopamine hypothesis' proposes that increased levels of dopamine produce symptoms of schizophrenia.

Other popular forms of chemotherapy include the treatment of anxiety disorders, commonly used to treat those who suffer from stress and panic attacks. Beta blockers for example, reduce anxiety by acting on the CNS, reducing levels of adrenaline and noradrenaline, or by binding to receptors of the heart, resulting in slower heart beat and a fall in blood pressure. This, in turn, should result in the person feeling calmer and less stressed.

Chemotherapy has proved successful as a means of treating a range of psychological disorders, and is widely available. Viguera et al. (2000) report that over 60% of patients with bipolar disorder improve when taking lithium.

Example of Question 5

Comments on Megan's answer

It is not clear from the start of this answer the ways in which the method is relevant to the assumptions of the approach (i.e. why is this method appropriate for the biological approach). There is a reasonable evaluation of the strengths and weaknesses of lab experiments in this answer but the issue here is that the candidate could have rote learned this answer and applied it to other approaches (e.g. cognitive). For candidates to access the top bands for this question, it should be clear as to how the methodology is appropriate to the approach as well as providing evidence of both strengths and weaknesses. Using relevant examples of research will help this.

There is only a statement of one method used by the biological approach here, along with a reasonable evaluation, and, for this reason, this answer would attract only **5 out of 12 marks**.

Comments on Tomas's answer

The methodology is clearly explained and is highly relevant to the approach. The answer has clear structure, and is generally coherent. The answer displays range and depth, and strengths and weaknesses are accurate and relevant. This is a very good answer in the time given, and while some strengths/weaknesses could have been more coherently elaborated, this is still a top band answer that would attract **11 out of 12 marks**.

CHAPTER 2 THE BEHAVIOURIST APPROACH (PAGE 30)

Example of Question 1 (a) and (b)

Comments on Megan's answer

1 (a) Megan has outlined two assumptions, which are relevant and detailed. This answer would attract **4 out of 4 marks**.

1 (b) This is a good overall description of the main elements of the SLT of aggression. All material is relevant to the answer, and is used effectively. There is good range, and depth by way of relevant examples. This is a top band answer that would attract **8 out of 8 marks**.

Comments on Tomas's answer

1 (a) Tomas has outlined two relevant assumptions of the behaviourist approach, but they are very brief and there is no attempt to elaborate them. This answer would attract only **1 out of 4 marks**, as there is not enough detail to warrant more than this.

1 (b) While Bandura's research is highly relevant in supporting the SLT of aggression, Tomas displays limited knowledge of the theory itself. Bandura's study is described accurately, and there is some implicit link with the theory at the end of the answer. There are several versions of Bandura's Bobo doll study and candidates should be careful not to muddle procedures as Tomas has done here. Due to the limited knowledge displayed of the SLT of aggression itself, this answer would attract **3 out of 8 marks**.

CHAPTER 3 THE PSYCHODYNAMIC APPROACH (PAGE 44)

Example of Question 1(a)

Comments on Megan's answer
Megan has accurately identified two relevant assumptions; however, these lack detail. Overall each assumption would need more detail to be able to access marks in the top band. This answer would attract **2 out of 4 marks**.

Comments on Tomas's answer
Tomas has described two relevant assumptions and these are detailed and accurate. This is a realistic outline of two relevant assumptions in the time available, and so the answer would attract **4 out of 4 marks**.

Example of Question 2

Comments on Megan's answer
Megan has produced a good description of free association, which is largely accurate and detailed. However, there is no link between the approach and the therapy, so unfortunately she is unable to access marks in the top two bands. This is a common mistake made by candidates, when the question clearly asks to 'Describe how the _____ approach has been applied in _____'. This answer would attract **6 out of 10 marks**.

Comments on Tomas's answer
Tomas has produced a good answer in the time allocated. The description of the therapy is accurate and reasonably detailed. It is generally coherent, and the material has been used in an effective manner. The link between the approach and the therapy is highly evident at the start of the answer. Tomas could have gained full marks by being a little more thorough, for example in his description of dreamwork. This answer would attract **10 out of 12 marks**.

CHAPTER 4 THE COGNITIVE APPROACH (PAGES 58 AND 59)

Example of Question 1(b)

Comments on Megan's answer
Megan's answer is accurate and well-detailed. She displays both range and depth of knowledge, and has made effective use of examples to illustrate her knowledge of the theory. The answer is coherent and material has been used effectively. The answer would gain the full **8 out of 8 marks**.

Comments on Tomas's answer
Tomas has provided a basic description of attribution theory. There is a range of knowledge, but this is described in a limited manner and is muddled in places. The material is relevant to the question and the use of examples does show some understanding. This answer would gain **5 out of 8 marks**.

Example of Question 3(a) and (b)

Comments on Megan's answer
3 (a) Overall this is a very strong answer. In terms of the strengths, two strengths are evaluated, are clearly explained, and relevant to the approach. Megan would receive **6 out of 6 marks**.
3 (b) In terms of weaknesses both are explained clearly and thoroughly, and so would also be awarded **6 out of 6 marks**.

Comments on Tomas's answer
3 (a) Tomas has started by describing an assumption of the cognitive approach, which is not needed in this answer which requires strengths/weaknesses; although it is accepted that some description may be necessary to 'lead in' to a relevant strength/weakness. In terms of strengths, two strengths are discussed, in fairly basic detail, and so (a) would receive **2 out of 6 marks**.
3 (b) In terms of weaknesses, Tomas has evaluated only one weakness, though in reasonable detail, and so would receive **2 out of 6 marks**.

Example of Question 5

Comments on Megan's answer
Megan's answer is accurate and well detailed. She has described two methods used by the cognitive approach and provided information about the strengths and weaknesses of both of these methods. Most importantly she has linked her discussion of the methods specifically to the cognitive approach and therefore gains **12 out of 12 marks**.

Comments on Tomas's answer
While the methodology is clearly stated in Tomas's answer and there is evidence of several strengths and weaknesses, the answer lacks relevance to the actual approach; in other words the methodology as used by the cognitive approach is not well explained. The method described here could apply to the behaviourist or the biological approach, and therefore for the answer to portray depth and relevance, it should have been put in context. For example, Tomas could have given an example of research conducted within the field of cognitive psychology that has made use of the experimental method. This answer would attract **6 out of 12 marks**.

CHAPTER 5 CORE STUDY 1 ASCH (PAGE 73)

Example of Question 2

Comments on Megan's answer
Megan's answer contains some information on Asch's procedures, but there is also quite a bit of information on the aims and the findings that don't receive credit here. Overall, procedural detail is superficial; **3 out of 12 marks**.

Comments on Tomas's answer
Tomas's answer is reasonably accurate and well detailed. It is at the bottom of the top marking band as it is missing a few key details such as the number of participants Asch used; **10 out of 12 marks**.

CHAPTER 5 CORE STUDY 2 MILGRAM (PAGE 79)

Example of Question 1

Comments on Megan's answer
Megan's answer is brief and the description of the context is superficial. It also does not have a clearly defined aim, so **2 out of 12 marks**.

Comments on Tomas's answer
When you initially look at Tomas's answer it seems accurate and well detailed. It's 'stuffed' with appropriate context! However, Tomas does not fully address the question as he has not included Milgram's aim, and this impacts severely on his mark. If he had included even a brief aim, it would have pushed the mark awarded into the top band, but examiners can only credit what is written down; **6 out of 12 marks**.

CHAPTER 5 CORE STUDY 3 RAHE *ET AL.* (PAGE 85)

Example of Question 3

Comments on Megan's answer
Megan's answer is accurate and well detailed. A plentiful number of findings are given and the conclusions are appropriate. Although the answer contains more detail on the findings than conclusions, there doesn't need to be an equal balance though slightly more detail on the conclusions would have given this answer top marks. As it stands this answer receives **11 out of 12 marks**.

Comments on Tomas's answer
Tomas's answer is superficial. The statements here are very vague; thus only **2 out of 12 marks**.

CHAPTER 5 CORE STUDY 4 BENNETT-LEVY AND MARTEAU (PAGE 91)

Example of Question 4

Comments on Megan's answer
This answer has covered a reasonable range of methodological issues, but they are discussed mostly in a basic way. A more thorough discussion of the issues raised would definitely improve the mark; **5 out of 12 marks**.

Comments on Tomas's answer
This answer includes some coherent evaluation of a few of the methodological issues, but overall the amount of discussion puts the answer in the 7–9-mark band. If Tomas had included more discussion of a similar standard, the mark could have been in the top band, so only **8 out of 12 marks**.

CHAPTER 5 CORE STUDY 5 LOFTUS AND PALMER (PAGE 97)

Example of Question 5

Comments on Megan's answer
Megan's answer describes some appropriate alternative evidence, but of the three pieces of evidence described, only one has been linked at all to Loftus and Palmer's research; **4 out of 12 marks**.

Comments on Tomas's answer
Tomas's answer is clearly structured and coherent. Each piece of evidence is appropriate and clearly linked to Loftus and Palmer's research. However, two-thirds of the answer is the description of the alternative evidence. If Tomas had just increased slightly his discussion about how the alternative evidence relates to Loftus and Palmer's research, he could have got the top mark. However, without these links to the core study, his mark is limited to **10 out of 12 marks**.

CHAPTER 5 CORE STUDY 6 GARDNER AND GARDNER (PAGE 103)

Example of Question 1

Comments on Megan's answer
Megan's answer is reasonably accurate but lacks a certain amount of detail. It contains both context and aim so it can access the top half of the marks; **8 out of 12 marks**.

Comments on Tomas's answer
Tomas's answer shows a very basic knowledge of appropriate context and a brief aim; **4 out of 12 marks**.

CHAPTER 5 CORE STUDY 7 LANGER AND RODIN (PAGE 109)

Example of Question 3

Comments on Megan's answer
Megan's answer is mostly inappropriate, with an obviously inappropriate conclusion. However, she would probably receive very minimal credit because there is an element of truth in that those in the responsibility induced group were given plants to care for and at the end of the research they did have a higher happiness score; **1 out of 12 marks** (just!).

Comments on Tomas's answer
Tomas's answer is exceptionally well detailed and all of his 'facts' are spot-on in their accuracy. In fact, he has probably written more than is necessary for the full **12 out of 12 marks**.

CHAPTER 5 CORE STUDY 8 GIBSON AND WALK (PAGE 115)

Example of Question 2

Comments on Megan's answer
Megan's answer demonstrates an accurate and well-detailed description of the procedures. She has wisely not tried to 'pad out' her answer with details that would not be creditworthy. However, her answer is on the short side and she has omitted many key details, such as some of the non-human animal variations in the procedures (e.g. testing rats so they couldn't touch the glass surface with their whiskers). A few more of such details and this could have achieved the top mark; **10 out of 12 marks**.

Comments on Tomas's answer
Tomas's answer starts off well, but it is limited by the fact that the majority of the answer relates to findings rather than procedures. Appropriate content is basic and limited; **5 out of 12 marks**.

CHAPTER 5 CORE STUDY 9 BUSS (PAGE 121)

Example of Question 4

Comments on Megan's answer

Megan's answer is really very superficial. It is merely identifying a couple of methodological issues that should be discussed further; **2 out of 12 marks**.

Comments on Tomas's answer

Tomas's answer demonstrates a clear and coherent discussion. The comments are well-structured and thorough. It's clear that Tomas has considered what could go in an answer to this question before writing it in timed conditions. He has included a quote in his answer, which shows that he has read beyond the textbook and studied the original article, adding his own details. A well deserved full **12 out of 12 marks**.

CHAPTER 5 CORE STUDY 10 ROSENHAN (PAGE 127)

Example of Question 5

Comments on Megan's answer

Megan's answer demonstrates a reasonable balance of describing the alternative evidence and using it to assess Rosenhan's research. If Megan had included either a slightly more thorough discussion or another piece of alternative evidence that was discussed equally well, this answer could be in the top band. As it is, this answer gets only **8 out of 12 marks**.

Comments on Tomas's answer

This is a very well thought out comment. It's a shame that there is only one piece of alternative evidence, as it means that the answer could never get more than 6 marks; **4 out of 12 marks**.

CHAPTER 6 APPLIED RESEARCH METHODS (PAGES 170 AND 171)

Question 1

Comments on Tomas's answer

1. (a) This answer has clearly identified an appropriate advantage and disadvantage of a field experiment; however, neither the advantage nor the disadvantage has been linked to the scenario, thus **1 out of 3 marks**.
1. (b) An appropriate issue of reliability is noted and linked to the scenario, but the method used to deal with it is not really appropriate and not linked to the scenario; **1 out of 3 marks**.
1. (c) An appropriate issue of validity is present, has been thoroughly discussed and is clearly linked to the scenario. However, there is no description of how the issue could be dealt with; **1 out of 3 marks**.
1. (d) An appropriate advantage and disadvantage of self-selected sampling. However, only the disadvantage is linked to the scenario; **2 out of 3 marks**.
1. (e) An appropriate discussion of a relevant ethical issue with many links to the scenario; a full **3 out of 3 marks**.
1. (f) An appropriate conclusion drawn from the median values and clearly linked to the scenario; **3 out of 3 marks**.

Question 2

Comments on Megan's answer

2. (a) An appropriate advantage and disadvantage are given and both clearly linked to the scenario; **3 out of 3 marks**.
2. (b) An appropriate issue of reliability and way of dealing with it have been noted, and both are clearly linked to the scenario; **3 out of 3 marks**.
2. (c) Although the validity issue comes from a flaw in the sampling technique, it is still an appropriate issue of validity! Both the identified issue and the way of dealing with it are appropriate and linked to the scenario; **3 out of 3 marks**.
2. (d) An appropriate advantage and disadvantage are given and both clearly linked to the scenario; **3 out of 3 marks**.
2. (e) A coherent discussion of an appropriate ethical issue is present with numerous links to the scenario; **3 out of 3 marks**.
2. (f) An appropriate conclusion is drawn from the bar chart and clearly linked to the scenario; **3 out of 3 marks**.

ANSWERS TO CROSSWORD ON PAGE 64

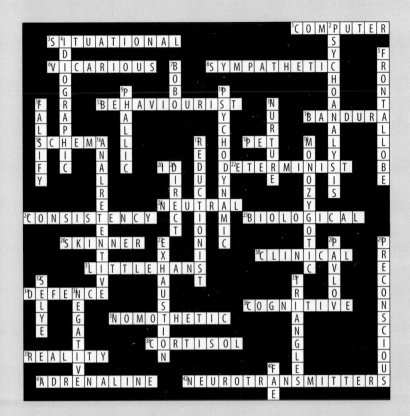

ANSWERS TO CROSSWORD ON PAGE 132

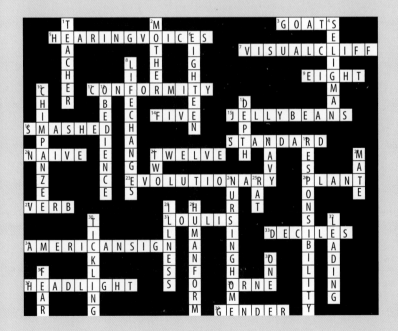

ANSWERS TO CROSSWORD ON PAGE 167

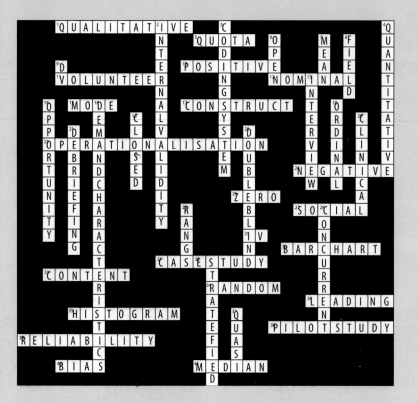

References

Adler, A. (1930). Individual psychology. In C. Murchison (ed.) *Psychologies of 1930*. Worcester: Clark University Press. ▸ page 104

Adolph. K.E. and Berger, S.A. (2006). Motor development. In W. Damon and R. Lerner (Series Eds.), D Kuhn and R.S. Siegler (Vol. Eds.), *Handbook of child psychology*: Vol 2: Cognition, perception, and language (6th ed.) New York: Wiley, pp.161–213 ▸ page 114

Adorno, T.W., Frenkel-Brunswick, E., Levinson, D. and Sanford, N. (1950). *The Authoritarian Personality*. New York: Harper. ▸ page 74

Arendt, H. (1963). *Eichmann in Jerusalem: A Report on the Banality of Evil*. New York: The Viking Press. ▸ page 74

Asch, S.E. (1946). Forming impressions of personality. *Journal of Abnormal and Social Psychology*, 41, 258–290. ▸ page 124

Asch, S.E. (1955). Opinions and social pressure. *Scientific American*, 193(5), 31–35. ▸ pages 68–73

Atkinson, R.C. and Shiffrin, R.M. (1968). Human memory: a proposed system and its control processes. In K.W. Spence and J.T. Spence (eds) *The Psychology of Learning and Motivation*, vol. 2. London: Academic Press. ▸ page 45

Badawy, A. A. (1999). Tryptophan metabolism in alcoholism. *Advances in Experimental Medicine and Biology*, 467, 265–274. ▸ page 21

Baddeley, A.D. and Longman, D.J.A. (1978). The influence of length and frequency on training sessions on the rate of learning type. *Ergonomics*, 21, 627–635. ▸ page 139

Bancroft, J. (1992). *Deviant Sexual Behavior*. Oxford: Oxford University Press. ▸ page 21

Bandura, A. (1986). *Social foundations of thought and action: A social cognitive theory*. Englewood Cliffs, N.J.: Prentice-Hall. ▸ page 18

Bandura, A. (2004). Swimming against the mainstream: the early years from chilly tributary to transformative mainstream. *Behaviour Research and Therapy*, 42, 613–630. ▸ page 18

Bandura, A. and Walters, R.H. (1963). *Social Learning and Personality Development*. New York: Holt, Rinehart and Winston. ▸ page 19

Bandura, A., Ross, D. and Ross, S.A. (1961). Transmission of aggression through imitation of aggressive models. *Journal of Abnormal and Social Psychology*, 63, 575–582. ▸ pages 19, 26, 152

Banyard, P. and Grayson, A. (2007). *Introducing Psychological Research*, 3rd edn. London: Palgrave. ▸ page 67

Baumrind, D. (1964). Some thoughts on ethics of research: after reading Milgram's behavioural study of obedience. *American Psychologist*, 19, 421–423. ▸ page 78

Beck, A.T. (1967). *Depression: Clinical, Experimental and Theoretical Aspects*. New York: Harper and Row. ▸ page 49

Beck, A.T. (1976). *Cognitive Therapy and Emotional Disorders*. New York: International Universities Press. ▸ page 48

Becklen, R. and Cervone, D. (1983). Selective looking and the noticing of unexpected events. *Memory and Cognition*, 11, 601–608. ▸ page 145

Bekerian, D.A. and Bowers, J.M. (1983). Eye-witness testimony: were we misled? *Journal of Experimental Psychology, Learning, Memory and Cognition*, 9, 139–145. ▸ page 96

Bennett-Levy, J. and Marteau, T. (1984). Fear of animals: what is prepared? *British Journal of Psychology*, 75, 37–42. ▸ pages 86–91

Berezckei, T., Vorgos, S., Gal, A. and Bernath, L. (1997). Resources, attractiveness, family commitment; reproductive decisions in human mate choice. *Ethology. ALQ*, 103, 681–699. ▸ page 121

Bergin, A.E. (1971). The evaluation of therapeutic outcomes. In A.E. Bergin and S.L. Garfield (eds) *Handbook of Psychotherapy and Behaviour Change*. New York: Wiley. ▸ page 37

Berns, G.S., Chappelow, J., Zink, C.F., Pagnoni, G., Martin-Skurski, M.E. and Richards, J. (2005). Neurobiological correlates of social conformity and independence during mental rotation. *Biological Psychiatry*, 58, 245–253. ▸ page 73

Bettleheim, B. (1943). Individual and mass behaviour in extreme situations. *Journal of Abnormal and Social Psychology*, 38, 417–452. ▸ page 104

Bickman, L. (1974). Clothes make the person. *Psychology Today*, 8(4), 48–51. ▸ page 145

Blass, T. (2004). *The Man Who Shocked the World: The Life and Legacy of Stanley Milgram*. New York: Perseus Books. ▸ page 75

Boden, M.A. (1977). *Artificial Intelligence and Natural Man*. New York: Basic Books. ▸ page 103

Bogdonoff, M., Back, K., Klein, R., Estes, H. and Nichols, C. (1961). The psychologic response to conformity pressure in man. *Annals of Internal Medicine*, 57(3), 389–397. ▸ page 72

Bouchard, T.J. and McGue, M. (1981). Famial studies of intelligence: a review. *Science*, 22, 1055–1059. ▸ page 13

Bower, G.H., Clark, M., Lesgold, A. and Winzenz, D. (1969). Hierarchical retrieval schemes in recall of categorized word lists. *Journal of Verbal Learning and Verbal Behaviour*, 8, 323–343. ▸ page 150

Bower, T.G.R., Broughton, J.M. and Moore, M.K. (1970). Infant responses to approaching objects: an indicator of response to distal variables. *Perception and Psychophysics*, 9, 193–196. ▸ page 115

Braun, K.A., Ellis, R. and Loftus, E.F. (2002). Make my memory: how advertising can change our memories of the past. *Psychology and Marketing*, 19, 1–23. ▸ page 97

Bremner, J.G. (1994). *Infancy*, 2nd edn. Oxford: Blackwell. ▸ page 115

Bridges, P.K., Bartlett, J.R., Hale, A.S., Poynton, A.M., Malizia, A.L. and Hodgkiss, A.D. (1994). Psychosurgery: stereotactic subcaudate tractomy. An indispensable treatment. *British Journal of Psychiatry*, 165(5), 612–613. ▸ page 7

Brown, R. (1986). *Social psychology: The second edition*. New York: The Free Press. ▸ page 104

Browning, C. (1992). *Ordinary men: Reserve Police Battalion 101 and the Final Solution in Poland*. New York: HarperCollins. ▸ page 135

Bryan, A.L. (1963). The essential morphological basis for human culture. *Current Anthropology*, 4, 297. ▸ page 98

Buckout, R. (1980). Nearly 2,000 witnesses can be wrong. *Bulletin of the Psychonomic Society*, 16, 307–310. ▸ page 96

Burger, J.M. (2009). Replicating Milgram. Would people still obey today? *American Psychologist*, 64(1), 1–11. ▸ page 78

Burger, J.M. and Cooper, H.M. (1979). The desirability of control. *Motivation and emotion*, 3, 381–393. ▸ page 72

Burrell, G. (1989). *Buster's Fired a Wobbler*. London: Penguin. ▸ page 123

Buss, D.M. (1989). Sex differences in human mate preferences: evolutionary hypotheses tested in 37 cultures. *Behavioral and Brain Sciences*, 12, 1–49. ▸ pages 116–121

Buzan, T. (1993). *The mind map book*. London: BBC. ▸ page 15

Capafóns, J.I., Sosa, C.D. and Avero, P. (1998). Systematic desensitisation in the treatment of fear of flying. *Psychology in Spain*, 2(1), 11–16. ▸ page 23

Carmichael, L.C., Hogan, H.P. and Walters, A.A. (1932). An experimental study of the effect of language on the reproduction of visually perceived form. *Journal of Experimental Psychology*, *15*, 73–86. ▶ pages 94, 95

Carson, R.C. (1991). Dilemmas in the pathway of the *DSM-IV*. *Journal of Abnormal Psychology*, *100*, 302–307. ▶ page 127

Cellerino, A. (2003). Psychobiology of facial attractiveness. *Journal of Endocrinological Investigation*, *26*(3), 45–48. ▶ page 121

Charlton, T., Gunter, B. and Hannan, A. (eds) (2000). *Broadcast Television Effects in a Remote Community*. Hillsdale, NJ: Lawrence Erlbaum. ▶ page 147

Chomsky, N. (1957). *Syntactic Structures*. The Hague: Mouton. ▶ page 98

Cohen, S., Tyrell, D.A. and Smith, A.P. (1991). Psychological stress and susceptibility to the common cold. *New England Journal of Medicine*, *325*, 606–612. ▶ page 84

Cohen, S., Tyrrell, D.A.J. and Smith, A.P. (1993). Negative life events, perceived stress, negative affect, and susceptibility to the common cold. *Journal of Personality and Social Psychology*, *64*, 131–140. ▶ pages 84, 108

Comer, R.J. (2002). *Fundamentals of Abnormal Psychology*, 3rd edn. New York: Worth. ▶ pages 6, 22

Cook M. and Mineka S. (1990). Selective associations in the observational conditioning of fear in rhesus monkeys. *Journal of Experimental Psychology: Animal Behavior Processes*, *16*, 372–389. ▶ page 91

Coolican, H. (1996). *Introduction to Research Methods and Statistics in Psychology*. London: Hodder & Stoughton. ▶ page 144,

Coolican, H. (2004a). Personal communication. ▶ page 144

Coolican, H. (2004b). *Research Methods and Statistics in Psychology* (3rd edition). London: Hodder & Stoughton. ▶ page 146

Cosgrove, G.R. and Rauch, S.L. (2001). Psychosurgery. Available at: http://neurosurgery.mgh.harvard.edu/functional/Psychosurgery2001.htm ▶ pages 7, 10

Craik, F.I.M. and Tulving, E. (1975). Depth of processing and the retention of words in episodic memory. *Journal of Experimental Psychology*, *104*, 268–294. ▶ pages 139, 143

Cunningham, M.R., Roberts, A.R., Barbee, A.P., Druen, P.B. and Wu, C.-H. (1995). 'Their ideas of beauty are, on the whole, the same as ours': consistency and variability in the cross-cultural perception of female physical attractiveness. *Journal of Personality and Social Psychology*, *68*(2), 261–279. ▶ page 120

Daly, M., Wilson, M. and Weghorst, S.J. (1982). Male sexual jealousy. *Ethology and Sociobiology*, *3*, 11–27. ▶ page 116

Davey, G. (1995). Preparedness and phobias: specific evolved associations or a generalized expectancy bias? *Behavioral and Brain Sciences*, *18*(2), 289–325. ▶ page 91

David, D. and Avellino, M. (2003) A synopsis of rational-emotive behaviour therapy (REBT): Basic/fundamental and applied research. http://www.rebt.org/synopsis.htm. ▶ page 48

Dawkins, M.S. (1990). From an animal's point of view: motivation, fitness and animal welfare. *Behavioral and Brain Sciences*, *13*, 1–61. ▶ pages 102, 114

deCharms, R. (1968). *Personal Causation*. New York: Academic Press. ▶ page 104

DeLongis, A., Folkman, S. and Lazarus, R.S. (1988). The impact of daily stress on health and mood: psychological and social resources as mediators. *Journal of Personality and Social Psychology, 54*, 486–495. ▶ page 84

Dement, W. and Kleitman, N. (1957). The relation of eye movements during sleep to dream activity: an objective method for studying dreaming. *Journal of Experimental Psychology*, *53*, 339–346. ▶ page 12

Dully, H. and Fleming, C. (2007). *My Lobotomy*. New York: Crown Publishing Group. ▶ page 7

Doms, M. and Van Avermaet, E. (1981). The conformity effect: a timeless phenomenon? *Bulletin of the British Psychological Society*, *34*, 383–385. ▶ page 72

Dunbar, R. (1995). Are you lonesome tonight? *New Scientist*, *145* (February), 26–31. ▶ pages xii, 117

Eagly, A.H. (1978). Sex differences in influenceability. *Psychological Bulletin, 85*, 86–116. ▶ page 72

Ekman, P. and Friesen, W. V. (1978). *Manual for the Facial Action Coding System*. Palo Alto, CA: Consulting Psychology Press. ▶ page 153

Ellis, A. (1957). *How to Live with a 'Neurotic'*. Hollywood, CA: Wilshire Books. ▶ pages 50, 51

Ellis, A. (1962). *Reason and Emotion in Psychotherapy*. New York: Lyle Stuart. ▶ page 48

Ellis, A. (1994). *Reason and Emotion in Psychotherapy, Revised and Updated*. Secaucus, NJ: Carol Publishing Group. ▶ page 51

Ellis, A. (2001). *Overcoming Destructive Beliefs, Feelings, and Behaviours: New Directions for Rational Emotive Behaviour Therapy*. New York, NY: Prometheus Books. ▶ page 51

Engels, G.I., Garnefski, N. and Diekstra, R.F.W. (1993). Efficacy of rational emotive therapy: a quantitative analysis. *Journal of Consulting and Clinical Psychology*, *61*(6), 1083–1090. ▶ page 51

Evans, P., Bristow, M., Hucklebridge, F., Clow, A. and Pang, F.-Y. (1994). Stress, arousal, cortisol and secretory immunoglobulin A in students undergoing assessment. *British Journal of Clinical Psychology*, *33*, 575–576. ▶ page 85

Evans, P., Clow, A. and Hucklebridge, F. (1997). Stress and the immune system. *The Psychologist, 10*(7), 303–307. ▶ page 85

Ferguson, S., Cisneros, F., Gough, B., Hanig, J. and Berry, K. (2005). Chronic oral treatment with 13–cis-retinoic acid (isotretinoin) or all-trans-retinoic acid does not alter depression-like behaviors in rats. *Toxicological Sciences*, *87*, 451–459. ▶ page 9

Ferrare, N. (1962). Cited in Zimbardo, P.G. and Ruch, F.L. (1975). *Psychology and Life*, 9th edn. Glenview: Scott, Foresman. ▶ page 104

Fick, K. (1993). The influence of an animal on social interactions of nursing home residents in a group setting. *American Journal of Occupational Therapy*, *47*, 529–534. ▶ page 155

Fillmore, C.J. (1971). Types of lexical information. In D.D. Steinberg and L.A. Jakobovits (eds) *Semantics: An Interdisciplinary Reader in Philosophy, Linguistics and Psychology*. Cambridge: Cambridge University Press. ▶ page 92

Foster, R.A., Libkuman, T.M., Schooler, J.W., and Loftus, E.F. (1994). Consequentiality and eyewitness person identification. *Applied Cognitive Psychology*, *8*, 107–121. ▶ page 54

Foucault, M. (1961). *Madness and Civilization: A History of Insanity in the Age of Reason*. Translated by R. Howard (1965). London: Tavistock. ▶ page 122

Fouts, R. and Mills, S.T. (1997). *Next of Kin: My Conversations with Chimpanzees*. New York: HarperCollins. ▶ page 100

Freud, S. (1900). *The Interpretation of Dreams*. New York: Macmillan. ▶ page 34

Freud, S. (1909) Analysis of a phobia in a five-year-old boy. In J. Strachey (ed. and trans.) *The Standard Edition of the Complete Psychological Works: Two Case Histories*, vol. X. London: The Hogarth Press. ▶ page 32

Gardner, R.A. and Gardner, B.T. (1969). Teaching sign language to a chimpanzee. *Science, 165*, 664–672. ▶ pages 98–103

Gardner, R.A., Gardner, B.T. and Van Cantfort, T.E. (eds) (1989). *Teaching Sign Language to Chimpanzees*. Albany: State University of New York Press. ▶ pages 100, 102

Gibson, E.J. and Walk, R.D. (1960). The 'visual cliff'. *Scientific American*, *202*(4), 64–71. ▶ pages 110–115

Gibson, J.J. and Gibson, E. (1955). Perceptual learning: differentiation or enrichment? *Psychological Review*, *62*(1), 32–41. ▶ page 112

Gilligan, C. and Attanucci, J. (1988). Two moral orientations: gender differences and similarities. *Merrill-Palmer Quarterly*, *34*, 223–237. ▶ page 159

Goffman, E. (1961). *Encounters*. New York: BobbsMerril Company. ▶ page 125

Haslam, S.A. and Reicher, S. (2008). Questioning the banality of evil. *The Psychologist*, *21*(1), 16–19. ▶ page 135

Hawkins, N.G., Davies, R. and Holmes, T.H. (1957). Evidence of psychosocial factors in the development of pulmonary tuberculosis. *American Review of Tuberculosis and Pulmonary Diseases*, *75*, 768–780. ▶ page 80

Hayes, K.J. and Hayes, C. (1952). Imitation in a home-raised chimpanzee. *Journal of Comparative Physiological Psychology*, *45*, 450–459. ▶ page 98

Heider, F. (1958). *The Psychology of Interpersonal Relations*. New York: Wiley. ▶ page 46

Heider, F. and Simmel, M. (1944). An experimental study of apparent behaviour. *American Journal of Psychology*, *57*, 243–259. ▶ page 46

Hill, D. (1986). Tardive dyskenesia: a worldwide epidemic of irreversible brain damge. In N. Eisenberg and D. Glasgow (eds) *Current Issues in Clinical Psychology*. Adershot: Gower. ▶ page 9

Hilts, P. (1995). *Memory's Ghost: The Strange Tale of Mr. M. and the Nature of Memory*. New York: Simon and Schuster. ▶ page 55

Hinde, R.A. (1974). *Biological Bases of Human Social Behaviour*. New York: McGraw-Hill. ▶ pages 86, 89

Hock, R.R. (2008). *Forty Studies That Changed Psychology*. London: Pearson Educational. ▶ page 67

Hockett, C.F. (1960). The origin of speech. *Scientific American*, *203*, 88–96. ▶ page 98

Hofling, K.C., Brontzman, E., Dalrymple, S., Graves, N. and Pierce, C.M. (1966). An experimental study in the nurse–physician relationship. *Journal of Mental and Nervous Disorders*, *43*, 171–178. ▶ page 79

Hofsten, C., von, Kellman, P. and Putaansuu, J. (1992). Young infants' sensitivity to motion parallax. *Infant Behaviour and Development*, *15*, 245–264. ▶ page 115

Hollway, W. and Jefferson, T. (2000). *Doing Qualitative Research Differently: Free Association, Narrative and the Interview Method*. London: Sage. ▶ page 37

Holmes, T.H. and Rahe, R.H. (1967). The social readjustment rating scale. *Journal of Psychosomatic Research*, *11*, 213–218. ▶ page 80

Hopfield, J.J., Feinstein, D.I. and Palmer, R.G. (1983). 'Unlearning' has a stabilising effect in collective memories. *Nature*, *304*, 158–159. ▶ page 35

Humphrey, J.H. (1973). *Stress Education for College Students*. Hauppauge NY: Nova. ▶ page 22

Jenness, A. (1932). The role of discussion in changing opinion regarding matter of fact. *Journal of Abnormal and Social Psychology*, *27*, 279–296. ▶ pages 68, 72

Jones, E.E., Rock, L., Shaver, K.G., Goethals, G.R. and Ward, L.M. (1968). Pattern of performance and ability to attribution: an unexpected primacy effect. *Journal of Personality and Social Psychology*, *9*, 317–340. ▶ page 47

Joronen, K. and Åstedt–Kurki, P. (2005). Familial contribution to adolescent subjective well–being. *International Journal of Nursing Practice*, *11*(3), 125–133. ▶ page 162

Jost, A. (1897). Die Assoziationsfestigkeit in ihrer Abhängigkeit von der Verteilung der Wiederholungen. *Zeitschrift für Psychologie*, *14*, 436–472. ▶ page 139

Kahn, R.J., McNair, D.M., Lipman, R.S., Covi, L., Rickels, K., Downing, R., Fisher, S. and Frankenthaler, L.M. (1986). Imipramine and chlordiazepoxide in depressive and anxiety disorders. II. Efficacy in anxious outpatients. *Archives of General Psychiatry*, *43*, 79–85. ▶ page 9

Kelley, H.H. (1967). Attribution in social psychology. *Nebraska Symposium on Motivation*, *15*, 192–238. ▶ page 47

Kerr, G. and Leith, L. (1993). Stress management and athletic performance. *Sport Psychologist*, *7*, 221–231. ▶ page 48

Kesey, K. (1962). *One Flew Over The Cuckoo's Nest*. New York: Viking. ▶ page 123

Kety, S.S. (1974). From rationalisation to reason. *American Journal of Psychiatry*, *131*, 957–963. ▶ page 126

Kiecolt-Glaser, J.K., Garner, W., Speicher, C.E., Penn, G.M., Holliday, J. and Glaser, R.(1984). Psychosocial modifiers of immunocompetence in medical students. *Psychosomatic Medicine*, *46*, 7–14. ▶ page 85

Klein, D.F., Zitrin, C.M., Woerner, M.G. and Ross, D.C. (1983). Treatment of phobias: II. Behavior therapy

and supportive psychotherapy: are there any specific ingredients? *Archives of General Psychiatry*, *40*, 139–145. ▶ page 23

Kohlberg, L. (1978). Revisions in the theory and practice of moral development. *Directions for Child Development*, *2*, 83–88. ▶ page 159

Kunzmann, U., Little, T.D. and Smith, J. (2000). Is age-related stability of subjective well-being a paradox? Cross-sectional and longitudinal evidence from the Berlin Aging Study. *Psychology and Aging*, *15*, 511–526. ▶ page 109

Kuyken, W. and Tsivrikos, D. (2009). Therapist competence, co-morbidity and cognitive-behavioral therapy for depression. *Psychotherapy and Psychosomatics*, *78*, 42–48. ▶ page 48

Laing, R.D. (1960). *The Divided Self: An Existential Study in Sanity and Madness*. London: Penguin Books. ▶ page 122

Laing, R.D. (1965). *The divided self*. Harmondsworth, Middlesex: Penguin. ▶ page 11

Lalancette, M.-F. and Standing, L.G (1990). Asch fails again. *Social Behavior and Personality*, *18*(1), 7–12. ▶ page 73

Langer, E J. and Rodin, J. (1976). The effects of choice and enhanced personal responsibility for the aged. A field experiment in an institutional setting. *Journal of Personality and Social Psychology*, *34*, 191–198. ▶ pages 104–109

Langer, E.J., Janis, I.L. and Wolfer, J.A. (1975). Reduction of psychological stress in surgical patients. *Journal of Experimental Social Psychology*, *11*, 155–165. ▶ page 104

Langlois, J.H. and Roggman, L.A. (1990). Attractive faces are only average. *Psychological Science*, *1*(2), 115–121. ▶ page 121

Langwieler, G. and Linden, M. (1993). Therapist individuality in the diagnosis and treatment of depression. *Journal of Affective Disorders*, *27*(1), 1–11. ▶ page 127

Larsen, K.S. (1974). Conformity and the Asch experiment. *Journal of Social Psychology*, *94*, 303–304. ▶ page 72

Lazarus, R.S. (1990). Theory-based stress measurement. *Psychological Inquiry*, *1*(1), 3–13. ▶ page 84

Leventhal, H., Watts, J.C. and Pagano, S. (1967). Affects of fear and instructions on how to cope with danger. *Journal of Personality and Social Psychology*, *6*(3), 331–321. ▶ page 145

Little, A.C., Apicella, C.L. and Marlowe, F.W. (2007). Preferences for symmetry in human faces in two cultures: data from the UK and the Hadza, an isolated group of hunter-gatherers. *Proceedings of Biological Science*, *274*, 3113–3117. ▶ page 120

Loftus, E. (1979). Reactions to blatantly contradictory information. *Memory and Cognition, 7,* 368–374. ▶ page 96

Loftus, E. (1996). *Eyewitness Testimony,* 2nd edn. Cambridge, MA: Harvard University Press. ▶ page 93

Loftus, E. and Ketcham, K. (1992). *Witness for the Defense: The Accused, the Eyewitness and the Expert Who Puts Memory on Trial,* 2nd edn. New York: St Martin's Press. ▶ page 93

Loftus, E. and Ketcham, K. (1996). *The Myth of Repressed Memory: False Memories and Allegations of Sexual Abuse,* 2nd edn. New York: St Martin's Press. ▶ page 93

Loftus, E. and Palmer, J.C. (1974). Reconstruction of automobile destruction: an example of the interaction between language and memory. *Journal of Verbal Learning and Verbal Behavior, 13,* 585–589. ▶ pages 92–97

Loftus, E. and Pickrell, J. (1995). The formation of false memories. *Psychiatric Annals, 25,* 720–725. ▶ page 97

Loftus, E. and Zanni, G. (1975). Eyewitness testimony: the influence of the wording of a question. *Bulletin of the Psychonomic Society, 5,* 86–88. ▶ page 96

Loftus, E., Miller, D.G. and Burns, H.J. (1978). Semantic integration of verbal information into visual memory. *Journal of Experimental Psychology, 4*(1), 19–31. ▶ page 96

Loftus, E.F., Loftus, G.R. and Messo, J. (1987). Some facts about 'weapon focus'. *Law and Human Behaviour, 11,* 55–62. ▶ page 54

Loftus, E.F., Loftus, G.R. and Messo, J. (1987). Some facts about 'weapon focus'. *Law and Human Behaviour, 11,* 55–62. ▶ page 144

Loring, M. and Powell, B. (1988). Gender, race, and *DSM-III:* a study of the objectivity of psychiatric diagnostic behavior. *Journal of Health and Social Behavior, 29*(1), 1–22. ▶ page 127

Lycett, J.E. and Dunbar, R.I.M. (2000). Mobile phones as lekking devices among human males, *Human Nature, 11*(1), 93–104. ▶ page xii

MacKinnon, D. (1938) Violations of prohibitions. In H.A. Murray (ed.) *Explorations in Personality.* New York: Oxford University Press. ▶ page 39

Maguire, E.A., Gadian, D.G., Johnsrude I.S., Good, C.D., Ashburner, J., Frackowiak, R.S.J. and Frith, C.D. (2000). Navigation-related structural change in the hippocampi of taxi drivers. *Proceedings of the National Academy of Science USA, 97,* 4398–4403. ▶ page 12

Mandel, D.R. (1998). The obedience alibi: Milgram's account of the Holocaust reconsidered. *Analyse and Kritik: Zeitschrift für Sozialwissenschaften, 20,* 74–94. ▶ page 79

Manstead, A.R. and McCulloch, C. (1981). Sex-role stereotyping in British television advertisements. *British Journal of Social Psychology, 20,* 171–80. ▶ page 162

Marshall, J. (1969). *Law and Psychology in Conflict.* New York: Anchor Books. ▶ page 92

Masserman, J.H. (1943). *Behaviour and neurosis.* Chicago: University of Chicago Press. ▶ page 22

Mayberg, H.S., Lozano, A.M., Voon, V., McNeely, H.E., Seminowicz, D., Hamani, C., Schwalb, J.M. and Kennedy, S.H. (2005). Deep brain stimulation for treatment-resistant depression. *Neuron, 45*(5), 651–660. ▶ page 7

McArthur, L.Z. (1972). The how and what of why: some determinants and consequences of causal attribution. *Journal of Personality and Social Psychology, 22,* 171–193. ▶ page 47

McGrath, T., Tsui, E., Humphries, S. and Yule, W. (1990). Successful treatment of a noise phobia in a nine-year-old girl with systematic desensitization in vivo. *Educational Psychology, 10,* 79–83. ▶ page 23

McNally, R.J. (1987). Preparedness and phobias: a review. *Psychological Bulletin, 101,* 283–303. ▶ page 91

McNally, R.J. and Reiss, S. (1982). The preparedness theory of phobias: the effects of initial fear level on safety-signal conditioning to fear-relevant stimuli. *Psychophysiology, 21*(6), 647–652. ▶ page 90

Meichenbaum, D. (1977). Cognitive-behaviour modification: an integrative approach. New York: Plenum Press. ▶ page 48

Meichenbaum, D. (1985). *Stress inoculation training.* New York: Pergamon. ▶ page 49

Menzies, R.G. and Clarke, J.C. (1993). A comparison of in vivo and vicarious exposure in the treatment of childhood water phobia. *Behaviour Research and Therapy, 31*(1), 9–15. ▶ page 22

Merckelbach, H., van den Hout, M.A. and van der Molen, G.M. (1987). Fear of animals: correlations between fear ratings and perceived characteristics. *Psychological Reports, 60,* 1203–1209. ▶ page 90

Middlemist, D.R., Knowles, E.S. and Matter, C.F. (1976). Personal space invasions in the lavatory: suggestive evidence for arousal. *Journal of Personality and Social Psychology, 33,* 541–546. ▶ page 143

Milgram, S. (1963) Behavioural study of obedience. *Journal of Abnormal and Social Psychology, 67,* 371–378. ▶ pages 74–79

Milgram, S. (1974). *Obedience to Authority: An Experimental View.* New York: Harper & Row. ▶ pages 78, 79

Miller, N.E. (1978). Biofeedback and visceral learning. *Annual Review of Psychology, 29,* 421–452. ▶ page 21

Mineka, S. and Cook, M. (1986). Immunisation against the observational conditioning of snake fear in rhesus monkeys. *Journal of Abnormal Psychology, 95*(4), 307–318. ▶ page 91

Mineka, S., Keir, R. and Price, V. (1980). Fear of snakes in wild- and laboratory-reared rhesus monkeys. *Animal learning and Behaviour, 8,* 653–663. ▶ page 86

Moos, R.H. and Swindle, R.W. Jnr. (1990). Stressful life circumstances: concepts and measures. *Stress medicine, 6,* 171–178. ▶ page 84

Morgan, L.C. (1894). *Introduction to comparative psychology.* London: Walter Scott Limited. ▶ page 101

Neto, F. (1995). Conformity and independence revisited. *Social Behavior and Personality, 23*(3), 217–222. ▶ page 72

Nicholson, N., Cole, S. and Rocklin, T. (1985). Conformity in the Asch situation: a comparison between contemporary British and US Students. *British Journal of Social Psychology, 24,* 59–63. ▶ page 73

Nisbett, R.E., Caputo, C., Legant, P. and Marecek, J. (1973). Behaviour as seen by the actor and as seen by the observer. *Journal of Personality and Social Psychology, 27,* 154–164. ▶ page 47

Öhman, A. (2000). Fear and anxiety: evolutionary, cognitive and clinical perspectives. In M. Lewis and J. M. Haviland-Jones (eds) *Handbook of Emotions* (2nd edn). New York: Guilford, pp. 573–593. ▶ page 90

Orne, M.T. (1962). On the social psychology of the psychological experiment: With particular reference to demand characteristics and their implications. *American Psychologist, 17,* 776–783 ▶ page 143

Orne, M.T. and Holland, C.C. (1968). On the ecological validity of laboratory deceptions. *International Journal of Psychitary, 6*(4), 282–293. ▶ page 78

Pajares, F. (2004). Albert Bandura: biographical sketch. Available at: http://des.emory.edu/mfp/bandurabio.html. ▶ page 18

Perrin, S. and Spencer, C. (1980). The Asch effect: a child of its times? *Bulletin of the British Psychological Society, 32,* 405–406. ▶ page 72

Perrin, S. and Spencer, C.P. (1981). Independence or conformity in the Asch experiment as a reflection of cultural and situational factors. *British journal of Social Psychology, 20*(3), 205–209. ▶ page 72

Peterson, L. R. and Peterson, M.J. (1959). Short-term retention of individual verbal items. *Journal of Experimental Psychology, 58,* 193–198. ▶ page 145

Piaget, J. (1970). Piaget's theory. In P.H. Mussen (ed.) *Carmichael's Manual of Child Psychology*, vol. 1. New York: Wiley. ▶ page 52

Pickworth Farrow, E. (1942). *A Practical Method of Self-Analysis*. London: George Allen and Unwin. ▶ page 37

Piliavin, I.M., Rodin, J. and Piliavin, J.A. (1969). Good Samaritanism: an underground phenomenon. *Journal of Personality and Social Psychology*, *13*, 1200–1213. ▶ page 107

Piliavin, I.M., Rodin, J. and Piliavin, J.A. (1969). Good Samaritanism: an underground phenomenon. *Journal of Personality and Social Psychology*, *13*, 1200–1213. ▶ page 143

Pole, N. and Jones, E.E. (1998). The talking cure revisited: content analysis of a two-year psychodynmaic therapy. *Psychotherapy Research*, *8*, 171–189. ▶ page 37

Popper, K. (1935). *Logik der Forschung*. Julius Springer Verlag, Vienna. Translated 1959 as *The Logic of Scientific Discovery*. London: Hutchinson. ▶ page 39

Premack, D. and Premack, A.J. (1966). *The Mind of an Ape*. New York: Norton. ▶ page 98

Rahe, R.H., Mahan, J.L. and Arthur, R.J. (1970). Prediction of near-future health-change from subjects' preceding life changes. *Journal of Psychosomatic Research*, *14*, 401–406. ▶ pages 80–85

Rahe, R.H., Meyer, M., Smith, M., Kjaer, G. and Holmes, T.H. (1964). Social stress and illness onset. *Journal of Psychosomatic Research*, *8*, 35–44. ▶ page 80

Raine, A., Buchsbaum, M.and LaCasse, L. (1997). Brain abnormalities in murderers indicated by positron emission tomography. *Biological Psychiatry*, *42*(6), 495–508. ▶ page 12

Rank, S.G. and Jacobson, C.K. (1977). Hospital nurses' compliance with medication overdose orders: a failure to replicate. *Journal of Health and Social Behavior*, *18*(2), 188–193. ▶ page 79

Regan, M. and Howard, R. (1995). Fear conditioning, preparedness and the contingent negative variation. *Psychophysiology*, *32*(3), 208–214. ▶ page 91

Rodin, J. and Langer, E.J. (1977). Long-term effects of a control-relevant intervention with the institutionalized aged. *Journal of Personality and Social Psychology*, *35*(12), 897–902. ▶ page 105

Roethlisberger, F.J., and Dickson, W.J. (1939). *Management and the Worker: an Account of a Research Program Conducted by the Western Electric Company, Hawthorne Works, Chicago*. Cambridge, MA: Harvard University Press. ▶ page 145

Rolls, G. (2005). *Classic Case Studies in Psychology*. London: Hodder and Stoughton. ▶ page 67

Rosenhan, D.L. (1973). On being sane in insane places. *Science*, *179*, 250–258. ▶ pages 122–127

Rosenthal, R. (1966). *Experimenter Effects in Behaviour Research*. New York: Appleton. ▶ page 141

Ross, L., Greene, D. and House, P. (1977). The false consensus phenomenon: an attributional bias in self-perception and social perception processes. *Journal of Experimental Social Psychology*, *13*, 279–301. ▶ page 46

Rotter, J.B. (1966). Generalised expectancies of internal versus external control of reinforcements. *Psychological Monographs*, *80* (whole no.609). ▶ page 104

Rubin, R.T., Gunderson, E.K.E. and Arthur, R.J. (1972). Life stress and illness patterns in the US Navy. *Psychosomatic Medicine*, *34*, 533–547. ▶ page 82

Sabbatini, R.M.E. (1997). The history of psychosurgery. Available at: http://www.cerebromente.org.br/n02/historia/psicocirg_i.htm. ▶ page 6

SANE (2009) Medical methods of treatment. Available at: http://www.sane.org.uk/AboutMentalIllness/MedicalTreatments. ▶ page 8

Sarbin, T.R. and Mancuso, J.C. (1980). *Schizophrenia: Medical Diagnosis or Moral Verdict?* New York: Praeger. ▶ page 127

Savage-Rumbaugh, S., McDonald, K., Sevcik, R.A., Hopkins, W.D. and Rupert, E. (1986). Spontaneous symbol acquisition and communicative use by Pygmy Chimpanzees (*Pan paniscus*). *Journal of Experimental Psychology*, *115*(3), 211–235. ▶ page 103

Savell, K.S. (1991). Leisure, perceptions of control and well-being: implications for the institutionalised elderly. *Therapeutic Recreation Journal*, *25*(3), 44–59. ▶ page 109

Schellenberg, E.G. (2004). Music lessons enhance IQ. *Psychological Science*, *15*, 511–514. ▶ page 147

Schneirla, T.C. (1965). Aspects of stimulation and organization in approach/withdrawal processes underlying vertebrate behavioral development. In D.S. Lehrman, R. Hinde and E. Shaw (eds) *Advances in the Study of Behavior*. New York: Academic Press. ▶ page 89

Schulz, R. (1976). Effects of control and predictability on the physical and psychological well-being of the institutionalized aged. *Journal of Personality and Social Psychology*, *33*, 563–573. ▶ page 109

Schunk, D.H. (1983). Reward contingencies and the development of children's skills and self-efficacy. *Journal of Educational Psychology*, *75*, 511–518. ▶ page 145

Schwartz, A.N., Campos, J.J. and Baisel, E.J. Jr. (1973). The visual cliff: cardiac and behavioral responses on the deep and shallow sides at five and nine months of age. *Journal of Experimental Child Psychology*, *15*(1), 86–99. ▶ page 114

Seckel, A.L. (2004). *Incredible Visual Illusions: You Won't Believe your Eyes!* London: Arcturus Publishing Ltd. ▶ page 111

Seligman, M.E.P. (1971). Phobias and preparedness. *Behaviour Therapy*, *2*, 307–320. ▶ pages 86, 90

Seligman, M.E.P. (1975). *Helplessness*. San Francisco: Freeman. ▶ page 104

Selye, H. (1936). A syndrome produced by diverse nocuous agents. *Nature*, *138*, 32. ▶ pages 4, 5

Selye, H. (1950). *Stress*. Montreal: Acta. ▶ page 4

Sheridan, C.L. and King, K.G. (1972). Obedience to authority with an authentic victim. *Proceedings of the 80th Annual Convention of the American Psychological Association*, *7*, 165–166. ▶ page 78

Sherif, M. (1935). A study of some factors in perception. *Archives of Psychology*, *27*(187), 1–60. ▶ page 68, 72

Singh, D. (1993). Adaptive significance of female physical attractiveness: role of waist-to-hip ratio. *Journal of Personality and Social Psychology*, *65*, 293–307. ▶ page 120

Skinner, B.F. (1938). *Science and behaviour*. New York: Macmillan. ▶ pages ix, 17

Skinner, B.F. (1948). *Walden Two*. London and New York: Macmillan. ▶ page 25

Skinner, B.F. (1954). The science of learning and the art of teaching. *Harvard Educational Review*, *24*(2), 86–97. ▶ page 24

Slater, L. (2004). *Opening Skinner's Box: Great Psychological Experiments of the Twentieth Century*. New York: Norton. ▶ pages 67, 93, 123, 124, 126

Smith, J.W. (1988). Long term outcome of clients treated in a commercial stop smoking program. *Journal of Substance Abuse Treatment*, *5*, 33–36. ▶ page 21

Smith, J.W., Frawley, P.J. and Polissar, L. (1997). Six- and twelve-month abstinence rates in inpatient alcoholics treated with either faradic aversion or chemical aversion compared with matched inpatients from a treatment registry. *Journal of Addictive Diseases*, *16*(1), 5–24. ▶ page 21

Smith, P. and Bond, M.H. (1998). *Social Psychology Across Cultures: Analysis and Perspectives*, 2nd edition. New York: Harvester Wheatsheaf. ▶ page 72

Solms, M. (2000). Freudian dream theory today. *The Psychologist, 13*(12), 618–619. ▶ page 35

Sorce, J. F., Ernde, R. N., Campos, J. and Klinnert, M.D. (1985). Maternal emotional signaling: its effect on the visual cliff behavior of 1–year-olds. *Developmental Psychology, 21*(1), 195–200. ▶ page 114

Spitzer, R.L. (1976). More on pseudoscience in science and the case of the psychiatric diagnosis: a critique of D.L. Rosenhan's 'On being sane in insane places'. *General Psychiatry, 33*, 459–470.

Spitzer R. L., Lilienfeld 5.0. and Miller M.B. (2005). Rosenhan revisited: The scientific credibility of Lauren Slater's pseudopatient diagnosis study. *Journal of Nervous and Mental Disease* 193 (11), 734-739. Available at http://www.ncbi.nlm.nih.gov/pubmed/16260927. ▶ page 126

Sternberg, R.J. (1995). *In Search of the Human Mind*. Fort Worth TX: Harcourt Brace. ▶ pages 20, 23

Storms, M.D. and Nisbett, R.E. (1970). Insomnia and the attribution process. *Journal of Personality and Social Psychology, 16*, 319–328. ▶ page 46

Stotland, E. and Blumenthal, A. (1964). The reduction of anxiety as a result of the expectation of making a choice. *Canadian Review of Psychology, 18*, 139–145. ▶ page 104

Suls, J. and Mullen, B. (1981). Life events, perceived control, and illness: the role of uncertainty. *Journal of Human Stress, 7*, 30–34. ▶ page 108

Symons, D. (1979). *The Evolution of Human Sexuality*. Oxford: Oxford University Press. ▶ page 116

Szasz, T.S. (1960). *The Myth of Mental Illness*. London: Paladin. ▶ page 122

Taylor, S.E., Klein, L.C., Lewis, B.P., Grunewald, T.L., Gurung, R.A.R. and Updegraff, J.A. (2000). Biobehavioral responses to stress in females: tend-and-befriend, not fight-or-flight. *Psychological Review, 107*(3), 411–429. ▶ page 11

Terrace, H.S. (1979). *Nim*. New York: Alfred A. Knopf. ▶ page 102

Trivers, R.L. (1972). Parental investment and sexual selection. In B. Campbell (ed.) *Sexual Selection and the Descent of Man*. Chicago: Aldine. ▶ page 116

Tschuschke, V., Anbeh, T. and Kiencke. P. (2007). Evaluation of long-term analytic outpatient group therapies. *Group Analysis, 40*(1), 140–159. ▶ page 37

Tulving, E. and Psotka, J. (1971). Retroactive inhibition in free recall: inaccessibility of information available in the memory store. *Journal of Experimental Psychology, 87*, 1–8. ▶ page 52

Van Cantfort, T.E. (2002). *Beatrix Gardner (1933–1995): her contributions to developmental psychobiology*. Paper presented at the First Annual Sandhills Regional Psychology Conference, Fayetteville, NC, 23 March 2002. Published online at: http://faculty.uncfsu.edu/tvancantfort/REPRINTS/BTGardner/Trixie%20Gardner3a.pdf. ▶ page 100

Veitch, R. and Griffitt, W. (1976). Good news, bad news: affective and interpersonal effects. *Journal of Applied Social Psychology, 6*, 69–75. ▶ page 145

Viguera, A.C., Nonacs, R., Cohen, L.S., Tondo, L., Murray, A. and Baldessarini, R.J. (2000). Risk of recurrence of bipolar disorder in pregnant and nonpregant women after discontinuing lithium maintenance. *American Journal of Psychiatry, 157*, 179–184. ▶ page 10

Wampold, B.E., Minami, T., Baskin, T.W. and Tierney, S.C. (2002). A meta-(re)analysis of the effects of cognitive therapy versus 'other therapies' for depression. *Journal of Affective Disorders, 68*, 159–165. ▶ page 48

Waynforth, D. and Dunbar, R.I.M. (1995). Conditional mate choice strategies in humans: evidence from 'lonely hearts' advertisements. *Behaviour, 132*, 755–779. ▶ page 120

Whaley, A.L. (2001). Cultural mistrust and clinical diagnosis of paranoid schizophrenia in African-American patients. *Journal of Psychopathology and Behavioral Assessment, 23*, 93–100. ▶ page 127

Williams, G.C. (1975). *Sex and Evolution*. Princeton: Princeton University Press. ▶ page 116

Williams, T.M. (1985) Implications of a natural experiment in the developed world for research on television in the developing world. *Journal of Cross Cultural Psychology, 16*(3), Special issue, 263–287. ▶ page 147

Witherington, D.C., Campos, J.J., Anderson, D.I., Lejeune, L. and Seah, E. (2005). Avoidance of heights on the visual cliff in newly walking infants. *Infancy, 7*, 285–298. ▶ page 114

Wolpe, J. (1958). *Psychotherapy by Reciprocal Inhibition*. Stanford, CA: Stanford University Press. ▶ pages 22, 25

Wolpe, J. (1973). *The Practice of Behaviour Therapy*. NY: Pergamon Press. ▶ page 25

Wurm, S., Tesch-Römer, C. and Tomasik, M.J. (2007). Longitudinal findings on aging-related cognitions, control beliefs, and health in later life. *The Journals of Gerontology Series B: Psychological Sciences and Social Sciences, 62*, 156–164. ▶ page 109

Yerkes, R.M. (1943). *Chimpanzees*. New Haven: Yale University Press. ▶ page 98

Yonas, A., Granrud, C., Arterberry, M. and Hanson, B. (1986). Distance perception from linear perspective and texture gradients. *Infant Behaviour and Development, 9*, 247–256. ▶ page 115

Yuille, J.C. and Cutshall, J.L. (1986). A case study of eyewitness testimony of a crime. *Journal of Applied Psychology, 71*, 291–301. ▶ page 96

Zimbardo, P.G., Banks, P.G., Haney, C. and Jaffe, D. (1973) *Pirandellian prison: the mind is a formidable jailor*. New York Times Magazine, 8 April, 38–60. ▶ pages 134, 143

Zuckerman, M. (1994). *Behavioral expressions and biosocial bases of sensation seeking*. New York: Cambridge University Press. ▶ page 161

Glossary/Index

Deep brain stimulation (DBS) A form of psychosurgery that requires no destruction of tissue. Electrical currents are passed via wires inserted in the brain to interrupt target circuits. 7, 14

Defence mechanism *See* Ego defence mechanism

Dehoax 75, 76

Demand characteristic A cue that makes participants unconsciously aware of the aims of a study or how the researchers expect the participants to behave. This may act as an extaneous variable. 26, 27, 28, 54, 56, 78, 140, 141, 143, 144, 146, 166

Dement, W. & Kleitman, N. 12

Dendrites 3

Denial In psychoanalytic theory, a form of ego defence whereby the ego simply denies the existence of something that is threatening. 33

Dependent variable (DV) A measurable outcome of the action of the independent variable in an experiment. 26, 136, 138, 140, 144, 146, 152, 153, 158

Depersonalisation 125

Depression A mental illness characterised by a lowering of mood, often accompanied by disorders of thinking and concentration, feelings of anxiety, and disturbances of sleep and appetite. x, 4, 6–8, 9, 14, 15, 52, 104, 126, 135

Depth perception 110–105, 129

Descriptive statistics Methods of summarising a data set such as mean, median, mode and range, as well as the use of graphs. 150, 151

Desensitisation hierarchy 22, 28

Determinist The view that an individual's behaviour is shaped or controlled by internal or external forces rather than an individual's will to do something (i.e. free will). x, 10, 14, 25, 28, 39, 42, 53, 56

Developmental psychology 52, 104–115

Diagnostic and Statistical Manual (DSM) This is a classification system of mental disorders published by the American Psychiatric Association. It contains typical symptoms of each disorder and guidelines for clinicians to make a diagnosis. The most recent version is *DSM-IV-TR*. 122, 127

Difference studies 146

Direct reinforcement 17, 18, 19

Discrepancy principle 89, 128

Displacement In psychoanalytic theory, a form of ego defence whereby the ego shifts impulses from an unacceptable target to a more acceptable or less threatening one in order to relieve anxiety. Also an element of dreamwork where the emotional or latent content of the dream is attached to something different in order to disguise its content. 31, 34, 42, 98

Dispositional attribution In attribution theory, accounting for an individual's behaviour in terms of their personality or disposition. 46, 47

Dispositional factors 46, 74, 77

Disputing 51, 56

Distinctiveness 47, 56

Distortion In psychoanalytic theory, a form of ego defence whereby the ego reshapes external reality so that it matches internal needs. 33, 129

Dizygotic twins Non-identical twins formed from two fertilised (or zygotes). 13

Dopamine A neurotransmitter produced in the brain, involved in sexual desire and the sensation of pleasure. Unusually high levels of dopamine are associated with schizophrenia. 3, 8, 9, 10, 14, 15

Double blind Neither the participant nor the experimenter is aware of the research aims and other important details, and thus have no expectations. 141, 166

Dream analysis Techniques developed by Freud to transform the manifest content of a dream back to its latent meanings. These techniques include free association and reversing the processes of dreamwork. 34–35, 36, 41, 42

Dreamwork In psychoanalysis, the processes that transform the latent content of a dream into manifest content. 34, 42

Drug therapy 8

DSM *See* Diagnostic and Statistical Manual

Dully, Howard 7

DV *See* Dependent variable

DZ twins *See* Dizygotic twins

Ecological validity A form of external validity; the ability to generalise a research effect beyond the particular setting in which it is demonstrated, to other settings. Ecological validity is established by representativeness (mundane realism) and generalisability (to other settings). 26, 54, 78, 96, 140, 154, 162

ECT *See* Electroconvulsive therapy

EEA *See* Environment of evolutionary adaption

EEG *See* Electroencephalogram

Ego Part of Freud's conception of the structure of the personality, the ego is driven by the reality principle, which makes the individual accommodate to the demands of the environment. 31–35, 38, 42

Ego defence mechanisms In psychoanalytic theory, the strategies used by the ego to defend itself against anxiety, such as repression, denial and projection. 31, 33

Ego strength The extent to which the ego can deal effectively with the demands of the id, superego and reality. 32

Electroconvulsive therapy (ECT) The administration of a controlled electrical current through electrodes placed on the scalp. The current induces a convulsive seizure which can be effective in relieving severe depression. 20, 123

Electroencephalogram (EEG) A method of detecting activity in the living brain, electrodes are attached to a person's scalp to record general levels of electrical activity. 12

ELIZA 103

Ellis, A. 48, 50–51

Empiricists The view that all knowledge is gained through direct experience i.e. learned. This is contrasted with the nativist view. xii, 110

Environment of evolutionary adaptation (EEA) The environment to which a species is adapted and the set of selection pressures that operated at this time. For humans, this is thought to be the African savannah approximately two million years ago. 86, 90, 116

ERP *See* Exposure and Response Prevention

Ethical committee A group of people within a research institution that must approve a study before it begins. 78, 108

Ethical issues An ethical issue arises in research where there are conflicting sets of values concerning the goals, procedures or outcomes of a research study. 27, 28, 66, 72, 78, 84, 90, 96, 102, 108, 114, 120, 126, 135, 136, 142–144, 154, 160–161, 166

Ethologist A scientific discipline where researchers seek to study and understand behaviour through the use of naturalistic observation. 100

EV *See* Extraneous variable

Evans, P. 85

Event sampling An observational technique in which a count is kept of the number of times a certain behaviour (event) occurs. 153

Evolutionary approach Explains behaviour in terms of its adaptive value. Any behaviour that is perpetuated must have been naturally selected and thus at some time was adaptive. 86, 113, 116, 118, 121, 130

Evolutionary psychology An approach in psychology which aims to explain human behaviour in terms of the theory of evolution (e.g. natural and sexual selection). 86

EWT *See* Eyewitness testimony

Exhaustion 4, 14, 15

Expectancy bias 91

Expectancies of future outcomes A concept in social learning theory; observational learning and vicarious reinforcement lead an individual to form expectations about the consequences of imitating observed behaviours in the future. 17, 18, 28

Experiment Any study where one variable (the independent variable, IV) is deliberately manipulated to observe the effect on another variable (the dependent variable, DV). Only studies with an IV and DV can be called experiments. 24, 25, 26, 28, 54, 56, 72, 108, 136–137, 164

Experimental group The group (in an independent groups design) receiving the independent variable. 84, 94, 105, 108

Experimental validity A form of internal validity, the degree to which the observed effect was due to the experimental manipulation

pleasure principle – an innate drive to seek immediate satisfaction. 31, 32, 34

Idiographic An approach to research that focuses more on the individual case as a means of understanding behaviour than looking at general behaviour and formulating general laws of behaviour (the nomothetic approach). x, 11, 25, 39, 40, 42, 53, 56, 62, 63, 80

Immune system A system of cells within the body that is concerned with fighting against 'intruders' such as viruses and bacteria. White blood cells (leucocytes) identify and eliminate foreign bodies (antigens). 4, 5, 15, 85

In vitro **desensitisation** *See* Covert desensitisation.

In vivo **desensitisation** Using principles of systematic desensitisation where a patient has direct experience of the hierarchy of situations from least to most fearful (as distinct from covert desensitisation). 22, 28

Independent groups design An experimental design where participants are allocated to two (or more) groups, each one receiving a different treatment. 95, 137, 141, 145, 157, 166

Independent variable (IV) An event that is directly manipulated by an experimenter in order to test its effect on another variable – the dependent variable (DV). 26, 136, 138, 144, 146

Indirect reinforcement ix, 19

Individual differences The differences between individuals in terms of, for example, gender, culture, personality, intelligence, mental health and so on. 116–127

Individualist A culture that values independence rather than reliance on others, in contrast to many non-Western cultures that could be described as collectivist. 46, 72

Inferential statistics Procedures (statistical tests) for making inferences about the population from which samples are drawn. 151

Informed consent An informed decision to participate in research based on comprehensive information given to potential participants about the nature and purpose of the research and their role in it. 28, 66, 84, 96, 108, 136, 142, 143, 154, 166

Innate Behaviours that are a product of genetic factors. These may be apparent at birth or appear later through the process of maturation. xi, 18, 20, 24, 25, 32, 38, 39, 42, 60, 90, 110, 112-3, 114, 128, 129

Instrumental conditioning/ learning Another term for operant conditioning. 99, 101

Intelligence x, 3, 13, 53, 110, 116, 146, 165

Inter-interviewer reliability The extent to which there is agreement between two or more interviewers in the answers they elicit from interviewees. 160

Inter-observer reliability The extent to which there is agreement between two or more observers involved in observations of a behaviour. 154, 165

Inter-rater reliability The extent to which there is agreement between two or more raters involved in rating of a behaviour. 127

Interactionists The view that development is determined by a mixture of innate and experiential factors, an interaction between nature and nurture. 110

Interchangability 98

Internal reliability A measure of the extent to which something is consistent with itself. For a psychological test to have high internal reliability, all test items should be measuring the same thing. 160–161, 165

Internal validity Whether a study has tested what it set out to test. 140, 154, 160, 165

Interval data A level of measurement where units of equal intervals are used, such as when counting correct answers or using any 'public' unit of measurement. 150, 151

Intervening variable A variable that comes between two other variables that is used to explain the relationship between those two variables. 84, 149

Interview A research method or technique that involves a face-to-face, 'real-time' interaction with another individual and results in the collection of data. 159, 164

Interviewer bias The effect of an interviewer's expectations, communicated unconsciously, on a respondent's behaviour. 41, 42, 156, 161, 165, 166

Investigator effect Anything that the investigator does which has an effect on a participant's performance in a study, other than what was expected. 141, 146, 166

Issues x

IV *See* Independent variable

Jenness, A. 68, 72, 128

Kanzi 100, 103
Kelley, H.H. 46, 47, 56

Lab experiment An experiment carried out in a controlled setting. Lab experiments tend to demonstrate high experimental (internal) validity and low ecological (external) validity, though this isn't always true. 26, 40, 54, 96, 137, 144–145

Laing, R.D. 11
Langer, E.J. & Rodin, J. 104–109, 129
Language acquisition device (LAD) 98

Latency stage In psychoanalytic theory, the fourth stage of psychosexual development which occurs between the age of 6 and the onset of puberty. During this stage little psychosexual development takes place. The focus is mainly on social development through peer interactions. 32

Latent content According to Freud, the hidden and 'real' meaning of a dream. 34, 35, 42

Leading question A question that, either by its form or content, suggests

what answer is desired or leads the respondent to the desired answer. 40, 54, 92, 94, 129, 141, 160, 165–166

Learned helplessness Occurs when an animal finds that its responses are ineffective, and then it learns that there is no point in responding and behaves passively in future. 104

Libido In psychoanalytic theory, the psychological energy or life force associated with the id. At each stage of psychosexual development, the libido becomes focused on a part of the body. 32, 39

Lie scale A set of questions in a questionnaire or interview to determine the extent to which the participant's answers are truthful, such as asking the person whether they are always truthful – anyone who answers 'yes' is lying and their answers in general may be untruthful. 160

Life change units (LCUs) 80, 82
Life changes 80, 83, 84, 108
Life events 79, 80, 84, 123
Linear correlation 82, 128, 148
Little Hans 32, 40, 41, 163
Lobotomy *See* Prefrontal lobotomy

Locus of control An aspect of our personality; people differ in their beliefs about whether the outcomes of their actions depend on what they do (internal control) or on events outside their personal control (external control). 73, 104

Loftus, E. & Palmer, J.C. 92–97, 129
Loftus, E. & Zanni, G. 96
Loftus, E. 54
Lonely hearts advertisements 120
Long-term memory 45

Longitudinal study Observation of behaviour over a long period of time, possibly looking at the effects of age on a particular behaviour (such as moral development) by repeatedly testing/interviewing a group of participants at regular intervals. 162, 163

Loulis 102

Maguire, E.A. 12
Manic depression 10

Manifest content The content of a dream that is recalled by a dreamer which, according to Freud, disguises the latent content. 34, 35

Masserman, J.H. 22

Matched pairs design An experimental design where pairs of participants are matched in terms of key variables such as age and IQ. One member of each pair is placed in the experimental group and the other member in the control group. 137, 141, 166

Mean The arithmetic average of a group of scores, taking the values of all the data into account. 87

Mechanistic approach 53

Median The middle value in a set of scores when they are placed in rank order. 66, 82, 150, 151, 166, 169, 170

Mediational processes 52, 56
Medical model 122, 130
Meichenbaum, D. 48, 49

Meta-analysis A researcher looks at the findings from a number of different studies in order to reach a general conclusion about a particular hypothesis. 51, 162

Milgram, S. 74–79, 128

Mineka, S. 86

Mode The most frequently occurring score in a data set. 66, 150, 166

Modelling The process of imitating another's behaviour. 19, 22, 26, 48, 49, 56

Models 17

Monozygotic Identical twins formed from one fertilised egg (or zygote). 13

Motion parallax As we move, objects that are closer to us move farther across our field of vision than more distant objects, providing information about depth. 110–113, 114, 115, 129

MRI scan Magnetic resonance imaging, produces a three-dimensional image of the static brain which is very precise. A magnetic field causes the atoms of the brain to change their alignment when the magnet is on and emit various radio signals when the magnet is turned off. A detector reads the signals and uses them to map the structure of the brain. 7, 12, 14

Multistore model Explains memory in terms of three stores (sensory (SM), short-term (STM) and long-term (LTM)). The transfer of data can be explained in terms of attention (SM to STM) and rehearsal (STM to LTM). 45, 55

Mundane realism Refers to how a study mirrors the real word. The experimental environment is realistic to the degree to which experiences encountered in the experimental environment will occur in everyday life (the 'real world'). 138, 140, 144, 146, 166

Mustabatory thinking 50, 56

Myelin sheath A white fatty substance that protects the neuron and speeds up the transmission of messages along the length of the axon. 110

MZ twins See Monozygotic twins.

Nativists The view that development is determined by innate factors, that most abilities simply need fine tuning but do not depend on experience for their development. 110, 113

Natural experiment A research method in which the experimenter cannot manipulate the independent variable directly, but where it varies naturally, and the effect on a dependent variable can be observed. 109, 137, 146–147, 153, 173

Natural killer cells 85

Natural selection The major process that explains evolution whereby inherited traits that enhance an animal's survival and reproductive success are passed on to the next generation and are thus 'selected', whereas animals without such traits are less successful at survival and reproducing and their traits are not selected. 86, 116

Naturalistic observation A research method carried out in a naturalistic setting, in which the investigator does not interfere in any way, but merely observes the behaviour(s) in question (likely to involve the use of structured observations). 102, 126, 152, 153, 166

Nature Those aspects of behaviour that are innate and inherited. Nature does not simply refer to abilities present at birth but to any ability determined by genes, including those that appear through maturation. x, 3, 11, 13, 14, 25, 28, 38, 39, 42, 43, 53, 56, 57, 60, 129

Nature–nurture The discussion about whether behaviour is due to innate or environmental factors. Such a debate is no longer appropriate as it is now accepted that both contribute and interact in such a way that it is not a simple matter of saying that one or the other determines behaviour. 11, 13, 25, 38, 60, 62, 110

Nearness scale 87, 128

Negative correlation Describes a correlation where, as one covariable increases, the other decreases. 32, 88, 148

Negative reinforcement In operant conditioning, escape from an unpleasant situation increases the probability that a behaviour will be repeated i.e. reinforces the behaviour. 17, 19

Negative triad 49

Neural networks A system of highly interconnected neurons which means that the whole network behaves in a way that would not be predicted from the behaviour of individual neurons. 35

Neuron A specialised cell in the nervous system for transmission of information. x, 3, 8, 9, 14

Neurotransmitter Chemical substances, such as serotonin or dopamine, which play an important part in the workings of the nervous system by transmitting nerve impulses across a synapse. 3, 8, 10, 11, 14, 122

Neutral stimulus (NS) In classical conditioning, the stimulus that initially does not produce the target response i.e. it is neutral. Through association with the unconditioned stimulus (UCS), the NS acquires the properties of the UCS and becomes a conditioned stimulus producing a conditioned response. 17, 20, 22, 27

Nightmares 34

Nim Chimpsky 102–103

Nominal data A level of measurement where data are in separate categories. 150, 151

Nomothetic An approach to research that focuses more on general laws of behaviour than on the individual, possibly unique, case (the idiographic approach). x, 11, 62

Non-human animals 25, 110, 111, 112, 114, 177

Non-participant observation An observational study where the observer is not taking part on the activity being observed, and therefore should be more objective than when participating. 153, 166

Non-verbal behaviour Communication which is not linguistic, such as smiling or leaning towards someone. 41, 43, 153, 155

Noradrenaline A hormone associated with arousal of the autonomic nervous system (e.g. raised heart rate), and also a neurotransmitter. 9

NS See Neutral stimulus

Nurture Those aspects of behaviour that are acquired through experience i.e. learned from interactions with the physical and social environment. x, 11, 13, 25, 38, 53, 121

Obedience A type of social influence whereby someone acts in response to a direct order from a figure with perceived authority. 74, 76–77, 78–79, 128, 131, 141, 145

Observation 133, 152, 153, 162, 164, 166

Observational learning Learning through imitation. 17, 18, 86, 91 See also Social learning theory.

Observational techniques The application of systematic methods of observation in an observational study, experiment (to measure the DV) or other study. 152–155

Observer bias The tendency for observations to be influenced by expectations or prejudices. 47, 102, 154, 156, 162, 165, 166

Obsessive-compulsive disorder (OCD) An anxiety disorder where anxiety arises from both obsessions (persistent thoughts) and compulsions (means of controlling the obsessional thoughts). 6, 7, 10, 14, 23

OCD See Obsessive-compulsive disorder.

Oedipus complex Freud's explanation of how a boy resolves his love for his mother and feelings of rivalry towards his father by identifying with his father. Occurs during the phallic stage of psychosexual development. In Greek mythology Oedipus unknowingly killed his father and married his mother. 32, 40

Oestrogen A female sex hormone produced by the ovaries, and by the adrenal gland. 3, 121

Öhman, A. 90

Open question A question that invites respondents to provide their own answers rather than to select an answer that has been provided. Tends to produce qualitative data. 158, 164, 166

Operant conditioning Learning that occurs when we are reinforced (negative or positive) for doing something, which increases the probability that the behaviour in question will be repeated in the future. Conversely, if we are punished for behaving in a certain way, there is a decrease in the probability that the behaviour will recur. x, 17, 18, 19, 20, 23, 24, 25, 28, 86, 99, 102

Operationalised Providing variables in a form that can be easily tested i.e. the constituent operations are identified. 24, 28, 136, 140, 144, 146, 153

Opportunity sample A method of obtaining a sample where by selecting people who are most easily available at the time of the study. 156

Optic nerve Transmits electrical impulses from the retina to the brain. 110, 112

Oral stage In psychoanalytic theory, the first stage (0–18 months) of psychosexual development when the organ-focus is on the mouth. 32, 33

Ordinal data A level of measurement where data are ordered in some way. 150

Orne, M.T. & Holland, C. 78

Overt observation An observational technique where observations are 'open' i.e. the participants are aware that they are being observed. 153, 166

Parasympathetic branch Part of the autonomic nervous system (ANS) involved in the restoration of the body's relaxed state ('rest and digest') following sympathetic nervous system excitation ('fight or flight'). 3

Parental investment Any investment by a parent in an offspring that increases the chance that the offspring will survive but at the expense of that parent's ability to invest in any other offspring (alive or yet to be born). 116

Participant effect A general term used to acknowledge the fact that participants react to cues in an experimental situation, and that this may affect the validity of any conclusions drawn from the investigation. 144

Participant observation A kind of observational study where the observer is also a participant in the activity being observed. This may affect the objectivity of their observations. 153

Participant variable Characteristics of individual participants (such as age, intelligence, etc.) that might influence the outcome of a study. 141

Paternity probability The probability of whether the child being raised is actually the biological offspring of the male doing the raising. 116

Pavlov, I. 17, 25, 27

Penis envy A girl's recognition of not having a penis, and her desire to have one. Leads to a process similar to the resolution of the Oedipus complex. 32

Perception The process of extracting meaning from sensory data. 45, 52

PET scans Positron emission tomography, a brain scanning method used to study activity in the brain. Radioactive glucose is ingested and can be detected in the active areas of the brain. 12, 35

Phallic stage In psychoanalytic theory, the third stage of psychosexual development when the organ-focus is on the genitals. The child

aged 3–6 years becomes aware of gender issues and gender conflicts. The resolution of this conflict results in the development of a superego (see Oedipus conflict, penis envy). Unresolved conflicts may result in a poorly developed conscience, homosexuality, authority problems, and rejection of appropriate gender roles. A fixation at this stage results in the phallic personality type who is self-assured, vain and impulsive. 32, 33, 42

Phineas Gage 163

Phobias/Phobic disorders A group of mental disorders characterised by high levels of anxiety that, when experienced, interfere with normal living. Includes specific and social phobias. 22, 23, 24, 27, 90, 186–187

Physiological psychology 81–91

Piaget, J. 52

Pilot study A small-scale trial run of a study to test any aspects of the design, with a view to making improvements. 150, 160, 163

Placebo A drug or other form of treatment that contains no active ingredients or therapeutic procedure. In order to test the effectiveness of a treatment, one group is given the real treatment while a second group receives a placebo. Usually this is a double blind procedure so neither the researcher or the participant know whether they are receiving the placebo or not. 9

Pleasure principle In Freudian psychology, the id's primitive desire to seek instant gratification and avoid pain at all costs. 31, 42

Popper, K. 39

Population *See* Target population. 156, 166

Positive correlation Refers to when, in a correlation, covariables both increase together. 82, 108, 148

Positive reinforcement In operant conditioning, a reward increases the probability that a behaviour will be repeated i.e. reinforces the behaviour. 17, 24

Postsynaptic neuron The neuron that is receiving a message, after the synapse. 8

Powerlessness 125

Preconscious Consists of information and ideas that could be retrieved easily from memory and brought into consciousness. Freud distinguished three levels of mind: unconscious, preconscious (or subconscious) and conscious. In this sense the preconscious is that area of the mind through which material must pass before it reaches the conscious mind. 31

Prefrontal cortex The anterior part of the frontal lobe, involved in 'executive functions' such as complex cognitive behaviours, moderating socially-appropriate behaviours, personality and goal-directed behaviour (motivation). 6, 12

Prefrontal leucotomy An alternative term for prefrontal lobotomy, named after the tool (a leucotome) used to severe brain connections. 6–7, 123, 163

Prefrontal lobotomy A form of psychosurgery where connections to and from the prefrontal cortex are severed with the intention of alleviating the symptoms of severe mental disorder. 6, 14

Premack, D. & Premack, A.J. 98

Presynaptic neuron The neuron that is sending messages across a synapse. 8

Presynaptic vesicles In a neuron, a small bubble where neurotransmitters are stored ready to be released at a synapse. 3

Primary-process thought In Freudian theory, thinking that is not organised, is concrete and emotion-driven, visual rather than verbal and, above all, irrational. 34, 35, 42

Privacy The zone of inaccessibility Privacy mind or body and the trust that this will not be 'invaded'. A person's right to control a flow of information about themselves. 142, 143, 154, 161

Private acceptance Changing one's personal beliefs or thoughts. The fact that an individual goes along with the majority (i.e. conforms) in public, does not indicate that they have changed their private attitudes or beliefs. 68

Productivity 98, 103, 145

Projection In psychoanalytic theory, a form of ego defence whereby one unknowingly displaces one's own unacceptable feelings onto someone else. 31, 43

Protection from harm Steps taken to ensure that during a research study, participants do not experience negative physical or psychological effects, such as physical injury, lowered self-esteem or embarrassment, as a result of the research. 142, 143

Pseudopatients 122–124, 126–127, 130

Pseudoscience xii

Psychoactive drugs Drugs that alter one's mental processes. 6, 8, 10

Psychoanalysis A form of psychotherapy, originally developed by Sigmund Freud, that is intended to help patients become aware of long-repressed feelings and issues by using techniques such as free association and dream analysis. ix, 33, 34, 36, 37, 38, 41, 42

Psychodiagnostic labels 124

Psychodynamic approach Literally an approach that explains the dynamics of behaviour – what motivates a person. The approach has become synonymous with Freud's theory of personality. Freud suggested that unconscious forces and early experiences are the prime motivators. ix, xi, 31–44, 48, 56, 60, 175

Psychological harm For example, lowered self-esteem, embarrassment or changing a person's behaviour or attitudes. 66, 72, 78, 135, 142, 161, 166

Psychosexual stages In psychoanalytic theory, the developmental stages that are related to the id's changing focus on different parts of the body. 32, 33, 38, 39, 42

Psychosomatic Relating to both mind (psyche) and body (soma). 80

Psychosurgery Surgery that involves severing fibres or removing brain tissue with the intention of treating disturbed behaviour for which no physical cause can be demonstrated. Modern psychosurgery techniques, such as deep brain stimulation, do not involve permanent damage. 6, 8, 10, 55

Psychotherapy Any psychological form of treatment for a mental disorder, as distinct from physical forms of treatment. 20, 23, 37

Psychotic A loss of contact with reality, consistent with serious mental illness, which typically includes delusions, hallucinations and disordered thinking. 8, 14, 126

Public compliance Publicly acting in accordance with the wishes or actions of others. 68

Punishment In operant conditioning, the application of an unpleasant stimulus such that the likelihood of the behaviour that led to it reoccurring is decreased. 17, 18, 25

Qualitative Data that expresses the 'quality' of things involving descriptions, words, meanings, pictures, texts and so on. Qualitative data cannot be counted or quantified but can be turned into quantitative data by placing them in categories. 37, 40, 41, 42, 55, 56, 66, 67, 150, 158, 162, 164, 166

Qualitative analysis Summarising qualitative data, for example by identifying themes and interpreting the meaning of an experience to the individual(s) concerned. 40, 55, 162, 164

Qualitative content analysis When conducting a content analysis the examples in each category are described rather than counted. 162

Quantitative Data that represent how much or how long, or how many, etc. there are of something, i.e. a behaviour is measured in numbers or quantities. 67, 150, 158, 162, 164, 166

Quantitative analysis Any means of representing trends from numerical data, such as averages (mean, median, mode or range). 162

Quantitative content analysis When conducting a content analysis the examples in each category are counted rather than described. 40, 55, 162

Quasi-experiments Studies (such as a natural experiment) that are 'almost' experiments but lack one or more features of a true experiment, such as full experimenter control over the IV or random allocation of participants to conditions. Quasi-experiments cannot therefore claim to demonstrate causal relationships. 146–147

Questionnaire Data is collected through the use of written questions. 87, 90, 105, 106, 117, 158, 160, 164

Quota sample A method of obtaining a representative sample where groups of participants are selected according to their frequency in the population. Within each group, individuals are selected using opportunity sampling. 156, 169

Radical behaviourists 24

Rahe, R.H., Mahan, J.M. & Arthur, R.J. 80–85, 128

Random allocation Allocating participants to experimental groups or conditions using random techniques. 146, 157

Random sample A method of obtaining a representative sample where a group of participants are selected using a random technique in such a way that every member of the target population has an equal chance of being selected. 156–157

Random technique Any technique in which there is no systematic attempt to influence the selection or distribution of the items. 157

Randomness 157

Range The difference between the highest and lowest score in a data set. 150, 151, 157, 164, 166, 169

Rapid eye movement (REM) sleep A kind of sleep when the body is paralysed except for the eyes. REM sleep is often equated with dreaming, though dreams also occur during other sleep periods. 12, 35

Rapid learning 90

Ratio data A measurement where there is a true zero point and equal intervals as in most measures of physical quantities. 150

Rational emotive behaviour therapy (REBT) A development of RET to emphasise the behavioural component of the therapy, i.e. that the aim of the therapy is to change a client's behaviour as well as their thinking. 50, 51

Rational emotive therapy (RET) A form of cognitive behavioural therapy where the client is encouraged to think rationally instead of irrationally and thus remove self-defeating habits which cause maladaptive behaviour. 2, 48, 50–51

Realism 138, 144, 146, 166

Reality principle In psychoanalytic theory, the drive by the ego to accommodate to the demands of the environment in a realistic way. 31, 42

REBT See Rational emotive behaviour therapy

Reciprocal inhibition Pairing two things together which are incompatible (such as anxiety and relaxation) so that one inhibits or eliminates the other. 22, 25, 28

Reductionism An approach that breaks complex phenomenon into more simple components, implying that this is desirable because complex phenomena are best understood in terms of a simpler level of explanation. x, 11, 38–39, 53, 62

Reflex response 17

Regression In psychoanalytic theory, a form of ego defence whereby the individuals returns psychologically to an earlier stage of development rather than handling unacceptable impulses in a more adult way. Anxiety-provoking thoughts can thus be temporarily pushed into the unconscious. Often confused with repression. 31, 42

Reinforcement If a behaviour results in a pleasant state of affairs, the behaviour is 'stamped in' or reinforced. It then becomes more probable that the behaviour will be repeated in the future. Can be positive or negative reinforcement – both lead to an increased likelihood that the behaviour will be repeated. ix, 17–19, 24, 28

Reinforcer Any response that creates reinforcement. 17

Reliability A measure of consistency both within a set of scores or items (internal reliability) and also over time so that it is possible to obtain the same results on subsequent occasions when the measure is used (external reliability). 72, 84, 90, 135, 155, 160–161, 165

REM See Rapid eye movement sleep

Repeated measures design An experimental design where each participant takes part in every condition under test. 4, 137

Replication If a finding from a research study is true (valid) that it should be possible to obtain the same finding if the study is repeated. This confirms the reliability and the validity of the finding. 26, 54, 96, 135, 146, 162, 166

Representation In psychoanalysis, an element of dreamwork which enables the latent content of a dream to be transformed into manifest content by translating thoughts and emotions into images. 34

Representativeness Selecting a sample so that it accurately stands for, or represents, the population being studied. 34, 154, 160

Repression In psychoanalytic theory, a form of ego defence whereby anxiety-provoking thoughts and feelings are excluded from the conscious mind. Often confused with regression. 31, 34, 36, 42, 43

Reproductive value The expected reproductive success for any individual from their current age onward. 116, 118, 119

Research methods 133–167

Resistance 4

Response-bias factors 94

RET See Rational emotive therapy

Retina The region of the eye containing photosensitive cells (rods and cones) which record light energy. 110, 112

Retinal image The image formed on the retina. 111, 112, 115

Retrieval cues 52, 92

Right to withdraw The right of participants to refuse to continue with participation in a study if they are uncomfortable in any way, and to refuse permission for the researcher to use any data produced before they withdrew. 27, 66, 78, 84, 142, 143, 154, 166

Rosenhan, D.L. 122–127, 129

Sample A selection of participants taken from the population being studied, and intended to be representative of that population. 72, 90, 120, 156–157, 162

Sampling procedures In observational studies, the method used to select when observations should be recorded e.g. time or event sampling. 152

Sampling techniques A method used that aims to provide a sample that is a representative selection of a target population. 117, 152–153

Scattergraph A graphical representation of the relationship (i.e. the correlation) between two sets of scores, each dot representing one pair of data. Also called a scattergram. 82, 89, 133, 148, 166

Schema A cluster of related facts based on previous experiences, and used to generate future expectations. 45, 49, 53

Schizophrenia A mental disorder where an individual has lost touch with reality and may experience symptoms such as delusions, hallucinations, grossly disorganised behaviour and flattened emotions. xii, 3, 6, 8, 9, 10, 11, 14, 122, 124, 126-7, 130

Scientific method The systematic process by which scientists produce and test explanations about the world using objective research. ix, xii, 10, 24, 52, 133–135

SD Standard deviation, a measure of dispersion that shows the amount of variation in a set of scores. It assesses the spread of data around the mean. 22–23, 25, 87

Secondary elaboration In psychoanalysis, an element of dreamwork that enables the latent content of a dream to be transformed into manifest content by linking all the images together to form a coherent story, further disguising the true meaning of the dream. 34, 42

Selective serotonin reuptake inhibitors (SSRIs) Commonly prescribed drug for treating depression. It works by selectively preventing the re-uptake of serotonin from a synapse, thus leaving more serotonin available at the synapse to excite surrounding neurons. 8

Self-selected sample Same as Volunteer sample. 66, 156, 166, 168, 169, 173

Self-serving bias A kind of attributional bias. Individuals prefer to make internal (dispositional) attributions about their successes and external (situational) attributions about their failures. 47, 56

Seligman, M. 86, 90, 104

Selye, H. 4–5, 10

Semanticity 98

Semi-structured interview An interview that is both structured and unstructured i.e. the interviewer has some pre-established questions but also develops questions in response to the answers given. 159, 162

Serotonin A neurotransmitter found in the central nervous system. Low levels have been linked to many different behaviours and physiological processes, including aggression, eating disorders and depression. x, 3, 8, 9

Sexual selection A key part of Darwin's theory explaining how evolution is driven by competition for mates, and the selection of characteristics that specifically promote reproductive success for any individual. 116, 130

Shaping A process whereby a desired behaviour is gradually conditioned by reinforcing behaviours that progressively move closer and closer to the target behaviour. 17, 25, 99, 100, 129

Sheridan, C.L. & King, K.G. 78

Sherif, M. 68

Short-term memory 45

Significant A statistical term indicating that a set of research findings are sufficiently strong for us to accept the research hypothesis under test. 149

Singh, D. 120

SIT *See* Stress inoculation training.

Situational attribution In attribution theory, accounting for an individual's behaviour in terms of aspects of the environment or external factors, such as another person's behaviour or luck. 46, 47, 77

Situational variable Any factor in the environment that could affect the DV, such as noise, time of day or the behaviour of an investigator. 141

Skinner, B.F. 17, 24, 25

Slater, L. 67, 93, 123, 124, 126

SLT *See* Social learning theory

Social desirability bias A tendency for respondents to answer questions in a way that they think will present them in a better light. 20, 156, 160, 161, 165, 166

Social learning theory (SLT) The basic assumption of this theory is that people learn indirectly through observing the behaviour of models (observational learning) and imitating such behaviour in similar situations if others have been reinforced for such behaviour (vicarious reinforcement). Continued performance depends on direct reinforcement. ix, 2, 17, 18, 19, 24, 26, 28, 29, 62, 67, 152

Social phobia A phobia of situations involving other people, such as speaking in public or being part of a social group. 22–23

Social pressure 68–73

Social psychology 52, 68–79

Social Readjustment Rating Scale (SRRS) 80, 81

Socioeconomic status (SES) A measure of an individual's or family's social and economic position, based on income, education ans occupation. 105, 108, 117

Specific phobia A phobia of specific activities or objects, such as bathing or spiders. 22–23

Spitzer, R. 126

Split-half method A method of assessing internal reliability by comparing two halves of, for example, a psychological test to see if they produce the same score. 161, 165

SSRI *See* Selective serotonin re-uptake inhibitor

Standardised procedures A set of procedures that are the same for all participants so as to ensure that any changes in the DV are due to variation in the IV rather than alterations in the procedures. Also to enable replication of the study to take place. 16, 136, 141, 166

Stanford Prison Experiment (SPE) 134–135, 142, 143

Stereotactic psychosurgery 7

Stereotypes A fixed, often simplistic generalisation about an individual based on some readily available feature, such as the clothes a person is wearing, rather than their personal attributes. 52, 53, 56, 109

Standard deviation *See* SD

Stimulus 17, 128

Stotland, E. & Blumenthal, A. 104

Stratified sample A method of obtaining a representative sample where groups of participants are selected according to their frequency in the population. Within each strata individuals are selected using random sampling. 156

Stress The subjective experience of a lack of fit between a person and their environment (i.e. where the perceived demands of a situation are greater than a person's perceived ability to cope). 3, 4–5, 9

Stress inoculation training (SIT) A form of cognitive behavioural therapy that trains people to cope with anxiety and stressful situations more effectively by learning skills in order to 'inoculate' themselves against the damaging effects of future stressors. 48

Structure (systematic) observations An observer uses various 'systems' to organise observations, such as behavioural categories and sampling procedures. 152, 164

Structured interview Any interview in which the questions are decided in advance. 159, 160, 164

Subjective Seeing things from a person's own perspective and therefore likely to be biased. 40, 55

Sublimation In psychoanalytic theory, a form of ego defence whereby anxiety-provoking thoughts are relieved by channeling them away from destructive acts and into something that is socially acceptable. 33

Superego Part of Freud's conception of the structure of the personality. It embodies our conscience and sense of right and wrong as well as notions of the ideal self. It develops between the ages of 3 and 6. 31, 32, 34

Suppression In psychoanalytic theory, a form of ego defence which is similar to repression. However, unlike repression the anxiety-provoking thoughts are consciously placed out of conscious awareness. 33

Symbolism In psychoanalysis, an element of dreamwork which enables the latent content of a dream to be transformed into manifest content by replacing elements of the dream with symbols. 34

Sympathetic arousal *See* Sympathetic nervous system

Sympathetic branch *See* Sympathetic nervous system

Sympathetic nervous system The part of the autonomic nervous system (ANS) that is associated with physiological arousal and 'fight or flight' responses. 3, 4, 9

Symptom substitution In therapy, the reappearance of symptoms in a different form possibly as a result of treating only the symptoms of a disorder rather than the underlying cause. 38, 48

Synapse A small gap separating neurons. It consists of the presynaptic membrane (which discharges neurotransmitters), the postsynaptic membrane (containing receptor sites for neurotransmitters) and a synaptic gap between the two. 3, 8

Synaptic gap or cleft The gap between a transmitting and receiving neuron, about 10 nm wide. 3

Syphilis A sexually transmitted infection (STI) caused by a bacterium. At first sores and a rash appear but these disappear in time giving the impression that the infection has ceased. If untreated the bacterium eventually causes serious physical and psychological problems which may ultimately lead to early death. 122

Systematic desensitisation A process by which a patient is gradually exposed to (or imagines) a threatening situation under relaxed conditions until the anxiety reaction is extinguished. 20, 22–23, 27

Systematic observation *See* Structured observation

Systematic sample A method of obtaining a representative sample by selecting, for example, every fifth or tenth person. This can be a random sample if the first person is selected using a random method and then every *n*th person is selected. 156

Szasz, T.S. 122

Tardive dyskinesia 8, 9

Target population The group of people that a researcher is interested in. The group of people from whom a sample is drawn. The group of people about whom generalisations can be made. Also sometimes just called the 'population'. 90, 156

Terrace, H.S. 102–103

Test-retest method A method used to check external reliability. The same test or interview is given to the same participants on two occasions to see if the same results are obtained. 66, 161, 165, 176

Testosterone A hormone produced mainly by the testes in males, but also occurring in females. It is associated with the development of secondary sexual characteristics in males (e.g. body hair), but has also been implicated in aggression and dominance behaviours. xi, 3, 14

Thalamus 3, 7, 14

Time sampling An observational technique in which the observer records behaviours in a given time frame, e.g. noting what a target individual is doing every 30 seconds. 153, 166

Transference In psychoanalysis, a problem that occurs when a patient may transfer their feelings about others onto the therapist. The therapist then has to deal with this as an additional 'problem'. 36, 98

Transmission 9, 98, 110

Tripartite personality 31, 42, 165

Tulving, E. 139

Tulving, E. & Psotka, J. 52

Twin studies Research conducted using twins. If nature is the major influence on behaviour (rather than nurture) than we would expect monozygotic (MZ) twins to be more similar than dizygotic (DZ) twins in terms of a target behaviour such as intelligence or personality. Such studies may look at twins reared apart to reduce the confounding variable of shared environment. 13, 146

Type 1 error Not believing something is true when it is, which could result, for example, in sending a person to jail who is innocent. 124, 129

Type 2 error Believing something to be true when it isn't, such as letting a criminal who is guilty go free. 124, 129

UCR *See* Unconditioned response

UCS *See* Unconditioned stimulus

Unconditional positive regard Providing affection and respect without any conditions attached. 51, 56

Unconditioned response (UCR) In classical conditioning, the innate reflex response to a stimulus, such as salivating when presented with food. 17, 20, 22, 27

Unconditioned stimulus (UCS) In classical conditioning, the stimulus that inevitably produces an innate reflex response, such as food producing a salivation response. 17, 20, 22, 27

Unconscious Lacking consciousness or awareness. In psychoanalytic theory, the unconscious part of your mind contains information that is either very hard or almost impossible to bring into conscious awareness. It holds your repressed thoughts which are too anxiety-provoking to allow into one's conscious. However, such material exerts a powerful influence over behaviour. ix, 31, 34, 36

Unstructured interview An interview that starts out with some general aims and possibly some questions, and lets the interviewee's answers guide subsequent questions. 159, 160, 164

Unstructured observations An observer records all relevant behaviour but has no system. This technique may be chosen because the behaviour to be studied is largely unpredictable. 152, 160, 164

Validity Refers to the legitimacy of a study, and the extent to which the findings can be applied beyond the research setting as a consequence of the study's internal and/or external validity. 26, 54, 78, 84, 90, 135, 138–141, 160, 165

Vicarious reinforcement/learning Learning not through direct reinforcement of behaviour, but through observing someone else being reinforced for that behaviour. 17, 18, 19

Visual cliff 110, 111–115, 129

Volunteer bias A form of sampling bias caused by the fact that volunteer participants are usually more highly motivated than randomly selected participants. 156

Volunteer sample A method of obtaining a sample of participants that relies solely on volunteers to make up the sample. 78, 156, 169, 170

Washoe 99

Watson, J.B. 24

Waynforth, D. & Dunbar, R.I.M. 120

Weapon effect In violent crimes, an eyewitness' attention may be drawn to the weapon held by a criminal thus reducing their ability to remember other details such as the criminal's face. 54, 144

Wish fulfilment 34

Wolpe, J. 22, 25

Yerkes, R.M. 98

Yuille, J.C. & Cutshall, J.L. 96

Zero correlation In a correlation, covariables are not linked at all. 148, 166

Zimbardo, P. 78, 134